THE REGAL SONS OF DOUGLAS

BY GIL LEFEBVRE

Designed by: Susan Harrison
Edited by Marcia Lefebvre and Julie Hersum

Library of Congress Control Number: 2018944460

ISBN 978-0-9672172-8-4

To my dear wife, Marcia

*Who has, once again, earnestly
and patiently indulged me
with her intelligent editing of
my coarse dialogue and scribblings.*

THE REGAL SONS OF DOUGLAS

BY GIL LEFEBVRE

TABLE OF CONTENTS

GIL LEFEBVRE

The Regal Sons of Douglas

"A true story to rival that of Forest Gump
that has circled the world."

Obsessing Rufina

"Suspense, Drama and Mystery in Post WWII Europe
and based on true facts that appear in headlines today."

Unto Caesar Unto God

Assessment of the merits of religious
activist policies in recent years

Not Too Far to
Have Never Been

Suspenseful Novel Wrapped in Romance
takes the reader from foreign battlefields
to the sunny beaches of Catalina Island.

Catalina Summer

A delightfully true and entertaining novel with riveting
Huckleberry experiences. Enjoy the voyage as it tales its
way around the Catalina Baseball Camp of the late 1950s.

PART III | **USC**

PART IV | **THE FINALE**

PROLOGUE

BREAKING NEWS

SAN DIEGO CHANNEL 10NEWS
Posted 11:33 pm, Oct 22, 2012
Story as reported by Dan Haggerty

SAN DIEGO – The ashes of a man who apparently died more than 15 years ago were found at a car wash in Ocean Beach on Monday.

The mysterious metal box was found at the OB Suds car wash near Voltaire and Bacon streets after someone cleaned out their car and left.

The box had only one clue in the fine print.

"The sticker on the box said they were cremated in 1995," said Liz Greene, who is with the Ocean Beach Mainstreet Association.

Inside were the ashes of Henry efebvre, who has been dead for 17 years.

"It kind of put me in a panic," said Greene. "It weighed a lot and I was worried because the bag it was in was kind of dusty. What was I touching? Was I being pranked?"

The car wash owner says it is not a prank. He found the ashes near one of the bays. When no one claimed them, he brought them to the Ocean Beach Mainstreet Association.

"Haven't been able to find the person or the crematorium online, so hopefully you can help us," Greene told 10News.

However, the online databases that usually help did not. Searching obituaries and entering the man's name on Google did not turn up any results. 10News searched for the crematorium – Secure Crematorium – and found one with the same name in Santa Ana.

"We never sold cremation to the public, we only did cremation for the mortuaries," said Chris Macera, the crematorium's director. "I'd have to find out the mortuary who actually took care of the family."

The crematorium told 10News they have no record of efebvre because it has been longer than 10 years. They said a document which is sometimes placed inside the box could offer more clues.

"I don't know," said Greene. "I hope we find his owner."

PART I

DOUGLAS

G Avenue Douglas Arizona 1916

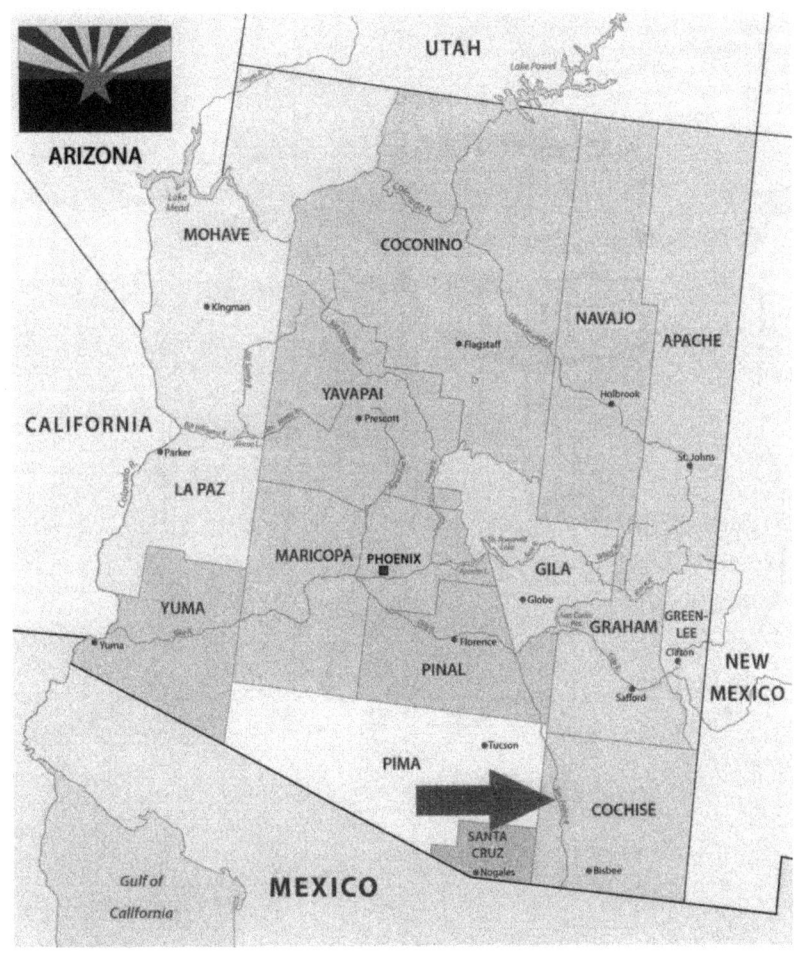

CHAPTER 1

STATE OF ARIZONA OCTOBER 30, 1915
COMING HOME

The air chilled in the late fall afternoon, finding its way to the southeastern tip of Arizona, a portion of land puzzled in by the New Mexico border to the east and the state of Sonora, Mexico to the south, just some fifteen miles outside of the booming smelter town of Douglas. Off in a distant and remote cattle range, muffled voices could be heard by six tired *vaqueros* sitting by a crackling fire, savoring their last bit of coffee while keeping watch over a small herd.

As the sun began to set, a rustling joined the muffled voices in the distance, quickly banishing the casual atmosphere. The cowhands perked, then tossed back the last gulp of dark liquid while dashing out the fire with what was left from the kettle. Hastily, they slid back into the leather chaps and vested jackets they wore to protect themselves from cactus spines. By habit, they belted on six-shooters, tightened the straps to their legs, and thrusted their rifles into boots next to their stirrups. The sombreros went on last as the cowhands—now armed with more ammunition than the average Texan—mounted their horses. All were aware that the taming of the American West was far from complete in this remote Arizona territory.

It had been only two years since Arizona acquired statehood and the effects of the Civil War still left a void in this desolate plain. Hostile Indians and Mexican *banditos* plumaged remote *ranchos*, ran off with cattle, and murdered and raped resistant settlers, ranchers, and farmers who stood in their way. Overloaded with plunder, they proceeded to cross that invisible line to the Mexican sand.

Here in Arizona, the law was enforced, but not as often by courts and reluctant juries as by the men elected as sheriffs who ruled as judge, jury, and executioner—the recipe for justice in this rugged land.

As the *vaqueros* rode out to challenge the cause of the distraction now rippling through the herd, the commotion they'd heard by the fire grew louder. Three of the *vaqueros* rode on up ahead to the bluff and from there spotted something coming their way. By instinct they quickly dismounted and nestled under the few starving bushes that had survived the unusually dry hot summer. With *pistolas* in hand, they readied themselves for anything.

Shadows came into focus, then closed in. The tracking cowhands burst out from their concealment with guns cocked and aimed. To their relief, only straggling, barefooted boys appeared, each with small packs and boots strung about their shoulders. Dusty, unkempt clothes draped their lean figures, and the stench in the air left no doubt they were in immediate need of a good washing.

The boys were undisturbed by their discovery and continued to pass out stories among themselves. To spoil the intrusion and get their attention, one of the *vaqueros* cleared his rifle from its boot and let off a round into the darkening the sky. With the sound of a cannon blast, it silenced their voices and did the job. The boys stopped so quickly that one stumbled and fell into thorny scrubs. While squinting to see the predicament they were in, one of the men called out, "*¿Qué pasa? Buenos días, chicos. ¿Donde*...where you going out here?"

Seemingly unbothered, a boy stepped out boldly and said, "We're from Douglas...just spent a few days in the Chiricahua Mountains."

"Doing what, *chico?*"

"Oh swimming, fishing, climbing about...trading with the young bucks up there."

"I see," the man said nonchalantly as he holstered his pistol and mounted his horse. "So you know your way around the territory then?"

"Yes," the boy snapped back confidently.

The rider now stretched out his words and rose the pitch to punctuate his point. "Theenn you must know you're trespassing on the San Bernardino Ranch!"

"Of course, we do. This is the short way home, some fourteen miles up the road. We live just off Fifteenth Street...really on Fifth."

"Okay then...*¿Como se llama?*"

"My name is Henry Lefebvre Jr."

"'Junior,' you say?"

"Yes, but my friends call me 'Hank.'"

"And your *compadres?*"

"This is my brother, Alfred, next to him is my other brother, Benjamin..." then pointing to the boy dusting off from the fall, "that be Josiah, our neighbor." The boys laughed at their friend's comical show. "Me and him are the best of friends, like our pa's."

"Well," The *vaquero* went on, "if you are not afraid of us, are you not afraid of the Indians and Mexican robbers out here?"

"Aw, no worry. You see, I carry a *pistola* in my sack here," Hank said, holding it up as proof, "besides, the Indians and most Mexican bandits know my uncle Joseph. He sells things to them."

"Like what?"

"Like blankets and can goods...even to Pancho Villa," Hank replied with pride.

"Okay, brave ones," the *vaquero* said while turning to his *compadres* and raising his hands off the saddle horn, "let me guide you to the ranch house and you can tell your stories to Mr. Slaughter. He sometimes takes a liking to kids and maybe even offer some food to get you back to Douglas.

"Just keep walking west, follow the sun as it goes down. In about two miles you will see his *casa*. You can't miss the white picket fence. We will ride ahead with these critters and tell Mr. Slaughter you are on your way. Is that okay with you, *chico*?"

"It is okay, *señor*."

"Then *vamanos*," he said to the other riders, and off they went.

Hank smiled broadly, then like a crowing rooster, boasted to the boys, "Maybe I speak Spanish so good they let us stay on the ranch." The other boys laughed.

"Yep. I'm sure that's it," Alfred said with a snarl. "More like you is the one that don't mind making a fool of yourself. You is always jumping into a fray first."

Benjamin echoed in, "Yup."

Hank shot back, "Benjamin, you keep on backing up Alfred and next time I'm going to leave you back home. You'll be going to school and that's not just a threat."

Josiah, the outsider now, didn't seem to find this part humorous at all and added, "Yeah, and if Hank doesn't let you come along, my mom won't let me go either."

Hank thought it was time to present his dominance once again. "Well boys, it's just that I'm the oldest and leader of the family, outside Pa and Ma. Trust me. That's all. And besides, who gets you through the mountains every time? It's me."

Sounding more like his father, Hank rambled on while the others walked faster to catch up "...who taught you how to swim, shoot guns, ride and climb mountains? Me, that's who. So there, quit complaining. You see, the telling is that Ms. Viola Slaughter makes good pies and has an ice house filled with ice cream and dries out some mighty tasting jerky, and Mr. Slaughter has so many cars...they say he never cared to learn how to drive. And, just maybe he has one of those Ham Radios. Maybe we can even hear a baseball game, and then there is this pond to swim in."

The boys all got so excited at that last thought that they began to double-time like the troops at Fort Huachuca. Hank whispered over to his best friend and life companion, Josiah, "I need to do this from time to time...give them all a vision of where we're going. I used to need one too, but now Pa says my instincts gets me there. You'd seen Pa's eyes light up like the Fourth of July when he be a-talkin' to me and my brothers about going anywhere. And he is always going somewhere. It's just that he never wants to stay there too long when he gets there."

Hank and the boys traveled on now with renewed resolve, tasting that cool ice cream and sensing a refreshing plunge into the Slaughter pond. Just a few miles to the west, the sun was about to take away the day as it eased behind Mule Mountain. Once they reached the white picket fence surrounding the grand house, they saw a man with a slouched Stetson sitting on the front porch. He wore a plaid shirt with Levi's tucked neatly into his tall boots. He stood to gesture, cajoling the boys to come on in.

Hank motioned Alfred to unlatch the gate. "Let's go on in and talk to the man." He was confident that the only one taken to such liberty and relaxed nature on Slaughter's ranch would have to be none other than Mr. Texas John Slaughter himself. Slaughter stood and greeted the boys in such a friendly fashion that Hank couldn't help but think of Christmas while looking at the white beard surrounding his broad smile. The man wasn't above Hank or Alfred in size, but that made no difference when he looked directly into Hank's eyes. Hank always thought eyes were the window into a person's character and this man's demanded respect. Hank imagined how many bandits and outlaws had looked into those tender eyes just before Mr. Slaughter rendered his final judgment.

"Welcome, boys. I'm Mr. Slaughter and this is my ranch. My foreman, Emiliano, tells me you were off in the Chiricahuas and just passing through."

Alfred, who always was slight on giving a conversation stood a little behind Hank, but Benjamin was much more giving and ended up on Mr. Slaughter's opened book as he plopped himself down on a large leather chair. Hank gave an embarrassed cringe. Seeing Hank in distress, Mr. Slaughter said, "No worry, son, just move it on over."

Hank remained standing, leaning against the porch post. Mr. Slaughter took a glance at the boy's ragged wears and chuckled a bit. "So, my foreman here says you have some mighty fine names. "I'm guessing you are Hank," Mr. Slaughter said when he offered his hand.

"Yes sir. That be me," Hank replied proudly as he shook the outstretched hand.

"I see you boys have already met my foreman here," Slaughter said, giving a nod to Emiliano as he stepped up on the large porch.

"So, Mr. Saughter, you know these boys' father?" Emiliano asked.

"Yes, I do. I know their father well." "How is your pa these days, Hank?"

"Well sir, he's just doing…well…I guess like always."

Mr. Slaughter smiled at Hank's clumsy response.

When Hank tried to answer again, Mr. Slaughter gave him a reprieve by cutting him off. "Yes, I know, boy. Nature does play funny things, doesn't it? Now take your uncle Joseph, your father's identical twin brother. They are so alike, yet not…" Slaughter smiled again, "I remember the last time I saw the two brothers standing together."

Looking out over his front lawn, beyond the fences and toward the horizon, Mr. Slaughter went on, this time sounding more like a preacher beginning a sermon, "Hank, your uncle Joseph is a collected, prepared, and principled man. I know him well. His handshake is all a man needs to do business together. Now, your father, mind you, well, he's less than that. He may come from the same pie, but he's a slice different. He loves to gamble, like me, but in poker, he's just too inspired to win," Mr. Slaughter lowered his voice now and looked carefully at Hank, "he likes the drink. Me too, but I'm a slight more tempered than Henry. You see, son, your pa's spirited, like a mare in heat that fancies those adventures out there," Mr. Slaughter said, pointing toward the ridge of the Chihuahua Mountain range.

Mr. Slaughter looked back from under the brim of his Stetson. "I guess a lot like you. Oh, your uncle Joseph likes adventure too, but your father's the one that doesn't think about security nor financial gain. No. Henry Lefebvre just likes the journey. He fights in the barnyards to make his mark. He'll even toil for wages in the mines where most men won't go. "But of course, Hank, you know this well. You've lived with him for, is it 15 or 16 years since you were born in Bisbee, up the road from Douglas?"

"That's right, sir." Hank answered, taken by surprise Mr. Slaughter knew about such matters.

"And you, Alfred?"

"I be much younger."

"How about you, Benjamin?"

Benjamin squeaked out, "I be even younger than Alfred says."

"Well then, there you are. And this boy here?"

Emiliano spoke up. "We found this one in a patch of thorny brushwood."

Everyone enjoyed a good laugh.

"My name is Josiah Jakubowski. I'm 16."

"You come from France?" Mr. Slaughter grinned, baiting the boy on.

"No sir…Poland, sir."

"Poland, you say. My, you're a long way from home."

"No sir. I'm Hank's neighbor…know him since, well…almost I was born, maybe," Josiah assured him. "We've done many things, he and I, around Douglas. Even his pa and my pa are good friends. They work alongside in the smelter."

"Okay then, settle down young man. I know of your pa too. Just funning with you son," Mr. Slaughter said, then turned the conversation back. "About Henry…what I'm trying to say is, just don't be hard on your pa, Hank. Take the good in him. I assure you there is a lot of that. Heck. I'd hire him in a minute out here on the ranch. He could come work for me anytime. How's your ma doing with all…what seven, eight, or nine kids?"

"Well sir, she be doing her chores, bakin' and cleanin'… sometimes for the neighbors or at the boardinghouse on Ninth Street—"

"Your ma is bueno, young man," Viola Slaughter said as she stepped out onto the porch, interrupting Hank, "I know where you boys and your sisters come from, but where your ma been from?"

Hank jumped in, "She never lets on where she be from. Pa says when she's mad, it sounds like she's from the White Mountain Apaches. Ma says Mexico, most of the time, but sometimes delights herself and says she's from Spain…maybe some fancy royal family," the Lefebvre boys smiled at each other, "but Pa says Ma likes to spin her dreams."

"So where are you boys traveling to today?"

"Well, Miss Viola, Alfred, Benjamin, and my friend Josiah are on their ways home."

"You best be getting on. Your ma might need you around the house or want you to spend some time schooling," Mrs. Slaughter added with concern.

"But I be traveling up to Tombstone to see my cousin, Charley. It's been going on two years now since he left to Mexico," Hank explained, "he be in Tombstone for a day…visiting his brother Albert."

"Oh yes. Charley and his young Mexican bride," Mr. Slaughter remembered with a smile.

"Yup, something like that. There's talk around the house about us picking up and going to California soon. It could be my last chance to see them for a while, since Pa and Uncle Joseph don't seem to get together much anymore. The Lefebvre family sort of split up after we buried my Grandpa Anton."

"Sorry to hear that, Hank. He was a good man. Anton and your grandmother, Amelia, were bakers from France, is that right?"

"Yep."

"Amelia still doing fine?"

"Yes ma'am. She's a-living with uncle Joseph just up the road in Pirtleville."

"There's been some talk of her going back to France?"

"Yes, ma'am—"

Mr. Slaughter interrupted, "Let's get these hungry boys some cooking's. They got a long road ahead of them. After eating, you can find a place by the pond to settle down for the night. Viola will get some morning grubs set up for you in the commissary out back."

As they stood to go, Mr. Slaughter asked, "By the way Hank. I heard the darndest thing. People tell me you won this year's Chiricahua race running bare footed from Douglas to the Chiricahua foothills and back. And that you beat all the others by two hours and thirty-five minutes? That so?"

Alfred found room to jump in, "That's right, Mr. Slaughter. You should've seen him and heard the crowd cheerin' him back in Douglas!"

Hank smiled shyly then simply stated as a fact, "You bet that was me."

"Well ain't that something. I also heard all you Lefebvre boys were good at playing baseball and football over at Sportsman Park."

"Yes sir. That be us."

"Well, you boys keep up the dream," Walking back into the house, Mr. Slaughter added, "by the way, Hank, tomorrow I'll be sending Emiliano here up to Tombstone on some business. Can't drive any of my cars. Right, Viola? But my foreman can and he can give you a ride, seeing how thirty-six miles is a long walk, even for a boy from Douglas."

Then Mr. Slaughter turned back with concern in his eyes, "Oh, and when you get back home…spread the news. I've heard Pancho Villa's army is about to battle with Carranza supporters. The US has made it known they is supporting Carranza in Agua Prieta. And you living just blocks away from the border and the fighting, best take cover for a few days. I've done a fair amount of business with Villa and he's a sensible man. But this President Wilson that turned coats on Villa... has now got him all riled up. That's not good, getting Villa all riled up like that. In fact, your uncle Joseph tells me that sometime back he sat and had a meal with Villa while selling him some blankets. Villa found out there was a problem with a spy in his army and shot that man dead right in front of the dinner table...so I hear."

Viola broke in, "Enough of that kind of talk. You'll scare the boys half to death, John Slaughter. Okay now, *vamanos*. Come on out to the commissary and I'll get you some jerky and pie. Then get some rest. Tomorrow, before you leave for home, maybe I can find some ice cream out back."

While getting up to leave, Hank hesitated and turned back.

Mr. Slaughter asked, "What's on your mind, son?"

"Well sir, about three nights back we were sleeping out under the stars and heard a howling noise that bothered us all through the night...causing us to lose some fair amount of sleep. At sunup we saw, some twenty yards up from us, was these three Mexicans, or maybe Indians, hanging from a tree. Don't know which, 'cause we didn't get too close. Their mouths were opened so wide that the wind passing through them made the howling."

Slaughter considered the predicament for a moment. "It's been a long time since I been sheriffing around these parts. Don't concern yourself, son. There must have been a good reason for the hanging.

"Now, go get some grubs from Viola. It makes her happy to see kids around with a full belly. And Hank, make sure you send the others on their way home and you leave with Emiliano for Tombstone in the morning...right at sunup."

"Yes sir. Good night."

Later, after settling down next to the pond, the boys went

for a swim in the buff. The water made their tired bodies come back to life and willing to eat more of the jerky and extra can of beans Viola gave them. They spread themselves out on their blankets under the stars. "Gosh," Hank said, "look up there. Those stars have been around for so long, it's hard to think that far. Look at them twinkle at us. Just think, there's kids far away out there in some other parts of the world that are looking up at them just like us. I wonder what they're thinking. Some years off, when we look up there, where will we be?"

"Hank, quit that philosophizing again. It hurts my head," Alfred said.

"I'm not philosophizing, Alfred. I'm just dreaming on those old stars. Without dreaming, what else is there to look forward to in life? It's all too magical. Just look up there."

"Aw, go to sleep, Hank. We got a lot of livin' going on right here."

"You think so, Alfred?"

As the boys lay and gazed into the moonlit sky hypnotized, perhaps searching for what was beyond, Alfred finally answered, "I'm sure of it, Hank. Those old stars will be there long after we're gone and forgotten."

"I sure hope it doesn't end up that way."

"What do you mean, Hank?"

"Oh, just that us boys from Douglas way out here will be long gone and forgotten."

CHAPTER 2

TOMBSTONE

The sun attempted its impression off in the distance over the Chiricahuas, streaming its way down on to the flat desert floral setting of Arizona's San Bernardino Valley. It soon squelched the chill of the early morning fall day, as was its custom about the same time each year.

This familiar feel in the air happened many times in Hank's almost sixteen years. Unlike the boys in some metropolitan city, out here where the Wild West still refused to convert to more civilized ways, Hank's existence was severely aged. His personal gridiron extended from the border town of Douglas, past the neighboring rural heights of Pirtleville, where the most influential men of aspiration and destination lived on sprawling cattle *ranchos*. It continued up north through the copper mining town of Bisbee (one time considered the largest city between St. Louis and San Francisco), stretching further north to Tombstone, where the Cochise County Hall of records and the 1915 style of justice played themselves out. But, the fateful flooding of Tombstone's silver mines derailed the legendary boomtown and set it into a rapid regression—spent it out, as will happen to antiquities. It wasn't just Tombstone. There were others—remote outposts that slipped past their prime, one by one, becoming mere ghost towns, yet still serving as photo ops for travel digests struggling to revive their fantasy fetishes for the old Western gunfights and double-dealings, promoting folklores that gave magical scenes advertised in dime store novels.

Just a few miles northwest was the fledgling community of Sierra Vista. This stalwart handmaiden to the federal government supported civilian housing for Fort Huachuca. The fort, established March 3, 1877, quartered the US Calvary and the unit that would later be known as the "buffalo soldiers," and which provided settlers and cattle ranchers security from a series of Mexican *banditos*, rustlers, and indigenous Indian raids. Local Indian tribes saw US policy of Manifest Destiny and the winning of the West as confrontation to their prevailing way of life. Legendary figures such as Geronimo, Cochise, and Narbona, along with Indian renegade scouts, found such an impression in American Eastern folklore that later, entire regions and counties branded their names.

This was Hank's playground—his perimeter. He'd wander about, find things to do, like ventures with his brothers and good friend, Josiah. It was their world and they made of it as they wanted. Of course, there were some guidelines—unspoken lines not to cross—but, like the wind that blew sand about the desert floor and into the remote canyons of this rugged land, they changed as fast and unpredictably as the climate.

Hank woke by the beckoning of the morning's radiance with a familiar anticipation of upcoming adventure and challenge. His day would not fall into the habits of the time clock, nor the routines of proper business. Much like his father, Hank would have none of that. No, no. Never out here. This day would play by Hank's rules, like the far-off explorers, inventors, or vagabonds before who regulated their time by natural impulses. Though he knew the smelter ran on time, Sunday church ran on time, as did trains bringing cattle, passengers, and building materials for folks who came to Arizona's boomtowns, these weren't enough for Hank, no, these were just mere considerations he learned to defray while running amuck. Intrinsically, Hank knew there would be more for him to gain from this Douglas upbringing, something far more supreme, more majestic to rule his life. Hank was inclined to think someday he might find out what that was.

But now, as he lay cuddled under a picnic table adjacent to the ranch pond, doubts about his future slowly crept in. He'd been troubled recently by the notion his family would soon be moving to a far-off place he'd yet to reckon with. California was all too confining a thought. His mere independence was about to come under assault by some big, developed city like Los Angeles or Long Beach, pinning and fencing him in with many obstacles. How would their rules fit his, him being not all French but shades of different colors?

Over the years, Hank had learned well the way of things in Douglas and other Arizona towns but he had no idea how to manipulate his predicaments out there in California, or if would there be any need.

As if choreographed by a barnyard rooster, Hank rolled over and greeted the day just as the Slaughter's commissary bell rang out. Thoughts of ham slabs, eggs, and buttered bread coated with preserves prompted Hank to jump to his feet and announce: "Boys, let's go! Eating time!" And that was all the motivation the boys needed to grab their belongings and rush off in the direction of the delicious smell of breakfast. Once fed, the boys thanked Miss Viola for her welcome and hospitality. She placed them in the trusted hands of Emiliano, who quickly skirted them out to the waiting automobile.

The engine chugged away while the foreman explained, "Look, *Amigos*. It's an Apperson Conejo—a Jackrabbit—and one of the best. It will take all you boys to the outskirts of

Pirtleville. From there it's a short walk back to Douglas. Then Hank, you and me will *vamanos* onto McNeal path to West Davis Road and on into Tombstone. I have business to take care of for Mr. Slaughter, and Hank has some things to do there with his cousin, Charley. *¿Sí, chico?*"

"*Sí,*" Hank faintly replied.

"So, get on up into the back seat, boys. Hank, you ride shotgun with me in the front." As Hank climbed into the front seat, he immediately understood what Emiliano meant. The 12-gauge sawed-off Remington shotgun lay neatly, for convenience, between Emiliano and himself.

Emiliano drove on. The ranch quickly became a blur by the yellow dust kicked up behind the car. The boys remained silent, likely so taken by the automobile ride they were speechless. Once the excitement wore out, however, they began chattering about the past few days' activities.

It was Josiah who took over the conversation: "Yup, it was my idea to follow that old Indian trail to one of those tall peaks of the Chiricahuas. That's why it was only right that I got to give it a name. Mighty fine name…'Josiah Peak.' From there we could see some far-off smoke coming from the Douglas smelter," Josiah bragged on, "it also was my idea, along with Hank's, to dive from that there cliff into that pooled up stream. And--don't forget—I'm the one whose caught the biggest trout this year. Now, didn't I?" he said, looking up to Hank for agreement."

Hank smiled, "Yep, right, outside of mine."

Then Benjamin jumped in, "Look at this I got here!" he said, reaching well into his pocket, searching it out. Once found, he displayed the object by holding it up high. "An Indian arrowhead! Maybe Cochise made it. What do you think, Hank?"

"Maybe. Then maybe not," Hank mumbled. After noticing Ben's disappointment and loss of flavor, he changed his mind, "Yeah, maybe it was."

Ben's spirited expression revived. "You really think so, Hank?"

"Yeah Ben, could be Cochise's very own arrowhead."

When they finally got to Franklin Street just a few miles out of Douglas city limits, Emiliano, who had yet to say any little thing, spouted out, "Okay, boys. It's out you go from here. Back to your homes. Now, *vamanos*. You go straight to the casa. ¿*Sí*? If you don't, Mr. Slaughter will mend my hide."

The boys filed out. Last one to exit was Alfred who turned back and said with concern in his voice, "Hank, what's to tell Mama?"

"Oh, just tell her the truth this time. Tell her I'm going to spend a day with Cousin Charley. He'll be in Tombstone for a day visiting Albert. I'll sleep in the barn for the night then find my way home through Bisbee. Be back in two days."

"Now Alfred. You stay at the house. No wandering off. Yah hear? Take care of Ma's needs and the kids, and tend to what Lily says. No snorting back at her until I get back. Okay?"

Alfred nodded, then turned to the rest of the boys. "Come on guys."

As they walked away, Hank yelled out, "And Josiah, you take care of them all."

"Yeah Hank. See you in a couple days."

Emiliano thrust his foot to the pedal and said, "Okay, let's get a-going."

Hank quickly reached into his bag and took out a pad of scratch paper. He dug a little more, finally finding a led pencil, and began to scribble about. With the noise of the Apperson and the bumpings of the road, Hank's efforts were quickly challenged. Hank didn't seem to mind; his persistence carried him on.

A few miles up the road, Emiliano overcame the noise carried by the automobile and loudly asked, "What you writing there down about, Hank?"

"Not writing anything…just drawing things."

"Things? What things?"

"Oh, Indians and cowboys and stuff."

"Why don't you wait when the car stops to do that, Hank? You can get it better. ¿*No, chico?*"

"I am no *chico*, Mr. Emiliano. I have fifteen years."

Emiliano laughed. "*Todo está bien.* It's all good then. So, *hombre*, why the cowboys and Indians?"

"To remember."

"To remember?"

"Yeah, to remember. I don't want to leave this territory and forget it all. And I don't want them to forget me."

"Why, are you going somewhere?"

"Yup. Think so. My pa's brother got him a-thinking it be better for him in California…get away from his doings here and his friends he doin' it with."

Emiliano chuckled. "I met your pa one time in a saloon in Douglas."

"Yah did?"

"*Sí.* He seemed like a nice fellow, for a gringo. He made me laugh."

"Well, I ain't no gringo, Mr. Emiliano. My ma says she's from somewhere around here, maybe Sonora. And Pa's from French, but born out in San Francisco. So says Grandma Amelia."

"So, you're a half-breed?"

"Maybe so. Maybe not so. I don't know where my French starts and my others begins. Ma never says."

"You know Spanish and English well?"

"Yes sir, I do."

"That's mighty good to know two languages, Hank."

"I suppose so."

"So, what's going to be your mark in this world?"

"Well, Mr. Emiliano—"

"*Hombre*, just call me Emiliano."

"Okay. I'm going to find that Dutchman's gold mine maybe. Not his, but a mine something like it."

"*Está bien, hombre. Pero...* but, what then...when you have all this gold...what will you do with it?"

"When I done that, I plan on helping somebody else get a better start. I just don't want to go through this world and let people forget me."

"What can you do for them?"

Hank didn't have time to answer. Just then, up ahead, a few cattle rambled across the road. While slowing down, Emiliano casually grasped hold of the shotgun with one hand, then pulled to a stop just short of the cattle. Four men came out on horses, edging their way in front of the rumbling auto. They didn't appear to be cowboys, for each carried side shooters and two of them brandished long rifles in one hand with tightened reigns in the other. They looked to be an ornery bunch for sure. Without flinch or hesitation, Emiliano took control of this dubious encounter by calmly unlatching, then slowly opening his door with one hand while holding tight to the shotgun with the other. He let the thick car door conceal his intentions and spoke to the riders in Spanish.

As they settled squarely in front of the car, Emiliano blocked the road. He switched to English with a Spanish spit and said, "*Amigo*, I hope you come as friends, yes? You see, I am Emiliano Gomez...foreman of the San Bernardino Ranch. My *patrón* is Texas John Slaughter and I'm about his business now, in the *Conejo*—that is his car," Emiliano gestered toward the Apperson and continued, "and my passenger is *hombre* Hank Lefebvre. His uncle, Joseph Lefebvre, is a personal friend of Senator Carl Hayden, retired sheriff of Maricopa County. I am sure you have heard of these men and what they do."

Emiliano lowered his gaze, "Now, I think if you are up to something unpleasant, you be like the dog, yes? *El Perro.* If so, you are barking up the wrong tree here, *amigos.*" Henry saw Emiliano's fists clench by his side. "Of course, I know I worry too much about *banditos* out here on this long stretch of road, so maybe I am sorry to question you about such things. I suggest you just move along. But, if you are like the dog, best you move out of this state. Maybe try your luck in New Mexico or even maybe Sonora." Emiliano didn't flinch as he awaited a response.

The horsemen coward their stature and looked at each other, conversing only with their eyes. Finally, they pulled back their steeds, made an abrupt about-face, and pressed on into the desert. Once they were out of sight, Emiliano stepped back into the car and reset the shotgun comfortably between the two of them and accelerated on up the road.

At that moment, Hank knew what it meant to be courageous. Emiliano's confident yet refrained defiance in the face of danger defined his character. Emiliano drove on as if nothing had happened, then after some time passed he broached the silence. "There is more to a man than what you draw in your pictures. No?" After a while he went on, "so, then, do you not go to school, *hombre?*"

"Well, my pa says school is all about counting for money. He says today he needs to make money in the smelter during the week, and on Sundays he needs to make money prizefighting. Boxing and gambling—"

"Maybe that's so, but you can't gamble what you can't afford to lose, no?" Emiliano said. Hank pondered on that for a few minutes until Emiliano announced, "Here's McNeal. Let's stop and have some lunch, *amigo*."

After eating, they got back into the Apperson, turned up the West Davis Road, and headed toward Tombstone. Emiliano took command of the conversation and shortened and concluded his thoughts from earlier. "You see, Hank. Our days our coming to an end. Yours are just beginning. This here country has changed. The wild days of Tombstone and the Wild West are beginning to change, too." Look at this automobile we drive in. Whoever made it needed an education. ¿*Sí?*" Hank took a moment to notice the details of the car as Emiliano continued, "And that person needed more than just knowing how to ride a horse, lasso a cow, or pick up a stray. The frontier's becoming full of farms where crops grow and miles of fences keep all kinds of critters in or out. All sorts of ways to make things easier for a new way of life. It's no good for an *hombre* to go with no learning any more. Just look at Tombstone or Bisbee. They be turning into ghost towns with only the past, no future." Hank had an idea he might be right about that. You say you don't want to be forgotten, don't become a ghost like in them ghost towns. ¿*Sí?* You know what to do?" Wondering how he would answer that question goofed Hank's mind throughout the silence of the rest of the drive.

They arrived at Tombstone late in the afternoon. As they drove through the small town, Emiliano said, "Hank, Mr. Slaughter told me to make sure you got back to Douglas tomorrow. I gave him my word. I intend to do just that. He also told me, 'Hank needs the reminding that people who come from this part of the world know a lot about each other, they care.' I say that is good advice. Try not to forget that, Hank… they care even more in Douglas.

"Look out here," Emiliano pointed outside, "even though some towns like Pearce done gone dry of gold specks—and here in Tombstone the same for its silver—the spirit of these places, and the history, will be passed on through people who struggled to come here looking for a good life with their families. Like yours did, in covered wagons. Trust me. I know Tombstone. It's like so many other towns in the early 1900s that wind their way through Southeast Arizona. They each have their own rules and pecking order. The whites is always good about setting up the rules and making sure their place is in the center of the town. And of course, business…always the good paying jobs."

Emiliano went on, "You know, Hank, us Mexicans never go into the mines here because that's where the high paying jobs are. Pero, but also the danger. ¿Sí? Mi amigo. The Mexicanos is just below them, even when they be coming down from Sonora mines, just miles outside of Arizona. Here they all got the secondhand jobs and homes. Not bad, 'eh? Better than the Chinese. They ain't allowed in most places around here to come into town after the sunset. They been allowed to build railroads and now many turned to doing the laundry business. Some went to making a profit with opium… shirting about the edges of town. Now the Indian, who once owned this land first just by being here, his time has passed. They now live on federal reservations that spot about the territory. When you see them most today, hombre, they be with the military at Fort Huachuca or Camp Jones in Douglas as scouts or meddling about outside of towns wearing loin cloths and riding about and trading trinkets, or bartering for their next meal.

"And you, amigo, half-breed, neither all Mexican nor Indian

or *gabacho. ¿Sí?* You don't know where you stand. Half this part and half of that."

Hank ended Emiliano's advice, "I guess so. We all survive together though. Sometimes, we be just people that walk on our own path."

Chuckling, Emiliano pulled up in front of his cousin Albert's house at the corner of Fremont and Third Street, a block off Allen Street and said, "Hey, this is where the gunfight at the corral happened."

"Yes, I've been here many times before," Hank said, jumping out and rushing to open the fence gate.

Hank's cousins, Albert and Charles, greeted them. Standing by Charles was his wife, Concepcíon 'Maria' Figueroa Lefebvre. Hank introduced Emiliano, and Maria asked in Spanish, "Emiliano, would you like to stay for dinner?"

"*Gracias. Pero no señora porqué,* because, I have much business to take care of for Mr. Slaughter at the county house. *Mucho gusto. Adios.*"

Emiliano turned to leave, then glanced over his shoulder and said, "Hank, I'll be back here by midday. *¿Bien?*"

Hank replied, "*Mañana.*"

They watched Emiliano start the car and make a U-turn, then a short right at Third Street, passing Allen Street before turning left on to Toughnut Street, toward the Cochise County Building.

CHAPTER 3

ICE CREAM AND THE OK CORRAL

Albert looked excited as he ushered Hank into his home. "Have a seat, rest here in my favorite chair!" Albert instructed Hank. "You and Charley have lots to go over. It's been too many years since you seen each other. And how about these little blessings they brought up from Mexico? This here is Doris Mae."

Hank reached over to shake the hand of Charley's daughter. She blushed and smiled at his greeting. After a moment of silence, Maria yelled out, "Charley Jr.! Come out here and meet your cousin Hank."

"What? There's more?" Hank asked.

"*Sí.* We wasted no time at the *rancho.*"

"Come on in here, Junior. Well, I'll be. You're almost all grown up," Hank said, while offering his hand.

Charley jumped in, "Yup. I've been telling him, I hope he grows just like his cousin Hank."

"Really? Why's that?" Hank asked with obvious pleasure.

"It's your temperament. I'm afraid he's showing signs of it already," Maria said with a smile. They all laughed at the thought.

Albert said, "Okay. That's enough carrying on. Maria, let's get on into the kitchen and gather up some cookings. Give Charley and Hank some time to get caught up. You boys have always been more like brothers then cousins," Albert said.

As Maria and Albert moved into the kitchen, Maria added, "Charley talked so much about Hank while we were down in Mexico that he drove me crazy. So, go on now, we'll get you some drink and food."

"So, Charley, what's this I've heard about you and Maria Figueroa Lefebvre running off to Mexico to join up with Pancho Villa's band of Villistas?

Charley laughed. "Oh yeah, well, there's a story about how we got there. You see, Maria and I wanted to marry, but for whatever reason her family said no. She was too young. I was too French. Who knows what else they were deciding to keep us apart. But we done married anyway. That's when her family said some threatening things to me. My pa, who done plenty of business with Villa in the past, asked him a favor…a trade of goods to take me and Maria under his protection."

"I had no idea."

"Yep. My father, your uncle Joseph, is so favored that Villa once said to me and Maria, 'mi casa es tu casa.'"

"So, you were at Villa's *rancho*… fighting with the Del Norte division, alongside Villa?"

"No!" Charley laughed, "Nothing like that, Hank. No, we just worked in the kitchen, pero, it was mighty exciting sometimes though. I even got to see his meeting with Emiliano Zapata the day he came up from the south of Mexico and visited Villa's *rancho*."

"Wow. What'd you think of Villa?"

"Villa?" Charley paused. "Well…I guess you could say he has a tender heart. And he can be an impressive, gracious man. But don't get on his wrong side. His temper is not something you want to be around for. By the way, Hank, be careful when you get back to Douglas. They tell me his army is about to attack Calles' men, who have the backing of US troops at Agua Prieta."

"Again?"

"Yep," Charley stuttered for a moment, catching his breath, "after a while, Maria wrote her mother to let her know about our baby, now a-growing up before our eyes. And, with the help of Villa and Grandma Figueroa's persuasion, we're back and all is forgiven. Pa got me a job and housing at Fort Huachuca. I'm the quartermaster there now."

"Really? How'd that come about?"

"You remember the store my pa and your pa had in Pirtleville?"

"Yep."

"Well, my pa talked to his friend, Senator Carl Hayden, and tells him, 'My son Charley knows the merchandising business better than anybody,' and that did it for me."

"So, you're going to be a big man at the fort."

"I hope so," Charley said with a proud smile."

"But, what about Maria?"

"Well, we knew she and the kids must bear out a little unfairness, them being part Mexican and all. Pa says that's just the way it is around here. Hopefully it changes soon. Besides, Maria is strong and her family is used to it. She has lots of love and support from them. It should work out...maybe just like other problems, someday it will go way."

Hank plowed in with a defiant prediction, "Little Charley Jr., you will someday become a famous musician or athlete or both. You'll see. Someday they'll be sorry for looking down on any of us."

Charley smiled. "You know, Hank? That's what I love about you. You're so positive about what you do. Nothing brings you down. It makes you challenge things more...gives you something else to prove."

"Maybe, but don't we all have something to prove out here in Arizona territory?"

"Okay. Enough of this patting each other on the back.

Come with me." Charley gestured for Hank to follow him into the next room. "Look here, Hank. See what my pa got us!" he said as he went over to a desk and whisked a cloth off the top like a magician. "A shortwave radio!"

"I swear," Hank said smartly.

"Now we can get the scores of the baseball games while they're playing, even play-by-play!"

Hank's eyes grew larger, enamored by the thought. He wondered if this was one of the new machines Emiliano had been talking about.

"After dinner we'll get Albert to show us how it works," Charley added.

"So, cousin. Now that you're working for the federal government, what do you hear about the war?"

"Which one, Hank? The one over in Europe?"

"Yep. We going to join the fight?"

"Na. The word is that it will all be over before that happens. They say the Allies have the Germans on the run."

"Hope so, Charley, 'cause I sure don't want to go over there."

"Don't worry, Hank. Like I said, it will be over soon."

"Hey, this is the first time I seen you look scared and such about fighting," Charley teased.

"Well, fighting with guns and knives are mighty different than fixing those masks on for poison gas. That's not for me, Charley."

"Well, no worry. That's what they're saying. No Americans need to go this time. It will all be over soon."

"Is anyone hungry for Texas-style enchiladas and beans?" Maria poked her head in and asked.

Hank felt his eyes almost popping out of his stomach. "Yep!" they both yelled while rushing over to the water bowl to wash up.

Albert's wife greeted them when they sat down around the table. She'd just came back from the laundry shop. "Hank, so good to see you. You're all but grown up."

"Well, maybe so, but unfortunately my size hasn't changed much since I saw you back here in Tombstone a year or so ago at Grandpa's funeral."

Albert broke in, "Yeah, too bad our families…our fathers don't seem to get along. It makes it so we don't get to see each other much. I heard your father is thinking about moving to Los Angeles, near the ocean. Is that so?"

"That's what he's been saying. So, I guess it's true," Hank replied in a low note.

"Look at it this way, Hank. You'll be with the movie stars and football games, and have a heck of a lot more places to see. I hear they even have a Pike where they got some thrill rides. And what about those girls wandering around on them beaches?"

"Saying all that doesn't really help much, Albert, 'cause my younger brothers and sisters and me won't know anybody, nor where to go from there."

"You'll figure it out. You always do. Okay, Maria, say your prayer so we can get to eatin'."

"How about you, Charley, being that you're the man in our growing family," Maria said with obvious love and pride for her husband.

Charley bowed his head and asked God to protect Hank in his new home, then gave thanks for dinner and asked God to please bless the hands that made it. After all had said 'amen' and made the sign of the cross, Hank jumped into the steaming hot Texas enchiladas with a fervor.

"Who made the tortillas?" Hank asked.

Charley answered, "They're really good aren't they. Maria learned from cookin' for Villa's family."

Maria blushed. "No, no."

"You know it's true, Maria. They loved your cookin'. Seemed to me like they didn't want you leaving and comin' back to here to Arizona."

After supper, the cousins sat around and talked a bit before Charley had an idea. "Hank, let's run to the ice cream parlor over on Allen Street. We can bring it back here for the family."

"I'm all in for that."

"Okay. Let's get going." The kids screamed with delight when Charley announced, "We'll be back with ice cream!"

Hank and Charley walked over to the corner of Fremont and cut through the field. Charley chuckled a little. "I'm so tired of hearing gunshots coming from here."

"What? What's going on?"

"On the weekends, this is where the tourists come to watch town folks acting like they're in the middle of the OK Corral shootout. We can hear all the shooting from Albert's back window. It drives me crazy."

They crossed over to Allen Street. Charley went on with a rundown of the town's failings since he'd been back from Mexico. "Tombstone ain't much of a town now. There be two cemeteries. One just outside of town, over there to the north—it's just for the tourists. The other's just off Allen Street for the local burials. A school house been built just up the street from that one. On weekends, sightseers are all about, buying film for their Brownie cameras, shooting photos of everything... like storefronts and the old saloon that's now the ice cream parlor. Anything that looks Western, from four-legged mounts to horse droppin's."

Hank Laughed.

"But now, in the middle of the week, all sorts of men come around...could be miners from Bisbee, farmers and ranchers from the San Bernardino Valley, or just rake and ramblers finding their way south. The military types usually stay down yonder in Sierra Vista, outside the fort gates. There's rarely Injuns or Mexicans or Chinese out during the night. They have their place outside of town. That's just the way it is here, and Hank, they've learn to live with it.'"

The cousins treaded further on down Allen Street, then came to the center of town. Hank and Charley crossed the street to the other boardwalk. Right before the ice cream parlor, they heard a loud grumbling interruption inside.

"Looks to be two skinners," Hank whispered.

"How do you know that?"

"'Cause I seen their kind of fellas in the Chiricahuas. Yeah, they're skinners alright."

"How do you know, Hank?"

"I can tell from their leathers."

Hank and Charley watched as one of the skinners grabbed a young Indian girl by the arm and yanked her about. "Squaw. You can't go in here. Get back home to your teepee! You and your kind need to stay out of town, it's after sunset. Don't they teach you that back on the reservation?" the skinner asked.

Hank noticed Charley glance over to him as though he knew this would not set well. Charley had seen Hank with that look a few times before and might have guessed what was about to take place. Hank stepped up and calmly said, "Mister, you can take your hands off this girl. She means you nothing...just wants some ice cream. That's all. There ain't a need for being rude, now is there?"

The man looked down at Hank and said to his companion, "Look here, Jake. This pint-size half-breed...telling me what to do."

Charley took a step back like he knew what was about to

happen. Hank had a reputation for getting feisty when some-one rubbed him like that.

Hank tempered up like old Villa and said, "I'll tell you one more time. Leave this girl alone. Let her go on her way."

"And if I don't?"

Hank leaned forward, looking up into the skinner's eyes to acknowledge the stand-off. Then with a swift, upward thrust of his left leg, he shoved the man backward with one stroke, then reached into his boot and flushed a switch-blade out, snapped it open, then paused to let the man see the new threat.

"Kid, do you really want this?" the skinner asked.

Hank held his position.

"Okay then."

"Jedidiah, you don't want this either," the skinner's friend said stepping in.

With a look of surprise, the skinner turned to look at the serious and unforgiving frown on his friend's face.

"Jake, you know I'm not afraid of this."

"Well, are you afraid of dying?" Jake hollered back. If you want to fight over this with this kid, then get on with it. But, mind you, this here is Henry Lefebvre's boy, and you never know what his pa Henry will do. They say he'll go bat crazy. He'll follow you to hell and back. There will be no place...not even in Mexico you can hide. Henry will find you over this. Now, just let this one alone."

After a long pause, the skinner slowly let go of the girl's arm. Jake spoke up again, "Okay, boy. No need for that knife. We'd be passing out of town now."

Hank continued to glare as both skinners backed their way out the door and vanished into the night.

The ice cream soda jerk gave out a loud sigh of relief. "Okay, Injun girl, you and that young fella deserve some special ice cream. On the house."

The soda jerk walked over to the ice cream selection, "Come on up here and pick what you want, then find your way back to wherever you come from."

Hank slipped his knife back in his boot and took pleasure escorting the girl to the counter. She picked out vanilla with chocolate toping. With her cup in hand she turned to leave, then stopped and stared at Hank. He could read the gratitude all over her face. She was gracious all right. It needed no saying. Hank gestured his hand like a conductor at the end of a concert signaling "its finished, and it's okay now."

The Injun girl walked out the store, and, much like the skinners, faded into the night.

"Now Charley, what does your family like?" Hank asked.

"Vanilla. Maria has honey at the house. It goes good with that."

"Vanilla it is. Give me two quarts," Hank ordered.

"It will be my pleasure," the clerk said, and while filling the tin he continued, "things are changing around here. Son, your generation and your kind of guts at least give us some hope. Here now, take the ice cream and have a good time tonight. You best stay off Allen Street though." Smiling, he finished with "you just don't know who you may run into."

Before they crossed the street, Charley kicked in, "Every time there's trouble, it draws to you. You're like a big old magnet. You could've looked the other way, yah know."

"But, I couldn't."

"Why's that?"

"Because, all my life someone makes some talk about me or my family, that, somehow we are lower than them. I can't let it pass or that be true, Charley. I'm just trying to stay ahead of the fella behind me. That's all."

"No Hank, you're just trying to stay ahead of the things said about your pa. There's a lot of comic in you, but a lot of fight there, too.

The cousins walked in silence for a bit, until Charley picked up the conversation again. "Your pa…I wished I had some of his gumptions. He's a funnin' guy. I hope my son grewd up something like him. My pa is different. Maybe he'd grow up a little like him too. You see, both are alike…strong men. But your pa strays from the farm a little more then my pa. So, I play music and you'd be challenging the neighbor for a race or a fightin' or whatever."

"That hit my funny bone!" Hank said and laughed.

"What?" said Charley, then they both broke out laughing.

They walked to Fremont Street, then to Albert's front gate. Inside, Albert and his wife sat on the porch swing. Maria sat on the steps with Charley Jr. and Doris Mae, all looking eager to taste some of the promised ice cream. Maria asked, "How was Allen Street tonight?"

"Oh, just like normal when Hank's around."

"What does that mean, Charley?"

"We'll tell you later. No sense now. By the way, Albert, you said you be showing us how that shortwave works. While Maria puts some honey on this here vanilla ice cream, Albert let's you, me, Hank, and the youngins go in and see what this voice machine does."

They all jumped to follow Albert into the house and over to the desk, slouching on what was available. "Here we go," Albert said, flipping one switch, then another. He turned the dial this way and that while static noise punctuated by a voice came out of the speaker.

As the sound crackled they picked up someone talking about the war in Europe. The room fell silent and Hank listened intently, hoping not to miss a word between the breeches in the transmission. When Albert turned the dial, the subject changed. It was baseball!

Hank yelled out with excitement, then they all hushed again. The world series results were in—the Red Sox's beat the Phillies!

The voice went on with more talk about the Red Sox's new pitching prospect, Babe Ruth. He could be really something for the 1916 roster. The voice then began talking about Shoeless Joe Jackson. The kids watched as Hank reacted to all the sports talk, his mind way far away with this guy on the shortwave, to any place but Tombstone.

When the shortwave became silent, Albert asked, "So Hank, what yah think?"

As if he had been brought back from somewhere in space Hank muttered, "Wow, Babe Ruth and Joe Shoeless."

"Hank, you're a babbling about Shoeless Joe Jackson?" Charley laughed a little at Hank, who was still in a daze.

"Hey Hank, you only occasionally wear those boots you got on there for exceptional situations like tonight, not to get your feet in the horse dung. The two things you have in common with Shoeless Joe is, you both play baseball, and you both despise those pioneers who design shoes. But for you Hank, there's just something about a being takin' away by the prevailing wings of the foot industry. Remember what you said to your ma?

Charley looked at Hank, but Hank didn't respond. "I remember after she kept at you to best wear your shoes more often, you told her, 'Ma, there is something perverse about taking something as natural as walking barefoot and enshrining it with leather stolen from the back of a cow, and at the same time enslaving a man's freedom that way. It wasn't a good idea for any man, let alone the cow.'"

They all had a good laugh. Then Hank mumbled, "Gosh. Think of it...all the way from Philadelphia and France. There's a mighty big world out there." No one looked surprised when Hank added, "And I want a piece of it."

"Maybe someday they'd be talking about you on the shortwave?" Charley agreed.

"Yep. Maybe they be," said Hank, with an air of certainty. "Yeah, I'd like that…even little Charley Jr. there, he be on the shortwave too."

"Yeah Hank—now, wouldn't that be something!" Charley said.

Doris watched Hank, perhaps understanding that with Hank, just about anything might be possible.

As the night wore on, Hank said his good nights, took a blanket and pillow offered by Albert, and found a comfortable place out in the barn among a bale of hay. As he'd done the night before, when he saw a star peek through a crack in the roof, he let himself wonder where he would be some years up the road. Would voices announce his name over the short-wave? All this was too distant for him to understand why these thoughts continued to play in his mind when he was all alone, just him and the stars. He never mentioned much of it, except with Josiah, for they seemed to think alike.

CHAPTER 4

BISBEE—JUST PASSING THROUGH

Saying his goodbyes to Charley, Maria, the kids, and Albert tested Hank. He had to hold back from carrying on with too much emotion. It would give him away. He knew somehow it would be too long before they would be together again. It had to be. Hank couldn't get much younger. No, life would take that away from here.

Charley saved Hank from such display of weakness by getting in the last word as they waited for Emiliano.

"Hank, no sightseeing there in Douglas. Villa is in a bad mood…going to be bullets flying about and across the border…just blocks away from your house, so stay low."

"Will do, Charley. Thanks for the advice. Vaya con Dios, Maria." With that, conversation ended and Emiliano arrived.

After Hank got in, Emiliano stepped on the gas and drove away. Up Freemont Street they went, heading toward Bisbee.

Hank kept looking back, hoping to fix the picture of them standing there waving in his mind, then the frame disappeared along with the town of Tombstone.

Once out of sight, Emiliano wasted no time broaching the subject of the night before. "So, *hombre*, they tell me you ran into some trouble last night."

"Where?"

Emiliano chuckled. "You know. In front of the ice cream parlor."

"Who told you this?"

"*Hombre*, this town is too small to be hiding anything."

"What did they say?"

"They tell me you pulled a stiletto on a skinner to save an embarrassed Injun girl."

"Well…maybe so but…"

Emiliano stopped Hank from treading on an acceptable reply. "No *amigo*, no need to explain. No. It was a brave thing to do. Pero, just be careful when you do, remember the stiletto is no match for the *pistola*. You must not hesitate too long."

"*Sí*." Hank agreed, wondering if that was a warning or a caution. No matter, it gave Hank something to think about for a few miles up the road. But that was it, there would be no more conversation about that. They chugged their way up a windy road beveling into the Mule Mountains that cradled the copper boomtown of Bisbee.

With conversation at a standstill and the car chugging on, Hank persisted with his sketches. Challenged again by vibrations at each bump, he calculated his strokes. This jinking strategy displayed so comical of a sight that Emiliano, who respectfully showed how much he fancied Hank's antics, chuckled just under his breath. It was not the merit of Hank's artful skill that got Emiliano's attention, but his amazement at Hank's staunch determination. He finally said so with a smile, "*Hombre*, is there anything that gets in your way, that sidetracks you?"

Hank stopped to consider his answer while looking out into the hillside, then turned to say, "Now that you mention it, no."

"Why *amigo*? Why do you think that's so?"

"Pa, he never taught me that."

"*Amigo*, what do you mean?"

"Well, my pa always says to figure how to do things many ways." Hank grinned eulogizing his father's antics.

"What else does this funny man, your father, say."

Hank thought for a few moments then sat back ready to sound just like his pa. "He says to me, 'Hank, you got to live life out or you might as well be dead. If you don't think big, you will always be small. It's what you are inside, not what others say of you.' Pa is interested in the man—who he is, not what he got, 'cause gotten can cost a man his pride.'"

"But don't he like to live in a big house like his brother, Joseph?" Emiliano asked sincerely.

"Oh yeah. Pa says he don't mind living in a big house, but a little cozy one will do just fine. He doesn't usually lay his head down to sleep anyhow. Pa says to let reason follow your instincts, and a house should not be the measure of a man. That be for others, not him." Hank paused to think on it more. "But...but, he does drink too much. That be his short-coming."

"So I've heard. That's his corral, I guess. And you, my friend, what do you think?"

"Well, I don't drink. The other...well, that's easy. I'm Henry Lefebvre Jr. That's what the certificate says. So not to be confused with my pa, they just call me Hank. And my last name is spelled so funny—being French and all—makes me say it more than twice before a person catches on. I was born in 1900. My mama got me born just up the road before moving on to Douglas, and there ain't been no regret.

"I got to make the best of what God give me. I'd seen better and I'd seen worst then me. I'd seen taller and smaller. So, that's what I do. It's like you said before, Emiliano. It's really about what's up here," Hank said, pointing to his head, "and what I try to think on is the good things. For it's the fellow up there who rides the horse."

Emiliano broke out into full laughter. "Oh, *amigo*, you are a funny one. And, like they say, them apples don't fall too far from the tree. You always got some answer don't you. Well, okay then, *hombre…*"

After some time riding out the bumpy one-lane road, digesting the mountain scenery covering most of the twenty or so miles between Tombstone and Bisbee, they finally crossed over the summit and snaked down the road through the scratched and sculptured peaks of the Mule Mountain Range.

Soon, outskirts of the town came into view. With telegraph communication systems blossoming and the war on in Europe, copper became a rich commodity. Bisbee found itself at the bright edge of the boom, with 10 percent of the world's production coming from there. In fact, it was the most populated town between St. Louis City, Missouri and San Francisco, California. And with the smelter of copper on the rise, Douglas—just a few miles south and serving as a connecter and train hub for the transfer of ore—offered new potential for laborers. Bisbee's population would later recede, but at that time it was a bustling city and soon to become the Hall of Records for Cochise County.

Seeing the few houses that rose above the bluff, Emiliano started in again. "So, *Hombre*, you say you lived here before. How was that?"

"Pa and his brother came here some years ago. They started out in Tucson in a covered wagon with just enough money given them by my grandfather. He be a Frenchman from France and owned a laundry and bakery in Tucson," Hank explained. "When gold was found, they traveled to Pearce, wanting to strike it rich. They tried their luck there. When nothing came up gold, they moved on to Charleston."

"Where? Charleston?"

"Yep."

"Rough town." Emiliano shook his head. "That's where the Clantons, the McLaurys, and Johnny Ringo hung out, and where Justice Burnett came from. He was later shot down in Tombstone."

"Yep. That be so. The brothers left sometime later and found their way to Bisbee for steady jobs in the mines, and that's where Pa met my ma."

They talked on, eventually entering a high mountain pass that traversed down into a canyon with more shackled homes, some mounted on stilts nestled in the crib.

Soon, the center of town came into view. This place was very different than Tombstone or other nearby towns. Bisbee had a cosmopolitan touch, highly unusual for an Arizona mining town and a result of eastern investors' influence on local culture. Its labor force combined a variety of ethnic and racial workers who each added bits of flavor and gave the impression everything was in harmony.

"You know what they say about Bisbee, Emiliano?"

"No *amigo*. What is that?"

"Is a duck a duck?"

"*¿Como?*"

"At first sight, you think 'here they got jobs, money, houses, a shopping district, and even a community recreation center like the YMCA.' It all looks so nice, above the water. But under the water, the duck's feet be a struggling to keep the duck afloat. The workers, no matter if they be Injun, Chinese, darky, Mexican, or half-breed's like me, they understand that the *gabachos*—the whites—they get the best of it all. But even with them, it makes a difference what country they come from.

"The Irish, Polack's, Germans, no matter, all have problems to where to they get to live. They fight over the pay, the job, the churches. My Pa says that's why we moved to Douglas. It's not that good, but for us, better than this place. But Emiliano, you must know this. You've been here many times before, no?"

"Oh no, *amigo*. Before working for Mr. Slaughter on his ranch in Sonora, most of my life I crossed the border only sometimes." Emiliano added with a laugh, "sometimes to rustle a few cattle from here and there, then ride back to Chihuahua to sell them to the revolution for a good price. On one occasion, I met Mr. Slaughter. He trusted me. I trusted him. I scouted awhile with him and we reached an agreement. I protect his ranch from my *amigos* across the border, and he takes care of mi familia. Now, he and Viola are mi familia."

"Emiliano, turn at the next corner. I want to show you something. It will take just a few momentos. Okay?"

"*Sí, hombre.*"

After making a left under the bridge, Hank gave directions toward the bustling center of town. "Let's stop here before we pass through. This was my family's favorite place on Sundays. I remember by the smell. You like sweet rolls, Emiliano?"

"*Sí, pero*, we could be in trouble here with me being Mexicano and *tu* a half-breed." He smiled cautiously.

Reading the concern on Emiliano's expression, Hank kidded back, "No problemo. The Vienna Bakery is just up Brewery Gulch. That's where the bars and all the whores and miners hang about. Ain't too particular there. But a few blocks over is the Copper Queen Hotel, visited by gentlemen and their ladies from back East. Two blocks to the right, now that's another story. There's where the up families move about the banks and shops. It's where the trolley ends and the automobiles begin."

"Okay, *hombre*. I'll take you at your word. You know this town." They made another left and drove past the Copper

Queen Company Store, then turned right at the intersection leading up to Brewery Gulch.

"There it is, the Vienna Bakery!" Hank cried out. They pulled into an alley and parked. Emiliano carefully set the shotgun between the back seats and covered it with his jacket.

"No problem here my friend," Hank repeated, "we can see the car from the bakery." After crossing the street, for the first time on this trip, Emiliano showed his discomfort. Perhaps being in a strange town made all the difference. When Emiliano reached into his pocket, Hank said, "No, *amigo*. It's on me," and gestured for Emiliano to have a seat. "I'll go."

As Emiliano slowly sat down, Hank noticed him scout the place out with a careful eye. Within minutes, Hank returned and placed two sweet rolls and glasses of milk on the table. "Here they eat as good as they smell," Hank said with a laugh. Emiliano tried again to take out some coins. "No, no *amigo*. I told you that it's on me," Hank said, feeling proud that he could do something for this grand man.

"So, Hank, you really lived here before?"

"Yes, yes. As I said, I was born here. Ma tells that she and Pa were married just up the gulch at Sacred Heart. My family weren't allowed to go to the white Catholic church, being that we was half-breeds and all."

Emiliano nodded and said, "Mexicans still ain't allowed."

"Yeah, I figured as much," Hank acknowledged, and went on, "We lived in an old frame house on the side of the gulch up on Chihuahua Hill. I remember there were floods from the monsoons and fires and the typhoid, and there was a rainmaker."

"You had one here too?

"Yep." Hank laughed. "Pa said, when the drought came he would appear, do a dance or two, then rain would come and he'd take care of his thirst in a gulch bar, then disappear when all that weather he caused gave so many problems." Hank sighed, "Pa and my uncle Joseph would go work in the mines. I remember my pa telling me, 'Boy, it's about time you be caring for your brothers and sister and mama while I'm gone.' My pa was French, but we were part this and part that…some Injun, Apache, Mexicano, or who knows. Like I told Mr. Slaughter, Ma never really says what she is. Pa, him being white, could go here and there without a problem. But the for rest of us, not so easy. Funny world we live in. *¿Sí?* Then we moved to—"

Before Hank could finish, trouble happened. Several angry looking men with wooden sticks, and even a few with rifles, marched by. They looked to be heading toward the middle of town. Hank and Emiliano looked out the window and saw large crowds gathering and beginning to line the street. Some threw rocks at the men marching down the street. Hank and Emiliano stood to get a better view of what was going on, then headed outside.

At the entrance to the company store, another group of men gathered and boldly waved protest signs. The two groups rushed to meet and thus began a vicious riot. Men with the sticks brazenly beat men with signs. Hank and Emiliano had nowhere to retreat. Before long, bodies of fallen men blocked the streets. The baker ran out, bumping into Hank.

"*¿Qué paso, Señor?*" Emiliano shouted.

The baker answered, "It's the Wobblies!"

"Who?"

"The Wobblies—the miners striking for better pay. They want to have a union like they done yonder in the towns of Jerome and Clifton. But the owners don't take to unions." Suddenly Hank heard ear-piercing gunshots, then shouts of distress, much like the wounded cries of an animal. More shots caused the startled crowd to run all about, up and down the gulch, hiding in alleyways or taking cover behind cars.

"I think it's time to go. *¡Vamos a ir rapidamente amigo!*" Emiliano called over to Hank. Crouching down for protection, Hank and Emiliano rushed across the street, then clutched the sides of building walls until reaching the alley where Emiliano had parked the car. "Get in, Hank!" Emiliano yelled now, then quickly grabbed his shotgun. "You know how to shoot?" Emiliano tossed the weapon over to Hank, "Shoot anyone who tries to stop us! You got that?"

"Yes sir." Hank answered, preparing a firm grip.

"Don't worry, it's loaded. Now, just do as I tell." This was new for Hank. He'd been at the other end of the barrel before, even had to pick a few buck shots from his backside but never had he prepared to shoot another man. Emiliano started the car, put it in gear, and accelerated up the alley, making a screeching right turn. Then he slammed the pedal to the floor—giving the car all it could take—and raced across an intersection, nearly impaling a man who dove out of the way just in time. From his side of the car, Hank got a glimpse of a man lying in the street, arms spread as if praising the sky, blood pooled about his body. Another man attempted to parry off blows set upon him by a crowd swarming in an excited and brutal frenzy of kicking and jabbing. But Hank glued his eyes on a wiry-brushed face of a man. It wasn't the face that was about to do him harm, it was the rifle he brandished.

While Emiliano changed gears to retreat, Hank's instincts took over. Hank focused on him like prey looking down the sights of a hunter's weapon. He lurched the shotgun as if blocking a line-drive ball coming directly toward his face and took aim. He'd shot a gun before, but this time he knew if he pulled the trigger, the response would kill a man. He thrust his hands up to prepare. All he had to do was pull his finger, fire, and defile the man's life. Time stood still while a standoff of nerves provoked a response. Somehow, though, Hank found himself reasoning with the man's eyes, much like he'd done many times before when animals readied themselves to attack. The man apparently saw the benefit of Hank's hesitation, and a boy's face behind the shotgun. He let down his anger just for that moment, giving Emiliano time to shift to the right gear and press on.

As the man faded back into the ruckus of the streets, Emiliano drove the car under the bridge, then turned left toward safety. They were on the highway now, proceeding out of town in the direction of Douglas, when Emiliano glanced over to Hank and calmly said, "Say, Hank. Your hesitation... maybe not so lucky next time." Then, as was becoming his habit, he brushed aside his comment, letting Hank work it out. "So much for passing through Bisbee for a sweet roll. Hey, *hombre?*" Hank was not sure if it was the humor in his statement or simply the huge relief of being past danger that caused them to both laugh out loud. Emiliano roared, "No matter, *amigo*, we're on our way to Douglas!"

They traveled on down the road. It wouldn't be long now, maybe only about a half hour or so before they reached Douglas. As they drove, the bumpy road felt peaceful, much like the rhythm of a familiar song being played under the rumbling car. "Stop here!" Hank yelled after they came around a bend.

"Here, *hombre?*"

"*Sí, amigo*. Right here, *por favor*. Now!" Hank pleaded like a kid in a candy shop.

"Okay, *amigo*. But where?" Emiliano patiently asked.

"There, park over there to the left of the road," Hank said, pointing.

"*Uno momento por favor. No problemo*," Emiliano said as he pulled the Jackrabbit over and did just as Hank asked. After this morning's events, they shared something now that made them more like partners.

Hank unlatched the door and jumped out. With raised arms, he said, "Look at that, *amigo*! Do you see it?" Both looked out over the panoramic view of the desert below. "There they are, the Chiricahuas to the east." Hank directed the scene as if serving as a guide. "Look at the Madrean's way out there, blending with those blooming storm clouds, giving us a glimpse of amazing orange fire colors. A raw beautiful art piece of nature, *¿Sí?*" Hank proclaimed.

Emiliano, followed his gaze out over the spectacular view they shared. Hank finally broke the silence. "This might be the last time I'll be able to see this. Look at that smoke streaming in the air. That's Douglas. That's where I'm really from. I might have been born in Bisbee, but I learned and grew up in Douglas. I learned all there was to know and I was free to do most anything there." Wistfully, he continued, "Now, who knows what's up ahead of me. It don't matter though. Douglas will always be my home. I can see Ma, Pa, family, and my friend Josiah, together, all of us there, no matter what."

"What else do you see, *amigo*?"

"Just look up into them clouds, Emiliano. There, do you see them too? Can you imagine the frontiersmen and Indians who lived here, the soldiers who fought here, the Mexicans, the missionaries, the settlers, the ranchers? How 'bout them farmers, struggling in the heat and cold of the rugged desert. Then there's the animals that prey about for food...I see them all. I see what was once Mexico, then a territory fighting Confederate battles and then the Union and, finally, becoming the state of Arizona. Pa told me about all of it. But even after that, nothing really changes much, 'eh, Emiliano?" Hank looked at his friend who nodded. "Not here in this part of the word, that's what makes it so special," Hank continued, "history passes by. But I hope not by a place like this. Like you said before, *amigo*, it's the relics left behind as markers that let you know where you come from and who you are."

Emiliano looked over at Hank with a new sense of respect. "*Amigo*, you are very old, for such a new *hombre*."

Hank became serious. "Emiliano, what makes men like the ones we saw in the riot, back there? The killing sometimes needs doing, but with the excitement, the jubilance of violence in their faces? What kind of men are they?"

In a somber voice, Emiliano answered, "In my life, I've seen that look on a man many times. I once asked a priest, 'Is man of God or of the devil?' He told me that it's up to each one to choose. For that's what life is about, the trials of despair and sacrifice. Out of it all, will we give into the good, or the bad of it? For me, a man who cherishes the thought of taking another man's life…I don't want him around, no matter how noble his cause." Emiliano finished with a slim smile, "So, *amigo*. Let's get going. I think you and me, we think out the problems for many men."

"Yes. Let's get on with it," Hank agreed and they both laughed, disguising potential embarrassment from searching too deep into their souls. Doing so, of course, could make a man vulnerable, letting down his play too early.

Now it was on to Douglas, a dozen miles or so on a straight and narrow road that went no other place ahead on the desert floor. A cautious thought strayed into the back of Hank's mind as they drove. Just five blocks from his house on Fifth Street was the Mexican town of Agua Prieta. It was there that Pancho Villa and his Villista army encamped—poised like rattle snakes, ready to strike a deadly blow to his Mexican opposition. Farther away from Douglas was Villa's opposition, a man named Plutarco Elias Calles. With the blessings of President Wilson (because of his flirtatious involvement in the Mexican revolution) and backing of the United States military, the die was cast for an altercation.

Hank knew—from stories of previous battles—that some bullets and cannon fire would miss their mark and surely make their way across the border, most likely killing a few of his Douglas neighbors. Sadly, this had happened before. Oh, some men could be faulted, the ones who had the audacity to stand on high buildings to view the attraction, the progress of the battle. They might be deserving of such a fate, but Hank had doubts about faulting those who huddled on dirt floors and under beds for protection. Hank was hopeful that when it was all over, his own flourishing family would be spared tragedy.

CHAPTER 5

DOUGLAS

The town of Douglas came in a vision to James Douglas, known as "Rawhide Jimmie," a name given to him during his travel to Arizona's Sulfur Valley one fine day. The idea of a smelter occurred to him when he approached the area where the Mexican border town of Agua Prieta collided with Arizona territory.

"Yes," he declared, "a new town should be built here for the overload of the Bisbee copper industry and Mexico's mining traffic."

The new town, Douglas, would include a railroad hub to serve both the ore producers in Bisbee and the cattle ranchers of the San Bernardino Valley. From here, their products could be distributed in all directions by rail. This idea lit a spark, resulting in speculation and migration of all kinds of characters, some with good intentions and some of the worst kind. Hastily, they arrived in this new, bustling seedling of a town where a person could take a chance, find his niche, get a second start in life, or, at the very least, make a meager living.

Douglas was never built upon cosmopolitan ethics. No. A town in this part of the West became a case for rugged, individual survivalist mentality. Smelter workers gambled, brawled, and scooted about the red-light districts down on Fifth and Sixth Streets, trying to find an easy touch of love.

The young town soon acquired a reputation that gnawed into the annals of western novels. That is, until the puritanical city patrons hired legendary Arizona ranger, Captain Thomas H. Rynning.

After closing the door of his former headquarters in Bisbee's Brewery Gulch, he headed for Douglas. Upon his arrival, Captain Rynning later noted in Westward Ho Magazine, September 1929:

I've been in many a tough town in my day, but from Deadwood to Tombstone, I've never met up with a harder formation than Douglas when we made the Arizona Rangers' home corral there in 1902. Cattle thieves, murderers, all the worst hombres of the United States and Mexico made their headquarters there. The dance halls were the worst I've ever seen on any frontier. Most of them was run by men who'd plenty notches on their guns, and their hangers. They were all just plain poison. It wasn't no ways safe, even for an officer of the law to walk along Tenth or Sixth Street after dark. Robberies were going on everywhere. People were being killed, even in the hotels. And at least half the deputy sheriffs were blackleg gamblers and killers.

Hank and Emiliano chugged along in the Jackrabbit until they met with a thick yellow fog invading the clear desert air. It menaced and clouded the view of Douglas down below. Some said the fog was from the smelter, others blamed it on wind whipping about the dust from Sulfur Valley. No matter, by the fog, Hank knew they were about to reach the outskirts of Douglas. Giving into this evidence, Hank placed his paper sketches and well-worn pencil back into his carrying bag and said, "Emiliano, you can leave me off at Fifteenth Street. It's only a short distant from my house on Fifth. After, you should go due east and you'll be back at the ranch."

"*Sí, hombre*, I know this, but it won't work that way. You see, Mr. Slaughter tells me to make sure you get all the way home." He chuckled a little. "You have this thing about running into trouble and sometimes not getting to a place you aimed at. So, for your safety and mine, I will put you back in your mother's arms. Maybe she's not so happy to see you, but Mr. Slaughter will be happy with me." Emiliano smiled broadly at his decision and drove on down G Street.

Douglas, the oasis in the in the mist of the dry desert, showed signs of concerns this day. The crowds that usually wallowed about the storefronts, restaurants, and freshly painted houses were gone. After passing the Gadsden Hotel, Emiliano spoke up, "Yep, it smells like Villa is about to attack alright." They slowly drove on until arriving at the corner of G and Fifth Street.

"There it is, *amigo*. My house is the third from the corner."

"So, it was as you said. You do live close to the border."

"Yep, just a football toss away."

"Best be careful in the next few days, *amigo*." After turning down Fifth Street, Emiliano made a U-turn to pull up directly in front of Hank's house.

"It's a bit small for all of us, but better than the tent city we used to live in," said Hank.

Suddenly, the front door burst open and remnants of the family ran out, shouting, "Hank's home, Mama! Hank's Home!"

When his mother reached the car, Hank said proudly, "Mama, this here is my good friend, Emiliano."

"Yes son, I know. Mr. Slaughter told Uncle Joe his trusted foreman would be taking care of you." Hank's mother looked at Emiliano, "*Mucho gracias, señor*, for getting my son home safely. I hope he didn't get under your skin too much along the way," she added with a smile.

"Oh no, señora Lefebvre. It was my pleasure. He is a fine *hombre*," Emiliano assured. It was obvious to the family that the two had become good friends.

"Would you like to come in for some lemon water?" Hank's mother offered.

"I am sorry, señora. I must be on my way. Mr. Slaughter has many things for me to do before the sun goes down. Emiliano turned back to Hank and said, "*Vaya con Dios*. And, *amigo*, you come my way again, I take you all around the San Bernardino Ranch…you and your *compadres*. *¿Sí?*"

"*Sí, amigo*."

With goodbyes finished, Emiliano lurched the car out onto the road and made a right at the corner. After watching the chugging car go out of sight, Hank's mother said, "Come on in now and tell us what's going on with our cousins in Tombstone. But first leave that dirty old bag of smelly clothes outside here on the porch. I'll scrub them for you in a while."

Hank dropped his bag where his ma pointed then pulled her to his side. "We done some trading up there in the Chiricahuas." He pulled some change from his pocket. "It's not too much, but it can help. Yes, Mama?"

His mother smiled brightly. "I'm sure glad to have you, Son. With Pa and all…I don't know if we'd could make it without the extra money you bring in. You is always thinking about us. I love you, Son," she said after giving Hank a big, warm hug. "Well, that's that. Come on in now, Hank. How about me fixing you tamales and warm up some tortillas. Then you could tell me what Charley's kids look like. Are they happy?" she asked while putting on her apron.

"Yep. I'm sure of it, Mama. In fact, did you know Uncle Joseph got Charley a job as quartermaster over at Fort Huachuca? And Charley Jr., he's grown so big. And Mama, you should see little Doris Mae. She's a daisy. When growed up, she'd be a fine-looking lady. So, Mama, what's been going on around here?"

"Well, Hank, you've come back at just the right time. Villa, he's back again and about ready to attack. In fact, he's already been known to take cannon shots around Agua Prieto," she said, as she took down a pan from the cupboard, "and by the sound of them, he's not far away. So, after you get your fill of eats, you need to go find your pa and get him back here before it all gets a-going. Your sisters, they be over at the boarding-house cleaning. Alfred, Bennie, and Gilbert were supposed to be out lookin' for Pa. They ain't made it back so far though, and we need wood to cover over the windows to stop the bullets like the last time Villa came to town."

"Okay, Mama. I'll go over to the Seventh Street cottages and get Josiah. His pa and ours ain't never an arm's length apart, doing what knows…probably hangin' out in the billiard hall, playing pool."

"Well, you just pass on through Sixth Street. Hank, I never know what's going on there with those two men…gambling and such."

"Don't you worry, Mama. Me and Josiah have some friends over there."

"You and that Polack. What you get yourself into, I don't even want to know. Just be sure you don't end up like your pa."

"Now, Mama. Pa ain't that bad. Why, even Texas John said so. In fact, he said he would hire him any day!"

"So, he did, did he?"

"Yep. That's what he'd told me just a day ago at his ranch."

"Well then, let him do it and maybe your pa will quit his ramble ways. I dare say it won't be too soon. Mind your manners now, when you prowl around with Josiah."

"Yes, Mama." Hank smiled and leaned over to gently kiss his on her forehead.

"Get to eating, then get to going. Time it's a-wasting and I'm sure your uncle Joseph's friendship with Villa ain't about to help us out this time."

"Yes ma'am!" Hank replied, and rushed through the meal so he could set out to look for his pa. At times like this, Hank needed to appraise his predicament. They way he saw it, Pa had the constitution to get work and be dependable, but here's where the bent came in: Pa was a rambler and a bit of a rake. He could add on to that layer of cake that he was a bit of a hustler, too, especially when he hung around with Big Mike. Yeah, Josiah's pa and his were gone for days at a time, but somehow they'd squeeze in work at the smelter between playing cards and hanging out in the billiard parlor. There was no arguing with their reputation. They were a well-known, fun-loving, likeable pair that let none come in their way, and they liked it that way.

Ma would put up with it. She only required Pa to be at the Immaculate Conception Church every Sunday, on time, and looking like the gentleman he wasn't. She was always so busy having babies—she lost one named Robert some time back. Buried him next to Grandpa Anton in the Douglas cemetery, around the corner. Hank's family was up to seven, for now. There was Hank, Alfred, Gilbert, and Benny. The girls-Mary, Lillian, Esther, and some others that didn't make it out of Ma's womb on time. They'd never met them, so Ma or Pa never brought those souls up much in conversation. Let it be, there sure was a bunch of them. They were a family and it ran this way. Pa, then Ma…the girls, well they worked with Mama most of the time at the boardinghouses, cooking or cleaning or what not, while still going to school like the boys. They all did most what Ma said.

Hank was the exception as far as school went. It fell to him to pick up the slack when his pa was gone. Alfred, though quiet and shy, was second in command. Lillian, being the smartest and second loudest, would think of herself as next to Hank. She never let the others boss her, no matter.

Now the finding of Pa was more a deed than a person first set eyes on, for who knew where he could be about. You see, the real reason—liquor—always got in the way of his good intentions. As usual, Ma had already sent out the other boys to find their pa, but they wouldn't follow through, of course, and Hank knew it was 'cause all they would do was find a sweet store or sneak into the movie house, a trick Hank had taught them one day. Instead, the boys would hustle around, scrape up a few pennies, then come home sure enough, sometimes happy, but always with no Pa."

Hank was more experienced in the business of "Pa lookin's" and always made sure to bring along his best friend. Josiah was built like his own pa, Big Mike, and knew more about tracking down these two fellows better than any of them. It always involved traveling about the town asking all kinds of questions. Yep, their pa's would leave clues and the boys usually ended up finding them and giving them a need to get back home...if only for a while.

So the first thing for Hank to do on this day was to tie in with Josiah over at the Seventeenth Street motel, where he lived and work part time with his second ma. She was less as-suring as a mother, but worked hard. Unwanting of her own family made her more social in her religious settings at Sacred Heart.

What was comforting for Josiah came from his girlfriend, Chata Armida. Her family came from a Sonora mining town and her father worked as a handyman for the motel. His fa-ther was also a close relative of Charley Lefebvre's ma, they kind of grew up together way back in Tombstone before Chata was born. Chata was just little taller than Hank, but not as tall as Josiah. She was a pretty Mexican girl alright, with the spirit of a bull, but stubborn as a mule. When folks ask about her coming from Mexico, she'd say, "No. I'm from here, just like most of you *gabachos*." And that would be enough to swat them down like flies. Chata and Josiah were always a match. They mostly wandered about the streets with the Lefebvre boys. That's the way it was in those days, especially in Douglas. Somehow, they all made it home. They were dependent on each other...had sort of a "community watch," that was their way of caring for neighbors, yet not getting in the way.

Hank walked quickly over to Sixth Street where the whores and gambling sharks preyed. Turning down offers, he continued along to Seventeenth Street where he figured Josiah would be waiting. Hank would later tell that each time they met was "a jubilant occasion, for they knew they was on to a new adventure." Hank had a way of leading and this day would be no exception.

Josiah greeted Hank with a handshake. "So, Hank. I heard you have this thing for a young Injun girl back in Tombstone?"

"Nah, who told you that?"

"Come on, Hank, everybody knows what you did to that skinner. Heard he almost got the best of you."

"Well he didn't, did he?"

They both laughed, happy to have another episode to jaw about. "Josiah, we got to go find our pa's. Ma is worried 'cause old Villa is around, talking about shootin' up Prieta. Need to board up those windows at my house. Let's get going?"

"Okay, Hank. But wait till I get Chata. She just finished cleaning Bungalow 28." Hank sat down to wait and shake off the yellow dust that lingered around in the late afternoon. It didn't take long for Josiah and Chata to come back around the corner. Hank thought Josiah was sure lucky to have Chata. Not only was she pretty, but usually nice and cheerful, always wanting to be a part of the boys' adventures.

"Let's ride the bikes. It will hurry up the looking," Josiah said.

They took off together. First stop was the Gadsden Hotel where the two pa's loved to get a drink together before deciding what to do. It was where the locals and important people connected. Even people like the next president of Mexico, Calles, would stop off at the Gadsden. It was legend that Villa, back when he'd befriended the Americans, would make a grand entrance by riding his horse into the lobby and up the hotel stairs. Hank was sure that was mostly stories to attract the tourist, but it was true that's where their pa's would start their daily talkin's." They rode a few blocks up to G Street, then down the dirt road behind the Gadsden. After leaning their bikes up against the hotel wall, they walked around to the front and warmly greeted their friend and porter, Pedro Cedrillo.

"*¿Qué pasa, Pedro?*"

"*Está todo bien, amigos,*" Pedro answered, then added with a smile, "Chata, you must not spend too much time with this half-breed and the Polack. By the way Hank, I heard you got into trouble again...this time over an Injun girl."

"No, no. Who keeps this thing going around? That was back in Tombstone."

"We know everything here at the Gadsden, hey *amigos?*"

They laughed together then Hank asked, "If you know so much, Pedro, where is my pa and Big Mike?"

"Sorry, haven't seen him or Josiah's pa for a few days back. I'll check with the bartender for you. He will know. *¿Sí?* Stay out here. No need for more trouble."

"Thanks, Pedro. We'll wait."

Hank began to tell Josiah and Chata about his cousin Charley's trip to Mexico and his work on Villa's ranch, but was interrupted when Pedro returned. "The bartender says they went just this morning to Bobbie's on Sixth Street."

"Oh no. He's sure?"

"*Sí*. That's what he says."

"Okay. Thanks, Pedro."

Pedro teased. "Now, Hank, you best stay away from those pretty Injun girls."

"Right. I'll keep that in mind, Pedro."

On the way to their bikes, Josiah patted Hank on the back. "See, Hank. No hiding from your bravery around here."

"Come on, Josiah. Let's go over to Sixth. Gosh, I hate that place," Hank confided as they rode.

"Why do they always end up there?" Josiah asked.

Chata jumped in. "They don't go there for the whoring. They just like sitting out on the front porch, drinking, and looking at all those rough characters walk about. Makes them feel like *macho hombres*…somebodies.

"Really? That's it? I guess that's what a life in the smelters brings." Josiah added. Hank finished the thought, "Sixth Street is only a part of Douglas. Thank God."

On the way to Bobbie's, whores passed them by without a look. Not just because of Chata's presence, but because they knew Hank and Josiah. There would be nothing going on there for them. They also knew from time to time the boys would be out hunting down their fathers. As Hank swung open the door to Bobbie's saloon, a large muscle-bound man stopped him and said, "No son, you can't come in here."

"Oh, it's you, Hank and Josiah," another man stepped out. "These here are Henry Lefebvre and Big Mike's boys," he said to the muscle-bound man. "What are you two doing down here? Hank, I bet you be looking for your pa. Ain't been home for a stint?"

"Yup. That's it."

"Well then, he's with his trainer, Big Mike."

"Over at the YMCA on Pan American Avenue?"

"Yep. And you best get there pronto, Kemosabe, 'cause Henry's prizefighting right now."

After giving their respects, the kids rushed to jump back on their bikes and hurried back across to G Street, just on the other side of the railroad station. While racking their bikes on the side of the gymnasium, they overheard a ruckus inside. Once they convinced the door attendant Hank's pa was the one fighting, he let them in. Inside, the boys found an intoxicated crowd yelling and storming about the bleachers and ringside. In the center of the ring, two fighters—Hank 's pa and another man—were putting the hurts on each other, with each punch landing—no matter on who. The packed crowd reached a crescendo with each violent blow. When the bell rang, the two fighters returned to their corners, mounted their chairs, then braced for buckets of water to be tossed over their heads. All the while, handlers solicited bets from eager men scattered about the gym.

Hank pushed his way up past Big Mike and noticed the sign announcing the Fifth round. "Hey, Pa. Doing good?"

Henry whispered in Hank's ear, "Son, almost got him where I want 'im."

"Yep, Pa. Looks that way."

"Heard about the Injun in Tombstone," Henry said.

"Aw, Pa. Not that..."

"Well, Son—" but Henry was interrupted by the bell. Giving Hank a final confident smile, he stood to meet his challenger and the fighters began again.

They threw raging, tearing, heavy blows at each other, first to the face, then back to the body. Hank watched, mesmerized. Blood flowed from the fighter's faces. The bell finally rang again for a two-minute respite. The men were thrashed again by buckets of water, and Henry looked at his son and spoke up, red liquid flowing from his mouth, "Son, I got him where I want him. This is the last round. Bet on that." He smiled as the clanging bell rang out announcing it was back to work for the fighters.

The fighters approached the center of the ring, touching gloves before continuing the beating. Henry delivered a right that should have put away a bigger man, but the opponent countered with a right, followed by a quick left, then finished with a crushing blow to Henry's body, and he to the canvas. Henry lay motionless until the count reached six. Then Henry turned over and pulled himself to standing. Still bent over, the crowd became ecstatic, waiting deliciously for a knockout. The men began beating each other again with smashing jabs and uppercuts, then one last flurry caused Henry to fall to the mat for the third time. Hank mumbled under his breath, "Pa ain't getting up."

At last the referee waved back the fighters, declaring the fight over, and the crowd went into an operatic roar. Big Mike crawled through the ropes to toss another wet bucket at Henry, who slowly came back to life. After rolling over and struggling up to one knee, Henry leaned into Big Mike. Only Hank saw the glimpse of a smile that came between the two friends. As Big Mike brought Henry to his feet, someone in the crowd yelled. "You bum! You could have taken him!" With the help of Big Mike, Henry stumbled to his dressing room. Hank, Josiah, and Chata mingled about until another fight began.

On their way to the dressing room, an angry man passed

and said to another, "It was fixed. Henry should have taken the other guy out in the early rounds." Finally, Hank saw Big Mike and his pa coming out of the locker room, both carrying stuffed bags and looking rather content considering what just happened back in the ring. In fact, Hank thought they looked quite happy and reluctantly considered that maybe the grumbling men were right about the fight being fixed. He hoped it wasn't true.

"Pa. You looked good out there, for a while."

"Thanks, Son. So, Ma wants me home?"

"Well, now that Villa's going about putting bullets in the air, she wants to board up the windows. It's not a bad idea. Right, Pa?"

"Yeah. Why not," Henry said, while giving Chata a kiss on the cheek. "You be taking care of Big Mike and his boy for me, Chata."

"They's good at doing that themselves, Mr. Lefebvre." She smiled back.

"Okay. Tomorrow then, Mike. Hank and me... we need to get home. Ma and the family needs me."

As his pa turned to leave, Hank leaned in to say, "Josiah, see you guys later tonight around ten o'clock at Eighth Street Park."

"Like always," Josiah replied.

Henry blurted out over his shoulder, "Keep your heads down. Villa means business." Then he added, "Hank, let's go get some ice cream first."

"Sure, Pa."

Once seated, Hank called out to the waiter, "We'll be having two chocolate malts with eggs!"

"Hank, let's talk."

"Little to tell, Pa."

But Henry raced on with questions. "Tell me about your

trip up to the Chiricahua mountains. I heard you spent the night at Slaughter's ranch? Nice fellow, that Texas John. But mind you, there's another side of him. And your cousin Charley, did you know what your uncle Joseph did for him…with Villa?"

"Yep, Pa. He told me so."

Henry looked up at Hank. "Boy, I am proud. Without you, I couldn't do all this." He noticed a puzzled look on Hank's face and asked, "What is it, Son?"

Hank stuttered, trying to find the right words. "Well, Pa it's just…you could've taken that guy out tonight."

Henry rested back in his seat as if considering his answer or stalling his reply. The waiter placed their malts on the table. "On your tab, Lefebvre?" he asked.

"No, not tonight. Here ya go. Keep the change." Henry told him with a broad smile. Then Henry took a sip of the delicious malt and looked at Hank, "Well, get to it, Son."

They sat together sipping their malts in silence until Henry began his explanation. "This is the way I see it, Son. A man's got to have priorities. I have come to know I'll never be the world champ at boxing. That I know for sure. I can carry on a good fight with the best of them, though. Those people back there, on occasion, will bet on me. Sometimes I win. Sometimes I lose. Win or lose, for me, it don't really matter. For if a man's willing to bet on another man's courage when he's not willing to get in the ring and fight for his own, well… he's getting his money's worth for just getting the thrill of what might be. That man can watch, be entertained for what he doesn't have. Son, we win either way."

Henry reached over into his sports bag and pulled out a wad of bills. "Look what we got tonight. Big Mike and I worked the fight, getting bets both ways. This here money is for Ma and you kids. And look. I got this shortwave radio to boot!" Henry gave a big smile as he pulled it out with a flourish. You see son, now we can listen to all the sports we want from home—Yankees, Boston Red Soxs, Giants, and Dodgers—just as they happen. Plus, news from around the world, even the war."

Hank stumbled on his words trying, not to stifle his pa's exuberance. "But... Pa...what about honor?"

"Precisely the point, Hank. I might never be a Rawhide Jimmy Douglas, nor for that matter a Texas John or Carl Hayden or Wyatt Earp. My education and past deeds are not up to that. Nor my drinkin', I might add, but I can have some comforts by trading in talents and letting people be entertained on what I do. Do you see, Son? Each one of us trades what we can do for those who can't do what we can. Think of the farmer trading a bottle of milk from his dairy for a dozen eggs. Each in his own way gets what they need. Sometimes, you do come up short."

"Like your card gambling, Pa?"

"Yep, that be true, Hank. Boy, I know that to be so, but the best of men love sitting around, smoking their expensive cigars over a game of poker. That could be something to win on, but I also get to know people... their instincts and qualities play out even when they lose. Some men make it rich by taking a chance."

"Yep, I guess they do," Hank agreed.

"Now look at your uncle Joseph, he does his own type of gambling. But his gambling is real estate or mining investments, calling it 'venture capital,' all the while, they be hoping—and yes, betting—the price or the profit goes up, not down. Me, I'm not as patient as they be. I'm not like the others out there," Henry said, pointing his hand toward the street. So, there you have it, Son. Education and instinct is what you need to make your mark. Honor and pride is good, but sometimes it gets in the way of making the best for you and your family. Now, tell me about the skinner you pulled on in Tombstone," he laughed and added, "and hey, what about you boys camping out by those men hanging from a tree?"

Hank couldn't help but be humored out of all the serious talk. Pa always did that to him. "Oh, no. Not going to talk on that again."

"Well then, how much money did you make up there in the Chiricahuas with Alfred, Bennie, and Josiah, trading fish with the mountain men and Injuns?"

"Some fair amount of change. I already gave it over to Mama."

"Good job. Proud of you, boy. Let's get from talking and get on home… haven't seen your ma and the kids for a while. She's right, we need to get ready for Villa's warring."

"My oh my, how time's a changing. Villa was once a good friend of my brother's, and now look. He's gone and got himself fightin' against the government of Mexico and US troops." Henry and Hank stood to leave. "Oh, by the way, about you signin' up for that military to go over there to Europe… you let those Englishmen take care of the fight they got themselves into it. No need to make their troubles ours. Boy, we've got enough on our table right here in Douglas. Mind you, Douglas might not be the best of places in the world, but it's better than most. Now, let's get you home to get those windows walled up and round up the family so none get killed like some of those townsfolk did the last time old Villa came through."

They walked together a short way before Hank pleaded, "Pa?"

"Yes, Son?"

"Are we still planning to go to California?"

"I think so, Son. Your uncle Joseph's got things all set up

in the city of Long Beach down there in the south of that big state." Henry must have noticed the concern in Hank's voice. "Listen, Son, you gonna like those sandy beaches. Yah hear? I was in California one time with Uncle Joe and your grandma and grandpa. It's plenty nice and there's a cool ocean breeze like nothing you've ever felt around these parts."

"You think then I'll be making some friends out there?"

"I'd bet on it, Hank. With your talents, you'd be making good friends. And besides, maybe Big Mike and Josiah will come live there once we get to telling them how nice and friendly California people be. But for now, Uncle Joseph thinks it's best we get out of town for a while. No telling how long." Henry stopped short, looked back over his shoulder, then said, "Tell your ma I'll be back around, after I do a little celebrating with the boys for coming out to the fight. Take some of this here money and the shortwave. Tell her I'll be home shortly."

Hank knew what that meant. No reason asking when. "Okay, Pa. See yah then."

CHAPTER 6

VILLA'S CURIO SHOPPING

Alice Gatliff, an American business woman, owned a thriving curio shop in Mexico, just across the border from Douglas, Arizona. Only a wire fence and a dried-up riverbed separated her shop from the Lefebvre's house on Fifth Street. That curio shop was where many of the Mexican revolutionaries hung out while scheming about politics, history, and the future of Mexico—all with a common desire to see change, but change in opposition to the Villistas' view. That's why Agua Prieta and its neighbors in Douglas became focal points for Villa's tirade with America.

Villa's arrival into town again caused Hank's ma considerable stress. She worried about the family's safety, and—as usual—couldn't wait around for Henry's help. "Alright, let's get to work now. All the windows on that side facing the border needs a covering. Remember what happened last time? Little Alfred almost got to heaven. The bullets from the fightin' just missed him and hit the pot over there." She walked over to pick up the dented pot to remind everyone. "Just think about it," Hank's mother's tender eyes shined through drops of tears, "this pot could have been you, Alfred." Frightened looks came over the children's faces. Then with a smile and an upbeat tone ma added, "But it wasn't now, was it? So, let's get to workin'. Girls, you start cleaning the floor 'cause were gonna to be sleepin' under the beds tonight. Think of it like camping out, but inside," she said with a laugh.

"Now all of you, if nature calls, empty the bowl out the back side. No matter, we'll take care of it in the morning. Hank—you, Alfred, Gilbert, and Benjamin—you boys take care of the boarding up."

"Mama, what about Pa?" Hank asked.

"Don't worry about your pa. You know he can take care of himself and Big Mike. They've been a team much longer than you and Josiah. And besides, like he said, he'd be back shortly. I'm sure after some games of pool, your pa will come back all blustered up and probably sleep through it all."

When the sun slowly caved into the west, Douglas seemed to stand still. Townspeople had locked themselves into their homes, and the few who ventured out moved quietly.

"Hank, we're about to have supper now. Eat some up, then get to running over to Sacred Heart Chapel."

"Aw, Ma," Hank protested.

"Go, *vámonos*. Make sure to light a candle to the Virgin for our family." She handed over fifteen cents. "Tell her I'd be doing it myself but I got my hands full. She'll know about that anyhow." Hank knew his ma never did anything important without checking in with the Virgin Mary. He thought somehow she knew her well. It was as if they were close friends, and times like this required Ma to make sure the Virgin heard her concerns. There would be no argument from Hank.

"Yes Mama. I'll be getting back real soon."

"And Hank no going to over Eighth Street this early. Maybe later, this being a special night. If you see Pa, help him find his way home."

"Okay, Mama." Hank did what his ma asked. He ran over to the church, went to the side alter, picked up a match, dropped the change in the box, and lit a candle. After relaying what Ma wanted to say and sensing nothing miraculous coming back, Hank turned to leave and found Father Sandwosky standing in his way.

"Good to see you, Hank. It's been some time."

"Yes, Father. It's been a while."

"The church football and baseball teams sure could have used your help this year."

"Aw, I know Father, but I spent so much time in the Chiricahuas working with the fire people and fishing and hiking."

"And I'm sure trading a few things in between."

"Well, yes. A man's got to make a livin'. Right, Father?"

"So, how's Adela—your ma—doing?"

"Good, workin' all the time."

"Yes, of course. She does that. Haven't seen much of the family here in church lately."

"Well, you know, Father, Ma don't go here anymore on Sundays. She's been attending Immaculate Conception for mass. Because, you know Ma is very superstitious. Must be the Injun in her. Ma says for the blessings she'll go here, to Sacred Heart. But for the teaching on Sundays, it be Immaculate Conception. I know, it don't figure none, Father, but that's the way she be."

"How's your pa doing?"

"He's doing just fine, Father. In fact, he got himself a raise for the patent him and Mr. Fuentes done for the smelter machines. He's also been fighting for money over at the Y. In fact, he won some and a shortwave just this afternoon."

"Well then, I'm sure the church will see something from him in the collection box."

"Could be."

"I'll let you go your way, Son, unless you want to give your confession?"

"Aw, no Father. Ain't done anything a boy my age needs to confess. But I'm sure I be needin' one real soon 'cause we're going out to California."

"Oh, that's right. I heard that from your uncle Joseph."

"Word sure gets around fast, doesn't it Father?"

"Douglas is a very small town and as a priest, I get the privilege to hear it all sooner or later. Now, you tell your ma, '*Vaya con Dios.*' You know what that means, Hank?"

"Yes, Father. You know we'd speak Spanish. For me, a bit less than Ma, but I know plenty."

"Okay then, *amigo.* You can pass theology and Spanish at your new school in California." He smiled warmly when he said, "No more questions. God be with you. Go on home and stay away from Eighth Street park tonight."

Hank sprinted pass Sixth Street where the red lights still glared at customers. At Fifth he slowed down after hearing a growling coming from the bushes. It sounded as if someone was calling out his name, so he stopped and cautiously looked over the hedge that lined the street.

"Is that you, Pa?"

"Yep Hank, it is." Planted comfortably with his back to a tree, his father called out again, "It's me, Hank. Come over here and sit down with me for a minute to rest our feet. Hey, Son. Let's just enjoy the setting sun and the rising moon so I can finish this little bottle they gave me at the celebration down at Bobbie's." He took a long gulp then screwed the lid back on.

"Yah know, Hank, funny thing is, this will be the second time I've seen old Villa come marching into Agua Prieta. About these wars, it's one thing to be in a fight with another man, but an army of men? For whatever reason, they fight for riches, for land, for plunder, for politics, and even for women.

Sometimes, maybe for country. And the people get all stirred up, like it's some kind of celebration. You can cut the excitement with a knife. Like that prizefight I had today, people enjoy being entertained and go about choosing this guy to win or that guy to lose. Why? Because, they want to be a part of it—but not bad enough to be in the ring doing the banging."

"Same as prizefighting, Pa?"

"No, Son. This fighting tonight is apples and oranges different. For, some won't ever go home again. They'll die out there by a bullet that doesn't even know their name, who they was, who their friends are, or even why they're fighting. That bullet is just like the gambling wheel. It hits on an unlucky guy's number.

"But, out here tonight, the game will be over for some of them doing the fightin'. Now, those generals and leaders of the war, they'll stay back in some room, planning flanking movements to attack here or there, to use this strategy or that. But once it starts, all reason disappears. Their well-planned strategies get pushed aside by the fog that gathers over the battle, where only survival counts. Whatever it cost to win comes into play. I've seen that in men…those wars, there's no sense in them. So, when the war runs out and there's no more bullets to fire or men to kill, the side that has the most still standing gets to go home. Most always the leaders of the winners or losers come out unblemished. Look at Robert E. Lee. The South lost to Grant, but they both get to be heroes and legends. And the fallen on the battlefields, they're out there buried neatly in a row with white headstones, nothing but names and dates to remember them by. You've seen them there in Fort Huachuca's cemetery. All those fine young men…"

"And you, Pa, what would you do?"

Henry took a few moments and then another drink.

"Son, I'd rather it be just me and my enemy in the street,

dueling it out. Only one of us would be inflicted and I would make certain of the reason I killed that man. After it was done, it would all be over. No harm to my neighbors, if my shooting be straight. Then I'd just bury him under a cactus plant out yonder. But that's never how it is. You see, tomorrow, townspeople will be up on building tops just to get a glimpse of the war, to see the cannon fire and rifle shots for themselves. For them it will be like the Fourth of July. Better than a Sunday picnic while watchin' a hangin'. They want to be a part of it, to see one side win. After the gruesome battle, the crowd will march together to the Gadsden, jubilantly drinking up the day's festivities. Say, that reminds me, Hank."

Henry paused, caught his breath, and took another swallow of the spirits from the bottle he held tightly. With that finished, Henry set back to rambling. "The newspaper reporters will write and the tourists will arrive from all over the country, even as far off as California and New York. From sea to shiny sea, like Kit Carson done. Yes sir! They will be a coming to buy anything that looks like souvenirs of what happened here tonight. It's great for commerce, the mayor says! So, why not have a parade like they done after them European wars."

It seemed as if his pa had come to the end of his conversation, so Hank, like he'd done many times before, tried to get his pa to talk himself out by asking, "And you Pa? What yah think about all this?"

"Well, I think that creatures of God, the kind your ma always talks about, should never get caught up in these here wars. Their credibility to their maker is lacking. How can we kill so many of His creation, then pray for His favors? That's all we need to know, Son…for certain, it's something to confess on."

Just as the sun sank beneath the desert horizon, father and

son could hear cannon shots miles away. The volleys continued for about an hour or so. Some said later that old Villa
was just getting his guns in the right range, attempting to get
the Federalies and Americans to show their hands—to reveal
where their defensive weapons were placed.

Villa had boasted the battle would be over quickly. That it
would be easy to overrun the opposition in Agua Prieta. But,
apparently he was unaware of how well his enemy had dug
in and the unlimited supplies afforded them by the American's twenty-second infantry regiment out of Camp Douglas.
Villa's troops had been marching for days. They were tired,
undernourished, and without water. Dysentery had set upon
his men who desperately drank from polluted ponds and pig
troughs. They were in urgent need of essential supplies that
had been blocked by the Americans.

At the first sound of cannons, Hank's mother coached the
kids to stay away from the boarded windows. "Just in case a
stray bullet finds its way in."

Apprehension swelled around the neighborhood. What
if the Villistas won? Would they ravage the city of Agua Prieta and then cross the border to do the same in Douglas? After
the cannon fire came to an abrupt halt, the quiet of the battlefield became eerie and even more frightening. It was as if
a volcano had rumbled, then went calm, all the while building up to a major eruption. Then it happened, just as Hank
and his pa stumbled into the house. Like the crashing of a
storm wave hitting the shore, the fire of bullets commenced
and the battle was on, blasting in one continuous chorus, like
millions of firecrackers erupting in a finale. Yet, this time it
seemed it would never end. Hank's mother counted heads as
the children dashed for cover under their beds, hugging the
hard dirt floor.

After a few hours, the battle stopped. Hank thought it

sought a breath of air to reset the strategy to counter attack, to flank the opposition, to play the game of war out. But this time, the silence lasted. Hank's pa quickly fell into a sound slumber, along with his brothers and sisters. Soon, only Hank and his mother were still awake. Ma prayed with her rosary, counting God's blessings.

"Mama, I be back soon. Don't worry," Hank said as he quietly slipped out the back door. Hank's mother didn't worry as much about him. She said this was 'cause he was so much like his pa—they could both look trouble in the eyes and somehow get away. Hank's ma knew where Hank was going and what he needed—to feel independent in the night air, under the stars, and become lost in his dreams. As for Hank, those dreams could take him anywhere in the world he wanted to be, like the geography books he read in the Douglas library. That was his freedom.

Hank found his way over to Eighth off G Street, out of range of those furious ballistic pallets. He continued walking up two extra blocks to the Eighth Street Park, a patch of dirt and dried grass that was much more than just a park to Hank and Josiah. It was their retreat, their encampment. A place to plan the next episode of their daily lives. They visited often, laughing and plowing over their next ventures while sitting around man-made fires, accompanied by anyone who dared follow. Hank knew Josiah would be there tonight as well.

"Those cannons must have sounded mighty loud at your place," a voice said.

"Hi Josiah."

From out of the shadows, Hank heard Chata ask, "Any of those bullets hit your house?"

"Nah, don't think so," Hank answered, "but I wasn't about

to go out front to check!" The friends laughed together. "The family is fine and Pa's sleeping it off. Big Mike make it home alright?"

"Yeah, like he usually does," Josiah answered. "So, what we got going on tonight?"

"We best sit by this here fire and take a rest, 'cause tomorrow, if this thing is all over, we've got to get moving. There's money to be made. Like Pa says, the tourists are packing up right now, planning on comin' to Douglas."

"Yes, they is!" Chata agreed.

"And we'll be ready to sell them whatever we find out there," Hank continued. We'd best get out early 'cause you know we got to fight off the others for the best stuff. And you, Chata, you stay home. Wait till we get back."

"Aw, Hank. Why me?"

"'Cause, you be afraid of what you see out there and get the uglies at night when you dream."

"No sir! Not me, Hank."

"Oh really?" Josiah laughed, then looked over to Hank. "Okay then. Let's test her."

"You two think you're so brave. You go about a-testin' me. I can take it," she challenged.

"All right. Come with us," Hank offered, while slowing down the fire. The three kids then marched themselves a few blocks through the cool dark night until they arrived at the Douglas Cemetery.

"Josiah, you watch Chata here. I'll be right back," Hank said, then reached over to ask, "Chata, let me have that scarf around your neck."

"My Scarf? What for?"

"You want to be tested or not?"

"Yes, but…"

"Okay, then give me your scarf."

Slowly, she slipped it off and gave it to Hank.

"Be back in a minute," Hank said, then vanished into the black night to plant the scarf.

When he returned, Josiah asked Hank. "All set?"

"Yeah." Hank answered, a little out of breath.

Josiah stood close to Chata and whispered for effect, "Now Chata, as you know, this is a cemetery, but not all of the poor souls here are really dead."

"What?" she asked, trying not to sound worried.

"One of our friends—well, to be honest, a lot of our friends—say there's ghosts out there walkin' around."

Hank got into it. "In fact, one of our friends—"

"Hector is his name," said Josiah.

Hank continued with a serious face, "Well this Hector guy went into this cemetery and never was seen again."

"You funin' with me? Nah, you guys are trying to scare me," she said suspiciously.

"Okay, Chata. Have it your way," Josiah said with raised hands, while turning and giving Hank a smile. Hank gulped hard to keep serious. "Here's the deal, Chata. You must go into that cemetery while Hank and I go back to the park. You go out there, find your scarf, and bring it back to us."

"Really. Just go find my scarf in the dark?"

"Yes, and if you can pass the test—"

"Okay, okay. I get your drift."

"Me and Hank will be back at the park waiting, getting warmed up at the fire while you get to lookin' for that scarf in there on some dead man's tombstone."

"Just maybe you'll find some ghost to help you out," Hank added.

Chata looked as though this testing thing might not be such a good idea. But then again, if she didn't go and find that old scarf, she would be out of luck going with the boys in the morning. With a brave face, Chata looked at the boys and said, "Okay, see yah boys soon."

She might have fooled them if she hadn't looked back. Josiah whispered to Hank, "She's as scared as a cat chased by a crow."

The boys weren't about to leave her completely alone, though. No way, not with bandits just a few miles across the border. They sat down ready to wait it out. Suddenly, startled by screams from Chata, the boys stood, looked at each other, then raced into the dark cemetery. Now the frightened ones, the boys began calling out her name.

Finally Chata hollered, "Over here!"

When they got to her, she was down on her knees looking at two eyes that seemed to be looking back from the grave. A muffled voice said, "Agua… por favor… agua." Once Hank's eyes adjusted to the dark, he could see the eyes belonged to a boy. A boy much like them. "*Agua… por favor… agua*," the boy said.

Hank thought he must have crossed the border then followed the dry creek to find his way to the peaceful, quiet cemetery. A sling of bullets still hung about his neck, and he had no hat or anything else to let on who he was or for which side he fought. Hank reached back into his pack, pulled out a canteen and handed it over to the boy.

The boy gulped almost all the water down at once, only pausing long enough to look the three of them up and down before finishing off the precious fluid. With that, the boy seemed to come to life. Shaky, he kneeled, then stood to say politely, "*Muchas gracias.*" Then, like a wounded sparrow suddenly healed, he took flight into the night. No one could tell where. Josiah gave Chata a warm hug and kept his arm around her tightly as they walked back to the park in silence.

After some time stoking the fire and looking off into the night, the sky suddenly lit up. Remembering what his pa had told him about war and fighting at night, Hank thought, "That looks like a bright flying saucer come down from some planet, or like the finale I seen after fireworks on the Fourth of July." It all ended with a crescendo of shots and blasts followed by billowing smoke that carried with it the odor of spent explosives.

The three friends continued to sit there together like they'd done many times before, staring into the flames of their small fire until it worked its way out. Tonight wasn't entertainment, though, because they knew people were out there dying and killing each other for unknown reasons, all the while thinking theirs was the right reason so that ultimately no one was to blame.

The thought of all this dying and killing was far more distressing to Hank than any ghosts out there in the cemetery.

CHAPTER 7

IN HARM'S WAY

The morning light peaked through a crack in the boarded window, annoying Hank as he attempted to sponge out the last drops of sleep hunkered under his bed, in retreat from the world. Sparkles of light from the well-placed crack fumbled about his face, however, causing him to finally give up on his efforts. As he stirred and became more alert, panic raced through his mind and his heart. He remembered the plans he and Josiah had made for the day and he quickened his efforts, hastily crawling out of his protective cave.

Hank noticed that he was the last of the Lefebvres to be moving about. Still dressed from last night's event, the only hygiene needed was to take care of his business out back in the family pot. Once finished, Hank stretched his body with his hands raised to the sky to greet the day, but the only reply was the smell of spent gunpowder that dulled the sweet dessert aroma he was accustomed to. Not even his ma's attempts to invigorate her clan with fresh strips of bacon and eggs frying in the pan could compete with that deadly scent.

Hank's mother was going about her usual routine: preparing breakfast for the family, baking for the boardinghouses, and carrying on to the girls about the cleaning they needed to do for the day. The peaceful hum of the morning was interrupted when Hank heard his mother say, "No way this old goat Villa is going to stop us from getting things done that need to be to keep this family going! By the way, Hank," she turned to him as he walked through the kitchen, "your uncle Joseph came by a little earlier this morning to make sure we were alright and asked about your pa. I told him Pa was... as usual..." she sighed "and that he did win some money and sent it home. He also mentioned you, Hank." With that, Hank's ears perked up and he listened keenly. "He said to me, 'Adela, I love the spunk of Hank, but it was told to me, from Charley in Tombstone, he just almost got into real trouble over protecting an Injun girl.' I told him I didn't remember anything of that kind in our conversations," Ma looked pointedly at Hank, "but I told your uncle Joseph that if you did that, it was a proud moment for the Lefebvres...defending some poor Injun girl like that. It sounded like my son alright."

"So, what did Uncle Joseph say to that?"

"He says that, 'Hank is a very talented boy, but it's unfortunate that he has some traits of his father.' And he said, 'Hank's temperament must be more achievement-guided and aimed toward a more positive way of doing things.'"

"Like what, Mama?"

"Well, like schooling and education."

"But Mama, I get my education from the streets everyday here in Douglas."

"Gosh, Hank. Don't go out against your uncle's concerns. He means well and he cares for us, when we needed him or not."

Just then Hank's father wandered into the kitchen. He had left for work but returned because the smelter was shut down, cautioned by the uncertainty of the war going on across the border. "So Pa, what's going on over the border?" Hank asked.

"Well, last night about midnight, Villa tried an all-out attack, apparently to surprise the Federalies and American troops. But, it looks like he didn't know they had floodlights, so when Villa attacked with his forces, they was shot down in large numbers. So, instead of trying it again, it appears old Villa's trying to cut his losses by moving on to Naco. Most likely, he'll aim to get some reinforcement there."

"Wow. Then it's all clear?"

"Yep. For a while, I'm thinking. I've been called back to the smelter later today. So Hank, whatever your plans, you best need to be back home by this afternoon."

"Okay, Pa. But for now, Alfred, me, and Josiah have some things to do."

Alright, get with it then, Son. But, mind you, get back on time."

"Yes sir."

Hank's mother called out, "Here boys. Take some carne asada and tortillas with you."

"Thanks, Mama," Hank said, and gave his mom a kiss on her cheek.

Hank's ma and pa had an idea where the boys were going, but didn't ask.

With Alfred and two large duffle bags, Hank took off to Eighth Street. Like clockwork, they found Chata and Josiah walking toward them with their own bags, obviously excited. Hank motioned for all to huddle around. "Now here's the plan. We go north to the end of Eighth, past Catherine Ave., then walk a mile more, cross the dry creek, go under the barb-wire fence. After a couple miles more, I think we should be far enough behind the line."

"What about the fighting and all?" Josiah asked.

"No worry. Pa says old Villa has moved on to Naco. There be a lot more of Douglas folks out there before us. We need to get a-going while the pickin's are still good. Now remember, no personal items. And Chata, you ain't gonna get sick on us now, are you?"

"I promise, Hank. I won't be."

"Okay then, let's get a-going."

Hank, Alfred, Josiah, and Chata walked up to Catherina Avenue, crossed over the dry creek, found the hole in the fence, then paced south until they saw, one by one, gruesome dead bodies scattered around. As they continued to walk, they saw even more bodies. Hank interrupted their silent stares. "Let's get at it."

"But they're all dead," Alfred whispered, as if not to wake them.

"Of course they is," Hank said with a shrug. "No worry from the dead. There's no more fightin' in them." With Hank's reassuring remarks, the three went about their business taking bullets and canteens from the bodies and cutting off insignias from officers' uniforms, though Villa's proved to be a motley army. Not many insignia's around, but they did find a few six shooters and plenty of nifty unique knives.

Hank called out softly, "Get them knives. They's a-goin' to sell real fine. Seems like all the rifles were picked up earlier, probably by the older guys, but that's alright." The three kids spread themselves out around the battlefield and kept on their work for a while when, unexpectedly, they heard the popping of gunfire. There was no telling where it was coming from; it seemed to come from all around, and it was coming in a fury. Hank yelled, "Josiah! Get down and stay put!" Then he grabbed Alfred. Hank knew if something happened to Alfred, his ma wouldn't like that very much.

Hank and Alfred found a trench and took cover. After waiting for a minute or so, Hank peeked over the dirt mound left by cannon fire. Popping started again and bullets whizzed by, opening on their position. Hank yelled, "I'll get them to stop the fire," and he tore off his jacket, wrapped it around a stick, then stuck it in the air. But the gunfire only increased with a furious pace.

"Okay, let's backtrack. I'll get up and distract them. Let them shoot at me. You and Chata move back like we come. Then me and Alfred will do the same until we get out of range then we'll get the hell out of here! Okay?" They all nodded in agreement.

"On three, Josiah and Chata, you move," Hank paused for everyone to focus. "One, two, three!" Then he rose up to take on the assault while holding Alfred down with his right foot.

Fire targeted on Hank. Josiah and Chata stayed low, moving quickly backward, then flinging themselves into another trench. Josiah yelled out, "Oh no! It's Chata! Hank, Chata's been hit!" Hank was now in a quagmire, knowing Chata and Josiah couldn't move because the Federalies now knew their position.

Hank called back, "Stay there, Josiah. Don't worry. I'll stop these guys. Alfred, lay low. Don't move until I do. Then take the bags back to the house, the way we come. Okay? Don't let them see yah. Make sure to do that, Alfred. I'm depending on you."

"Okay, Hank."

Now it became a contest to win. Hank never minded the risk, if that's what it took to win. His father bred that in him. Hank popped out of his cover and began a rampage of his own, running in a zig-zag fashion to give the Federalies a moving target away from his brother and friend's location on the torched battlefield of the dead. All the time Hank dodged fire, moving fast and jumping into this trench, then another, bursts of fire riveted around him as he jumped over dead warriors scattered about. Once secured in a deep entrenchment, Hank decided to make his final plea by showing himself. Anything to halt the firing. He made his last gesture for survival by flinging himself out from cover and running zig-zag toward the gun-fire with his hands up high in the air.

The Federalies dropped their guns and stood with open mouths. One of them called out, "*¡El es loco en la cabaza!*"

The ruckus caught the ear of an American lieutenant from Fort Douglas who stood to ask, "What is going on here?" He turned to his sergeant. "Give me your field glasses!"

"Yes sir!"

The sergeant quickly handed over binoculars to the lieu-tenant who snapped them up to his eyes. After scanning the area, he yelled, "Cease fire!" Shots continued to ring out, so the lieutenant yelled out his command again—only this time louder: "I said, cease fire, *amigos*! And pass it down the line!"

The captain of the Federalies looked over in disbelief. "Why, Lieutenant?"

"'Cause, that's Hank Lefebvre out there! I'd know him from a mile away. His pa and I play poker many times. That there is a Douglas boy. His pa is very noticeable around these parts and you don't want him takin' a bad feelin' on you. Trust me, Lefebvre can be as mean as all of Villa's army."

The captain smiled, "And *¡muy rapido!*"

"He sure is, Captain. That kid can run, like a flash of lightning."

"*Sí*, Lieutenant. He sure can."

"Now Sergeant, get some of your men out there and move them kids off the battlefield. Not tomorrow, Sergeant. I mean now! Before some lugnut around here does more killin' and shoots the lad. His name is 'Hank,' so call him out."

The sergeant rushed out with his men, calling, "Hank, Hank! We are the US Army!"

Hank, expecting the worse, lay face down in the dirt. But when he heard his name called, he stood tall. "That's me. I'm Hank, sir. And those are my friends back there. Please get some help. One of them is hurt!"

Both ran back to the trench where Josiah was holding Chata. The sergeant yelled back, "Medic. Medic!"

"It looks like she took the bullet in her left shoulder!" Josiah said.

The medic appeared and quickly took out his tools for a quick examination of the injury. "Yes, she caught a bullet. Not too bad. Went right through. Let's get her out of here."

When they started to climb out of the trench, Josiah stumbled. "You alright, Josiah?"

"Oh, I'm okay, Hank. Just got this hurtin' in my leg."

The medic took charge. "Stay put, boy. Let me take a look." The medic took out scissors and cut away Josiah's pant leg.

"He's hurt, alright. There's a bullet wound in his thigh. He's losing a lot of blood. I need to put a tourniquet on him."

"No! No! Hank, don't let them!" Josiah yelled, with fear in his voice.

"Let the man do what he thinks is okay," Hank commanded, while trying to hide the concern on his face. Josiah nodded at this assurance from his friend and became still as they carried him over to a truck waiting to drive them to the clinic.

Just then the American lieutenant arrived on the scene. After a quick observation, the lieutenant squelched the medics' work. "Stop! No! Get the damn tourniquet off his leg. Now, medic! Just apply pressure. Bandage the leg tightly and get him quickly to the Douglas clinic."

At the clinic, Hank gave the front desk his father's smelter ID number and said that Chata was his sister. That's all it took for the medical help to get busy.

Hank remained in the lobby until the doctor came out to tell him that both Chata and Josiah would need to stay over for a day or so.

"How are they?" Hank asked.

"Well, Chata is okay. Just a shoulder wound. Josiah…we'll know more tomorrow."

Apparently sensing Hank's apprehension, he added kindly, "Don't worry. We'll take care of your friends."

"Can I come and look in on them later?"

"Yes. But not today. Try in the morning." The doctor turned to leave, then came back. Hank, they're all talking about you. What you did out there probably saved their lives."

"Oh, I don't know about that. They be strong persons themselves. And besides, they'd done what I did. Friends do that kind of thing for each other here in Douglas. Right, Doc?"

"Yeah. I suppose so. Now, you get home. Your ma's going to be lighting candles at Sacred Heart for you and your sister, Chata," the doctor said with a smirk.

"You knew about Chata, Doc?"

"Yes, of course, Hank."

"And about the candles?"

"Yes, about that too. Mind you, Son, your mother's been here many a time with your father—him bleeding from here and there—and she's always talking about them miracles answered by the candles offered at church. I keep telling her there's no reason to bring your pa here. Just take him to Sacred Heart Chapel, light a candle, that will do it and make my day somewhat easier." Hank and the doctor shared a laugh at that, then Hank said his thanks and goodbyes.

As he walked out of the clinic and ploddied his way back across town from Sixteenth Street, then back to Fifth, Hank thought about the day and what it meant to him. He lamented about his friends, independence, and his future. Mostly, though, after all this, he thought: "How can I ever leave Douglas?"

CHAPTER 8

TONIC MEDICINE MEN

When the townsfolks ascertained that Villa had moved on west to Naco and out of firing range, they became overcome with excitement. Tourists began flooding in. Those spectators and makers of legends intended to get either hot news releases from live witnesses, or authentic relics to cherish and take back home and place in their libraries and offices. These relics would simply add to curious assets already staged on coffee tables intended to incite conversations, waiting for someone to ask: "What is this doing here?" so the owners could enthusiastically recite: "Well, let me tell you…"

That's exactly what Hank, Chata, Alfred, and Josiah were counting on. They had the real relics from the battlefield ready to offer to a sorted variety of collectors.

When Hank and Alfred returned home later that evening, Hank's father told them, "You know, boys, there's something magical about what comes from the battlefield. Those relics make people feel better about themselves—like a tonic, or a charming dose of medicine to take back home—and makes them feel a part of something they never were really part of."

Hank knew what his pa was leading up to. "Yep. Just like you fighting to entertain some rich onlookers. But no worry,

Pa, we'll get a fair price out of it."

"I'm sure you will, Son, but before you offer up its value, you best look into the buyer's eyes. It's a lesson I learnt from all those poker games at Bobbie's Log Saloon. If a buyer shows a keen interest, then you give them a keen price. That's what I call capitalism. Yah see Hank, a man of low education, like us, can learn something from dealing with men of means." Henry laughed and then rambled on, "Hank my boy…"

"Pa, you sound a little 'Irish.'"

Henry Laughed again, "Yep, guess I do, Son. Maybe I'm just pickin' up expressions said by Lloyd Brenner." Taking on a serious air, Henry continued, "Mind you, I've had my share of unlucky streaks with the game of chance. But Son, I do know this, when you're winning, folks will say, 'Henry, you sure know what you're talking about.' And I can guarantee you, a man who says that, he's plum crazy, or more likely wants something bad out of me, 'cause, I don't know what I'm talking about most of the time. And that is a fact, Son."

After breakfast the following morning, Henry said, "So Hank, you and the boys go get about your business now and later today we need to talk about me leaving to California in a few days."

"Really, Pa, that soon?"

"Now Hank, don't worry. You just get out there to G Street with Alfred and Benny. Douglas is a bustling today. There's lots of money to be made."

As Hank started out of the house, he yelled back, "Come on, Alfred and Benny. We'd got work to do!"

"Be right with you, in a few minutes," Alfred replied.

As Hank gathered up the hard-earned knives, insignias, and other relics they'd scraped off yesterday's dead, he said, "Dang, Alfred. You done a mighty fine job of getting all our bags back to the house."

"I did what you told me, Hank. I even had to come back twice to fetch them while all the shooting was going on."

"By the looks of this, we've got a few hundred dollars' worth here," Hank said, while patting Alfred on the back.

Hank went into the kitchen to pack a lunch for the boys while he waited for Alfred and Benny. He overheard his father say with pride,

"Adela, we've raised some brave boys, haven't we? Not only was Big Mike praising Hank for being so brave, you know what else folks been saying?"

Henry didn't wait for her to figure it out. "They say that Hank's real fast. I mean *real* fast at a runnin'. Big Mike says them folks been chirping it up this morning at the Elks Club and the PD Store…even at the Gadsden. Yep, they said, 'Henry and Adela have some kind of boys there.'

"Now, I ain't putting down the girls, Adela. No, they do their part, sometimes even better than the boys, working for all the family. I'm just saying, we done well. I admit to my shortcomings, but when we go to California, I promise, that will change. You'll see, Adela. Joseph got me a fine stable job out there. He told me yesterday that I should go there and get a house ready. He said, he'll take you and the family to Benson, pay your way by train to Los Angeles, and by that time, I'd be able to pick you up in a car."

"I pray you're right about this move, Henry, 'cause, I surely am going to miss Douglas. This will always be home. California is so far away from friends and all. And us being a mixins'…well I'm just a bit worried. That's all."

"Now Adela, don't you fret. Remember what it was like when we first came to Douglas from Bisbee in that covered wagon? It all worked out fine and it will even be better in California. Even Joseph said so. Now, you know Joseph and his good business sense. He's rarely wrong."

All this California talk gave Hank indigestion until he called out, "Okay Alfred, find Benny—*¡pronto, amigo! ¡Ándale! ¡Arriba!* What's holdin' you up?"

"This is what's holdin' me up," Alfred yelled back while dragging two stuffed bags down the hall.

"Wow. Okay, load these into the newspaper wagon we used to sell papers in Pirtleville, and let's get a-going." Hank decided that since Josiah was still laid up in the hospital, they needed to bring Benny and his sister as well. "Mama, can Lily come help today? She's the next oldest to me and knows how to represent things in a selling manner."

"No, Son. I be needing her at home."

Hank begged, "Aw, Ma, just Lily?"

His mother sighed, "Okay. But you best take care of her, Hank."

"Dang. She takes care of herself just fine," Hank joked. When his mother smiled and kissed him on the cheek, he knew it would be alright.

Off they went with Alfred pulling the wagon full of goods, Hank carrying two packs, Benny in charge of lunch sacks, and Lily straggling along at a distance.

They had planned all this out the other evening while setting back together at the Eighth Street Park. It was Josiah that suggested they should have someone walk up and down G & Tenth Street to cover tourists heading toward the Gadsden. The others could set up in front of Phelp Dodge Merchandising Department Store, just off G on Tenth, to cover the Douglas business district.

"No need to cover the bars and whorehouses. They wasn't there to take anything back home with them," Hank said, causing them all to have a good laugh.

So, that's what they were about to do, absent Josiah. Chata

had left the hospital that morning and insisted she was well enough from her flesh wound to go along so there would be plenty of them to sell their battlefield treasures.

Lily and Alfred were charged with targeting anyone who looked out of place in Douglas, mostly by checking what kind of shoes they wore. Their father had taught them that trick. In the early stages of planning, Josiah had given them a sales pitch: "Ask them if they was from out of town and needin' something to take back home. Then tell them we have things left behind by Villa after the fightin' in Agua Prieta and if they be curious, ask them to walk around the back of Brophy's building where we'll show them authentic Villa relics for sale. Then leave it to Hank to make the sale."

Hank took another inventory of their collection. "We've got a fine bunch of knives and *pistolas*, but shame there ain't no rifles. Just as well though, even if we grabbed them first, the older boys be fightin' for them." All in all, Hank was pleased there was still plenty to sell.

The day turned out to be quite a bit hotter than expected for the time of year. As the kids continued planning their sales in the sweltering heat, Hank knew the weather would make trading difficult as people became irritable.

Probably because he was the oldest and often watched his father find ways to benefit from the difficulties, Hank came up with the idea of enticing tourists with cool lemonade. This would encourage them to walk the few blocks over to barter with him for the best deal. Sure enough, business picked up after that.

Soon only the most expensive souvenirs were left, and that's when a well-dressed business man and his friends took the bait.

"We've been over at the Gadsden and heard you kids had some interesting things to sell." After he stepped up to take a look, he turned to Hank, "So, you're the boss of this operation?"

"Yes sir, that's me."

"We also heard you kids did some brave things to collect these souvenirs." Hank's father had warned him about the flattering and he wasn't about to get distracted. The man set a price on two engraved Mexican knives and one fine leather belt, but Hank didn't agree and set his own price. As the stranger became irritated and loud—even mocking Hank's Douglas accent—Hank held his ground.

Seeing that his tactics wouldn't give him his price, the man showed his temper and threatened to turn them into the military if Hank wouldn't agree. Hank simply stood with his hands crossed over his chest and slowly shook his head no. When the man asked to see the belt again, Hank offered it up, and the man grabbed it away. Hank was losing patience with this strange sort of businessman. Coiling up like a rattlesnake, Hank's hand flinched, ready to reach inside his boot. Perhaps sensing Hank's determination and growing anger, the man was shrewd enough to back down.

"Hold it there, kid! Just testing you," he said, flashing a sunshine smile that broke Hank's spell and quieted his disposition. "Alright," he said, "I'll buy it at your price." In fact, the man did better than that and bought all the remaining knives at a price higher than Hank had previously set. Hank looked more perplexed than angry when the man asked, "What's your family name, son?"

Alfred jumped in to answer, "It's Lefebvre, sir."

The man smiled even wider and chuckled, "I should have known, should have put two and two together. You're Henry Lefebvre's boy."

"Yes sir."

"Well, well. I heard what you did out there to save your friends while the Federalies were firing. Son, you're a big story over at the Gadsden."

Hank noticed the flattering again and didn't let himself relax quite yet.

"Mama mia!" the man said loudly, then turned to his friends, "They sure make them brave and smart out here in Douglas."

"You bet they do, mister. Thanks for buying at a fair price. The family will put it to good use," Hank said, arrogantly.

"Listen, Son. I like you. You've got spunk. In fact, I'm going back to the Gadsden to help pump up your business. How about that?"

Hank smiled politely as the man handed him his business card.

"Lefebvre, if you ever come to Los Angeles and need a job, look me up. You got that?"

"Sure, mister. It's a deal, if I do."

After the man's friends gathered up their cache and walked back toward the Gadson, Hank read the card: "Santino 'Sonny' Cardinale, PRODUCE." He handed it off to Alfred. "Save it. Someday, who knows…"

As the sun slid toward the west, Hank said, "Alfred, sales are slowing down. Most of the tourists are getting too much of the drinks. They're hiding out in the bars so you and Benny take care of what's left. I'll hold on to most of the money. Chata and I need to get to the infirmary and see how Josiah's doing."

"Don't worry," Alfred said proudly, "I'll watch over the business."

When they went off together up Tenth Street, Hank noticed the anxious look on Chata's face. "Don't you worry, Chata. Josiah is getting the best medical care available in Douglas. If you work for the smelter, they take care of their own." Hank secretly worried that sort of thing might not happen in a big city like Los Angeles.

When they asked the receptionist at the clinic if they could visit Josiah, she recalled the story of how he'd arrived there. "You crazy boys. And you, Chata, what do you do with them?"

"I do what Hank and Josiah does," Chata boasted.

The receptionist laughed, "Okay, follow me. Josiah's been itching to get out of here, so you both keep him calm. He needs to stay here for a few more days, for testing and observation."

They both nodded in agreement. When Josiah saw his friends, he straightened himself up and surreptitiously wiped his tears. Hank and Chata exchanged a concerned glance. Josiah's skin color was a dishwater-gray with red blotches that floated around his burley cheeks. His usually long, flowing locks of hair were now flat and straggled with perspiration. His obvious joy at seeing them overwhelmed the moment. Hank tried to say something clever to break the silence when Chata rushed to take hold of Josiah's sweaty hand and remained quiet.

Hank was speechless. It was Josiah that finally spoke, easing their pain. "So, did we make some money off the tourists today?"

"You bet!" Hank blurted out, giving hope to the situation. "Yes, we did, and you should've seen them all, Josiah! It worked just like you planned it. We made almost three hundred dollars!"

"Three hundred?"

"Yep. And we met this businessman. At first he didn't

much like our price. Then he must of thought about the qualities we done to get them, and bought up most of the best ones. He even went back to the Gadsden and bragged about what fine stuff we had to offer, so others would come by. We almost sold all of them—at good prices too! There's a few left, but it was a good day."

Josiah became more animated. "Wow! Got to be one of our best. What do you say, Hank?"

"Yep. I think so."

Just then the doctor came in. "I see the co-conspirators of this adventure have come to visit your roost."

"How's he doing?" Hank asked softly.

The doctor took some time to respond. "Well…let's just say Josiah is not quite ready to leave. It might be a little while. He needs more testing and rest. Maybe in a few days things will come along fine." Josiah smiled what looked like a forced smile at the worry that had come into the room.

"Time to give him that rest, Hank," the doctor said while checking his pulse.

"We'll be back soon," Chata said while leaning in to kiss Josiah's forehead. Josiah didn't seem to hear and slurred, "Three hundred dollars, well I'll be…"

When Josiah's eyes closed and he looked peacefully asleep, the doctor motioned for Hank to come with him out in the hallway. "I gave him some medication. It will help him rest."

Hank looked back at Chata struggling to take her hand away from Josiah's grip. Tears flowed from her eyes until Josiah gave a half smile, then she said goodbye.

Hank and Chata followed the doctor to the next room where—to their surprise—they were greeted by Big Mike, his wife, Loriana, and Hank's mother and father seated around a table. Hank and Chata joined them and the doctor spoke up. "First, you can thank the lieutenant for not allowing the medic to put a tourniquet on Josiah's leg. Secondly, all of you can help Josiah's condition in one way or another by being positive, because there is hope. You see, infection has set in and we don't know what course to take. Here in the Douglas infirmary, we take a wait-and-see approach to these kinds of wounds. Not like old Dr. Goodfellow, who operates right on the spot."

He continued, "I have a specialty doctor from Tucson who's looking at our patients in Fort Douglas. He's going to come here on his rounds and get a better look at Josiah's leg wound, but until then I recommend we take time to see how Josiah heals on his own."

"So, what does all that mean?" Big Mike asked.

"Three things, Mike. The best scenario is the infection reacts to the medicine we've prescribed. If not, he might lose a leg. Second option would be amputation to stop the infection from spreading. The worst-case scenario would be the infection spreads too quickly to save his life." The family and friends around the table gasped, then all were quiet as a sense of shock filled the room. Staring at the table and ceiling, everyone held back tears, stealing scrambled glimpses at one another, each face seeming to search the others for answers that none had.

For the first time, Hank thought life looked mighty peculiar and strained. He'd always felt Josiah and he were invincible. Now it seemed no words could set things straight in his mind. As Hank looked around the table, he watched Big Mike and his wife search each other's eyes. Then Hank glanced over at his pa and wished that he would come up with one of his quick-fix formulas, or maybe show his readiness to strike out, but there was no one he could turn on here to feel his blow. Oh, Pa had his religion to turn to, but it usually was another card in his hand to play out a bluff when needed. Hank knew his ma had her providence, prayer, and candles to give her relief. But what about the doctor, in the center of all this? There was no recluse for him. He stood alone, depending solely on his education, medical science, and experience. Wasn't he, at best, just giving into probabilities and odds. Wasn't he the real gambler here? Who would he be able to blame? It was if everyone in the room were wearing different glasses to see the same situation.

Hank's thoughts ricocheted back. What did it all matter, anyway? In the end, it was all about Josiah's fate. Put all of them thoughts in a glass, mix them like a chocolate malt, and add a banana and egg. It all didn't matter. What mattered was the fate of his friend, Josiah.

On this sour note, the family and friends slowly chipped themselves away from their seats and walked out, looking embarrassed at not knowing how to respond to each other's sadness. At least not yet, because to do so would only give away their worst fears. No, that wouldn't even surface. Not at this moment. Like that infection, they needed time to work things out.

CHAPTER 9

ONE FOR THE GIPPER

The busy week went by quickly. As planned, Hank's father left for California to set up a place for the family to follow. The biggest worry turned out to be Josiah. Though his health was improving, the infection was turning out to be as stubborn as Josiah. The doctor had prescribed rest, but whenever the swelling and fever went down just a little bit, Josiah would get up and try walking. Then his impatience would cause the infection to come back with a vengeance, putting him back in the infirmary.

The kids made a lot of money from the sale of relics, and after splitting three ways with Chata, Josiah, and the Lefebvres, each received $132—a nice business profit for those days. Even Uncle Joseph was proud of their efforts. Still, Hank couldn't help but feel a cloud of gloom settle over him. His father's departure put a reckoning on Hank. He tried to keep it in the back of his mind, but there was no denying it was really going to happen—there would be no use trying to cover it up. He would force a laugh now when telling people, "The Henry Lefebvre circus is going to California."

A few days after Pa had left, Hank's mother received a telegraph from him saying it was time for the family to pack up and move to California. He assured her that Joseph would take care of the house and other lose ends and would get his family to Benson where they would board a train to Los Angeles. Hank's mother called all the family together to explain more of what she'd read in the telegraph from their pa about California. She tried selling them on the move.

"Now listen to what Pa writes in this here telegraph. They have these beautiful sandy beaches near where we're going to live. It's just south of Los Angeles in a place called 'Long Beach.' Pa says we won't be far from Hollywood, where celebrities from the movies hang about—"

"They try to get into the movies too? Like we do?" the boys interrupted.

Ma smiled. "No, not like that boys, not in the back door, but *in* the moving pictures on the screen, as actors. There's these buildings and shopping centers. Like G Street, only much bigger. Here, in all of Douglas and Pirtleville together we have about 16,000 people. Pa says that they have 770,000 people around Southern California! Ain't that something?"

Ma went on building up the family's excitement, "And there's a Pike for rides, shows everywhere, and a place called the 'Rose Bowl' for sports and all. There are plans to build a sports stadium for bigger crowds, maybe even for the Olympics. Just imagine, all that right next to a small Methodist College named University of Southern California. And they play football games there, boys!"

Then Ma's voice became stern. Looking straight at Hank and Alfred, she said, "They have lots of schools for you kids. That includes you, Gilbert and Benjamin." Ma didn't need to mention the girls on this topic, because they were never truant from school. "Pa's letter says there are strict rules that make sure kids go to school. It's about time for you boys to take to learning. It's important. But, I need to tell you, they don't speak like us. And if you think because your mama is not so French like you and your pa…well, they are not like here where we just mind our ways around these parts. There, they have places for whites and the Mexicans. There's only a few Negros and not many Injuns. And most of the whites speak very good English.

"So, you best know, I don't want you telling anyone about your mama…where she'd come from. There will be no Spanish-speaking when we get there. Yah hear? We be French. They like French people. And you boys will go to school," she repeated.

"Pa says that Hank, you and Lily will go to a place called 'Long Beach Polytechnic High School'—some fancy name, isn't it? The rest of you will follow them later—if we still live there." She began to fold up the telegraph, but stopped. "Oh, and Pa writes here, 'there's a billiard parlor next to the university campus.'" The kids groaned, "I know," she said, "that might not be so good. We all know your pa will buddy up with that place, sure as anything. So, Hank, like always, you—being the oldest—will have to keep a keen eye on your pa and take on more responsibilities for the *familia*. Hank?"

"I understand, Mama."

Lillian asked, "What about horses?"

"Yes, there are some horses, but most of them are for the movies."

"Oh, I forgot this part!" Ma grew animated, "Pa says they have this place you can see from Long Beach called 'Catalina Island.' It's just twenty-six miles out at sea. He even said that all the world's most famous people go there for vacation. Pa says we'll go there too, someday." Once again, Ma folded up the telegraph and said, "So there you are. Now, get to packing. Put away things we don't need now that we're a-going to California!"

In all the excitement, Hank almost forgot about Josiah still lying in the infirmary. It sounded as if Ma and Pa had it all figured out—what the family would be doing in California, but Hank still didn't feel so sure. There would be new rules, new schools, new friends and who knows what more in California. The idea of moving still didn't appeal much to him. Back here in Douglas, hadn't he found all he really needed?

The kids emptied the room and Hank and his ma were left alone. "Why such a sad look?"

"'Cause, Mama, you beguiling us about going to California got the others excited, but it won't make me happy."

"Now, Hank. Where'd you get that fancy word, 'beguiling'? And whatever does it mean?"

Hank grinned. "I picked that one up from one of Pa's friends when I was waiting for him outside of the billiard parlor. I think it means, 'trying to make me feel good by charming me.'"

"Aw, Son. Trust your mama. I promise it will all be good for a change. You'll see. Maybe you best get down to the infirmary and say your goodbyes to Josiah and Chata. That might help make you feel better. You can always write each other, Hank."

"Nah, Mama. You'd know we'd never do that."

"*¿Por qué?*"

"'Cause it would be too personal."

Hank's mother hugged him and as she pushed him away, said "Okay, *mi hijo*. Then get going to see Josiah. I don't want you around here, dragging down the rousing I just gave." She smiled and whispered, "*El mismo,*" letting him know that down inside she felt the same as him about this move. "Now, *vamanos mi hijo*. Go see Josiah. It will make things better. *¿Está bien?*"

"Yes, Mama."

Hank turned to walk out when his ma spoke again. "Oh, Hank, I almost forgot. That thing you did in Tombstone. I go along with what they all been saying, it was a noble thing to do. But your knife…it must stay here in Douglas. I'm thinking it might not seem as needed as it is here."

"Okay, Mama." He thought for a moment then chipped in, "I know what to do with it. Don't worry. What about my *pistola?*"

"Best keep it packed neatly, Hank. Take it with us. Never know if we might need it along the way or when we get to California."

Hank left and skirted his way across town, staying away from the business on Sixth Street. Not that he minded the business—but he didn't want to face the locals asking where his pa had been this last week. Hank wasn't in a mood to put up with all the explaining that would require, so he took the short cut straight across town, picking his way through back-yards and alleys till he found his way to the infirmary.

Miss June was at the reception desk and looked up with a warm smile. "I'll be with you in a few minutes, Hank, just have some papers to put away."

Hank was glad she knew his first name by now.

When finished, she said, "Good morning, Josiah's been asking for you. He says you're going to California real soon."

"Yes ma'am. That be the case."

"Chata is in the garden out yonder waiting for you. And Josiah's ma and pa just left a short time ago."

The concern in Miss June's normally cheerful voice gave Hank a sinking feeling. Hank started to put two and two to-gether and spoke up on his suspicions. "So, is Josiah doing fine?"

"Well, I can't say, Hank. It's not my place to answer those kinds of questions. The doctor and Father Sandowsky are with him now. Maybe they will fill you in." Perhaps seeing

Hank's deep concern, she added, "Let me go and ask them if it would be okay for you to come in now."

"Oh, please Miss June. Would you do that? 'Cause, my family is about to pull out of Douglas. We're going to Benson in the morning to pick up a train to California. I just got to see him before I leave. Is it okay if I wait in the garden with Chata while you check?"

"Of course. Go be with her while I ask."

"Thanks, Miss June," Hank replied sincerely.

Chata didn't seem to notice as Hank walked into the cool air of the garden. Her head stayed down as she softly chanted and held tight to her rosary beads. Hank remembered that Ma lit her candles when times were tough, when she had no answers. Now Chata held her beads. He sat down alongside, breaking her trance. Chata turned and asked, "Josiah's not doing so well, is he?"

"I'm not sure yet. But the priest is in there," and trying to sound cheerful, Hank added, "maybe he wants to know why Josiah's family has missed mass so much lately. Let's wait on it til we hear from the doctor."

A few minutes later Miss June walked over. "Hank, Chata, the doctor said it's okay to go in now."

Chata gathered her sweater and purse, then held onto Hank's hand as they were led into a screened area. Instead of Josiah, however, they found a man in a white tunic seated behind a small desk. He stood to greet them. "Hello. I'm Dr. Myles from Tucson. I've been treating your friend, Josiah. I'm told you're the brave lad and young lady who went all out to get Josiah here." Hank gave Chata a sheepish look, knowing they probably shouldn't have been out there in the first place.

"First, let me say, both of you must thank that fine lieutenant for his excellent medical advice." The doctor motioned for them to sit on the two chairs facing the desk, then took his own seat. "I was told someone wanted to put a tourniquet on Josiah's leg to stop the bleeding, but the lieutenant said no. That was the right answer because the bullet didn't pierce an artery. A tourniquet would have stopped the circulation in his leg, causing gangrene and most likely resulting in amputation or even possibly the loss of life."

"Yes sir, we've heard that before."

The doctor went on, "Now, that's the good news. My concern here is the infection. The treatments we've tried to this point haven't been beneficial to his condition, which has only worsened. There is nothing left for us to do but to stay the course…give him rest and see what happens—"

"What are you saying to us doctor?"

"Well, Josiah is in a serious state right now."

Hank didn't like the sound of that and persisted, "So, Doctor, what are his chances?"

"Well, if I must give you an answer, Josiah has about a fifty-fifty chance of surviving the infection." Hank sat in stunned silence, but Chata didn't hold back her despair. Her cheeks trembled and her big brown eyes filled with water as she clutched even more tightly to the cross on those precious beads. "Now you just wait a moment here," the doctor said sternly, "you see, this is where both of *you* come into the picture." Chata took a breath to stop crying as the doctor kept talking. "In Arizona, we still practice in frontier ways, and usually we are right. But we can learn a few things from those Eastern doctors too, and they give a lot of credence to psychology these days."

"Psychology?" asked Hank.

"Yes, even though few really understand it fully, the Eastern doctors believe psychology can have a favorable affect in practical medicine."

Once again, Hank couldn't wait for the doctor to make his point. "What does that mean for Josiah, Doctor?"

"Well, now this is where you two can help." Chata's eyes got bigger with curiousity. "You see, Josiah is in a depressive state right now. He believes the worse, and for good reason. But having you and Chata visit him might improve his spirit, but *only* if you both appear optimistic to his recovery. I know it will be hard on you, but I want you both to go in and talk to him. Don't show him your fears. Give him a more optimistic presentation."

The doctor looked at Hank, "Josiah tells me you are leaving for California. And that for quite a long time you and he have been the best of friends—like brothers. Now he looked at Chata, "And Chata, Josiah says he knew he would marry you the first time he saw you." Hank and Chata looked at each other briefly as the doctor continued, "You both have so much influence on him. Go in there. Make him feel he has a future. Something that will make him want to fight to live. Now can you do that? Can you go in there without tears and pep him up?" The doctor looked at them gingerly, then added, "You will put on your best face in there, won't you?"

Hank reached over and held Chata's hand firmly. "Yes sir. We will."

"Okay, good. Miss June!" the doctor called out. "Please come in here." After a few awkward minutes, Miss June came in. "Nurse, please take Chata and Hank back to visit Josiah."

They walked in silence toward the back of the infirmary as Chata wiped her tear-stained face with a sleeve. Hank straightened his back as the nurse twisted the knob and opened the door to a small, poorly lit room. Seeing Josiah laying on the bed looking out the small window, Miss June cheerfully announced: "Look who's come to visit!"

Josiah turned as much as his bandaged leg would allow. When he saw Chata and Hank, the corners of his mouth lifted in what looked like a forced smile. Smartly, he said, "It's about time you come back again."

"Nonsense, Josiah. They said you needed a rest, and all we do is get you in trouble. Like you is in right now," Hank smiled and tried to chuckle. Josiah returned a knowing smirk at the truth in that statement. "And besides, we was so busy selling the rest of them souvenirs I told you about... made another forty-two dollars! Gave some to your pa. Now ain't that a smart thing to do?" Hank asked with extra pep in his voice. "Look at you a-laying there, thinking you be a-dying or something. What you been doing? Watching blue birds out the window?" Josiah smiled a big, healthy smile then, but Chata remained quiet.

"And look at your beautiful girlfriend, come to see why her boy is being laid up, being lazy, not out there in the streets a workin' for her." Josiah reached for Chata, who no longer held back, and they embraced. Uncomfortable, Hank continued with his ruse, "Did you see the pretty ribbon in her hair?" Chata gave up all pretense and tears fell uncontrollably. She laid her head on Josiah's chest and started to speak, but her voice quivered and she went quiet again.

Concerned they were heading where the doctor didn't want them to be, Hank turned the conversation in another direction. "Josiah, you heard the news? We Lefebvres are about to leave to Los Angeles."

Josiah's turned his attention away from Chata's sobs. "For real this time? You sure, Hank?"

"Yep. For sure. Pa got us a place in a city called 'Long Beach,' just a fair amount of miles away from downtown Los Angeles...kinda like the distance from Douglas to Pirtleville." Chata stopped crying now and stood up next to Hank. Taking her cue, Hank pulled up two chairs for them to sit alongside the bed.

"Listen to this, Josiah. Ma says I have to go to school at some place called 'Polytechnic High.'"

"No way!"

"Yep. That's what she says."

"Well, I know you, Hank. That ain't going to happen. No way. You're going to find mountains somewhere around California and disappear with Alfred, just like we done in those Chiricahuas for days, a-hunting, swimming and messing with Injuns." Hank agreed, happy that for now his efforts to get Josiah's heartbeat up and get him thinking on something besides dying had been successful. "Hank, we'd known each other for how long?" Josiah reminisced.

"Don't remember, 'cause we'd been too young when we met up."

"I sure don't know who I'd be spending time with when you be gone."

"Josiah you'll always have Chata. She'd make any boy happy, now wouldn't she?"

Chata and Josiah smiled at each other. "You bet. But Hank, what am I going to do, me and Chata, without you?"

"Well, there's the grand theatre they is a-building. You can sneak in with Chata when it opens. Just like we did at the YMCA. The store still gives out food in the back when the selling is too bad around town. And soon you'll probably want to join the National Wild Service Workers in the Chiricahuas, marry, and retire."

"You think so, Hank?"

"You bet I do."

"Well, wonder if I don't make it out of this room, Hank?"

"What did you say, Josiah? I didn't hear that out of my best and only friend's mouth. Now, did I? No, I didn't."

"What do you think, Hank?"

"About making it out of this place?"

"Yeah, what if I don't?"

"Well, since you asked. Here's what I think: Mama tells me, 'Hank,' she says, 'you been very noble up there in Tombstone with that Injun girl, and I hope you'd be the same in California. But that knife you be holding in your boot, it's staying here in Douglas.' I said, 'Okay, Mama, but who'd I give it to?' I been thinking on the way over here that my friend Josiah, he'd be needing it to protect Chata from all them other boys who want to be with her." All three laughed quite a bit at the thought of that. Even Miss June chuckled as she passed by.

Hank reached down into his boot and pulled out the pearl-handled knife, "a fittin' for a chief," he said while giving it to Josiah. "Now be careful with this, don't be drawing on a man with a pistol 'cause Emiliano tells me the bullet is much faster, but if you do, better be quick about it."

Josiah reverently took the knife and held it close. "Gosh, thanks Hank."

"Sure thing, Josiah."

Hank was about emptied out of talking and realized he'd have to say his goodbyes. "You know, Ma says I'd be a-writin' to you, but, I told her probably not. That's not what we men do much of. Maybe a word now and then. Besides, Pa will probably keep a-talkin' somehow with my uncle Joseph and your pa about things going on here in Douglas. And I'd want to know, 'cause Douglas will always be my home."

Realizing he was about to leave his lifelong friend, Hank looked into Josiah's eyes with sadness. Josiah seemed to understand and said, "I'll bet you that when you get to this Long Beach, you'll find some troubling there. I know you Hank, better than anyone. You just remember how we'd done it, that will carry the day."

When the boys shook hands, Josiah added, "If I don't make it out of this bed, remember who we be."

"Who's that, Josiah?"

"We'd be the Sons of Douglas. Now, ain't that so, Hank?"

Hank clinched his jaw to hide his grief and tugged out a reply. "Yes, Josiah. The Regal Sons, that's who we be, the Regal Sons of Douglas. But you will be a-comin' home soon. I know this, 'specially with Chata nursing about you that way. I'll be seeing yah both someday, after I find my way. Maybe then you two can come out to California to see me?"

There was no answer. Just a silent prayer that crept in like an evening fog that seemed to gather in the back of their minds.

Hank left then and closed the door behind. When he walked toward the exit, the doctor took hold of his arm and asked, "So, how did it go in there?"

"About what you expected, Doctor, not so good."

"Hank, don't let this stress you too much."

"No sir. Don't you worry about me. You see, I've seen men hanging from a tree, for good reason, and men dying out in those fields, for a cause. Now, a man's dying in the infirmary, given to gambling with science...odds being about fifty-fifty. But me, get all bedangled about it? Not a chance, Doctor. Ain't we all dying a little from the day we're born? It's on our way that we make our mark. I know about mortality, Doctor. Dang thing, it's just life. My pa says it's about my invincibility on the way to dying that I need to worry about." Hank turned toward the door. "See yah, Doctor, next time I'm in town."

Hank walked out the door, savoring his remaining moments with deep breaths of Douglas air. Despite all his bolstering, he knew in his heart that if Josiah gave into the ghost, a big part of himself would die with him.

CHAPTER 10

THE NEW FRONTIER

The first chapter of a story, like the landing of Christopher Columbus on the shores of the Americas, or the advent of travel from sea to shining sea and other accomplishments in history, has one thing in common: It's the beginning of the end of a tale. Somehow, Hank understood this and planned to take full advantage of his situation.

The closer the morning came to leave for California, the more Hank—at the advanced age of sixteen—felt confident that his Douglas upbringing had prepared him to meet any obstacle modern metropolitan centers like Los Angeles could deal out. The way he saw it, it was Hank Lefebvre's story—he just hadn't yet filled in the lines. It would be the dreams within dreams and the Southwest frontier values that motivated him to make his mark, that would not soon be forgotten.

As they went through the ritual of packing to travel, the family acknowleged some of the empty feelings they had with each. They felt as though they were leaving something important behind. And though they felt a sad sense of loss, a hint of excitement mixed with caution and uncertainty also filled the air. Hank always felt the latter when he took his journeys, like when they first began their escapades to the Chiricahuas, but what mattered most now was just that maybe this time they would never come back. So it was at exactly five o'clock in the morning, just as the sun bloomed for the day, when two shiny automobiles arrived outside the Lefebvre house on Fifth Street. Uncle Joseph had arrived to bring the family to the Benson train station. A big smile came across Hank's face as he raced out to meet the chugging autos and saw not only his uncle, but his good friend stepping out from the *Conejo* to greet him.

"*¡Hola, hombre!*" Emiliano said, "I heard that it would take two cars to get your family to the train station, so I asked Mr. Slaughter if I could help out and here I am."

The rest of the family scrambled out of the house, carrying only their personal belongings. Uncle Joseph would take care of the furniture and other loose ends later. He guided the girls and Ma into his automobile where he loaded their cases, then directed Emiliano to take Hank and the boys in the *Conejo*.

Once loaded, the family took off on the caravanned trip some seventy-three miles to Benson. They would pass through some of the same terrain that Emiliano and Hank had taken just a few weeks earlier, through McNeal, but this time bypassing Tombstone.

As they pulled out from their home and turned down G Street, Hank kept vigilance—along with all the family—gazing out the automobile window as if time stood still. Each block they passed honored a story they had lived, each building had been an episode. Maybe more so for Hank and his mother since they'd lived there longer and took on extra burdens when Pa had gone fleeting about, which had been more than just too often.

Once they passed the Gadson Hotel and came to the end of town, the road opened up to the expansive vista of the San Bernardino Valley. Hank, sitting in the shotgun seat again, broke the silence. "You know Emiliano, every time I get to this part of town, where it empties onto the desert floor, I remember the ships I've read about. Once they pass the breakwater to the open sea, my heart skips…so much freedom out there."

"You're right, *hombre*. Me too. I don't always like being locked in the city. No matter how big or small, the San Bernardino Valley makes you feel that way…freedom…yes."

Running out of air with that conversation, Hank took the pencil he always kept handy and tore into his carrying bag for a piece of paper and book. He placed the paper on the cover for support and started on a sketch, drawing fast to put this moment in place before it was gone. The bumpy road made drawing more of a task, but it didn't matter much to Hank. He knew what he had drawn, even if others wouldn't. This drawing was for himself, and that was what mattered.

Hank continued to pluck away at his picture until Emiliano spliced into his concentration. "*Hombre*, sorry to hear about your Polish friend Josiah and his girlfriend being shot."

It took some time, but Hank finally fell out of his artwork and said, "*Gracias, amigo.*" It took a few more moments to clear a quivering in his throat. He wouldn't allow quivering to give him away as too soft-hearted, so as Hank often would do, he found an antidote to explain his disposition.

"You know Emiliano, we'd all be dying everyday anyhow. It's just at different times. Ain't that so?"

With that remark, Emiliano broke into laughter. When his amusement calmed, he said, "*Amigo*, you are a funny one." He kept up his laughter and when it finally subsided he added, "you, *hombre*, when people talk about what you do and say, it makes them happy and they laugh so much. I'm sure it's because there is a piece of truth in what you say. Yes." Then all went quiet once again except for the roar of the *Conejo's* engine and the rumbling of the tires breaching bumps in the road.

The scenery on this day was different than on previous drives through the valley. Rains had come early this morning, which kept the dust down and the desert clear. Now the flora crept in the valley with vibrant colors, making the trip all the more pleasant.

Hank continued with his drawing while his brothers chatted in the back seat about California and what they would see and do. This was mere speculation because all any of them knew was what Ma had read from Pa's telegram. Uncle Joseph, who said he had only passed through California when he was very young, couldn't help with the details either. Like the rest of them, Hank began brewing his own ideas as he continued his art in the front seat and tried to blur out their chatter.

"*Hombre*, if you keep that up, maybe you be traveling the world to draw everything or take pictures of places and people, maybe even the Pope," Emiliano led again into a conversation.

"Yeah I'd like that…to take all those pictures," Hank stopped to look over at his friend.

Emiliano seemed to enjoy the bond he and Hank had developed. "Yeah *hombre*, Hank Lefebvre, captain of the world!" he said, which made Hank grin.

"*¡Sí, sí*, captain of the world!" Hank repeated, and they had a good laugh together. Up the road a bit more, Hank noticed their location. "Hey Emiliano, it was here that the *bandito* took exception to us."

"*Sí, hombre*. You are good. It was at this very spot."

"What happened to them Emiliano? Do you know?"

"Yes, *hombre*. For their unfortunate act of robbing a train, the killing of a passenger, and *pistola* whipping another, the sheriff chased them down and hung two of them. The others got away—somewhere in Mexico. There's no telling where they is now."

That silenced Hank and he went back to drawing. Once they reached the outskirts of Benson, Uncle Joseph pulled over his lead car and stopped and motioned for Emiliano to pull up next to him.

"Emiliano, you and Hank take the boys to the diner in town and get them something to eat. Going to be a mighty long trip to California. I'll run over to the train station, get right with the train tickets, and unload the luggage. Then the girls and Adela will come back to eat with you. Don't worry about the paying. I'd take care of that when I come back."

"Okay, Mr. Lefebvre." Emiliano called back and pulled his car forward to drive on.

The *Conejo* passed by a diner busting with business. "*Hombre*, this must be the place." Emiliano circled back and parked the car. The hungry boys hopped out and Hank ushered them into the restaurant. They'd barely sat down when a nice-looking lady came over to take their orders. Hank and the boys were delighted to be able to order sandwiches and cola. When the waitress returned, her smile had disappeared. As she stood beside their table it became apparent she was having difficulty finding the right words.

"I'm so sorry, señor, but the owner has told me that we can't be serving your type in this restaurant."

Hank got the jist of what she was saying and began a staunch defense of his family's rights. He stood to give her some words to repent on. But Emiliano quickly brought things to order. He stood tall next to Hank and commanded, "No, *hombre*. Not here. Not over this thing. It's bigger then you and me, *amigo*, and somewhere up the road it will be settled, but not here and not now, yes *hombre*? This is what makes the mind of a *gabacho* different then us. Let's get a-goin' down the street to the market and buy us some meat and jelly and potatoes plus some of that cola. Let's have a picnic until the train comes. Okay, *hombre*?"

Emiliano's verdict calmed Hank's hankerings and he forced a smile as he said smartly, "Yes. Let's take our business down yonder." And then he marched the younger boys out of the diner to the street.

Emiliano hung back and Hank heard him say softly to the waitress, "*Señorita, está bien.* We know what you face. We know what is in your heart. We want no trouble here." Then Emiliano drove them on over to the train station, which turned out to be a fine idea because a market was just across the street with a nearby park where they could sit and eat lunch.

When Joseph arrived at the diner with Ma and the girls, the waitress told him about the problem and that he had just missed Emiliano and Hank. She suggested they were probably down the street, eating at the park.

When Uncle Joseph found Emiliano and the boys, he herded Ma and the girls over to join in on the picnic, then took Emiliano aside to ask, "What was all the commotion back there about?"

Emiliano explained the situation and described how Hank had stood up for the family, but that he'd advised otherwise since Adela and the kids would be coming around soon. Joseph said he saw the wisdom of his decision. "Well done, Emiliano. I can see why Mr. Slaughter trusts you. He's always sure about your instincts. He says you're less passionate than the rest, yet fair and firm when you need be." Joseph looked over at the kids and Adela enjoying themselves. "Funny thing is, Emiliano, I'm from European stock. My brother and I can go anywhere, but our children are mixed. They can't go about like Henry and me. How do you make any sense of that? I'll never know. But out here, to avoid problems, we just go by what is. Someday it will change."

"Yes, Mr. Lefebvre. I told Hank that very same thing." Emiliano smiled. "I've become mighty fond of your nephew. But he needs a-watching 'cause, he can be a hot enchilada, with a soul like an Apache warrior!"

Joseph smiled now. "Yes, that's something to watch out for—the good and the bad that comes with it."

Emiliano added, "Still, if I was a gambler, I'd place my bet on him."

"Yep, Emiliano, He's a lot like his father, my brother. Henry's too impatient, and too passionate about things."

Emiliano stopped him short from going on. "No sir. It is not my business to say, but I will. Hank's like you both in many ways. He's *mucho grande plato*. You two Lefebvres mixed together, what a feast he'll be. Yes?"

Joseph chuckled. "Maybe so, Emiliano. Maybe so."

"Let's go and eat, *amigo*. Yes?"

"Yes. Let's," Joseph agreed.

While waiting together on the station platform, Hank overheard his uncle talking to his mother. "Adela, I know you come from good stock. You've been through some difficult times, but always manage. I trust you'll continue to try and take care of my brother. You know Henry's ways as well as I do."

"Yeah. I swear, Joseph. That man... sometimes... but I still love him."

"I know you do, Adela. You've be putting up with him for so long. This could be a new start for him, you and the young ones."

"Thank you, Joseph, for trying your best at Henry's rehabilitations. That stubborn man means good, but always brings in the other."

"Well, from time to time, if you need money Adela, I'll be happy to chip in, but don't never let Henry on to it. He thinks I've sworn him off. So, let's leave it that way. We have our differences, but he'll always be my brother."

Soon the train pulled into the station and everyone hugged Uncle Joseph and Emiliano goodbye, then boarded the train. Once the luggage was loaded and the train about to pull out, Hank looked out the window to see his uncle frantically signaling with an envelope in his hand. Hank rushed back out to the platform.

"I almost forgot. I promised Doris Mae I'd get this letter to you," Uncle Joseph said. Hank thanked him and put the letter in his jacket pocket, then hurried back inside.

As soon as Hank found his seat, the train began to tremble and strain, then crackle as it attempted to accelerate the connecting cars. As the engine pulled—then finally chugged—its way forward away from Benson Station, all that was left in sight for Hank was his uncle Joseph and Emiliano waving goodbye. Hank felt it was a pleasant moment, seeing he had such a fine friend and uncle to send him off, out there into the world, and knowing he had a vision and something to work on.

The train traversed about the mountains for hours, dipping into tunnels and pitching while turning around another bend in the tracks, clicking further away from Arizona and toward its California destination. Hank's brothers and sisters seemed to be having fun, secured by the fact that their pa was going to greet them at journey's end and take them to their new home.

Hank had taken a window seat next to his mother, who was seated along the aisle. While Hank took in the sights, he also noticed a well-dressed man wearing a top hat across the aisle from Adela who had begun to look intently at her. Welcoming a brief rest from the day's travels, Adela had closed her eyes by this time and didn't seem to notice the man.

A few minutes later, she awoke, apparently startled from his stare. Hesitantly, the man gulped and then spoke politely, "May I, ma'am?"

"Yes. What is it?" Adela asked.

"Well ma'am, I was wondering. You see I was in that diner earlier today with those boys who appear to be with you right now on the train, and I noticed some trouble—"

"I know what's bothering you," Adela said. When he looked even more stressed, she eased her tone and gave him a warm smile. It clearly enamored him. Hank's ma was always good at that. She then asked, "Your name, sir?"

"Oh, sorry. It's Mr. Warner, ma'am."

"Nice to meet you. My name is Mrs. Adela Lefebvre. You may call me Adela. My last name is hard to pronounce." With introductions over, she continued. "Well, Mr. Warner, the restaurant staff thought incorrectly that my boys were half-breeds and couldn't be served. But my son, I was told, explained they were no such thing. For, we are French. We'd had a Mexican ranchero drive us here to Benson. That's all." Hank began to listen more intently now.

"My son felt he needed to protect our driver's integrity because of course our driver isn't a Mexican revolutionary hoping to invade the United States, like we've all read in the newspapers. You know, about Germany and Mexico getting together. No sir. Our driver is just a loyal, trusted hired hand of the one and only Mr. John Texas Slaughter. Now of course, you must've heard of him? You've heard of John Slaughter, now haven't you, Mr. Warner? Respected Arizona sheriff and cattleman?"

"Oh, yes ma'am, who hasn't? He's legend in these parts."

"Yes, he is." Adela piled it on. "He's also a good friend of my husband's, and of Arizona Congressman Carl Hayden as well."

"You don't say," Mr. Warner replied.

"Yes sir," Ma said smartly.

Hank wondered if Mr. Warner was impressed by her name droppings.

She continued, "So, Mr. Warner, we all had a wonderful picnic at that park next to the station."

Now Hank couldn't help but notice his ma had just straight out lied. He thought she'd probably learned from his pa that sometimes there are some mighty good reasons to stretch the truth. And besides, now his ma had a new friend to talk to on their way to California. Hank knew his ma was about to rob this man's mind of all kinds of good information. He kept his eyes on the outside landscape as they went on, but his ears perked like a rabbit.

Adela continued, "We just come from Douglas to join my husband. He has a business concern in Los Angeles. There's a home waiting for us in Long Beach."

The man seemed impressed, then went on about his own ventures. He told Adela he was in the movie business and had investments in property because California would soon reach over 800,000 in population and in fact, by 1920, many thought the population would reach one million.

He spent quite a bit of time explaining how important it was to invest in property, because Long Beach was growing like New York's Coney Island. Hank wasn't sure what that was, but it must have been good or the man wouldn't have brought it up.

"Because of the war in Europe, Long Beach is now home base for the West's US Naval fleet. A lot of military and their family live there, and tourists are coming from all over the world because the weather is so warm and sunny." Mr. Warner's voice grew even more animated when he said, "And Adela, Long Beach also has a Pike and an amusement park where people come to swim and stroll along beautiful beaches, not to mention Catalina Island! Mr. Wrigley, the chewing gum man, he bought Catalina and now's thinking about building an entertainment casino to help bring all kinds of celebrities to the West Coast."

When he paused, Adela let him know she knew about that casino. "So, I've heard, Mr. Warner. Please go on."

"Well, ma'am. Then there is the movie industry in Hollywood, which I have an interest in. And there's the oil! They're digging and exploring for it in a place right next to where you're going, in Long Beach. It's called 'Signal Hill.' Nothing more than an orange grove now, but Adela, I believe there's oil there, down deep under those trees. I really do!"

"Wow," Hank thought as he listened to all the amazing things Mr. Warner was sharing.

The man finished by saying, "Guess what else, Adela?"

"I have no idea. What might that be, Mr. Warner?"

"They've even planned to build a coliseum in Los Angeles—just like they had in Rome—to play sports for the Olympics one day!"

"You dear say. My, my," she added.

Hank never recollected his ma talking that way back in Douglas. No way. Still, he saw no reason to ding the turkey twice. But that coliseum thing…well it stuck into Hank's mind. "Wow, just think about playing, running, throwing or whatever they do in coliseums, with hundreds—no, thousands!—of people cheering you on. Now, the Pike could be fun, but that coliseum, that would be something real special," Hank thought.

Little did Hank know it was right then—on that train—that a seed had been planted in his mind, and it would grow.

PART II

LONG BEACH

Long Beach Pike

Chapter 11

City Of Angels

The day shed the last of its light as the train approached the La Grande railroad station in downtown Los Angeles. Hank couldn't make out much, even from his window seat, but it was clear that in this town there would be more of everything.

The train ride had made Hank feel like his entire life was moving toward a destination in this new country. But that notion vanished as soon as the train's engine stopped and it was time to help Ma gather the kids and all of their endeared bundles of suitcases that represented all they'd treasured from their Douglas years. While stepping off the rail car, an unfamiliar scent found them right away. Hank leaned over to his ma and said, "Isn't it funny? Wherever you travel, you find a strange aroma that stands out and stays in your nose, for who knows how long, until you get used to it." After one look at the station's oversized building, Hank added, "Mama, it feels foreign here. Are we in Turkey?"

"No," A chuckling passenger's voice echoed as he passed by, "it's just a foreign style of architecture."

Then Hank noticed a familiar face. "There's Pa!"

Pa came to them with the wide-open arms of a lunging linebacker, greeting and hugging them all, one by one, until he got to Ma, who he squeezed especially tight for a long time.

"Look at all of you!" he said, then announced to a large, bulging, red-cheeked man beside him, "See, I told you, Michael, they were a fine-looking bunch!" Turning back to his family he said, "I bet you might be wondering who is this gentleman that has so generously volunteered to help drive us to our new home in Long Beach? Wait now, till you hear him speak. That will give you a clue." Henry grinned and pointed at the man. "My good friend wants to say hello to all of you."

The burly man stepped forward in his long overcoat, and with an exaggerated smile and a heavy accent declared: "I'm very happy to meet ye. Look at all ye lads and damsels. You're the wee mother of course. 'Tis Adela, isn't it?"

The family stared up at the man awkwardly.

"No really, guess his name…anybody?" Henry couldn't seem to wait for a response.

Hank replied, "He must be Irish."

"You have a good ear, me boy," the man said.

Pa jumped in, "Believe it or not, his real name is Mr. Michael Ireland." Then Henry went from one Lefebvre child to another, saying each name. He started with Benny, the youngest, and worked his way up to Hank. "Now this here is Hank, the one I've been telling you and Clifford so much about. He'll be leading the family soon, you'll see."

Michael greeted Hank with a crushing handshake. "Pleasure to meet you, son. Your pa's let us all know what a fine young lad you are, especially your courage and sporting skills." Hank looked over to see the pride in his pa's eyes and nodded.

"Well then," Pa said, "Let's get packed into the cars we have a waiting for us and be on our way. Boy, do we have some surprises for all of you back at the house. It's not far from here, just a little over an hour's drive."

The group careened through the bustling crowd until they found two parked cars waiting beside the front curb of the station. Tucked under the windshield wipers of both cars were folded sheets of yellow paper. "I'll take care of this." Michael said, as he slipped the papers away into his pocket. While the family loaded their belongings, Michael walked a few cars up and started a conversation with a policeman. After a few moments, Hank noticed Michael handing something to the officer. They both smiled when he turned to rejoin the group. "No problem folks. Everything can be fixed—this is LA!"

Ma, and Pa got into one car with Hank and the boys packed like sardines in the back seat, while Lily and the girls got into the other car with Mike. Mike took off in his car and Pa followed with Ma riding shotgun.

Ma asked Pa, "So, Henry, where did you find the fine Irish fella you'd been drinking with today."

"At the pool hall."

"Oh no. Henry, not another billiard parlor?" she challenged.

Henry started in on his alibi. "Well, you see Adela. When I was coming in on the train to LA, I knew I had to find my way around, just how to get from here to there. So, I asked the conductor if there was a pool parlor near the downtown station. I told him I was on my way to Long Beach and that most likely the men that hang around the pool halls knowed what's going on and where'd I need to go. So, the conductor said, 'Yep' there was. And not to worry 'cause it wouldn't be out of my way. I just needed to take the trolley close to the Shrine Auditorium on Jefferson Boulevard, across the street from the Methodist University of Southern California. When I got there, I was to ask for Clifford Girard. He even wrote down the directions for me.

"So, Adela, I did just that. He said to say 'hi' to Clifford for him, and to let him know that Roger the conductor said I'm okay. He also said this Clifford Girard owns and runs the pool hall and...well, he did know all about LA. You see, Cliff had growed up workin' with trains in Minnesota and pretty much all over the West Coast. He got sick and because the train company let him travel for free, he packed up his family and came out here like us." Henry paused and caught his breath. "That Cliff sure is a funny guy. You'd know, when he arrived at the station it was New Year's Day, so he put up his family in a downtown hotel and went straight the Rose Bowl football game!" Henry laughed. "Can you believe that? And they never saw or heard from him till he came back—two days later."

"Sounds like someone I know," Adela said sarcastically.

Paying no attention to her remark, Henry went on. "Yep. Now if Cliff comes to likin' you, well, he'd do just about anything for yah. So, I go a-visiting that pool hall. Don't worry, Adela. There's a sign that says 'no women allowed,' just like there is in Douglas.

"Of course there is." That ain't what's been worrying me, Henry. Adela said, rolling her eyes.

"Now Adela, don't you go that way. You'd know us men need our time away after working all day. So, we'd be sittin' there having a beer and this man pulls up a stool next to me. A friendly sort, and starts up a conversation. He says, 'Hi, I'm Mike.' I noticed he speaks a might peculiar. Then I found out why. He says, 'I'm Ireland.'" Henry chuckled, "You know Adela, I thought he was funning with me, until this bartender breaks in, after listening to us talking, and says with a smile, 'Yes, that's his real name—Michael Ireland.' Then he joked, 'We'd love to forget about him here.'

"Then he puts his hand across the bar and says. 'Who shall you be?' I said, 'My name be Henry Lefebvre, from Douglas, Arizona.' And he says, 'Well, I'm Cliff Girard, owner of this place.' Then I says, 'Nice to meet you. Roger the train conductor said to say hi for him.' Then Cliff asked, 'Roger?' I says, 'Yep, Roger.' Then Cliff says, 'Roger and I spent some time together on that old railroad. 'What might you do for a living Henry?' Cliff asked me, so, I told him that Douglas is a small town outside the mining town of Bisbee, near the Mexican border. And that I'd worked in the smelter before, but here in California, I'm going into the construction business. That's when I took out my wallet and pulled out my new business card, Adela." Henry pretended to show her a card. "He looked it over and says, 'Really? You speak fluent Spanish and French?' I says 'Yep' again, 'but,' I told him, 'I'm not too good in English.' Then Cliff took on a big smile when he says, 'You and Mike Ireland—he speaks only English and we still can't understand a word he's saying except 'give me another drink,' isn't that right, Mike?' Mike nods, 'Right ye are, Cliff.'

"Then I told him, 'I made some money elsewhere by prizefighting at the YMCA.' Well, Adela that did it! After that, Cliff goes on burstin' about his prizefighting career. Within minutes, we'd become best friends. He says. 'Henry Lefebvre, we're going to get along just fine.' I says, 'Looks that way. Then he says. 'If you need to know anything about Los Angeles, I'm the man to come to.'"

"Well now, Henry, haven't you been just too busy these last few days," Adela said.

Hank took notice that his pa's rambling speech was a bit slurred and wondered whether he'd been talking with that Mr. Girard over just one beer. But Ma never seemed to mind much. She'd never take to scolding pa. She always said she was happy for what she had with the kids, and that there was always a roof over their heads. Even if Pa did have his ways, she loved that about him and for what he provided.

As they drove on, Henry kept talking, building excitement with each breath. "Listen, Adela. With Cliff's help, we've got the girls and boys in a good neighborhood in Long Beach.

There's a great school for Hank and Lily. They say it's the biggest high school west of the Mississippi, with some three thousand-plus students. It's called 'Long Beach Poly Tech High School.'" He turned to the back seat. "Hank, listen to this. They are notorious for sports, known all over the country. You'd be a star there right away."

"Sure, Pa," Hank agreed nonchalantly.

"And the youngers will have fine schools too."

Adela pepped up now and asked, "How about the house, Henry?"

"Oh, now this is even better. We be renting—thanks to Joseph's contact—on Twenty-third Street, just three long blocks from the high school, and only walking distance from the younger kids' school. It's just some miles from the Pike and the beach."

"About the house," Adela primed Henry again.

"Well, that's the best part Adela, it's got wooden floors all over. Not like them dirt floors in Douglas."

"Well, if that doesn't beat all," Adela said with a big grin.

"Listen to this everybody. Anybody guess what else it's got?"

From the back seat, Alfred spoke up, "Aw, Pa. Quit playin'. Just tell us."

Henry paused and the anticipation built. "We got ourselves an indoor outhouse! Well, it's not really an outhouse. It's what they call a bathroom."

"No way!" everyone shouted back.

"Yep. This is California. Just think, you couldn't hardly find jobs back in Douglas. Well just look around here. Everybody works! It's booming like it was when we'd just got married in Bisbee. Remember, Adela? And how it was in Douglas?" He looked at Ma. "We'd always keep ahead of the goings on in business, now don't we Adela?"

Hank saw his ma smile wide—like it was floating so high, only the roof of the car could restrain it.

As the cars rumbled along toward Long Beach, the traffic thickened and the lights of LA never disappeared. Squashed up against his brothers Alfred, Gilbert and Benjamin, Hank tried to get some sleep, but couldn't get a wink. The excitement among the boys grew while they tarried toward Long Beach. After reaching San Pedro and turning south onto Pacific Coast Highway, Henry explained, "The fishing boats dock and unload the days' catch from the Pacific Ocean here." It was too dark to really take it all in, but Pa kept talking anyway. When they passed an area with bright spot lights, Pa said, "That's the US Naval Fleet Headquarters. You be seeing a lot of them sailors on leave from their ships down at the Pike."

They finally entered the city of Long Beach. They knew because the big sign said so. After traveling a while further, up this street, then another, the lights faded much like in Douglas once you'd pass the Gadsden Hotel. When the cars stopped, Mike shouted out the window, "We're here!"

Though restless and tired, Henry, Adela and the kids said good night to Mike and thanked him for his help, then rushed to see their new home. Henry gave a few more details while walking quickly up the path. "It has three bedrooms. One for the girls, Lily, Mary, Esther, and one for Hank, Alfred, Gilbert, and Benjamin. Now, you two, Hank and Lily, you being the oldest can fight about who gets which room, but, mind you, the room in the back with the porch—that be for your ma and me. Okay then." Henry finally took out a key, opened the door and reached in to turn on the light.

While the kids scrambled about the house plotting out their own spaces, Hank and Adela rested on the couch. When exhausted and the long day's journey had finally seemed to catch up to the kids, Henry called them back into the living room. "Okay, kids. I know it's going to be all new for you—much different than Douglas—but in time you'll find friends and places to go here. We'll all work together as a family, help each other out. And Ma, there's a lot of fine churches in these parts for you to light as much candles as you want." Everyone cheered. "There's also a hotel and restaurants on every corner for all you kids to make extra money. Oh, I almost forgot. Cliff told me there'd be a surprise for us in the kitchen."

Adela's eyes widened and she stood and walked to the kitchen. "Oh my goodness! Henry, look at this! Everyone rushed in behind her. "A brand-new refrigerator!"

"Well, open it Adela." When she did, everyone leaned in to see the inside full of food. "Anybody hungry?" Henry asked.

"I am, Pa," Hank said.

"Okay everyone. Let's eat!"

Hank remembered this as the best and worst night of his life. He was the oldest, and the family would depend on him a lot as they adjusted to this new life in California. His ma and pa had told him so. And still, there was no doubt about it, he missed Douglas and its ways. After the meal, everyone found their rooms. Though sparsely furnished, they were comfortable, and before "good nights" were over, each family member had tested out the new in-house plumbing.

Hank almost fell asleep before remembering the envelope Uncle Joseph had waved him down with before the train left Benson. Sleep wouldn't come until he knew what his cousin Doris Mae had to say, so he tiptoed his way to the closet, found his jacket, and pulled out the envelope. Then he quietly walked out to the dark front room, fidgeted around for a lamp switch, and turned it on. Peeling back the seal, he took out the neatly folded paper. He wasn't sure why, but it had a texture and aroma that seemed so friendly. He carefully unfolded the letter and read.

> *Hi Hank,*
>
> *It's me, Doris Mae. I was told, in my class in Tombstone, to start writing a diary each day for school. It would help my grammar. That was too dull for me. So, I'd decided to write you because, I know'd the troubles you had with your father and wanted to let you know how much my father Charley likes you and your pa. So much so, he'd said he'd like Charley Jr. to grow'd up and be just like his cousin Hank.*
>
> *Now, what I know is, that my grandpa Joseph and your father be identical twins. Our side of the Lefebvre family is musically inclined and your side is athletic. We call your family the California Lefebvres now. Your father and Grandpa Joseph were very close. It is said that when one would have a pain, the other would feel it, even though they lived miles apart. Grandpa Joseph supported your family when your pa went on a drinking binge and stayed away from home in Douglas and paid for hospital cures for your dad. Even when grandpa sent your father away to rehabilitation. After he was gone a long time the family set up a party for him when he'd returned. But when he came home, grandpa drove to the train station to pick your pa up. And when his bother Henry got off the train, he was drunk. They had a fight right there and Grandpa Joseph said he never wanted to see him again. But he arranged with Aunt Adela to have your pa go to California, to get away from his Douglas friends and start a new life out there. We like your father, even with his faults. And we love all our cousins but, you Hank, are special to my father, me and my brother Charley Jr. I'd like to keep writing you and maybe you could write me back because, I know you'll always be doing good things, like helping out that Injun girl here in Tombstone.*
>
> *My best to your family,*
> *Doris Mae*

This letter was really something special and got through to Hank like nothing else ever had. He'd been battling with his past, living always in the present since the day he was born. Folks had told him he made the best of every situation and he found it easy to make friends—people were always happy to have him around. But here in Long Beach, California, he wasn't as certain. He had too many questions lurching in the back of his mind. For the first time in his young life, he felt his future might be at risk because here in Long Beach, things didn't seem as clear. The terrain was so different than the Southwest, and the rules he'd always lived by might need some changing. But he wasn't about to give up on life without at least competing. What Josiah had told him in that hospital room in Douglas, and now what Doris Mae said in her letter, would make all the difference in his outlook. Now he had not only a cause to fight for, but a legacy to pass on. As Hank fell asleep, he realized this idea was a very scary proposition.

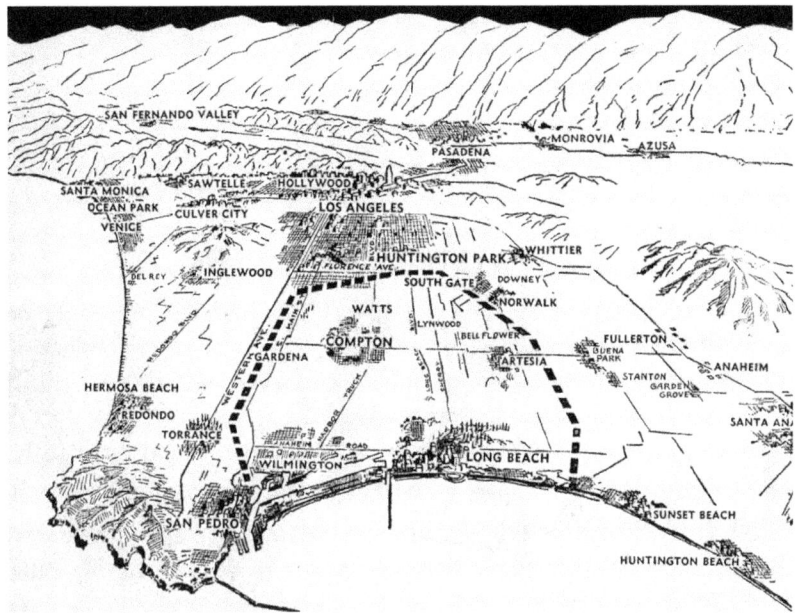

Long Beach California 1919

CHAPTER 12

COTTON CANDY & SALT WATER TAFFY

L ong Beach, less than an hour south from the bustling city of Los Angeles, evoked a rural atmosphere with mostly unpaved dirt streets, yet its population nearly exceeded 17,000. Like Douglas, there were trolleys, but instead of providing passage for commuters to jobs at the smelter or brewery, at the time of Hank's arrival in 1916, trolleys were mostly employed for the convenience of vacationers. Scores of midwestern and eastern tourists were attracted to the warm, comforting off-shore breezes of Long Beach, which provided an antidote for extremely cold and sometimes uninhabitable winters. Tourists exchanged chilly existences for the warmth and natural grandeur of the Pacific's crashing waves upon miles of wide sandy beaches—a coastline that stretched south all the way to Belmont Shores. With the addition of Long Beach's most recognizable attraction, the Long Beach Pike, the appeal was irresistible. Beginning at the end of Pine Street and cornered by Ocean Boulevard, just a chip shot away from Pleasure Pier, the Pike's games and side shows gave the area a circus atmosphere.

Music blared through loudspeakers as visitors munched on juicy hot dogs and whiffed the scent of popcorn and salt water taffy wafting through the air. Games for prizes were carefully positioned for the promenading boardwalkers to challenge those wanting to indulge, while well-wishing spectators gathered, eager to cheer them on. The more photographic observers and beach gawkers were consumed with viewing hundreds of bathing beauties from all parts of the world as they dashed to and fro the water's edge, some dodging under umbrellas, hoping to tame the bristle of the sun, others pursuing tans to elicit envy from hometown friends.

Just when tourists thought they'd had their fill of leisure, there was the famous Long Beach Coaster. In plain sight from miles down the coast, it beckoned and tempted patrons to come experience the thrill of their lives. The coaster thrusted jubilant riders about in high-speed cars, as they screamed at each turn to mellow their fears. Mind you, this coaster would not be surpassed by any other roller coaster in the world for the fright it offered—and rightly so. From its infancy, the coaster incurred a dubious reputation for the fact that from time to time it would derail, flinging unsuspecting passengers out into the deep blue Pacific Ocean. But no matter—especially for the locals—that's precisely what made the ride so formidable and challenging to one's pride.

When night came to play, there was always the enchantment of a seaside hotel within walking distance from the shore. If you were given preference for a reservation, most likely the luxurious Virginia Hotel would be your destination. Its architecture was designed for the exclusive hospitality of the guest, because, as advertised, every room had magnificent panoramic views of the Pacific.

After taking in the sights and having a good night's stay, the active visitor wanting to participate in more strenuous exercises wouldn't have far to go. The Bathing Spa was just a few steps from the breakers. Although the name was somewhat misleading, for it was really a giant indoor plunge with high and low diving boards that all the tourists enjoyed. If all of this didn't serve to exhaust an appetite, the open market right up on Main Street would do the trick.

Unlike Douglas, which had fulfilled its growth years ago, Long Beach was about to burst into an internationally respected industrial center—with a population to match. In fact, in the early twenties, Long Beach would become the fastest growing city in the United States, especially after oil was discovered under Signal Hill on June 23, 1921. The seaport of Long Beach accommodated the permanently stationed US Naval fleet as well as a prosperous fishing industry and allowed all kinds of building materials and merchandise to pass through its wide harbor, and it soon became America's second largest port of entry. In 1929, when the Ford Motor Company opened its Long Beach assembly plant, the population, which had already quickly moved up the charts, skyrocketed. Downtown hotels and business buildings sprouted up overnight. Among those new ventures was the iconic Villa Rivera. Built in 1921, it still stands tall today as the pride of Long Beach.

Lefebvre's Christmas mornings were always wonderful treats, full of suspense, excitement and surprises. Even though December was months away, when Hank woke up to his first California morning, it would be no different. The crowing roosters gave Hank few clues as to where he was. This first wake-up call of his new surroundings didn't feel any different than in Douglas. But, in his early attempts to rally toward a nature break by stepping on the wooden floor and walking outside, he was greeted by the fresh scent of a cool, moist ocean breeze. Finding no place of relief, Hank's mind woke quickly from its slumber. In time, the whole family would begin, just like Hank's early morning entry into the new land.

On this morning, Hank's pa was noticeably focused and collected in his new front room. When all family members were accounted for and present, Henry, acting as the captain of the Santa Maria just discovering land, stood front and center to address his crew. He surveyed the possibilities that lay ahead for the family, amusing the kids when he referred to Hank as his "first mate," while ma sat comfortably in her new-found retreat—the living room rocking chair. She swayed back and forth, listening intently.

"Mama, you're rocking with a fresh sense of pride that we'd got this far from home without trouble finding us yet!" Hank said. Ma laughed, but Pa showed disgust—he'd been interrupted. "Sorry, Pa. Just thought I'd mention."

"No matter, Hank." Henry went on, "Now, before you kids start into the schoolin', we all need to chip in and work—even more than what we'd done in Douglas. You see, we have space behind the house where we be starting a farm. Not a big one, just one that will provide our needs until we get our feet wet around here. I have a couple of friends in LA that will help bankroll some of our start-up costs, old Ireland and Cliff."

Hank thought Pa was talking about them as if he had known them for years. Pa did have a funny way of picking friends fast.

"You'll get to meet Cliff soon, once we get things together and have some time to spend a day in the city." Henry laid out the plan for all of them. The older girls would look for jobs at one of the department stores something around the hotels. "Hank, they have this open produce market that people bring their goods from all around here. Some sell to a company from LA, the others distribute the riper products to the market down off Main Street. Sounds like something you, Alfred, and Josiah done well with in Douglas. What do yah say?"

"Right, Pa. We'd done good with that."

"Then maybe you best wander over there so you can get a feel of the place." Henry stopped for a moment, then said,

"Alfred, you and the younger boys, probably need to get to taking care of the farm. You're too young for much else."

"Okay, Pa, done," they answered.

Henry turned toward Hank. "Son, please try to keep that temper of yours down a notch."

"Sure, Pa. I know what you mean. I'll try my best."

"Adela, you stay put around the house. Manage the farm and such. Your days working in the hotel are over. The younger girls can help with chores, and mind you, all kids and I mean all..." Now directly talking to Hank again, "Hank, when you're not working, you best be in school, 'cause here the law will find you if you don't. We'd be might tired of being distracted, trying to find you gone on some trip for days here and there, then attempting to ask the police to let you be. It's going to be different here, 'specially for you Hank."

"I know, Pa," Hank said, trying to hide his desire to laugh.

Henry smiled too and added "Oh, what the heck, Hank. You be just you." Then Henry put on his tough act and pointed to the rest of the family. "Now, you Lefebvres get to getting things in order. I have some business to take care of." With that he strutted over to Adela, gave her a kiss on the cheek, and turned to leave, much like Santa Clause putting his finger to his nose before rising up the chimney. After a broad and convincing smile, he offered a swirling wave goodbye and finished by saying, "Things are going to be just fine here. Now, get going."

Henry always had a mission to slip away to, like a sailor drawn to the sea, or a soldier departing the security of his outpost. When he left on to another adventure, he never much stayed around to see to it that things actually got done. He wasn't into that. Instead, he would move on to the new mission that seemed to keep his soul alive, that would give him purpose. "To stay relevant," he would say, "that's what makes history." And he'd jump at the chance to do anything that enforced his relvancy. Now some folks thought this a bit peculiar.

But it got Hank to thinking. Ma had bought him a brown leather notebook on his last year's birthday. She'd said, "Hank, some day you will know why I got you this present." However, until now he'd had little use for it. The lines got in the way of his drawings that he created to keep records of events passing through his life. Here in this new land, though, maybe it would be a good idea to write things down using his words, "Cause things kinda get entangled more than you'd think, especially since I'm not sure of the rules out here," he thought. "Maybe, if I write things down, they'll make some sense."

Hank wondered if would he be able to find anyone in this new place that cared about what was going on, like Emiliano, Josiah, or Chata? He wasn't feeling down. He rarely did. He just needed time to reflect. Everything that went on in Douglas was behind him. Here, the future was a mystery. A bit like that fog bank at sea he'd read about. Until it broke, a person couldn't navigate beyond. You just continue on, trusting something was out there for you. Hank knew he wasn't the timid type. There was no doubt he'd plug in. He was certain he'd find it. So, he went to his room, pulled the leather-bound book and a pencil from his bag, and walked out the back door to find a comfortable place under the shade of a nearby tree. It was still early, far short of midday, so while the family was buzzing about, he began to write.

After a while, his ma, while working in the kitchen, stopped to look through the window. Seeing Hank under the tree writing, she dropped what she was doing to come slide up next to him. "What yah doing, Hank?"

"Just writing, Mama. Like you said I would someday."

She looked like she could hardly contain her happiness. "It's a good thing, what you're doing. Writing down things makes you see them different. So, who you be writing to?"

"Oh, nobody really. Just myself I guess, putting my thoughts into words."

"Well you might want to add in Doris Mae. Joseph said she wrote you a letter. At least you got someone to keep you in touch of the goings-on in Douglas. You could tell her what our side of the family is up to."

"Yeah, Mama. I'll do just that."

"Well, when you finish up there, Henry "Hank" Lefebvre Jr., it's time we all quit for the day and get a-goin'!"

"Where to, Mama?"

She stood to announced. "To the Pike!"

"The Pike?"

"Yep and the beach. I've got a few pennies saved up. Let's have a day of it." When Hank shut his book, Ma instructed, "Now, Hank, put a date on it before you put it away. To remind when you said it."

"Yep. Good idea, Mama. I'll do that now."

"Tell your sisters and the boys to stop what they be doing. Oops, I almost forgot, Hank. No more frontier talking here. No more saying, 'be doing this or be doing that.' We've got to learn to speak from the best around here."

Hank laughed. "Right, Mama, like when you was talking with the man on the train saying, 'I dear say.'"

Ma smiled, not the least embarrassed. "You got it, Hank." Grinning, she whispered, "and you got to keep them ears from perking. You're overhearing too much adult conversations."

The news spread around the house like a prairie fire with a gust of wind. "We're going to the Pike on Mama!" Adela had it all planned. They would walk a few blocks over to Atlantic Boulevard, across to Pine Street, pick up the trolley, and end up in front of the boardwalk. After she had the girls pack a light lunch for the boys to carry, they were on their way.

It was just a few long blocks of marching under an unusually warm day—not overbearing at all for them. The family had been accustomed to walking long distances in the hot sun back in Douglas. Although, this wasn't the familiar dry heat, but one mixed with moist, fresh ocean air that savors, comforts, and invites you on. And it did just that today, as the Lefebvres, in cadence with Ma's tempo, reached the trolley stop.

The family waited patiently until a trolley appeared. When it stopped to let off and welcome new passengers, Adela politely asked the conductor, "Going to the beach?"

"This is it. Jump aboard and find a seat," he answered, and they did.

As the trolley chugged and clanged on its way, the feel and scent of the ocean's salty air became more intense, building suspense among the brothers and sisters. The only knowledge they had about the beach was from photos in the Douglas library, so they were excited that, out there, in a few more minutes, would be the Pacific Ocean!

"Do you think it's bigger than the streams in the Chiricahuas?" Hank teased.

"I sure hope so," Alfred said. They were laughing and giggling when it appeared. They caught just a glimpse at first, as if a curtain in a theater was slowly sliding open in anticipation of the eager audience. When the ocean finally came in full view, the Lefevbre children opended their mouths wide with excitement.

"Good Lord. Now, look at that!" Ma exclaimed. "There it is, and as far out as you could see."

"Look at them there boats, big boats! And is that an island out there on the horizon, just floating around?" Benjamin added.

"Silly," Lily jumped in, "islands don't float around. The

only way out to that piece of land is by boat. That's where this Wrigley Gum guy is building a world-famous casino. Right, Hank?"

"Don't know about that, but just look at those waves!" Hank answered.

When the trolley slowly grinded to a stop, the conductor announced, "Here's where you get off for the beach. It's only a block up to the Pleasure Pier then it's just a spit to the Pike."

"What shall it be, Hank?" Ma asked. He knew she counted on him to get the rest of the kids moving in the right direction. She always said she regarded Hank's enthusiasm as a virtue. Hank decided it would be the beach first. The rest of his siblings followed his lead after glancing back a moment to Ma for her approval.

"Yes, to the beach. Let's get a-goin'!" and forgetting her disguise, she added, "¡Vamonos! ¡Vamonos!" With this as their battle cry, all the kids rushed to escape their trolley seats, and were soon trouncing onto the wooden planks of the boardwalk.

As advertised, the beach was full of people—some with blankets laid alongside stuffed bags of this and that; some under umbrellas; and some just stretched out to meet the sun on its terms. Excited adults, acting as if children, raced in and out of the water, playing, as if each wave was chasing them in, then bravely they would chase the wave back out. Mind you, all this with as little clothing as the law would allow. This was where this flock of Lefebvres looked totally out of place. They paid no mind as they traversed their way down toward a mound of sand at the water's edge then plopped down to stare, taking in the delights that were, until then, mere fiction.

"Wow," they muttered between themselves. Hank added, "It sure is big."

Perhaps knowing it would propel him to action, Lily asked Hank, "Do you think the water is warm?"

Hank grew a big, wide grin on his face. "Why don't you and I just find out?" he said, as he tore off his shirt, kicked off his boots, and grabbed Lily by the hand. She begged, but there would be no resisting Hank's determination. He thrusted her up and within a few steps they were both in the ocean. When Lily emerged and yelled out, "Come on in kids! The water is so refreshing!" one by one, all of Hank's brothers and sisters found their way into the crashing surf. Hank looked back to see his ma smiling wide, nylons pulled down about her ankles, and wiggling her hands in the warm sand.

"Look at Mama, Lily. She be in heaven seeing her kids just having fun," Hank said.

They played on in the ocean awhile till Adela called out: "Best get out and let the sun dry you off. The Pleasure Pier and Pike are just over yonder. And remember, no Spanish today."

Hank asked, "But Mama, we be mixed and sometimes...."

"Shush," Ma said with a smile. "That's our secret, Hank. And don't you go telling Pa, 'cause he'll be funning with me forever, calling me a white mountain apache again."

"Okay Mama. You got a deal—no Spanish here."

After drying out, the family walked up onto the boardwalk and strolled toward the pier. As they closed in, they were overwhelmed by the crowds. There were sailors in uniforms, beachgoers in bathing suits, and camera-carrying foreigners with funny, flowered shirts and cut-off pants, looking far more out of place than any from the Lefebvre clan. Groups of people strolled around, buying hot dogs and hamburgers and piling globs of mustard, catsup, and onions on top, then spilling it on their clothes as they tried walking and eating. What a sight. When the scent from the variety of food options gave the family hunger pains, Ma said, "Look here, no buying anything. We got our peanut butter sandwiches and apples and such. Need to save them pennies for the Pike."

They traveled to the end of the pier and saw many 'NO DIVING' signs posted along the way, yet, several young men defied the sign's warnings. Hank thought this was probably because girls in bathing suits huddled around clapping and cheering after each young man tried to outdo the last by twisting and turning before splashing down below.

Then Alfred pointed, "Hey, Hank. Look at that. There's even a sign that says, 'NO FISHING,' but all those people over there have polls dipping into the water."

Hank laughed. "Them signs must only be for the tourists."

Ma suggested they find a bench to rest a while and eat together, like they did in the park back in Benson on that fine last day in Arizona. When finished, Hank called out, "Onward, let's get over to the Pike!" The family agreed, dumped out their trash in a nearby container, and raced back to the boardwalk.

Soon they all turned their attention toward the big roller coaster, standing so high on the skyline that it wasn't hard to find. The screams from the riders were so loud, the family could hear them over the roar of the breaking surf. Music played in the background like a circus was in town and the large crowd made it difficult to stay together. Carnival-style barkers stood outside colorful booths, beckoning their attention as they passed by. Some called out, "come in and see the Wild Man," or come "ride this" or "throw that." The commotion of fun and smell of popcorn and cotton candy was intoxicating. The family stopped and watched the large machine that pulled salt water taffy over and over again as if mesmerized. Shouts from a nearby jolly-looking man broke the spell.

He begged Hank to come on over. "Hey, kid. I bet you can't take this ball and knock down those stacks of milk bottles."

Hank took the bait. "Sure, I can."

"Oh, really? Yah think so?"

"So, what if I do? Then what?"

"Well, Son, you get to pick out one of those cutesy dolls and give it to your sweetheart" the man explained.

Hank smiled. "I don't have a sweetheart. I left them all back in Douglas. Haven't been here but a day."

The man smiled back. "You're a confidant critter."

A sailor with a pretty girl hanging on his arm obviously heard the challenge and said, "Hey, kid—"

"Don't be takin' me too lightly, sir," Hank shot back. He'd had enough of the 'kid' talk.

Seeing the disposition he'd created, the sailor quickly qualified his remarks. 'Okay, okay. Well, do you have a name you wouldn't mind sharing?"

"Sure. It's Hank."

"Okay, then. Hank, I'm your friend, not your enemy, least not today."

Hank smiled and relaxed a little. "You can do that, Hank? Knock all those bottles down with that ball?"

"You bet I can, sir."

"Okay, I'll give you the twenty-five cents, and if you win, you give the doll to my girlfriend here."

"Why would I do that, sir?"

"Because, as you say, you don't have a girl here—yet. And I do. See here?" The sailor put his arm around the girl. And it will cost you nothing to prove your point. Okay then?"

"It's a deal, sir," Hank said, grinning at all the onlookers who'd gathered around. They, along with all the Lefebvres, rooted him on.

The sailor said to the jolly man, "Here's twenty-five cents.

Give those balls to my friend Hank here."

Hank took the balls in his hands, gripped and squeezed them a few moments to feel their weight, then without hesitation he reared back and threw his first pitch. Like pins in a bowling alley thrust to a strike, the milk bottles flew, leaving nothing but air. The crowd yelled and erupted into applause. With a flair of flirtatious arrogance, Hank said to the sailor's girlfriend, "Go ahead and pick out your doll, ma'am."

Now there were others in line to bet on Hank's throwing talents. Eventually it occurred to Hank that a little commission would be in order and he began making deals—a nickel a throw—and plenty of willing customers lined up. Hank threw balls and won practically every cutesy doll on the shelf until, finally, the jolly man took Hank aside and said, "Kid, please do me a favor and go down there a bit and try some other game. You're killing me here."

Hank's newly acquired fans cheered and followed him down the boardwalk. He stopped at the sight of a colorful lady who pandered to the crowd with her bulging, low-cut dress. Adela said to the girls, "The last time I saw something like that was on Sixth Street in Douglas," and the family had a good laugh.

When the lady saw that Hank and the crowd aware of her flaunting, she said sweetly to Hank, "Why don't you come over here and test out your manhood by shooting these plates to pieces. If you do, you can pick out whatever you want from those prizes hanging up here."

Hank had become the attraction. His new-found fan club egged him on, "You can do it! Go for it Hank!"

Once again, Hank arrogantly announced, "Who's going to back me at this rifle shooting gallery?"

A navy officer, in his perfectly pressed and tailored uniform stepped forward. While his wife and kids stayed close by his side, he raised his hand to say, "I will. Let's see what this boy—oops, sorry—" the officer quipped to correct his statement, "let's see what this young *man*, Hank, can do with a gun."

Hank's family watched with surprise as all the sailors and tourists came around just to see what their Hank could do with a rifle. The officer handed the plump lady some money, then held out a dollar bill to Hank. "This is for you, if you break all of the plates."

Hank smiled and said, "Like takin' candy from a baby, sir." The crowd laughed.

"You think so, Hank?"

"Yes sir. Only question I have, is she going to put enough bullets in that there rifle to shoot all them plates down?" The crowd roared at this last statement of confidence.

"You got the money, honey, I'll give you the bullets," the lady told the officer in a seductive tone.

The officer said, "Fill 'em up, ma'am, and make sure it's the rifle that shoots live rounds."

Again, the crowd laughed and cheered. The lady appeared to consider, then said, "That will be five dollars, mister."

The officer turned to his kids to ask, "What do you think? Is it worth it?"

After looking at all the tantalizing prizes hanging about, his children in chorus said, "Yes, Daddy, please. Let Hank try."

"All right," he mumbled under his breath. "What have I got myself into?" He reached into his pocket for his wallet to pull out three one dollar bills. "Here you are, miss."

"I hate to take money from the military that we all love. But I always do. It's for fun, right?" She added while loading the rifle and handing it over to Hank.

"Ma'am, please step back a little."

"Yah need to set up your aim?"

"No ma'am. That's not it. I just want to make sure you won't be getting hurt when I start a-shootin'." The moment she backed away, he pulled the trigger. Bam! Bam! Bam! Fingers went into ears as pottery flew, while Hank continued firing at every plate in the place. Everyone went silent, it was an incredible sight. When Hank stopped shooting and the smoke cleared, there wasn't a plate left standing.

"Well now. That's something! I've never seen that kind of shooting before. You must be in the army," the busty lady said.

"No ma'am. I'm just from Douglas."

The jubilant officer encouraged his kids to go get whatever prize they wanted. "Here Hank, here's an extra dollar. I've seen a lot of shooting but today, none better. How many in your family?"

"Well, here, there is seven…no eight including Mama."

"Well then, here's enough money for all you to ride the roller coaster," he said, while counting it out and handing it over. "Now Hank, you're not scared of the coaster, are you?" The crowd laughed and started wandering away.

"I don't know, sir. Haven't been up on it yet."

"You learned to shoot like that in Douglas?"

"Yes sir. That's where I grown up."

"Really? That's around Tombstone and Fort Huachuca, isn't it?"

"Yes sir. I have friends and cousins in Tombstone and another cousin is quartermaster there in Fort Huachuca."

"You don't say. I'm sure you've heard about Wyatt Earp and that OK Corral shoot out? Nah, maybe you're a little young for that."

"No, but my pa did."

"Really? How about Texas John Slaughter?"

Hank jumped at that. "My pa plays cards with him in Tombstone and Douglas."

"Really?"

"Yes sir. You see, you'd be talkin' about my home now," Hank said proudly. "I'd stayed just some weeks back at Mr. Slaughter's ranch in the San Bernardino Valley. You must be some kind of history officer?"

"No, but I love reading those dime novels while I'm at sea. Like to have you visit me on the base and talk some more about the dying west."

"Oh, it ain't a-dyin' sir, just not moving forward."

"Love to talk to you more about that, Hank, here's my card. Take it."

"Sure will. Thanks, sir."

"You can get a hold of me at the main gate of the naval base. Now kids. Say thanks to Hank." They did, and sauntered down the Pike with arms draped around their winnings.

"On to the roller coaster!" Hank's brothers and sisters yelled and ran on ahead.

Ma refused to get on the roller coaster, and explained she just wanted to watch. But all the others clamored to get in line. Once they bought their tickets and stood watching with worry, Hank teased, "You know what makes the ride so much fun is, I hear it goes off the track sometimes, right out into the ocean. Best know how to swim," then asked one of pale-looking girls who'd just staggered off the ride, "Where's the best place to sit in the cars?"

"For you? In the front seat. And make sure to let go on the turns," she called out while turning away with a sinister smile. When it was their turn, that's what the Lefebvre children did. After rushing by people to the front seats and sitting down, the attendant lowered the bar to lock them in.

The roller coaster began slowly, like the trolley, clanging noisily as it climbed higher and higher. So high that riders could see up and down the beach in every direction. Hearts would begin to wonder what they'd gotten themselves into. It was too late to turn back though, because by then the coaster had hit the summit, and after a last-minute pause, went roaring down so fast that the mind couldn't catch up. Hank felt foolish for chiding his siblings in line. He decided he'd never been as scared as right then on that rickety old coaster. The Lefebvre kids screamed along with the others, but never let go. In a few minutes it was all over, but Hank's breath was still out on the tracks. They all tumbled out and were greeted by Ma, smiling, obviously relieved to see her children make it out alive.

"Now wasn't that fun?" Hank asked when he'd caught his breath. "Let's do it again!" Benjamin yelled. But no one took him up on the offer.

Just as they were leaving, a man stepped up and said to Hank, "I'll give you a couple of dollars if you and the family go into my Wild Man show. But you got to yell like the devil when the Wild Man comes out on stage. That way more people will pay to come in, okay?" They did, except for Ma. And the kids screamed on cue at the ugly Neanderthal-looking guy. The man was happy with his investment, sure enough, the crowds came in too.

By the time the tired family left the Pike, everyone carried something: the girls had dolls, the guys had either wallets or water pistols. They'd ridden the coaster, had lunch on the Pleasure Pier, met a fine officer's family, saw many friendly people, and swam in the Pacific Ocean. "What a day to remember." Hank wrote in his book.

To the letter he wrote to his cousin Doris Mae, he added: "*P.S. If that wasn't one of the best days, how about this: we all ate cotton candy and salt water taffy for the first time ever.*"

CHAPTER 13

THE JACKRABBITS

The California Lefebvres had been in Long Beach for over six months now. The younger boys had kept busy clearing and putting together the farm out back, planting all kinds of fruit trees, along with corn, tomatoes, cabbage, and other unfamiliar types of vegetables. The joke around the house was that Pa didn't really understand the fine art of growing crops in the mild California weather, but kept on planting anyway. Soon, the farm grew into a ranch when Henry started buying pigs and goats and even two cows. When he added chickens and crowing roosters to chime in with others in the neighborhood, no one ever missed early morning calls to breakfast.

The girls had successfully completed their interviews and now worked steady in department stores and hotels around town. Hank's ma didn't stay home as much as Henry expected, accepting neighborhood housecleaning when offered the opportunity. Hank and Alfred helped at the outdoor market, furthering their education in the produce business. "Food products are the staple of American success. People got to eat. That's never going to change with the times. No need to try something new." At least that was Henry's persuasion. In addition to working at the outdoor market, Pa's LA pool hall friend, Mr. Girard, arranged for Hank and Alfred to work for a local produce distributor, Mr. Kiesler. They'd make deliveries for Mr. Kiesler in a small truck, every other day, to customers throughout the neighborhood. Pa made good on his plan to start his own construction business, when he was around. But Hank wasn't sure how much building was actually taking place because Pa kept leaving the family's battered car in the garage and taking the E-Train to LA. It all felt somewhat familiar to the family. Like he did in Douglas, Henry would disappear for days at a time.

After a while, it became evident that there were serious issues with certain people who didn't like Mr. Kiesler selling his produce in the booming southern part of Long Beach. That area was growing quickly, due in part to the growing number of lumber shipments arriving each week from Santa Barbara and other northern California logging towns. To ward off trouble from the unhappy competitors, Mr. Kiesler asked Henry for help with his LA connections. Henry jumped at the chance and thought it would be a great idea to bring Hank along with him to finally meet this new friend, Mr. Girard, and show him around Los Angeles. So, off they went. After a trolley ride to the Los Angeles terminal, they hailed a taxi to Mr. Girard's Pool Hall, located just across the street from the Methodist College of Southern California.

"They call themselves 'Wesleyans.'" Pa explained.

"'Wesleyans'? What's that?"

"They be a religious people who believe a man's given talents by God, instead of sticking around the church all day, a-praying."

"Like Mama?"

"No, Hank. These fellas feel the need to get out and prove their worth. No drinking. No smoking. No messing around."

Hank laughed. "I suppose that leaves you out, Pa."

Pa smiled, "Rightly so, Son," then added with a smirk,

"on some accounts anyway. But, they got something going on about sports, you can bet on that. They be trying to play in the Rose Bowl someday."

"What bowl, Pa?"

"The Rose Bowl, Son!" Henry couldn't contain his excitement. "Listen here, Hank, the best football teams in the country come to play in the Pasadena Tournament Park. That's east of Los Angeles over there in the town of Pasadena. They play on every New Year's Day, since 1902. Crowds come from all over to see who is the best college football team this side of the country. USC, as they call themselves, want to prove they be the best, but they got to get there to prove it. Also, there's a lot of money to be made doing it. People like to bet on football games. At the pool hall, Mr. Girard takes a lot of those bets on who's going to win the Rose Bowl or even high school football games. Lots of money…lots of money."

"And you, Pa?" Hank smiled.

Pa laughed. "Yes. I'll be one of them. You know me, Son."

"Yep. That's what Mr. Slaughter says."

"What? What did old Texas John say about me?"

Hank chuckled. "Well, he said, you're a good man and he'd hire you in a minute, but you had a temper towards fighting and no patience for a hand of poker, not to mention your drinking habits. He right, Pa?"

Henry laughed. "Rightly so, I guess, if Texas John says," Pausing to consider, he added, "yeah, me and Big Mike, we'd have all kinds of fun back there in Douglas." Once they arrived at Girard's Pool Hall, Pa said, "Wait outside here on the sidewalk, Son. Let me talk to Clifford to see if it's okay for a boy to come on in."

"Sure, Pa. I'll wait."

After a minute or two Henry stepped back out and motioned for him to come on in. Hank couldn't see much at first. Eventually his eyes adjusted to the dim lights and he saw smoke hovering over the pool tables, lingering about the ceiling. The tart-based cigar smell immediately clogged the senses and made his eyes water.

"Cliff, this here is my boy I been telling you about."

"Come on over here, son," Mr. Girard called out, then looked Hank up and down in a stern fashion. "So, this is Hank…not a mighty too tall, but your pa says you're stocky and can put up a good fight."

"Yes sir."

"If you fight anything like your pa, you're a jim-dandy," Mr. Girard continued talking, as if Hank was just one of the boys when he pointed toward the customers. "Hank, here are our local players. Some are real good, others just pay the rent."

As he looked around the room, Hank noticed most had narrow brimmed hats with pinstriped suits that didn't fit their oversized bodies. They'd didn't say much, just stared at pool balls slicing around the tables. Most looked like a tough bunch; a few looked a bit timid. Holding tight to a glass of some drink or another, they all took to cussing almost every time someone made a shot.

"Yah see Hank, these fellas come here to get away from their job or just hangout away from wives." He leaned in, chuckled and whispered, "Have a few of the gangster types come here from time to time talking about business while shooting pool." Then Cliff spoke a little louder, as if to put some on notice, "No rough stuff goes on here, though. No, none of that. We collect all firearms at the door. That ways the hot heads and poor losers don't cause trouble in here. I tell them to take it outside. What they do out there, that's none of my concerns. But not in here. That kind of trouble could cause the police to shut me down. My establishment is known to be a respectful and friendly place. I rent the tables and let them bet on the games. Poker games are upstairs. I got my eye on the future, Hank," he talked softly again, "when prohibition comes in, I'll make more than just a livin' here."

Henry took the pause as an opportunity to break in, "Mr. Girard here came from Minnesota. He was a fine athlete."

"Your dad here says you're going to be a great athlete. Well, I hope you do, and someday help those Methodists across the street make it to the Rose Bowl," Mr. Girard said.

"Maybe them. We'll see. It'll be some school for sure."

"I hear a lot of confidence in your words, Hank."

Henry spoke up. "Yep. Sometimes a bit too much." They all had a good laugh, then Henry said, "Thanks, Cliff for showing Hank around. We need to get on our way to the produce district. We've got some business there to take care of."

"Oh really? You're on your way over to Central and Olympic?"

"Yup."

"Well now. Be careful. They're a rough bunch—truckers and produce guys. I wouldn't say this to nobody else, but I know they're organization men with Eastern connections. Henry, they can get tough. So, mind your p's and q's. You can use my name if need be. Some of the fellas come in here a lot. And you best be a little more polite than you are here." He chuckled. "That going to be hard?"

"No problem, Cliff. I understand how it goes."

"By the way, Henry, you can use my car. Needn't be riding around paying for a taxi. That reminds me. This friend of mine wants to sell his car, at a very reasonable price. You should take a peek at it. It's better than the one you have in your garage down in Long Beach."

"Okay, thanks. I'll take a look later today."

"Good, he'll be more than happy to show it to you."

"Thanks, Cliff."

Mr. Girard tossed his keys over, and Henry and Hank took off.

"Now Son, Mr. Kiesler justs want to be sure he can sell his produce in the right parts of Long Beach and is looking for this LA produce distributor to give him the okay. Understand?"

"Got it, Pa."

"Just let me handle it. Try to stay out of the conversation. This will be good for you—getting to see how to handle these big shots."

As they drove up to the corner of Central and Olympic, busy forklifts, trucks, and tractors moved in and out from storage bays alongside a large concrete building. Long lines of cars were parked in a crowded, fenced-in lot. Henry saw an open gate and turned in. Immediately, they were greeted by a uniformed security guard who waved them to a stop. Henry whispered, "Look at that, Hank. Last time I seen something like that rifle he's a-carrying on his hip was on a Pinkerton man riding shotgun on the bank-run stage coaches."

"What's your business here today, sir?" The guard asked.

Henry gave a short description of the situation and the guard directed them to park over in front of the main office. "Go on in. They'll tell you where from there."

"Okay, thanks," Henry replied and did as he was told. He parked the car then they climbed the stairs to the reception table.

A nice-looking lady asked what they were there for and Henry repeated his reasons. She picked up the phone with one hand and motioned for them to have a seat with the other. "Geno will be with you in a minute." After about five long minutes, a rather rough character, who looked like he'd received more hits than Henry, came out to meet them. Hank couldn't help but notice the man's big forehead, overgrown eyebrows, and suit that looked a lot like the ones patrons at Girard's Pool Hall wore, also in need of a good tailoring and ironing. He wasn't sporting a hat, but wore an overgrown tie that floundered its way over an ambitious waste line, dammed in by a stout belt. His shoes were Daisy two-toned oxfords that Hank remembered from a Sears catalogue.

"What's on your mind?" the man said.

Henry introduced himself and described Mr. Kiesler's problem.

The man laughed. "Yeah, I know what's going on down there in Long Beach. You see, mister…"

"It's Lefebvre—Henry Lefebvre. And Mr. Clifford Girard said to say hello."

"He did, did he?" Geno laughed. "Great guy. I like the man. I come in all the time to his place. But you see now, Henry, this Mr. Kiesler fella hasn't been contributing enough to his security lately. He's getting too independent. And that's not good for the boss's business. It's the deal we offered. You tell that Mr. Kiesler, if he'd don't start living up to the handshake we have with him, well then, we're going to have to shut him down. Capiche? He'll be getting no more produce from us this year."

Henry tried to reason. "Look, Mr. Geno. Mr. Kiesler is just getting by. Maybe if you could make some other kind of arrangement, he'd be willing and able to pay for your security, but this other guy's running him out of business and—"

Geno stopped Henry in his tracks. "Now look, Henry. We can be friends, but this is business. This is the way it's done here in LA."

"But that's not the way we do it in Douglas."

"Okay, Mr. Whatever-your-damn-name-is, if that's the way you want to be, then—"

It looked as if they were about to become permanent

enemies when Geno stepped forward and announced, "You better find your way back out that door, mister!" But before Henry could counter-punch Geno's bad manners, a large entry door slammed open, allowing a group of five men to rush in.

"That son of a bitch! I've had it with these guys!" the man in the center yelled out. He continued to yell louder and louder as the group rushed past the three of them into the adjacent office, slamming the door closed. Henry, Hank, and Geno froze and stared at the men through the window in the wall that separated them. The irritated man pounded on the desk while throwing things all about the room.

Hank took hold of his father's arm and leaned in to whisper, "Pa, let's get out of here."

Suddenly, the out-of-control man looked through the glass, stopped, and stared at Hank while throwing his hat and overcoat onto the desk. He called one of the other men over and said something while pointing directly at Hank. Almost immediately the door flung opened and the messenger said, "Hey, Geno. Boss says to bring the kid and this guy into his office."

"Why?"

"Why do you care, Geno? Get them in here now!"

Hank whispered again, "Pa, I think we bought some real troubles. We're in it now."

Geno escorted them into the room and stood directly in front of the boss's desk. Hank felt as if they were about to be given the details of their execution, when, unexpectedly, the angry man smiled a big grin. Then he plopped down in his big leather chair behind the desk and said, "Yes, yes, I'd recognize you anywhere. Hey guys," he said to the other men, "this is Mr. Henry Lefebvre, legend of Bisbee and Douglas. Hell, he's been hanging out with Texas John and gambling with the best in Tombstone. And hey there, boy! Remember me? I gave you my business card back there in front of the Gadsden Hotel. Did you read it? It said, 'Santino Cardinale, Produce Distributor, Los Angeles.'"

Hank let out a huge sigh, followed by a relieved smile. "Yep. You bet. And we sold you those Villa knives and fine leather belts you liked. At a fair price, I might add."

"Yes, you did, Son. I have them knives hanging over my fireplace in Beverly Hills." Santino stood and yelled over to his men, "You see? You glugs, if you had half of the heart of these two men, we wouldn't be having this problem. Nobody would be thinking of moving into our territory. Nobody! Okay?"

Hank thought this Santino guy could make a rattle snake bite themselves out of fear, especially when Geno and the other men say, in chorus, "Okay, Sonny. You're right, Sonny."

Mr. Cardinale turned back to Hank and his pa. "So, my friends from Douglas, what can I do for you?" Henry stuttered for a moment, apparently surprised to learn about Santino's experience with his son, then he quickly recovered and explained the problem with their friend, Mr. Kiesler. When Henry finished, Santino said loudly for all his men to hear, "If these men speak up for this guy in Long Beach— this Mr. Kiesler—then that's good enough for me. Now Geno, you were respectful to my friends out there in the lobby, weren't you?"

Geno mumbled meekly, "But boss…I didn't know they were your friends."

Henry jumped in to offer his assistance. "No, Mr. Cardinale. He was fine with us, plenty respectful."

Santino chuckled. "Okay then, Geno you're off the hook. But from now on, whatever he wants, tell him we'll work with him—this Mr. Kiesler fella. As long as he gets along with the Lefebvres, he has my blessings. I swear on my father. Now, go tell him that, Geno." Santino sat back down. "Sit. Please, Lefebvres, just for a few minutes." After they did, he asked, "Something to drink? No?"

Hank was relieved when his pa answered, "Thank you, Mr. Cardinale. But I'll have to say no to that, got a lot to do today."

"So, how's life in Douglas?" Santino asked, but didn't wait for an answer. "I love that place. Reminds me of the old days in Italy. If I didn't always have to be here in LA to run things, I'd have some fun hanging around you Arizona folks."

"Well, we be living in Long Beach now and I've gone into the construction business," Henry explained.

"That's good, an honest living. So, Henry, how about this *hombre* you have here," he said, looking over to Hank then back to his bodyguards. "Listen to this. Neither the Villistas or the Federalies could shoot this *hombre*. He was faster than them bullets, running a hundred yards across open fields at the Battle of Agua Prieta. They mistook him for one of Pancho Villa's bunch. Can you believe that! All just to divert fire and save his friends. Would you do that for me?" Santino looked around at his men, "No, I don't think so! But Hank here did. That virtue and character belongs in a book."

To one of his men leaning against the door, Santino said, "Believe me that's a true story. I was there just days after Villa attacked at Agua Prieta, just a few yards from their home in Douglas." Laughing now he continued, "This Hank here has more gumption than most of my men. I told him if he ever came up to LA, he should look me up. Well, he did. And now that we've taken care of his friend's problem down in Long Beach, tell me Hank," as he turned back, "what are you doing out here in California?"

Henry took over for his son, "Well, Mr. Cardinale…"

"No, Henry. It's 'Sonny' to you. We're friends."

Henry smiled. "Now that I've got this construction business, Hank needn't be chasing after Villa's wars for souvenirs to sell. Best get him back into school. And Sonny, he'd might be playing a little football, baseball, and even running some track at Long Beach Poly High."

"Fine school I hear, Poly High, especially in sports. Well then, I'll be looking for his name in the papers. May even put a bet on him."

Hank pointed to the *Times* on the corner table, "I'll be in that paper. You watch for me there, Mr. Cardinale."

"That goes for you too, Hank. Call me 'Sonny.'"

"You bet," Hank agreed.

"Great, now that we got that all settled, let me get back to my business. Oh, before I do that, so Henry, how you getting back to Long Beach, on the E-Train?"

"Actually, Sonny, we borrowed Cliff Girard's car to get here from his place, but yeah, from Girard's Pool Hall we'll take the E-Train back to Long Beach."

"Okay, okay. No need, Henry. Hey, Geno, tell Rocco to come in here."

Geno yelled out, "Hey, Rocco!"

"No, no, Geno. Don't yell. It's not professional. Go get him."

"Yes boss," he replied, then left.

After a few minutes, a man rushed in. "What do you want, boss?"

"Rocco, take the best car we have available, follow the Lefebvres, back to Cliff's place, then give my friends a ride to where they want to go. Just make sure they get back safely to Long Beach."

"Right, boss."

"And Geno, you try being extra polite with this Mr. Kiesler. Capiche? With a wave of his hand, Santino added, "Now get going, both of you." After Geno and Rocco left the room, Santino walked Henry and Hank to the door. While shaking hands goodbye, he said sincerely, "Sorry for the misunderstanding at the beginning. You see, you came in at a bad time. Believe me, we're trying hard to become more professional and business-like around here. But it's not going to happen overnight."

When Henry rushed in to the billiard parlor tell Cliff the story of their business meeting, Cliff laughed and patted him on the back. Then Henry and Hank jumped into Santino's Cunningham sedan with Rocco at the wheel. Henry rode shotgun and started in right away with, "Jackrabbits!"

"What? What jackrabbits, Pa?"

"Hank, the story goes like this. When spring rain came to Long Beach sometime back, there was so many jackrabbits running around the Poly High track and athletic fields, the track team decided to call themselves, just that—The Jackrabbits. Then the football team was tired of being called 'The Beachsider Boys,' or sometimes 'The Breakers,' so they hooked on the new name for themselves. That's what Long Beach Poly High calls themselves now. Mind you, the school's been around a while. It started back in 1895. And, like I wrote in my letter to Ma, it is the fastest growing and largest high school this side of the Mississippi River. Now, that's saying something. So, there you be. You're going to have a lot of competition, Hank, more kids then Douglas."

"But Pa, we'd had more talent in Douglas, just not enough teams to play against."

"Well now, that's one way a looking at it, Son."

Rocco hadn't spoken during the drive when Henry drew him into the conversation. "You see, Rocco, this boy of mine, he backs down to nothing. Let me tell you a story to prove my point. My son Hank here, with his best friend Josiah and my younger son, Alfred, captured a bear up in the Chiricahuas… made him a pet." Even though he'd told it many times, Henry still laughed at the story. "One day that old bear made the mistake of biting this Indian boy, and that done it. They had bear meat for cookin'."

Rocco and Henry laughed heartily together at the story. Then Pa became serious again. "Now, Son, when you get home, wander on over to Poly High, look around the place. Ma says it's time for you to get your schoolin', like I told Sonny you was going to do. And we don't want to let Ma, Sonny, Mr. Girard, or the Arizona Lefebvres down now, do we?"

Hank smiled a little. "Okay, Pa. I promise. In the morning, I'll go take a look around."

That night Hank had plenty to write in his notebook. After detailing the sights of LA and meeting Pa's important new friend, he ended with, "Nothing in the world scares me now… except maybe me. I don't have any notion as to what I should be looking for at this Poly High. But what I do know, I'm starting to feel the burden of people expecting things from me. It might just bind me in a little too much…sort of corral me in. That might be good for others, but I'm not so sure it'll be good for me."

CHAPTER 14

CRISTINA

With all those roosters crowing away, the family found it hard to sleep late, even if they wanted to. On this morning, the additional aroma of Ma's special school-day breakfast of eggs, sliced ham, and fried potatoes topped with her famous salsa convinced Hank and Lily to wake especially early, dress quickly, and hurry to the kitchen. As Ma spread homemade strawberry preserves on freshly toasted bread, she wore a smile from ear to ear. She could have been thinking what Pa said about the meeting with the LA produce guy yesterday, but most likely she was happy that Lily and Hank would be looking around Poly High today while she officially registered them as students. Ma was always proud of her kids, and because Lily and Hank were the oldest, she hoped they'd set a good example for the younger ones.

When stomachs were full and dishes done, off they went, walking all the way from Twentieth Street to Atlantic Avenue. On the way, Ma chirped out stories to Hank and Lily about herself and Pa's hard times in Bisbee, and even about their early life in Douglas. One thing Ma never got into was where she'd been before Pa came along. Pa leaked it out occasionally by mistake, so Hank was sure Uncle Joseph knew, but the story rarely trickled down to the kids.

They arrived earlier to school than the other students, and

when Hank asked a passing teacher where everyone was. She answered, "It's too early for most students. The only ones who arrive at this time would be athletic teams. But the main office is open so go on in."

Inside, Adela introduced herself as Mrs. Lefebvre to the school secretary and told her that they had recently come from Douglas. She explained she was there to enroll her children in high school, and asked if she might meet the principal. He'd just happened to overhear her request through his open office door and called out, "Yes, Nellie. Send them in." He looked genuinely happy to see them. "Did I hear you say you've come all the way from Douglas, Arizona?"

"That's right," Adela said, as they entered the office.

"Well, that's a long way from here."

"Yes, it is."

"You know, Douglas made the news a few months back with the revolutionary Pancho Villa and such," the principal added when he motioned for them to have a seat.

"Yes, it did."

"So, what made you come to Long Beach?"

"Well, we just needed a life change and heard about the business opportunities here on the West Coast."

"You made the right choice, Mrs. Lefebvre." He then focused his attention toward the kids. "Lily, is it?"

"Yes, sir."

"So, Lily, what are you interested in?"

"Business, sir."

"Business? Good choice young lady. And your name is Henry?"

"Yes it is, sir, but I'm a junior. My pa is Henry too, so they call me Hank."

"Then Hank it is. And you're interested in—?"

"Sports sir—mainly football," Hank answered before the

principal could finish.

The man seemed delighted at both their answers. "Long Beach Poly High has wonderful teachers. Now, as far as football is concerned, Hank you better get to practicing because our sports teams are outstanding, especially in football. We've got a new coach named Mr. Eddie Kienholz. He's building an excellent team to take on the California Interscholastic Federation, better known around here as the C.I.F.

"And Lily, like your mother explained, I'm sure you've taken notice of all the new business going on here in Long Beach. You've picked a good career option. Now, why don't you kids walk around campus and get a feel for the place while I escort your mother over to the administration office to fill out some paperwork. It will take her some time, so look around. Oh, and by the way, if you go by the cafeteria, you'll find some free milk and cookies to enjoy."

By now, more students were arriving in the same way it rains, slow drops at first, then a lot all at once. Hank and Lily found themselves stuck in the middle of a rush of students to their lockers. Wearing boots and well-worn Levi's, Hank looked out of place here at Long Beach Poly, and more like a rancher on vacation. But Lily had carefully prepared her wardrobe by watching young ladies shop as she worked in the department store—she was dressed to the hilt. Lily's lovely light brown hair, fair skin, and flawless complexion made her look the kind of girl who fit in. Her clothes even fit well. Hank thought sometimes a little too well. When he noticed some of the guys paying special attention as they walked by, he decided to kid Lily about it. "Them boys, what are they thinking, sneaking looks at you that way?"

Nearly under her breath, she replied, "You should be ashamed of yourself, Hank, with that type of talk. For once, please just shut your mouth."

Despite his out-of-place wardrobe, Hank was feeling mighty comfortable sizing himself up against the other guys. It wasn't until he came upon some boys with letterman jackets standing and snickering at a young Mexican girl that his mood would dramatically change. As the flustered girl fumbled to open her locker, Lily looked at Hank's face and whispered, "Oh, God. Not this again."

The lettermen teased, "Hey Cristina. What a hot chili bean. You could be in my burrito—salsa and all."

As the girl turned, avoiding their looks and comments, she dropped her books and a paper bag split open. Gym clothes floated to the ground. Without hesitation, Hank walked over and dropped to one knee and helped the girl pick up her belongings. A pair of panties had fallen out of the torn bag and the ruffians roared at the sight, dealing out another round of insults. Well, that was it for Hank. There would be no turning his temper back.

After Hank helped the girl get her locker open, he turned around to confront the ruffians. There was an unusual stillness and odd silence in the air as he silently made his intentions known, then he said, "Hey guys. I hate rude behavior in a person. I won't tolerate it. Now, you either apologize or let's get to fightin'. I think you bumbos need a lesson in manners right now."

Apparently these boys had never seen the likes of Hank's fire when he got all caught up. By his tone and body language, no one could mistake his intention to carry through with his threat. They didn't seem to want Hank's kind of trouble here in school. Besides, by now a large group of students were gathering in the hallway and all eyes were on the lettermen. As they backed away, one said to Hank, "Calm down, guy. Things might have got a little out of hand here."

"No need trying to apologize to me, fella. It's this girl who needs them words," Hank said.

"Sorry, miss," one boy said softly.

The girl nodded, then hung her head again when one of the boys passed and said, barely under his breath, "Hick-bean-er-lover. You can have her."

Hank turned and said to the young girl, "Don't pay them any mind. They been brought up that way. They'll change someday."

Lily helped the girl put her gym clothes in the locker when Hank asked, "*¿Cómo te llamas, señorita?*"

At Hank's Spanish, she smiled and asked, "You know Spanish?"

"*Poquito, pero,* but let's not tell anybody. Okay?" Hank begged with his inviting smile. He always had a persuasion with the girls and never shied away from flirting when the occasion arose. It did its charm, for she let down her defenses. "My name is Cristina Cordovez. *Y tu, ¿Como te llamas?*"

"Mine is Hank Lefebvre, and this is my sister, Lily. We're new here."

"They don't care much of Mexicanos around here," Cristina said sadly.

"Hank smiled. "So I see. But they will."

"Why?"

Hank stepped close to say proudly, "'Cause I'm going out for the football team."

"Are you a freshman?" Lily asked. "I am."

"Yes. Maybe we'll have a class together," Cristina replied.

"Hope so. See you later, Cristina," Lily said.

Hank and Lily started to walk away, then turned back to ask, "*Sí, pero, primara, ¿donde*… where is the football field?"

Cristina gave a big smile. "Oh, so you're going to play football here and you don't even know where the football field is?" Hank blushed. Cristina laughed and told him, "Just go out that door at the end of the hall, turn right and keep going. Can't miss it. It's the one with the grass and goal post at each end."

Hank felt happy with himself, knowing he'd made her day a little better. "Okay, I'll find it now." Flirting with her as he backed away, he said, "I'll see you around. Hey Lily, let's go find the field."

Once outside, Lily started in on him. "The Injun girl, now the Mexican girl, who's next, Hank?"

"Lily, you got to stand up for girls in trouble. Don't you know that by now?"

"I bet they was all good looking, like Cristina."

"Now what are you saying, Lily? I only help good looking girls?"

Hank smiled, but then said, "No, it's just that I know the frustration of being what we are, Lily. You don't mind, 'cause you're so white-skinned. But when you look like an Injun or Mexican they treat you different. Like Mama says, we all be French. So we be French in Long Beach, I guess. Then later we'll go back to being half-breeds when no one cares. Look, what happened in Benson. I'm not going to let it happen here."

"Okay, Hank. Now, get off that high horse you're riding and let's go!"

The school's first period classes had just begun when they found the football field.

Hank just had to walk out to the middle and stand on the fifty-yard line. Lily trailed behind and when she caught up, he announced, "Here's where I'll be, Lily!"

"What do you mean, Hank?"

"You know, Lily. I'll be here, playing on this field against the best."

Brother and sister stood still, gazing out at the enormous grandstands as Hank thought about the possibilities.

A fit looking man with a whistle around his neck, walked onto the field, breaking Hank's illusion. "Got to be a coach," Hank whispered.

"What are you kids doing out here?" he said.

"Just looking for my spot, sir."

"Your spot?"

"Yep. I'm going to be playing football for Poly. And I'm just getting comfortable with the surroundings."

"Really."

Lily looked down at the ground, hiding her embarrassment. The coach asked, "Well then, who might you be?"

"Henry Lefebvre Jr., sir. But everyone calls me Hank."

"Okay, Hank Lefebvre, you best get your butt off this field for now, because we have a PE class coming on to play touch football in about five minutes!"

"Sorry, sir. Maybe I'll get into your class, Mr...."

"Call me Coach Tipton."

"Sorry, Coach," Hank said, while walking off the field.

As the class ran onto the field, a skinny, frail-looking boy dragging a bag of footballs ran up to Hank and Lily. "Hi. My name is Forrest Smith. I'm the freshman football manager. I saw what you did for Cristina, the Mexican girl. That was real good of you. She's so nice and pretty. Those boys got on her the first day she came to school and haven't stopped. I also heard you want to play football here at Poly."

"You got that right," Hank said.

"Well, if I can help with anything...hey, just let me know. A manager's got a way of getting things done around here."

"Thanks. I'll keep that in mind."

"By the way, you any good, Hank?"

"Just watch me, Forrest, then you tell me. This here glamorous girl is my sister, Lily. Make sure you say hi to her out there on campus."

"I will. Well then, bye folks. Nice to meet you, Lily."

Lily just shook her head. While walking off the field, Hank said, "Well, if that don't beat all, Lily. First day here and we got all the bases covered."

"What are you talking about?"

"It's going to happen, mark my words."

"What's going to happen?"

"Aw, never mind Lily, you won't understand."

They found Ma outside the administration office looking concerned. "The principal asked me why there's a difference in age and you're both signed up as freshmen. I told him that Hank missed a few too many school days back there in Douglas and that got Lily caught up in grades." Ma turned to Hank and added, "I heard there was a little rustling going on in the hallway after you left the principal's office."

Lily explained in detail. When she finally finished, Ma said, "That's why we love yah, Hank. But try staying away from the rescuing of girls for a little while.

Lily kicked in again, "Mama, you should've seen that Mexican girl. She was real pretty. That's why Hank got to saving her virtue."

Hank laughed. "No it's not, Lily! Besides, you'd never saw that Injun girl in Tombstone, now did you? She could have been prime ugly. I didn't take much notice. But, no matter. She needed respect. Ask cousin Charley. He'll tell yah."

"I bet she wasn't as ugly as all that," Lily teased.

Mama jumped in. "Hush you two. Here's your class schedules. Lily, when you go to work this afternoon, get Hank a pair of those popular sneakers. These boots don't work here."

Later that night, Hank couldn't put the day's events out of his mind, so he decided to take his ma's advice and put his thoughts into words and sent them off to Doris Mae. It didn't take long for his cousin to write back.

Dear Hank,

Being raised in Southern Arizona, people are either white, black, or Mexican. Since we are part Hispanic and part French, we not considered white or black, so we're considered Mexican. And today, there's nothing worse than when kids play and call us dirty Mexicans. We're never asked to white people's parties. Why even at Fort Huachuca, they have two pools, one for the whites and one for the blacks. But for Mexicans, we can only go swimming on one day. The day before they empty the pool to clean it. At school, even though my dad is French and the fort's quartermaster, we have to stand in line at the water faucet until all the whites finish drinking. It was such a handicap that one day my mother said, 'Hide the tortillas Doris Mae!' I asked her what she meant. 'Yes, Doris Mae, from now on you just tell them you don't speak Spanish. So, that's what we do. We even flunked all our Spanish tests on purpose because we didn't want them to think we were Mexican, just French. So, I know how you feel living there. And how you have this instinct to protect the Indian and Mexican girls, as if they are sisters. They tell so many stories in the family about you and your father. But Hank, the good of you always comes through. Like I said many times before, even my dad says he wants Charley Jr. to grow up just like you. Do your best out there in California, because my brother always talks about you.

Keep in touch,
Your Cousin, Doris Mae

CHAPTER 15

PROSPECTING FOR GOLD

*D*ear Cousin Doris Mae,
    No doubt my pa is a funny and peculiar character. He loves sporting events, not only for the bravado, for don't all of us Lefebvres, but mostly for the adventure, challenge, and the testing of a man's character. He says those things help a person to do better in life…not to mention the stakes of winning. I guess that's the gambler in him. Both Ma and Pa have always had some get-rich scheme going on. But it's not necessarily to get gold. That doesn't seem to make no difference to them. They're not afraid of losing. There's not that much to lose. No, if he wins what then? You can't buy a dream. He enjoys the idea of moving on, waking up to another race with the sun. Where's the thrill of life without that?

    Okay there's the kids. But they're just part of the packages you toss in the back of the covered wagon. To be sure, throughout Pa's life he hasn't made a lot of bank deposits and investments like Uncle Joseph, 'cause that don't mean much to him. It's the philosophy, he says, that he treasures and lernt by all his travels around the Southwest and the fine people, that keep him going with just a handshake and their word.

    But I must admit, time's begun to play him out. The bruises from all those prizefights and the all-night goings-on in the saloon are catching up. Before, the pretty girls encouraged him, being a handsome man and all, but lately, even they've left him alone. Age done some of that.

Now, don't get me wrong, he'd always love Mama and us kids. And he'd battle for us with his life. But what makes Pa so special is that he's cut from a different pie, or maybe even a whole different flavor. It's made him a man of his own thinking and believe me, he's played his part well, one of those living legends that adds color to frontier stories. But now, after seeing the struggles of living, fightin' and dying that he'd been accustomed to daily around Pearce, Tombstone, Bisbee, and Douglas, life has taken a toll. I'm not so sure he could stand for the ten-count in the fourteenth round anymore. He struggles to grapple with the rope in the fourth, able to pull himself up just to get a-beaten down again.

What I love about Pa, he has no regrets. He says what he'd got from Douglas wasn't gold and riches on the outside. What he got was better. The gold he mined is on the inside of a man. That's what he hopes to pass on to each of us kids, the confidence and the knowings to carry on our own through troubled times. The skill to survive shows a man's worth, not money nor a fine home, nor the store-bought clothes a man wears to show off and all. What makes a man happy is respect. That's enough of a reward, that's the noble gift, the one to cherish. And in my lifetime, I'd be most happy to do the same for my brothers and sisters.

Pa struggles through life, not as a tragic figure, but one, so stated by the educated Mr. Clifford Girard, of a "delightful, pugnacious, jubilance sort." Now, what that means, I really couldn't tell you entirely, but it sure has a proper sound to it. What I can tell you, Pa always keeps his chin just above water level and everybody loves sitting around and letting him talk on and on about his past, about him rubbing elbows with the best of the West. Oh, Pa laughs that he's picked some cactus from his backside a few times, kickin' around those Arizona boomtowns. He's also confessed to the vices that attracted men like him to those towns.

Mind you, he's not finished. Not by a long shot. Pa's still on a mission to do something grand. Much like them men who say someday we'd be getting to the moon. I told him, once he got there, he'd only find another galaxy to go after. Pa laughed at that saying, "There's some truth to that, Hank."

But lately his faith is fading, his direction unclear, his health's become a traitor and age won't let him be. His barnyard fights are faded memories. His leaky tank needs refilling by the hour, and there's never enough in the engine to get him to the next station. He's gone for longer escapes now, sitting on a barstool with some anonymous patron who's willing to listen to another tale for the price of the next drink. Sadly, sometimes he's become the jukebox man in Girard's Pool Hall that plays on into the night, his ballads becoming but background music to songs; both have something in common—they've been overplayed.

Mama says she'd been preparing me for the day when I should take on more of Pa's duties around here, being I'm the eldest, then Lily, Esther, Mary, Alfred, then Gilbert, and Benjamin. She says, "Hank, you best get out there and get some schooling. You best start making your mark." And that's what I aim to do. I'm going to Long Beach Poly High today. I'm going to let them know that Henry Hank Lefebvre will begin, and like my drawings, I'll stake my claim here in California. I'm going to do something so they will never forget I'd been by this way. Now, Doris Mae, you just keep on telling Charley Jr. to go on out there and do the same. He's a fine one. Tell him I be thinking about you and him.

Cousin Hank

Hank and Lily's first day at Long Beach Poly High was in the late spring of 1916. Ma gave out their class schedules. Of course, Lily was dressed to the style of the day. Hank wore those sneakers his Ma had his sister buy at the department store. They made Hank feel much shorter than he was.

Fortunately, their first two periods were together and Lily directed Hank where to go after that. Fourth period was the only one Hank was excited to get to because that was PE and he had a point to make. No matter what, he belonged on that football field, and Hank wasn't going to be shy about it. He never was. Even though football was his focus this day, he did hope he'd pass by Cristina to give her a "hi," and maybe she'd smile and say "hi" or at least let him know that she was aware he was alive. Or maybe he was more like his pa, and less like Josiah in these matters, rarely liking one girl at a time.

Hank felt small coming into this big, new school and seeing so many new kids, but Lily helped distract him by talking to him and figuring out where they both needed to be throughout the day. Then she left and he was alone in this jungle, trying to get around. He didn't look for familiar faces to help because he didn't know any. At that's what he thought, until a voice came up from behind to rescue him from his obscure fate. "Hank! Remember me? Forrest Smith? You need some help around this place?"

"Yep. Reckon I do, Forrest."

"Okay then, let me check out your class schedule. Ugh. You've got Miss Ellis for third period English. What a drag, don't mind her grumblings. She's like a spinster. They say she can't find a male to help with that issue. Hey, you got fourth period PE with Coach Capron. He's nice. He coaches the frosh football team, of which, I'm the team manager."

"Yeah, that's right."

"Yes sir, and I've been promoted to sixth period spring football practice. Fun stuff and we have a few of those varsity guys in that class with me. The same bunch that messed with Cristina the other day. At least they're not in your fourth period PE"

"Don't really matter." Hank shrugged.

After Forrest gave Hank directions, he offered, "At lunch, look for me and Cristina out on the grass back of the cafeteria, okay?"

"Sure. See yah then," Hank said trying not to let Forrest know that his heart beat faster thinking about Cristina and lunch.

The bell rang and kids rushed around, flinging in and out of doors. Then just like that, the halls were empty, as if the rooms had inhaled the students. Finding his stride, Hank walked into the third period classroom. Opening the door, he found students already busy copying down what the teacher had written on the board, while she stood at the podium and checked each chair on every row. In all that silence, the door slammed shut behind him, confounded by a gust of wind that made for a pronounced backdrop for his late entry. Some in the class stopped, noticing his tardy disposition. A few of the girls giggled and were quickly silenced by Miss Ellis's strong reproach: "Shut that noise down, girls." But, this only put a spotlight on Hank's embarrassed presence.

The teacher spoke in an authoritative voice, "You must be the new student. May I have your name please?"

Hank's voice broke, not from lack of confidence—he certainly knew who he was—but from the manner in which the question was thrown at him. "I'd be Hank Lefebvre. A new student, ma'am."

"Good morning. However, your name is listed in my roll book as 'Henry La-fee-beerr.'"

"No ma'am. It be pronounced 'La-fever.'"

The teacher snapped back, "When addressing me, please state my Christian name. Miss Mary Christine Ellis. Just "Miss Ellis" will do for you. Now, let's try that name again."

"Well, Miss Ellis, it's Henry Lefebvre. My last name sounds

like what you have when you get the flu. 'La-fever.'"

"The "b" is silent?"

"Yes ma'am. Sorry, I mean, yes Miss Ellis. No need to mention the letter "b." Since my pa's name is the same as mine, and I be a junior, they just call me Hank."

"Okay then, Hank, please find an empty chair." Hank looked around the room, hoping to find Cristina. No luck, but a charming blonde-haired girl looked only too happy to point out the chair next to her in the back row.

"Kate, would you please show Mr. Lefebvre what it is we are doing here?"

"Yes, Miss Ellis," she answered and then began proctoring Hank. "Every morning we come in and write in this book. You have one in your desk. You must put down the date and write your thoughts—whatever you want to write on that day."

"On anything?" Hank said, looking puzzled.

"Yes, on anything," she said, then giggled.

"Okay then."

Hank shrugged, then took out the book and began writing, fitting in quite well now, he thought.

"Time to stop," Miss Ellis announced soon after. The class looked up and put their pencils down as instructed. Then Miss Ellis wandered around the classroom with her eyes and started calling on individual students to read aloud what they'd just written. One student described what he'd done over the weekend. Another revealed what she planned to do this summer.

Hank started to relax and leaned back in his chair until Miss Ellis announced: "We have a new student here this morning. Hank Lefebvre, what have you written in your journal today?"

There was an awkward pause before Hank spoke. "Well, really not much. You see, Miss Ellis, I just got here a few months back and—"

"I understand, but what did you write that was on your mind this morning?"

"Oh, just one thing is on my mind, Miss Ellis."

"And what is that Hank?"

"Football, Miss Ellis."

"Football? That's it?"

"Yes ma'am, Miss Ellis."

The class sat up straight, surely aware of the scorn Miss Ellis was about to inflict on Hank.

"Football? That is it? 'Football' is not even a complete sentence."

"But it is to me, Miss Ellis."

Looking infuriated to a fright of almost biblical proportions, Miss Ellis started in on a discourse as to why the world was going to hell in a handbasket. "There must be something more than football in a young man's mind. Now isn't there, Hank?"

Hank thought a moment for a satisfactory answer to her question. "Yes, Miss Ellis, there is something more."

She seemed pleased at herself for encouraging him to think deeper, until he answered, "Girls, Miss Ellis."

The class roared with laughter. Fortunately, Hank's savior of the moment was the bell, protecting him from further verbal abuse. The class stood and packed their books, then began to file out of the room when Kate approached Hank. "So, you're going to play football?"

"You bet. Maybe the frosh team."

"You on the team?"

"Not yet. But, I will be."

"Is that so? Well, Hank, what position do you play."

"Anything. But I'm best at halfback or defense."

Kate snapped back, "I wouldn't be so sure of that, Hank, 'cause my boyfriend plays halfback and next year's varsity is already set. That's the way it is here. Frosh to varsity."

"Well, you tell your boyfriend he'd better get workin' real hard, 'cause I'd be one step behind trying to take over his position."

Kate wasn't happy with that, but Hank's handsome smile and overbearing confidence apparently won the day once again. Oozing with charm and almost flirting she said, "We'll see then. Wish you the best, Hank."

On his way out, Miss Ellis stopped him at the door. "Hank, you might play football well enough to get along in life, but your language skills need immediate attention."

"Miss Ellis, I'd be working on that. My ma says that very same thing. See you tomorrow, ma'am." Hank smiled, knowing, much like Pa could do, he'd quickly won over and befriended his new English teacher.

Hank survived his way around school for three periods and now it was finally fourth. After finding his way to the boy's locker room, he was assigned a locker by the teacher's assistant, better known as the TA. The TA gave out instructions about requirements for PE clothes, which was anything other than what you wore to school that day. Then he directed Hank to stand on a painted number on the outside edge of the basketball court while he took roll.

Soon Coach Capron walked over wearing a green ball cap with the letters "LP" printed in gold. The front of his sweatshirt read: "Jackrabbit Football," in colors to match his cap, and Hank felt excited at the idea he'd arrived at the epicenter of American high school football. The coach instructed the class to go out to the sideline of the manicured football field.

"Okay, Skins and Shirts, touch football this morning. But first, we have a new student here today. Where are you Henry Lef-a-bev-ree?"

Hank raised his hand high. "I'm him, Coach."

"Okay, Henry."

"No, Coach, it's Hank."

"All right, Hank. You're on the Shirts team. They need some help." The coach smiled and the boys laughed.

"Yes we do, Coach!" the TA echoed, then announced: "Okay boys, let's get to the calisthenics."

After plenty of push-ups, jumping jacks, and running in place, the coach blew the whistle and pointed to the field. The TA dragged a heavy bag of footballs behind Coach Capron, who carried a local newspaper under his arm, a whistle around his neck, and clipboard in hand. Once he found his favorite spot on the sideline bench, he sat down to read while the game of touch football progressed.

Coach Capron stared intently at the sports section. Some time passed, then the TA came and stood. "What's the problem?"

"Coach, the game is getting out of hand."

"What?"

"Well, the Shirts are killing the Skins!"

"Really?"

"Yep. The new kid, Hank. There's no stopping him on defense or offense. That would be okay, but someone's going to get hurt out there. He's not tall, but he's real stout, Coach. Too much for these boys."

"You're kidding, right Billy?"

"No, Coach, watch, just watch for a few minutes. See there? Hank's on defense and watch the boys try to block him. See, he's sending the blocker back like he's been shot out of a cannon—right on his backside!"

The coach stood now. The Shirts had the ball and lateraled to Hank. No one touched him, let alone put two hands on him.

Hank had Coach Capron's full attention now, and after a

few more plays he called out, "Hey Hank, come on over here. The rest of you keep playing."

Hank trotted over. "Yes, Coach?"

"Son, have you played a lot of football where you come from?"

"Yes, Coach. We have some good players back home."

"And where was this home, Hank?"

"Douglas, Coach."

"Where is this 'Douglas'?"

"Out yonder, Coach."

The coach started smiling now. "Does the 'out yonder' have a name, like a state?"

"Oh yes, Coach. It's Arizona."

"Arizona, you say. Well then, since we've made a breakthrough with your geography, I can tell you, Son, you have some natural potential."

"No sir, Coach."

Coach Capron took off his baseball cap, looked into the empty stands with puzzlement, then turned back. "No sir, you say! What the hell do you mean, 'no sir'? Are we having a conversation or what? Am I missing something here, Son?"

"Well, Coach, I have 'potential' you say, but…well, Coach, potential is for those boys out there."

"Oh really? Is it? So, what can you do now?"

"Well Coach, I be the fastest boy in football for forty yards. Not a man in the world going faster—in football that is."

"Really? You're sure about that?"

"Yes, Coach."

"Okay." The coach turned to another boy and said, "Billy, run back to my office and get my stopwatch and get this boy some cleats. What size you wear, Hank?"

"Size eight. But no need, Coach. I can run in these here sneakers."

Coach Capron chuckled and said, "Okay. Billy, just get the stopwatch—pronto."

"Got it, Coach."

The coach marked off forty yards and told Hank, "I want you in a three-point stance. We're going to see how fast you really are."

Billy came running back with the timer and Coach Capron told him, "Okay, Bill, you get down there at the forty-yard line, and Hank, you get in your stance. When my hand goes down, Billy's going to start the watch. And Billy, make sure to stop it the moment he crosses the line. Okay, let's go!"

Hank got into position with Billy at the forty-yard line. Coach raised his hand, then swiped it to the ground and Hank was off—new sneakers and all. After he passed Billy, the coach yelled, "What's his time?"

Billy yelled back, "Four-something!"

"Four-something what?" Coach shouted, then waved for them both to come back over to him. "Give me that damn watch, Billy!" Then mumbling almost under his breath, "Holy shit."

Billy whispered, "Coach, you're not supposed to say those words out here."

"Billy, I only say them in exceptional situations, and I'd say 4.5 in sneakers, on grass, in walking clothes, is more than exceptional. Let's try that again guys."

After three more attempts, and getting the same results, except one at 4.4, Coach Capron admitted, "Hank, you might just be right."

Not hiding his excitement, Coach Capron yelped, "I like a boy who's sure of himself, especially when he can back it up. No more fourth period PE for you! We'll put you in sixth period frosh football spring training. That okay with you? By the way, what position do you like to play?"

"No matter, Coach. Whatever position you need me for."

Coach Capron stared at Hank in disbelief. This Lefebvre kid was good, but his attitude was like the cherry on top of the ice cream sundae.

Hank got lost at lunch, but found Lily just before the bell chatting away with some girls. On their way home, she told him about her new friends. Almost forgetting Cristina, Hank was very attentive to what his sister said because Lily usually made some pretty nice-looking friends.

Sitting around the dinner table that night, Ma asked everyone to share what their first day at school was like. When they got to Hank, he said, "I'd be playing some football for Poly's frosh team and Miss Ellis said my language needs immediate attention." Hank new both Ma and Pa would be proud.

CHAPTER 16

FRESH PAGE

L ong Beach School District board members made the popular decision to "promote athletic programs to reflect the state's recognition of the educational community." That really meant they planned on beefing up football recruitment at their flagship high school, Long Beach Poly Tech. Their first step was to bring Coach Eddie Kienholz in as varsity coach. His reputation for winning games created excitement in the spring of 1916 leading into the fall football season. Because of this, Hank found himself in a favorable, yet extremely formidable situation. When he learned this, he figured all he had to do was attend classes, mind his own business, and perform well at whatever position the coach wanted. His pa once told him, "a cork in water always finds its way to the top."

With that in mind, Hank was about to take on his first day of sixth-period freshman football practice. However, there was still some leftover cards he needed to put in play. Hank knew he'd better get a handle on it before it got worse, but that would have to wait until sixth period.

Lily's job at the department store and all those discounts, plus her ability to put on the charm while doing local housekeeping work, provided the family with well-stocked closets. But, she was never one to hold back on joking with Hank that he was way too big for his breeches, although, she knew ma relied on him more each day as Pa's condition grew worse. Hank easily slid into his role as head of the family, having no trouble telling the younger brothers how they should be conducting themselves. This attitude made his ma even prouder. However, Ma wouldn't let up on her desire to be known as "the lady from France." She'd talk big about shopping in Paris, or having a stroll on the Champs-Élysées after attending Sunday mass at Notre Dame. Soon, most everyone outside the family was convinced she'd been brought up in Europe. She even spent time learning how to pronounce French words, not many, but just enough to continue the charade. The kids knew better, and in lighter moments around the house, Hank would tease, "Aw, Mama, Pa says you be from the White Mountains Apache tribe." That would get Ma's predictable reply: "What does your pa know anyhow?" The family enjoyed making her defend her new-found heritage, and she would tell even more stories.

Hank stepped up his letter writing to his cousin, Doris Mae. Even though she was much younger, he enjoyed hearing about what was happening back in Douglas, Fort Huachuca, and Pirtleville.

On one warm spring morning, a few days after their first day at school, Hank was on a mission and told Lily they needed to get to school early because he had things to do.

"Like what?" she asked.

"Like, none of your business, nosey."

His sisters laughed and tried to upset Hank enough to revel the secret. Lily teased again. "All the girls think you're cute."

Hank wasn't taking the bait. "I don't care about that."

"Oh yeah. What do you care about?"

"Football! I'd be a great player. You'll see."

"And what's that going to do for you?"

"Fame—just you wait and see what that will do, Lily. Remember, you heard it from me first, way before it happens."

Very little talking went on between them as they walked to school in the early morning hours. On campus, Lily ran into her friends. Knowing full well what Hank was up to, she left him and took off with them.

Hank went directly to the main hall lockers. Trying to look as casual as possible, he leaned against the wall waiting for Cristina's arrival. He watched as she walked toward him. Unlike Ma, there was no pretending who she was. She wore a bright yellow skirt and crisp white blouse laced with embroidered colorful flowers. Her brown skin and complexion glowed while long, dark black hair flowed underneath a scarf that matched the outfit. Even though she had all those other attributes that make a girl so enticing and appealing to a male, Hank was most impressed by her character. It was obvious to anyone that she would be proud to share where she came from. As she approached her locker, Hank made another entry into her life.

Stepping away from the wall he said softly, "Good morning, Cristina."

She appeared startled at first so Hank was unsure how to proceed. Maybe she reacted in such a way because he'd surprised her, or the chivalry he'd shown a few days before just wasn't that memorable. Or maybe it was unusual for a boy to be so pleasant to her on campus. After looking at him carefully, she said, "Oh, it's you."

"I guess it's me," he said, then laughed. Trying to be clever and make conversation, he added, "At least that's what my mama called me, when I'd woke up this morning."

She smiled sweetly. "I never got to thank you for rescuing

me from those football players the other day."

"Well, that's what I'd like to talk to you about. I really—"

"Good morning, Cristina!

"Yes it is, Forrest," she answered.

As Forrest approached Hank, he said, "We've met before. It's Henry… no sorry…Hank Lefebvre, isn't it?"

"Yep. That's me."

"Coach Tipton says you'll be practicing with the frosh team today at sixth period."

"Yep."

"Well, you're in for a surprise. Remember those lettermen you humbled the other day? Thought you'd like to know, there're from the varsity team Coach Kienholz is rebuilding. They'll be scrimmaging with the frosh JV teams today. So, best look out for yourself. The story is, there's this click of players who have cheeky girlfriends who don't like the idea of you taking a position away from their boyfriends. Homecoming queen votes will be coming up soon, and everybody knows girls like to huddle up to their athletic boyfriends who'll get the students to vote for them."

"That don't bother me," Hank muttered.

"Just wanted you to be aware of those guys, even more about the bee that's up in those girl's bonnets. Oh, by the way, Cristina, I have some things to do in the biology lab during lunch today…won't be able to meet up with you." Whether he knew it or not, Forrest just gave Hank the opening he'd hoped for when he said, "Well then, how about it, Hank? Mind taking my place and having lunch with Cristina?"

Hank stumbled to find the words. He recovered enough to say, with a slight blush, "If it's okay with Cristina."

"I would like that," she said with a smile.

Forrest dashed off and Cristina added, "I have got to get to class and you should too, Hank. I will meet you later, outside of the football field entrance. There is a nice patch of grass there. We can have lunch and talk."

Happy he'd completed his first mission of the day, Hank said, "Okay. See you then, Cristina."

In Hank's third period he found the class once again quietly writing in their daily journals. Then, as before, Miss Ellis prompted the class to discuss their thoughts. Some read about personal situations they or members of their family were facing. Others, about their future after graduation, but most of them wanted to talk about the war going on in Europe. They were obviously concerned that if the US got caught up into that mess, the draft would affect the Long Beach community.

Once the teacher worked her way around the room she turned and said, "What's your opinion, Hank?"

"It don't matter much to me. My folks came from Arizona when it was nothing but a territory and a man needn't be thinking of fighting off somewhere in a far-away country. Let them take care of their own problems. Here in the United States, if the politicians keep on changing their minds about who they are fighting for or against, it makes things a might complicated. Now look at old Villa. In my part of the world, he wasn't such a bad guy to Americans. Why did they have to go and turn coats on him like that?"

Miss Ellis broke the stunned silence. "And you know this, Hank, how?"

"How? I'll tell you how. Because my cousin Charley done lived with Villa, before being the quartermaster at Fort Huachuca. Even my uncle Joseph did business with the man before the US Government decided different about him. When the revolution came, things fell apart…against his family, against the Villistas, and even Mexicans against gringos."

Miss Ellis's mouth dropped. "And this is where, Hank?"

"Douglas, ma'am. We lived just five blocks from the

border along Agua Prieta."

The bell rang and students reluctantly filed out. Miss Ellis asked Hank to stay for a few minutes. "My, my, Hank, you have got some stores to tell."

"Yes, ma'am. I guess I do."

"We need you to team up with one of our better language students. Right?"

"Probably so." Hank smiled.

"Let's get your English in order. Because, Mr. Lefebvre, I want to hear more about this frontier you came from."

"Thank you, ma'am. I'd see to it. I'd be looking for such a student."

"You do that, Hank. Let's get that done—pronto." She smiled back.

Between classes Hank ran into Lily surrounded by her giggling friends. After telling her he had some business to attend to at lunch, Lily said, "No problem, I've got the girls to talk with and who are you going to be doing this business with, Hank?" Lily, of course knew the answer but liked to get under his skin.

"Not for you to know."

"Well then, you go on your way to this business lunch with Cristina."

"What? How'd you figure it out, Lily?"

"Hank, this may be a bigger school than Douglas, but it also means a lot more gossiping goes around. That is, if you keep your ears open."

"Like you usually do, Lily."

"As you say, Hank."

The lunch bell rang and Hank found his way to the lush green grass, just a short distance from the football field entrance. He plopped down and waited to open Ma's bag of delicious treats. It didn't take long to see Cristina walking toward him. Everything about her was beautiful. The steps she took allowed her body to follow in perfect harmony. She certainly was a combination of poetic charm and character, reminding Hank a little of Chata. Cristina sat down, spread out her skirt, and began pulling out her lunch from a small leather bag. She opened a tin container that revealed two warm tamales; another container held the salsa. After looking at Hank's expression, she offered, "Would you like a taste?" He laughed. *"¿Qué?* What's so funny, Hank?"

He held up his finger and said, *"Mira, mira."* Then reached into his bag to pull out tamales, salsa, and a cup of chili. *"El Mismo.* The same."

"So, you and your *poquito* the other day, when I asked if you spoke Spanish, was not a put-on?"

"Put-on? An act? No, no not me. My ma says she's a little bit of everything, *pero*…but I can tell, she makes her tamales and salsa just like your ma."

"So, the other day was true?"

"Yes, but not what you might think, 'cause to be honest, Cristina, I wasn't only wanting to protect you, but also…see, my younger sisters are treated like that sometimes. Now, my older sister, Lily, having light-colored hair, she fits in anywhere, and because of the situation, we do like my cousin Doris Mae in Arizona—we pretend to be more French than Mexican. The name of Lefebvre is French so we can be whatever way we want, depending on the circumstances. Now you, Cristina Cordovez, well that's a tough one to get away from. And your hair…" Hank began to blush, thinking he might have taken this too far.

She smiled and said, "You do not like my hair?"

"No, no. It's not what you think," Hank said with embarrassment.

"How do you know what I think?" she teased.

"Okay, yes Cristina. I think you have beautiful hair."

They laughed and enjoyed their lunch for a while, then Cristina asked, "What should we do, bright one, Mr. Hank Lefebvre, football player?"

"Well, I been squalling with Injuns, Mexican *banditos*, *gringo* thieves and a lot of other just plain bad people from time to time, and there's one thing I know for sure: in any people, there are good ones and bad, so I make no trouble over a person not like me. Only when they don't show respect. And you, Cristina?"

"Unlike yours it is hard for me and *mi familia* to put on. We are what we are, not in Mexico, but here in the United States. Trying, like you, to make it through to a better world for us, but we do not pretend. Enough of this. So, why do you want to play football?"

"'Cause I'm good at it. Also, my pa is good at sports and I love the game, and competition. Maybe it will take me somewhere."

"Where would that be, Hank?"

"My pa is gettin' on. I need to do something to take care of *mi familia*, much like you I suppose. I want to do what it takes to be successful, be able to enjoy life and hopefully make others, like me, have it easier."

"You have ambitious goals, Hank."

"I know," he answered, finishing the last of his lunch.

"But Hank, do not let that ambition trap you in. It will, you know."

Hank was a bit stunned. Cristina's remark made a point that left him thinking—without an answer. As they packed up, Forrest came over and sat down. "Hello, you two."

"Hey, Forrest, how's your grade in Miss Ellis's English class?"

"An 'A' of course. Why?"

"That's good, 'cause Miss Ellis says I need to work on my language skills, seeing I come from a frontier town." They all laughed.

While looking at Cristina, Forrest said, "Okay, we'll all work on Hank's language skills."

Cristina smiled and added, "Yes, I would like that. We will work on it together."

"Maybe Syriana would want to help," Forrest offered with a shy smile.

"I will ask her, Forrest." Seeing Hank's puzzled look, Cristina added, "Syriana is my younger sister, by a year. She is very smart. Right, Forrest? And very pretty."

Forrest smiled and scratched his head without giving his thoughts away, while Cristina stood to leave. "See you both later. If not today, tomorrow here for lunch. Okay?"

They all agreed. Hank couldn't stop looking at her as she walked away. Even after she turned the corner, he didn't let up on his stare.

Finally, sixth period came. After checking in, getting equipment from the manager of the frosh team, which of course meant Forrest Smith, Hank hurried his way out to the football field. The sun was shining bright on this warm California spring day. Hank thought, what a refreshing way to begin a new chapter in life. It would all start right now, today.

The varsity warmed up at one end of the field while the frosh-JV teams at the other. After a while Coach Tipton, along with Coach Capron, told them to take a knee. "Coach Kienholz would like to say a few words to you guys before the scrimmage with his varsity team."

Hank was surprised how young he looked. Way too preppy, he seemed out of place for this brawling type of sport.

But when Coach Kienholz spoke, it was all football. He talked about teamwork and discipline, explaining they were the future of Poly football. There would be one goal this season— to win. But winning the right way, with fundamentals and dedication to preparation. Again and again he came back to teamwork. "Do your job. Do it with heart. Someday, some of you boys will become as well-respected as Bullet Baker, our quarterback, who represents us and the quality of our football program. Bullet, along with some of our other players, are being heavily recruited by major colleges. Think about it. Just maybe one of you boys may get that chance to play for a fine college, or even play in that new Los Angeles Coliseum that's just a few years away from completion. Or, you might even play in a Rose Bowl game. But it all starts here. Right now!"

The players seemed pumped by his rousing speech, especially Hank.

As the teams took the field, the varsity team moved over to the Home side, while the frosh-JV teams converged along the Visitor side. Poly's Jackrabbits varsity team took the field on defense first, easily defending the freshman teams' attempts to advance the ball. This went on for a half hour.

Coach Tipton and Coach Capron kept looking at their respective clipboards and said they were playing different players in different offensive schemes to see how they would best penetrate the varsity defense. Hank stood on the sideline, waiting for his name to be called. Losing patience, he walked up to Coach Tipton and said, "Coach, put me in."

"No, Lefebvre, you're not ready yet. Have a seat."

"I'm in shape for this, Coach!"

"Okay, maybe. We'll see."

It was time to switch. The varsity went on offense and the frosh defense. In the first play, Bullet Baker ran an end run and went untouched for six points.

Coach Kienholz was obviously pleased. "Okay guys! That's how it should work!"

After another half hour of scrimmage, with the varsity putting in new plays, Coach Tipton said, "We can't stop these guys. Okay, why not. Hey, Lefebvre, get in there and play safety. Are you ready?"

"Sure Coach, I'm ready!" Hank answered as he raced onto the field.

Just before a play, Coach Kienholz blew his whistle and yelled, "Hey Tipton! Your safety isn't wearing his headgear!"

"Sorry, Coach," Hank said, as he rushed back to pick it up.

"I'm not sure you are ready, Lefebvre. I don't want you injured in a scrimmage."

"No sir. I'm ready, Coach."

"Okay, okay Lefebvre," the coach said reluctantly, "safety it is."

Kienholz saw this and told his best receiver, Jim 'Jazz' Lawson, to "go long. Give this kid a streak he won't forget." Then he smirked.

Baker called the play, the varsity lined up, and he barked out the signal. The center snapped the ball and the play was on. The all-American, Jazz Lawson, gave Hank a fake post-turn inside, then ran right past him. Hank turned to make the adjustment while the ball spiraled high above. Hank's quick acceleration allowed him to catch Lawson just as the pass flew almost out of Lawson's reach, barely catching it in the tips of his fingers. Now a step ahead of Lawson, Hank turned back and jumped, taking the ball right out of Lawson's hands.

Hank took the intercepted pass and started running it back. Hank wasn't, by far, a big player at 5'6" and 170 pounds, but his blinding speed, agility, and sturdy build allowed him to keep low to the ground. He weaved his way through the varsity defenders and burst through those few that could get a hand on him. Finally, he broke into the open field and from there, none was left fast enough to catch him as he ran across the goal line.

"DAMN!" came out of Coach Kienholz's mouth. Being of a genteel nature outside of football, that was a word of many meanings and not often said by the coach.

Then from Coach Capron over on the frosh sideline, "SHIT! Did you see that?" Coach Capron said, with a smile from ear to ear, as Forrest followed close at his heels, reminding him that high school coaches should not speak that type of language (but this time kidding). "Shit, Son. That's the best I've got."

Then Coach Kienholz came across the field, patted Hank on the back and said, "Nice piece of running, son. What's your name again?"

"Lefebvre, Coach. And you be seeing more like that, I guarantee."

"Looking forward to it, son. Lefebvre, you'll get that chance here at Poly. I do declare."

When practice was over and the teams walked to their lockers with headgear in hand, Hank noticed the letterman who'd called him a "beaner-lover." Maybe it was the adrenalin from the game or the confidence from his performance, but Hank decided to deal with the problem right there and now. He asked one of the frosh players, "Do you know who that kid is?"

"Sure, everybody knows him. He's Herb Mitchell. He played varsity last year."

Hank called out, "Hey, Herb!"

"Yeah?" the guy said as he looked back.

"You Herb?"

"Yeah, what do you want?"

Hank walked up close to say loud enough for the frosh team to hear. "You remember me?"

"No. Who are you?"

"I'm that beaner-lover."

"What?"

"The beaner-lover. Remember, Cristina, in the hallway?"

"Oh, okay, yeah, yeah I remember. So?"

"Well, this isn't about the girl, it's about me. You go on saying or thinking anymore the same way and we'll settle this once and for all."

"Oh, yeah?" Herb said.

"Yeah, right now then," Hank said, then rushed him. Both boys threw wild punches, but Hank got a good right hand in and bloodied Herb's mouth.

Coach Capron ran over and pulled them apart. "What the hell is this all about?" he asked, while holding them.

"He knows," Hank answered.

With a scowl, Herb said, "No telling coach. It will be settled," and he walked away.

The coach asked Hank to stay behind as most of the players filed inside the gym. Before he could lecture Hank, they were interrupted by a man clapping and yelling from the grandstands. "That be my boy!"

Managing not to stumble, the man swayed his way down the bleacher steps, evading the field benches, and walked up to the coach.

"That be my boy, Coach. You best mind your manners and best keep his best interest in mind or you'd be hearing from me rightly." After a quick, "Great day, Hank!" the man turned and walked away.

When he was out of sight, the stunned coach turned to Hank, "We got an issue here, son?"

"What do you mean, Coach? What you getting at?"

"Well, who is that man, for starts?"

"That's my pa. He'd been coming to this country by boat, then with Mama by covered wagon, fighting Injuns, Mexican *banditos*, murderers and slackers of no good. Played poker and fought with the best of the legends of the Arizona territory, while whoring in the mines of Bisbee, and mostly since I was a kid, in them smelters around Douglas. I'd be mighty proud of that man. What he done here today, don't matter. What you'd just seen here, Coach, was the bottle, not the man. No issues here, Coach. No need to worry, 'cause Pa's never going to get better than this," Hank said with a smile.

Hank's attitude and humor brought the remaining freshmen players and the coach to laughter. While walking back to the locker room, one of the guys asked, "Hey Lefebvre, where the heck is Douglas?"

"Out yonder," Hank said with a wave of his hand.

Forrest leaned into Hank and said softly, "I think you got the team and Coach's interest in more ways than one." They laughed, then Forrest asked, "Hey Hank, about your pa. All that true?"

Hank smiled. "You bet."

As they walked into the locker room, Hank's voice began to fade, but you could still hear, "So, let me tell you how these skinners backed down one night at this ice cream parlor in Tombstone, just because this fella mentioned my pa's name…"

CHAPTER 17

FLU BUGS AND ASPIRIN POISON

Hank's dreams blossomed into the 1917 football season. As a sophomore, his swashbuckling defensive performance on the gridiron led coaches Tipton and Capron to start him in the backfield with even greater success. However, this didn't make the fiery, brash Hank Lefebvre any more popular with the girlfriends of his teammates. Their chances at being nominated homecoming queen slowly evaporated as Hank's performance on the football field outshined that of their boyfriends. But that never troubled Hank during his whirlwind spiral up the Poly depth charts. Time was all that prevented him from being promoted to first-string halfback.

After just a short stint as Poly High's football coach, Eddie Kienholz proved he could not only recruit quality talent, but coach them to become highly sought after by major colleges at the highest NCAA level. Bullet Baker and his supporting cast of talented fullbacks and linebackers were destined to go on to play with some of the most prestigious gridiron programs on the West Coast. USC, Stanford, University of California, and Oregon sent letters offering scholarships, creating a new era of sports recognition at Long Beach Poly, and generating opportunities for future stars to make their mark.

While Hank's celebrity around Poly took flight, his personal life took to the headlines as well. And it was all about

Cristina. Hank and Cristina teamed up with Forrest and Syriana to enjoy many activities in downtown Long Beach. School social bees, as they do, fluttered about with the latest rumors to keep themselves relevant as critics. As far as Hank's sister Lily was concerned, she had plenty of comers to the house with hats in hand, begging for a date. The group could all be seen sunning at Alamitos Bay Beach or strolling together and flirting about the Pike. Of course, Hank always took the limelight, winning more bears and trinkets than the hustlers at the Pike were willing to give out. But because he usually garnished quite a crowd, there was little opposition from vendors.

One hot afternoon, Hank, Cristina, and Forrest walked along the sandy beach and placed towels down a short distance from the breakers. They pulled out some snacks to munch on, passing the time until Syriana could join them after work at the downtown department store. Cristina suggested a swim, and without waiting for an answer, got up from her towel and began peeling off her clothes. Her skirt came off first, leaving Hank and Forrest to imagine what else was she would reveal. The boys tried not to stare at her as she casually undressed. Even Forrest shied away as she unbuttoned her blouse, though she seemed to take no notice of them.

As Cristina's blouse fluttered down to the towel, all that was left was a Mexican beauty wearing nothing but a smashing white swimming suit of stretched ribbed jersey hugging her curves, with a plunging neckline dropping into a deep V-neck. She turned and began a lavish strut toward the waves bursting on the shore. Hank thought it peculiar she wasn't even wearing that rubber cap most girls wore on such occasions, making her all the more sensual.

"Have you ever seen something like this, Forrest?"

Forrest shook his head "no" without breaking his stare.

"I've never seen such a thing either. Sure not around Douglas 'cause there ain't no Pacific Ocean near there." They laughed together but couldn't keep their eyes, let alone their thoughts, off Cristina's athletic body.

Just before she plunged into an oncoming wave, she turned back, giving the boys one last innocent, yet seductive, frontal view. She was something to admire as she beckoned for them to come on in the water with her. Since her legs were uncovered, and at that time, one might warn, "demanding attention from the opposite sex," Forrest and Hank looked up and down the beach for the "censor police," who were known to patrol the area with measuring tape in hand. These censors would calculate the distance between the bottom of a girl's bathing suit and her knee. Too much bare skin could result in a hefty ten-dollar fine, or even a haul off to jail. However, lately, mostly out of comfort, many women didn't care to follow the rules. Besides, far too many men enjoyed the view. So the modesty rules, in time, faded away.

Hank never saw a girl so sure of herself, so brash and unassuming with such qualities about her. She was special alright. When Syriana arrived and saw Cristina swimming out beyond the breakers, she giggled then said, "Boys, you look positively bewildered."

Watching Cristina prancing in and out of the waves, Hank replied. "That girl is a unique cut of God's creation, ain't she?"

"Yes, she is," Syriana answered, and then she proceeded to repeat Cristina's performance, undressing until all that was left was another skimpy bathing suit—this one a dark, shimmering blue. Syriana ran down to meet the crashing waves with her sister. What a sight—the two of them, having all that fun and independence. For weeks, Forrest would remind Hank of what a great day that was out there on the beach.

Hank's play on the frosh-JV team hadn't gone unnoticed.

On those casual strolls along the Long Beach boardwalk, a Jackrabbit fan would often comment as he passed by, "Hey Hank, how about next season's Poly Football?"

Hank enjoyed saying, "With Coach Kienholz and our quarterback, Bullet Baker, I see a championship a-coming soon."

Another fan would ask, "How about Eddie as a coach?"

"No need to concern yourself. I've never met a coach who loved his players more. Eddie Kienholz is a fine man of good reputation... and might I add an amazing educator and coach. Our team's getting better every day."

"And you, Hank?"

"Oh, I'd be there, playing varsity for sure, by this coming season."

"You will, Hank. The news around town is that you'll be one of the best."

"Amen to that," was Hank's usual response.

1918 was the year that Poly became the preseason favorite...predicted to take the league and then CIF championship. After Bullet Baker played out his senior year, Chet Dolley would inherit control of the quarterback position along with leadership of the team. However, all those plans were for mice or man. Circumstances would prevail the next two years that would not only alter Hank's dreams, but also the history of Poly football.

The war had been going on across the sea in Europe since 1914, and—though hotly debated—the idea of America's entanglement had, by 1918, become a predictable prospect. President Wilson made his decision to take America to war. In preparation for a military offense, the government sent out draft notices. Among thousands of others, Coach Eddie Kienholz's number was up. For him and many other colligiates, there would be no more hullabaloos on Friday nights, nor Saturdays on the gridiron; instead, their time would be spent on the Fields of Flander.

With the loss of the captain of Poly's ship, Chet Dolley, Bullet Baker's back-up, took on some coaching duties. But it was sophomore coaches Tipton and Capron who steadied the Poly varsity team of 1918. Back when Kienholz came to Poly, his team had been practically gutted by graduating seniors. Since then, he'd systematically built up Poly as a league contender, and 1918 was supposed to be the year when Poly would show the country's high schools what it had. But here again, another unforeseen event began to spiral out of control.

It appeared as a simple cough and in many cases the victim was deceased by the end of the day. Because of its international influence, it was labeled The Influenza Pandemic Virus of 1918. By the time it finished running its course it had killed more people than had been killed in all of World War I. The scourge of the flu worldwide was estimated at ten to forty million. In the United States alone, over 675,000 people were causalities of the deadly virus. Making things worse, a rumor spread that aspirin was the antidote, so millions of Bayer Aspirin customers filled their day impulsively gobbling abnormal amounts of the pill as a panacea. That overdose of medication led medical professionals to commonly register a cause of death, as "due to aspirin poisoning."

In Long Beach, something entirely inexplicable was happening, however. Though there were some fatal casualties to the flu, rates of death were far less than other parts of the country. Some medical researchers speculated it must have had something to do with the fresh ocean air. The Poly football team, unlike others in the league, were quite healthy and ready to roll. They entered their promised triumphal year with all the fanfare, but after rattling off three consecutive and impressive wins, they ran out of teams to play due to the problematic flu. The Jackrabbits even played the Navy Adult Base Team in its search for competition. But that would be enough of that. The CIF stepped in and cancelled the rest of the 1918 season, allowing seniors of all schools an additional year of eligibility. Bullet Baker got all-American Honors for his short season accomplishments and then moved on to future USC prowess.

For Hank, it would be a year squandered. His dreams and plans to move up and take part in the drama and guaranteed heroics of the 1918 Poly football year was not to be. For now he had to wait it out, writing often to Doris Mae concerning their health, but usually digressing about his predicament related to football. His letters to Doris Mae now became more than just notes connecting family. They became a ritual, a sanctuary where he felt safe expressing his feelings. "I have the charm and presence of my pa alright, it's the patience of Uncle Joseph I need more work on."

Returning home from an especially enjoyable Sunday at the beach, Adela called to Hank, "Henry Hank Lefebvre!" and Hank knew that was an illuminating clue that something was about to dramatically change in the Lefebvre household. "Henry Hank Lefebvre, let's you and I go out and feed the chickens," she said. Out there they'd have fewer distractions or piercing eyes and ears from the rest of the Lefebvre clan, and less of a chance of being overheard. Once outside, Hank's ma said, "It's about your pa. I know his failings and I know the good of the man. He's worked hard, fought hard, and played hard, but was always there for the family. He never let us down. Now, he has to pay his due…your pa has silicosis."

Hank looked up, "Mama, what's sila…whatever that word is?"

"The doctor says it's a progressive, fatal disease. He's got this scaring in his lungs from all those diggings and smelting in all that stuff flying about for too long back in Arizona. The doctor says he got to cut down on the workin' and his other ways for sure. So, Hank, it might be time for you to go out and get a real job, along with your schoolin'."

"And football, Mama?"

"Football's okay, if you can manage it. But, the family's going to need some extra money."

"Well, if that don't beat all," Hank said softly. After thinking about it for a while he added, "Don't you worry, Mama."

"Well I do Hank, 'cause you'd might be going to war someday or one of the kids, or maybe even catch that flu bug, or something else. So, I do worry. And just maybe, Hank, when us women get to vote, we might have some say in them matters."

Hank gave her a warm smile and hug. "Don't you worry about nothing, Mama. Besides, have I ever let you down?" That seemed to perk her up. Hank usually could do that, tell a person not to concern themselves because he'd make it all turn out right. It didn't occur to him then, but his ma knew. He was much like his pa, just at a different time and place... yet a bit more temperate.

When Pa came home, the two sat down together and had a long talk. Henry agreed to stay around the house more, deciding to work in the oil prospecting digs in local orange groves up on Signal Hill, with his good friend, Ed Doheny.

"Maybe, Pa, it's time I go down to LA's produce district and take up Sonny Cardinale's offer."

Pa said that would be a good idea. Hank could ride the streetcar downtown on weekends and the upcoming summer. "That just might do it, Son." Henry smiled at Hank for thinking things through, the way he did. After a few moments, he added, "I got a good idea. You know son, I could also come up with you on the weekends. I can work for Clifford delivering, to make some extra money, 'cause I'm thinking prohibition is coming. Those temperance ladies, they be making a fuss about the drink. When that happens, Clifford's going to need some help."

Hank grinned. "Pa, we're always seeming to be on the same page, but we'd be just in different chapters, that's all." Hank's pa would laugh and laugh at that.

CHAPTER 18

THE MAKING OF THE LEGEND

1918 came and went, the war in Europe was over, and Coach Eddie Kienholz returned from his tour of duty on the Western Front. "All I thought about on that battlefield was my wife, family, and Poly football." And that was good news for the Jackrabbits. Eddie stepped right back in where he left off as Poly's head varsity coach, meeting a bunch of impetuous, hungry players itching to show their grit on the football field. The offensive cast he so painstakingly nurtured to score with impunity before his departure were many of the same faces, except for Bullet Baker. Listed on the roster were names like Miller, Chet Dolley, Phil Tierman, and Jazz Lawson. However, there was another name that caught Coach Kienholz's fancy this year, standing as a new addition to that impressive offense. It was that start-up he recalled who'd dazzled Poly fans with his freshman/sophmore play—none other than Henry Lefebvre, sometimes called "Laffy," or just plain "Hank," but lately most often called by his new nickname, "The French Flash."

As they stood on the sidelines during practice, Eddie said, "So that's the kid who made the incredible interception and return when we scrimmaged the frosh-varsity teams two years ago? Dang, it doesn't seem that long."

"Yep. That's him, Coach. That's the same kid. He's a proven. The kid's the real deal. Inside or outside, from the wing position, he's a speedster with a punch. Lefebvre's smart, swift, and sturdy, with a great sense of humor. You're going to love this kid. Granted, he does come with a very colorful past." Coach Tipton laughed then added, "He's going to be a real positive influence on the varsity team, Eddie. If it wasn't for that damn flu, we could've done it all last year. I mean CIF champs and everything. Got some new faces here, but this team will come together."

Just then they heard a voice yelling from the bleachers. "Welcome back, Coach!"

"Who the hell is that?" Eddie asked.

Tipton replied, "Oh, that's Hank's personal cheering section—his father. But no worries, Coach, 'cause Henry Lefebvre Sr. there, now he's a man with notorious connections."

"What the hell do you mean by that?"

"Well, the story is he's been known to hang about regularly with some real notables…from both sides of the street. The types found in pool halls and the produce district. He's also got a reputation from back in Southeast Arizona's smelter and mining towns of Bisbee and Douglas. That's where Hank grew up. Yeah, that boy's got some great stories to tell, makes the team laugh about his pa's exploits. Lately, Mr. Lefebvre works for Ed Doheny, the oil man over on Signal Hill. The guy's supportive of the team. Hank's father just hits the bottle too often. But, I might add, he's well-liked around here."

"Seems like an ominous character."

"Yeah, but don't mind him, Eddie."

"Is that going to be a problem with his kid?" Coach Kienholz asked, nodding toward the bleachers.

Tipton laughed. "Not at all. But best not go there when talking with Hank."

Eddie seemed convinced and smiled. "Okay, let's get this team rolling."

And they did just that.

Straight out of the gate, the 1919 edition of Poly football gave the local newspapers something to write about. Coach Eddie Kienholz was noted as a defensive specialist, but he even admitted, "I just need to get the team to learn how to score." And right from the get-go the team proved they learned that fast and well. The Jackrabbits' first game put the pedal to the metal. They came out scorching opponents. First beating Compton High 71-0; then Whittier High by 69; the next victim was Whittier State 56-7; all in preseason play. When it came to league play, they did just as well, defeating Los Angeles Poly and Uptown's Los Angeles High, then taking a forfeit from Jefferson High. The whirlwind continued with the Jackrabbits' defeat of highly regarded Coronado High in San Diego by a score of 59-0, followed by a decisive victory over a well-coached Pasadena team on Thanksgiving Day.

Each week, local newspaper articles became addictive reading for thousands of Long Beach sports fans. The beach community celebrated each victory, rushing out to city street corners on chilly Saturday mornings, waiting on curbs for the morning paper to meticulously relay the previous night's game. Could this really be ballyhoo land, the year Poly would break out as prophesied for the past three seasons?

The backfield consisted of Chet Dolley, Phil Tierman, Pete Coleman, Miller, Jazz Lawson, and now Hank Lefebvre, "The French Flash." These were popular names and mentioned as often as Cracker Jacks, Ford Motors, and Coca Cola in Southern California's collegiate press. These heralded stars not only scored crossing the goal line, but in 1919, Poly's players played both sides of the ball, which made stats and acclamations hard-earned.

Hank stayed around the locker room after each game to

celebrate and wind down with his teammates, usually one of the last to leave. Eventually he'd find his way out to the parking lot to meet up with Forrest, Syriana, and Cristina. They'd walk together back to Hank's house on Twentieth Street where, without fail, his ma had snacks for everyone to enjoy as they sat around the backyard and talked way into the night. Hank's pa would revisit each of Hank's runs with his friends while playing an eternal game of poker at the kitchen table. Then, when the lights went out in the Lefebvre home, Hank would sit alone with Cristina on the back porch, looking up at the stars while they held hands, sneaking in kisses and dreaming about the future. Hank couldn't help but wonder how this would all play out, thinking somehow answers were up there, in those flickering lights.

The CIF playoffs were not in question now and the Poly campus became rampant with enthusiasm. Excitement seeded its way into every classroom. Even Hank's English class was marked by the score of last week's game. It was obvious Miss Ellis had taken a special interest in Hank. "I would like to talk to you for a few moments after class, Hank."

"Sure, Miss Ellis." After the bell he approached her desk with a warm smile.

"Well, Mr. 'Man-On-Campus,' what are you going to do with your new-found popularity?"

"I'm hoping to go to a fine college, ma'am. I'll be the first on my side of the Lefebvre clan."

"That's an excellent goal, Hank. I am so proud of you and your English. It needed so much attention to begin with, but has come along. I enjoy watching you share wins with the all the people around you. I am also impressed by your steadfast affection for your ma, and the special relationship you have with your pa. I like how you include your sisters, especially Lily, your younger brothers too, and that you consider what they will learn from all your efforts. But, you know, Hank, they will all go their separate ways someday and you may be alone. I think you know this. I see it in your writings. So, I just want you to realize how much I enjoy following your journey."

Hank smiled broadly. "Thanks, Miss Ellis. That's important to me."

"And by the way, that friend of yours, Forrest, he deserves a lot of credit for sticking in there and helping with all that frontier talk."

"Yes, Miss Ellis. I'm aware of that and so is he," Hank said with a chuckle.

"Good then, Hank, you go and win that CIF title for all of us."

"We will, Miss Ellis. I can assure you of that."

"Oh Hank, before you go, I've got something for you." She reached into her desk drawer to pull out a wrapped package and handed it over.

"Well, don't just stand there. Go ahead. Open it."

Hank carefully pealed back the paper to find a large book of poetry. He respectfully turned a few pages.

"Poetry, Miss Ellis? I don't know much about that."

Miss Ellis smiled. "I know, Hank. However, as life takes you on adventures, you'll find a need to open it and take a careful look. For now, just think of this book of poetry as something you borrowed from me. Besides, I'll expect it back with notations when you become famous."

"I hope so, Miss Ellis. Thanks so much for taking your concern with me."

With glistening eyes she motioned with her hand and said, "Go on now, Hank. Get on your way and win that title."

And they did. The team entered the playoffs on Thanksgiving Day and found the offense a bit studded, however ended with a 21-0 victory over well-regarded Santa Monica High's stiff defense. It had taken some time for the Jackrabbits to get their mojo going, and they joked in the locker room, "too much turkey legs slowed down the offense." But fortunately, the defense showed up. Next, it would come down to Poly's first ever CIF championship game. On paper, this looked like it would be a close one, but suspense never arrived that night. Poly scored 47 points and Fullerton High scored… none, and Long Beach Poly claimed their first CIF championship.

With that as Saturday's headline, the papers sold out the minute they hit the streets. The beach community celebrated throughout the weekend, reveling in their beloved football team's exploits. Could it really be possible? The team performed way beyond anyone's wildest expectations, giving them an invitation to the state of California's finals at Tournament Park in Pasadena. Long Beach Poly was now just two wins away from becoming the first ever state of California champions. Would that be too much to dream of? Hank wrote Doris Mae all about it. *"I still can't understand those stars shining up there in that big old sky. There's got to be something more."*

And there was. They beat Dinuba in the state semifinals 41-0, and that put them into the first ever state finals with Berkeley High. Butterflies flew in the stomachs of Poly fans at the suggestion of such a thing happening. State champs? They were happy enough to win CIF.

After the Dinuba victory, Hank's pa asked, "Do you think we can do it? Win the state championship?"

"Well, Pa, we're going to play the game like we're used to playing. Mind you, Pa, they got to be as good as us. They made it there just like us—by winning big."

The pundits and odd makers had Poly High in a runaway, and that made their fans a little more comfortable. On game night, just under 12,000 fans sat on pins and needles, biting nails and making deals with God. Poly scored first on an early fifty-five-yard touchdown run by quarterback Chet Dolley. The game was set for a blowout. But, it was not to be, as Berkeley came back to score seven points. Now what was supposed to be a Poly-controlled game became a defensive struggle. Then Hank scored on a run from outside the thirty, giving Poly the lead as the gun went off for the half.

After re-adjusting to Berkeley's defense, Poly came out in the second half drooling for a victory but—low and behold—Berkeley scored again, making it 14-14. From there Berkely's defense took over. Then, with less than minutes to go in the fourth, quarterback Chet Dolley heaved, in desperation, a long, high pass to all-American Jazz Lawson, who leaped over his defender to make a spectacular catch and went in to score. "YES! YES!" the crowd yelled wildly. Poly had won in a thriller, 21-14. The first ever California championship.

That night, the jubilant Lefebvre family members celebrated in Hank's backyard, while scores of friendly neighbors crawled up and onto surrounding fences to watch the happenings. When the celebration died down, Hank asked Alfred to look with him at those stars way out there.

"Oh, come on now, Hank. You been looking at the stars for years now. What good has that done you. They ever talk back and tell you anything? I don't think so."

"Well, maybe you're right, Alfred, but they get me to thinking there's something much bigger out there than here. What it is, I don't know. It's just too big up there to contain my mind."

"What's so big, Son?" Henry asked, coming out on the back step. When his boys didn't answer, Henry announced: "Now you folks come on in here. Mama made us a cake for the state champ victory."

They found their way in and gathered around the colorful cream-frosted cake. Ma asked Hank, "What do we do about the singing or saying before I cut into it."

Hank shrugged. "Not sure, Mama."

"Maybe a prayer, not a song?" she offered.

"Why's that, Mama?"

"You know what I'd done yesterday, before the big game?"

"Not sure, Mama."

"After you left the school with the team, I went to church."

Hank smiled, knowing what she was about to reveal.

"I can see it in your grin that you know, Hank."

"Yup, Mama, I'm betting you went to St. Anthony's and lit a candle to the Virgin."

"Yes, Son. I did."

"Well, that Virgin done a good job calling down that Hail Mary that Chet threw up." Everyone laughed. "But Mama, you're going to need to light some more of them there candles at St. Anthony's, 'cause we're not finished."

Everyone joined in then, "*¿Qué?* What are you talking about, Hank?"

"Something even bigger is in the works. Coach Kienholz says the season might not be over yet! Something so big that no high school team has ever achieved."

"CIF champs, first state champs, what can beat that?" Pa asked, adding, "Hank, have you been drinking from my bottle?" That got more laughter. "Son, what are you talking about here?"

"Okay, Pa, how does 'American Southwest championship' sound?"

"What the heck are you saying, Hank?"

"We might be playing for the Regional National title!"

After a few moments of stunned silence, Henry asked, "And who might we'd be playing against, Son?"

"Not telling you. You have to give it a guess."

The family pitched in various suggestions until Hank had enough. "Okay, okay. For now, it's a secret. But after tonight I'm afraid it won't be. Anyway, it'll probably be in the headlines of tomorrow's sports sections, if not on the front page of every newspaper this side of the Mississippi. Sooooo…"

"Just tell us!" they begged, and gave Hank some playful jabs.

"Phoenix, Arizona!" he announced.

"What? Can't be! Why, Phoenix High hasn't lost a game in six years!" Henry shouted.

CHAPTER 19

THE LEGEND AND THE BIG 102

The Jackrabbits scorched their opponents in a rampage—or, as Hank called it, a "warpath,"—by winning all twelve games and outscoring the other teams in the league by 406-21. Believe it or not, fourteen of those twenty-one points were scored in one game, so that Poly scored an average of forty points in eight games, shutting out nine other teams to win both the CIF and state of California championships. If that success wasn't enough for Poly's story to travel around the USA, savvy football promotors seized on the profitable potential of American high school football and took things up a notch by having Long Beach Poly play the first ever American Southwest championship game against the as-yet unbeaten Arizona State champs. Organizers knew Poly had the momentum, but the Arizona team had just beaten both Texas and New Mexico's state champs. Furthermore, the Phoenix Coyotes' impressive record posed an ominous threat because, as Pa cautioned, "The Coyotes have never lost a game in six years!"

When news got around that on January 10, a cross-state line rivalry game between the Long Beach Jackrabbits and the Phoenix Coyotes would be played on Poly's hometown Burcham Field, Californians went into orbit. Sports fans across the country were intrigued to find out who had the

Henry 'Hank' Lefebvre

best American high school football program, and local merchants and vendors were thrilled about the unlimited commercial potential this game would offer.

Now, for members of the Lefebvre family who came from Arizona's southeast corner, just two hundred miles or so from Phoenix, the upcoming game took on a special flavor. Pa announced: "Can you believe it? Hank, your game is going to be covered by every newspaper in Arizona and all our friends and relatives back in Douglas will be reading all about it."

Hank tried not to show too much concern when he said, "But Pa, I hope we do well, 'cause that game with Berkley was just about all we could handle, at least on that night. And Coach Kienholz has been stressing this will be a close game for sure. He wants us to work harder on our defense."

The week before the game, letters to editors of the California newspapers were filled with praise for the Jackrabbits. So many that the local post office decided to toss them all in a box and have the carriers deliver directly to the school office. Gamblers set betting lines, and places like Girard's Pool Hall were overwhelmed by an increase in business. Sonny asked Henry to "tell the kid the boys in the produce district have some scores to settle with Arizona buyers. We're going to place dough on Poly. I know he'll do us right. Make sure to tell him to run like he did 'cross those fields just outside of Douglas, when the Federalies and Villistas were taking shots at him."

Then there was Doris Mae's letter. To escape all the excitement around the house, Hank walked outside to the back steps and sat down and read in quiet.

We are so proud of you. My brother Charley is especially proud that you're going to be playing in the big game against Phoenix. It means so much to him. He's growing so fast. The doctor says, from the size of his feet he can tell Charley will be at least 6'2" tall. His hair is black as the night but his skin is light. His teacher's say he's a genius. He's so good looking. I think he looks like Tyrone Powers. And, he's talented. He can play so many instruments, but the sax is his favorite. He's also a very good baseball player. After high school, he wants to sign a professional baseball contract. Grandfather's good friend, Carl Hayden, says that after Charley graduates, he'd love to give him a congressional appointment to West Point. Can you beat that? Charley wants to come to California and see you someday up the road. My pa brags all the time at his job in Fort Huachuca, saying, "that California star football player Hank Lefebvre is my cousin." Then there's all your friends in Douglas talking about how they knew all along that you would be something special. Josiah says to tell you that "this is one of those times you two talked about in the hospital. For you to do it. Show them who we are. And when you do, tell them you're one of them Regal Sons of Douglas." He said you'd know what he meant. And there's Emiliano. He's edging into misery with excitement.

There was more, but Hank slipped it under the steps to read later when Pa walked out on the back porch and sat down.

"What's going on over there at Poly, Hank? I seen a lot of people moving around town lately," he asked.

"A lot, Pa. They're building new bleachers for a crowd of 17,000. It looks like a stadium of sorts now. Even Fox Studio is coming around just before the game—with actor Slim Summerville and Bobby Dunn—to film a football comedy. And there's stunt planes practicing a flyby to drop the game ball." Hank slowed down to caution his father's optimism. "Pa, you should've seen those Coyotes at our school rally. They be a husky bunch of kids, bigger than any of our players, that's for sure. Coach Kienholz says size doesn't matter but he feels it will be a real close nail-biter."

"What are Poly's chances, Son?"

"Well, they might have size on their side, but we got the speed and heart. We'll win. Don't you worry, Pa."

The crowd filed in early, around 12:00 p.m. for a 2:15 p.m. game. The stadium and surrounding areas had all had the trimmings of a circus, with thousands of students, visitors, and tourists mingling about. Sidewalk vendors sold everything from cotton candy to team photos, giving plenty of souvenir choices for fans to take home and show their friends that they were there. Coast-to-coast broadcast stations had hook-ups, so sport fans could listen to the play-by-play while huddling around the comfort of their home radio receivers. Poly students handed out hastily printed newspapers with huge headlines such as: "EXPECT A CLOSE GAME!"

Right on time, at 2:15 p.m., with a packed crowd of 17,000 inside the stadium and a few more thousand standing or picnicking on the grass outside, fans readied themselves to witness the sound and fury of one of the most spectacular high school football games ever played. From the moment it started, the frenzied crowd screamed on and on, so loud—it was said—they could hear them all the way from Catalina Island.

Later that night, after all the hoopla around the Lefebvre house subsided, family and friends sat around in the backyard. A few neighbors hung over the fences, hushing each other to hear Forrest read the advance copy of a local newspaper. "Listen to this, Hank" he said. Then he read loud enough for all to hear:

Fans were told to expect a close game. Well, they didn't get what they came to see. No sir! There could be no doubt about who was the best team in yesterday's battle of the giants. For the game was a brutal dominance, a one-sided event, an amazing game that will forever pass into high school football history. The Jackrabbits immediately let the visiting Coyotes know that this day was not going to be for them. Poly scored a touchdown every four minutes of the game. They won by the unbelievable score of 102-0. Leading the lightening offense assault of fifteen touchdowns was Phil Tierman, with 333 yards and five touchdowns, followed by "The Flash" Henry Lefebvre's 205 yards and four touchdowns. They scored so fast and so many times that Lefebvre and Tierman even let their lineman score some. And Poly's defense was just too good—too many players to mention for fear of leaving out one name.

The local merchants had pledged to give away gifts to any player who scored a touchdown. Well, they best have a lot of those gifts in inventory. And for the Arizona juggernauts—the Coyotes—they whimpered out of town. 'We had no alibi,' the Phoenix captain said. 'We're going back to Phoenix and tell the people we were so outclassed that any hope of scoring vanished just five minutes into the game.'

One LA sports analyst said, 'Arizona's team was lucky to escape town with zero.'

"No question about that," Hank added.

Forrest read on:

This 'Big 102' game will be legendary. The 1919

Long Beach 'Poly Eleven' will always be remembered as the bunch of guys who would never accept defeat. This was truly a defining game for Poly High athletics. It will serve as a plum line, a grand standard for performance of excellence for all future Jackrabbits—something to live up to."

"What do you think?" Forrest asked, as Hank looked up into the dark massive sky sprinkled with sparkling stars.

Instead of answering, Hank turned to his brother and posed a question: "Remember Alfred, when we stayed that night at Texas John's ranch and slept out next to the pond, under them same stars?"

"Yep. Sure do, Hank."

"Well, Alfred, I wondered then if there was somebody, years before us, looking up there, praying on the same question."

"What's question's that, Hank?"

"Will they remember or will they forget? You know, I think it's one of them kind of nights. One that should stick with everyone forever. But how long do you think it will take for them to forget, Alfred? How long will it take them to forget what we did down here today? Will it take a few years or will it take a few more?" Or, does it even make a difference up there, who won or who lost?"

The question quieted some of his family and friends for a few moments. But when others went back to celebrating, Cristina, Alfred, Forrest, and Hank sat together in silence, still searching for answers amongst and beyond those stars.

CHAPTER 20

ROARING TWENTIES

B efore the rooster got the urge to send out his bugler cry—usually when the sun showed its first sub-
tle glimpse of light—to make its claim that it hadn't
disappeared into the galaxy the night before, Hank and his
pa were out and on their way in the chilly morning air that
swirled around the cozy beach community.

Henry now worked for Doheny on Signal Hill and Sonny Cardinale hired Hank for the summer in LA's downtown
produce district. Each morning before he headed off to the oil
fields, Pa would drop Hank off at the streetcar depot. At the
end of Henry's "shift," as he liked to call it, he'd drive up to
LA and wait at Clifford's until Hank could hitch a ride from
one of Sonny's guys who were going that way. Hank always
made it to Clifford's, thanks to some workers' fraternal quest
to visit the popular pool hall quite often now that prohibition
had become law. Eventually, Hank and his pa would drive
back home to Long Beach. It was a long day.

On this morning, while sitting in the comfort of the LA-
bound trolley, Hank had time to think about past events
during the four years since they'd left Douglas. A lot had
changed. It was 1920 now and all seemed good for him and
the family. They'd stuck it out together. He smiled thinking
about their farm and how it had grown by leaps and bounds,

with probably more animals than the Griffith Park Zoo. And, after the Big 102, he and the rest of the "Long Beach Eleven" had become extremely popular around the city of Long Beach. The teammates were revered on campus and around town as members of a special football team. Hank's future seemed bright. Much like his pa, he looked at things like the Big 102 win as opportunities. But, he had also learned to keep his passions in check—a quality he acquired from his uncle Joseph.

Hank was happy to see his brother Alfred take on more of the family chores now that he was getting older. The girls also were getting big enough to step up their efforts, especially Lily, who's charm certainly was infectious. She schooled the younger sisters on the nuisance of business and social life, taking a lot of concern off Ma. Hank thought that since they were in the new modern age of the 20s, life seemed to be changing so fast, you had to accept it or get left behind out on the street.

When Hank starred out the window of the trolley, glaring back were miles and miles of orange groves, one after another. He knew most of those ripe, juicy fruits would end up on Cardinale's trucks headed for his distribution center. Hank smiled again at the thought they'd soon be in his hands, to be counted, packed, and sent on their way to potential buyers all over the country. When the trolley slowed toward the LA terminal, he grabbed his bag, then stepped off as it rolled to a safe stop. The station was only a mile or so walk to the Cardinale produce distribution center. Once waved in by the now familiar and friendly security man, Hank found his way to the warehouse, ready to spend the day unloading, packing, and weighing produce with fellow employees. He clocked in, threw his bag into the locker and went to work.

Mr. Cardinale was out of town for a while so Rocco was temporarily overseeing the daily warehouse operations. Today's schedule told Hank to start unloading a train of crated

Sweet Florida Orange Juice that had arrived the night before.

The sun finally broke through, with the forecast to be in the high 90's by late afternoon. Hank always looked forward to the workout of unloading the trains, for he was never opposed to physical exertion. The way he looked at it, conditioning would make him stronger for his upcoming senior year of Poly football. With the bonus of being paid for the effort, what else could be so good? And like always, his optimism and grand smile combined with his reluctance to complain and willingness to take on the task ahead—whatever it may be—along with his charm, which was much like Lily's—infectious—made others happy to work with him. After only a few weeks working in produce, Sonny noted Hank's industrial attributes, take-charge attitude, and natural leadership instincts and promoted him to foreman over older boys who also just worked the summer months. When Hank caught on to a challenge, he—like his pa—took the position: "you best do things right." Meaning, "my way or hit the road." Everybody does their job and tows their load. "No slackers here," Hank would say.

But there was one particular guy who constantly challenged Hank, even on simple jobs like unloading, crating, and stacking crates on trains. To make matters worse, Sonny's nephew, Tony Valachi, was that guy. Stanford student and member of the fraternity's boxing team, he was three years older and resisted whatever Hank asked of him, bringing an attitude of indifference each day. That was okay, Hank understood family was afforded special favors, but he also knew the more he let this kid play out his ego games, the more they would only serve to undermine Hank's position, especially with the other workers taking notice.

One day Hank had enough of Tony's antics. While loading a Cardinale truck, Hank took Tony aside and let him know that the cartons were not properly stacked on the skids. He would need to do it over. Tony refused and let his attitude show. "Maybe the high school football tooker could do a better job."

"So, Tony. Do I have a problem here?" The others stopped what they were doing around the loading bay to listen in. Before Tony could say another word, Hank added, "It's just that they say I'm 5'6" and slight on pounds in the Poly football programs, and you Tony are what, 5'11, 190 lbs. or so?"

"What are you saying, Hank? That, I'm a bully to a pip-squeak football mouth?" Tony said.

"No, Tony. I'm the one with the problem. You see, I'm always being disrespected because of my size, and guys like you always look to smaller guys, like me, to try and show what a big man you are. As I said, that's my problem and I'm used to dealing with it.

"So, look, bozo, get the lead out of your deadbeat body because if you don't get your ass in there and redo that load, then one of them other guys has to. I don't care about your family favors, your Stanford college cronies or your fraternity boxing buddies, that's not in question here."

"Oh, so that's it, Hank?"

"Yes, that's it. Tony, maybe we should settle up right now."

"Okay, tooker. I'm ready."

"Me too, Tony."

Workers overheard the heated conversation and came running to watch the impending confrontation. Hank took off his belt and handed it to one of his crew and told him to cut it in half. He did and gave it back to Hank who wrapped it around his knuckles, and Tony did the same. "After this, you'll be in that truck restacking. Okay?"

"Okay, tooker, but if I win, you'll be the one in the truck stacking."

"Deal. Anyone with a watch? Three-minute rounds, three rounds."

Someone said they got it, then Hank said, "Let's go. Round one."

Tony danced around and gave a few impressive jabs, then smiled before going straight for the head. Hank lowered his stance and Tony missed. Hank went to Tony's belly and dug a right hand under his ribs, followed by a left. As Tony bent over from the crushing belly shots, Hank followed up with an overhand right to the jaw. Tony went down like a rock and for the rest of the day, what do you think happened? Tony restacked the truck.

Just before quitting time, Hank was summoned up to the main office. When he got to the door, Hank saw Rocco standing in the middle of the room, fists up, bouncing around, pretending to be a prizefighter with a broad smile encompassing his face. "Come on in Hank!" he said, while he went to sit behind a large desk stacked high with papers.

Rocco had a stout, pugged-nose profile and wore clothing that took displeasure at being wrapped around a body it was never intended to fit. He asked Hank, "So, what do you think?" while turning around and displaying himself in a suit. It's Sonny's new thing. You see? Go 'head Hank and sit down."

While Hank did, Rocco went on, "You see, Sonny says that times are changing with this prohibition and women suffrage. This temperance movement and women pushing for more say has caused a lot of us married guys problems. Now us men of the house wear skirts!" He laughed at his joke and went on, "but you see, what Sonny wants is that we go legitimate, for us to be businessmen. No more bootlegging. All it does is create easy money and gangsters, like the Iron Man, Joseph Ardizzone, who always looks for an edge. Him and guys like him want to start wars over territory…who gets what.

"Sonny's gone to New York to settle this. He doesn't want any part of this booze business. He's got produce, trucking and meat packing. After prohibition ends, booze will all be regulated and the price will drop. So, he hopes The Accountant sees it his way and allows him to go legit. Now, look at us bazookas. We're sitting behind desks now—legitimate."

Changing the subject, Rocco continued, "Hank, Sonny's really taken to you and he knows you want to play football at Stanford or whoever, maybe for the Trojans, get an education, and then maybe you'll work for a legitimate business. And then there's the thing about your father. He's a fine man, but his time is up. So, I called you in to let you know Sonny and I got your back and we'll always be here to help…when needed. Okay, Hank? By the way, where did you learn to fight like that? They told me you're some winger."

"Well, Pa and I spared a lot when he was getting ready for fights back in Douglas."

"He taught you good. Don't worry about Tony. I think you gave him a needed lesson on respect. Now, take my car and get over to Clifford's and get your pa on home. I'll catch a ride over there later. I heard the mayor and a few of the LAPD's are upstairs gambling. Your pa's good, but the temperature of the game is too hot for him. Now, go then."

"Okay, Rocco." Hank started to leave then turned back to see Rocco waving his hand for him to go and that there was no need for thanks.

Hank drove over to Jefferson Avenue and to Clifford's Pool Hall. Once there, he found his pa's car in front and he parked nearby. As he walked up to the entrance and stepped inside, a rather stormy looking fella dressed in a pin-stripped suit with greased-back hair met him. All his cosmetic tailoring, couldn't dispel the man's intentions, however.

When he approached, Hank quickly got the idea he must be Clifford's new bouncer. "Are you looking for someone?"

"Yes sir, my pa."

"Who might that be, kid?"

"Henry Lefebvre, sir."

Just as the man was about to reply, Clifford walked over and greeted him. "Hank! Good to see you. How's work at Cardinales?"

"Fine, sir."

"You want to come on in, shoot a game of pool?"

"No sir. Just looking to get Pa. Got to get going home."

"Well Hank, he's in the middle of a big game upstairs," Clifford said, then turned to the rough upstart bouncer to say, "Mika, this here is Hank. Go easy on him. The Lefebvres are friendlies."

Mika shrugged his shoulders and stumbled to be polite. "Good to know you, Hank."

Just as they were about to go upstairs, two customers who were dressed as if they just left a downtown business meeting walked in. They followed the routine and waited patiently as Mika asked for their coats and firearms. Hank thought it must have been some business meeting when both pulled out weapons strapped to their back hips, concealed by coats.

As Mika placed them in a locker vault next to the coat racks, Clifford said, "Go on in boys. Billy will set you up if you want a game, or just play some pool. Upstairs, we got a big one in play, so unless you want to meet the limit, well, that's your choice."

The men nodded and motioned it would just be pool.

"Fine, there's a couple of games going on and Louie will be around to take your orders and get you in."

As they walked away, Clifford said, "Well, Hank, things have changed around here. With this bootlegging, business has picked up. About the security, well, because of the legal issues, we need to be vigilant on who we let in. Plus, we need more security because if some fella up there doesn't take to losing and decides to whisk down too many spirits, he might grab for a shoot-out.

"As we always have, we aim to run a peaceful place here. None of that stuff for us. In fact, the mayor and half of LA's police department are up there playing right now with your pa. Their taking a break now though, so, it's a good time for you to go up and say hi." Hank hesitated. "Go ahead kid, no problems, your pa's winning today."

"Okay, thanks, Mr. Girard," Hank said, as he walked up the stairs.

At the top, Hank almost choked on cigar smoke billowing out of the vent above the door. After a soft knock, another security-looking man opened the door. This time it was Michael Irish who spoke to the others in Hank's defense, "Look here, guys. Look who's coming to say hi to his pa."

Some of the guys were setting around a large green card table with a low hanging ceiling light, surveying the play. Others were standing about sipping on drinks. "It's Henry's boy! One of the Eleven from the Poly Big 102 team! I won some money on that game," Michael said.

The mayor asked, "Is that so? Look who we got here, Chief. Those boys put Long Beach and, may I say, Los Angeles—hell, probably all of California—on the map with that stunning game. What, it took you four minutes to get your first touchdown!"

"What do you boys from Long Beach got in store for us this coming season?" the police chief asked.

"Well sir, we lost Tierman and Dolley to USC, but we got a powerful team coming back to fill in. Miller's still with us…a great line with Bagro and such. And we have this fella who played great football last year as a freshman. You're going to hear a lot about him, Morley Drury. He does it all. Whatever Coach asks of him. He's big, somewhere around 180 pounds and six feet tall. He can run, pass, block—whatever you need. He came from a poor family and been working in the shipyards for a year or so after elementary school, but now playing with us."

"And, you, Hank, I understand that you're quite the speedster."

"Well sir, that's what they tell me," then Hank added, "I try to let the other team take notice of me."

"Yeah, some noticing, boy," The mayor continued. Like four touchdowns in the Arizona game."

One man asked, "How you keeping in shape?"

"I'm working through the summer, lifting and such. But Pa's keeping me from being too big-headed for my own good."

Henry smirked. "That's the tuff part."

After a pause in the joking, the mayor asked, "You going to USC after you graduate?"

"Not sure, sir. I hadn't been asked yet." When the men began dealing out a new round of cards, Hank said, "Well, Pa. We've got to get back home."

"Son, can't do that right now, 'cause I got a lot of these men's money here on the table, got to let them get a chance at winnin' some of it back."

"No such thing, Henry", the mayor jumped in, "you just get going home. We know this was no set-up to get you running away with our money while you're winning. No, go on home, Henry. We'll get another shot at you for sure, another time."

Henry looked around the table at the others nodding in agreement. "OK, but we'll just play one more hand. I'll be right down, Son. Get the car warmed up," Henry said, while tossing Hank the keys. "Now, go on son...be right down, after we play out this hand." It was settled.

"Okay pa. I'll be waiting in the car."

Sitting in the front seat, Hank reached into his pack to find a piece of paper and pencil to sketch. Soon, a man came running out the door of Clifford's parlor, then continued to the side parking lot. Two large, angry-looking men followed and ran him down, throwing him to the ground. After kicking the man a few times, one of the men shouted, "Pay up, Tom! Find the money or this is just the start." Then he gave one more kick to the man's face as if to make his point. Blood gushed and pooled on the pavement.

Hank opened the car door and shouted, "Hey there! What's going on?"

The men gathered themselves and calmly walked away, and Hank went over to help the bloody guy to his feet. "What's this all about?"

"Oh nothing, kid." The man struggled to get himself up, stumbling, but once he found his stride, he walked away, then turned back. "Hey, kid. Thanks. They might've about killed me."

Hank went back to waiting and almost fell asleep in the middle of a drawing, but was startled awake by his jubilant pa banging his hands on the hood of the car.

Smiling cheek to cheek he said, "The keys, Son!" Hank handed them to his pa, slid over, and they were off.

"So, Pa, how'd it go?"

"Well, thanks to you we'd got to the last hand and I cleaned their clocks. Yup, we did it Hank. It was a good day. Gonna buy some more chickens for the farm."

"Pa, you know, while I was waiting for you, I saw some guy being roughed up in the parking lot."

"You did? Oh yeah, I heard about that poor Tom. He'd

lost a lot the other night and they come to collect their debt."

"Who are they, Pa?"

"Who knows? Probably some bozos who get paid for collecting debts. Heck, Hank, we'd had harder times in Douglas. I remember the story where this man took old Texas John, while cheating, and old Slaughters went across the border, put pistol to his head, and the man paid up."

"Pa, I don't want that to ever happen to you."

"Now son, this is the rip-roaring twenties now. There's a lot of opportunities out there and the law is working on the edge, just like everybody, to make a fast buck, they look the other way. Heck, I got more beatin's in those prizefights at the Douglas YMCA. This modern time is the new frontier, Hank, and someday it's going to come to an end. But we Lefebvres got to make our mark here."

"And just what is our mark, Pa?"

"Well, Hank, now look what you've already done out here in California. You made people here and back in Arizona respect you. Just listen to those fellas talking about what you're doing. You're making your mark, Son, and your brothers and sisters be part of it too." Henry turned his attention to the road but continued to carry on some more about his winnings. Hank paid little attention though, as he'd had a long day and the rumbling of the car's engine sang him to sleep.

CHAPTER 21

CLIMBING MT. EVERETT

At the end of summer, Long Beach Poly's football team wasted no time getting back to what it did best. Reporters would often ask Hank for his take on the upcoming season. "What our team does best is reload." And reload they did. Harvested from last year's frosh-sophomore teams was a list of potential talents that would fill the holes left by last year's graduates, gone on to become valued assets to NCAA Division 1 university football programs around the country. However, a large portion of those famous Poly players ended up at the once underrated, unassuming small Methodist college, better known as USC.

This 1920 team was not yet heralded to be as successful as the 1919 Big 102 team (of course, who could ever be?), and would have their own mountain to climb. The 1919 team had set a high bar that would lay a challenging path for them. It was as if Jack and those seeds he bartered for on his way to the market, once planted, grew by leaps and bounds—and expectations for bigger triumph followed. The sky was now the limit!

Poly was the preseason headliner for high school football's CIF Southern Section sports in 1920. Reporters described how dominant a force the team would be compared to others in the California Interscholastic Football Southern Section:

"Poly's team is led by former "102" stars, Henry "Laffy" Lefe-bvre, Jazz Lawson, an impressive upstart, Morley Drury—and Kienholz's impregnable defense is ready to meet the task.""

As the season got underway, Hank wrote Doris Mae:

> *We've just repeated what we done the year before. We're running up scores against opponents so easy that it looks like there won't be no teams left to play or no teams interested to play us in the playoffs, 'cause, we beat them all. Rumor has it that Coach Kienholz might just decline to play in the CIF playoffs altogether. He says promotors are set to place us against an out-of-state team and if we win that, we'd be playing for the National American High School championship. How about that!*

> *That would be wonderful, Hank!* Doris Mae wrote back. *But beating Phoenix by a score of 102 to 0, for the local folks here in Arizona, by one of our own, from our own neighborhood of Douglas, now, that will be hard to beat.*

Sure enough, their plans came together when Poly declined to participate in the CIF playoffs, instead agreeing to play a Northwest champion team from the state of Washington—Everett High School, coached by iconic Enoch Bagshaw. It was said, "His teams played college football with a grammar school spirit." Under Bagshaw, Everett teams had lost only one game in eight years, and that was only by one point. "They play 'smashem-style' football. His team is in the finest condition and his Spartan tactics include long, drawn-out workouts, with only seventeen players. Plus, Coach Bagshaw doesn't allow for any timeouts, even never allowing a bucket of water on the field during those practices."

The winner of the game between the Jackrabbits and Everett would then play East Technical High School of Cleveland,
Ohio for the National High School Football title. But still, the
devil was in the details. California's federation had their own
plans for Poly's post-season play. Since Poly leapfrogged over
sanctioned playoff games, CIF notified Poly: "Go ahead and
play Everett, but your school will be suspended from playing
any other CIF teams during the next football season."

Long Beach Poly Jackrabbits, endeared with the idea
of playing for the national title, became indignant, even irreverent, over the ban. In fact, many stated the Jackrabbits
deserved a hearty commendation because with seconds to
finalize the deal, a key Everett player and captain, Leslie
Sherman, had his eligibility come into question. It was discovered he was twenty-one years old and, under CIF rules,
ineligible to play. He'd been allowed to play in the state of
Washington because their rules stated that if a player reached
maturity during the playing season, he could play out that
season. After long discussions, the paramount of the game,
Long Beach Poly gave in and dismissed their opposition to
allowing Sherman to play.

So, in back-to-back years, the stage was set for Poly to play
another "HIGH SCHOOL GAME OF THE CENTURY"
on Saturday afternoon, December 17, 1920 on Poly's home
field. Again, the grandstands would need modification. This
time to accommodate 3,000 more seats for the expected
20,000 excited fans. The Long Beach City Council even declared a city holiday, so its citizens could come celebrate along
downtown's Ocean Street and share in the Mardi Gras-style
festivities. This was monumental for the city and state of California's athletic prowess, not to mention the obvious benefit of
thrusting Poly into the national sport conversations.

For Hank Lefebvre, the upcoming momentous opportunity

was clouded by a personal critical decision he would need to make. Just two weeks back, in a rough game, both Hank and Jazz Lawson suffered severe leg injuries. Now in the 1920s, physical therapy had yet to breach the embryonic stages, so much of the prognostication was pure speculation.

So, with only two weeks' of recuperation and strained attempts to get his leg ready for the Everett game, his participation was called into question. He'd been a star in the Big 102 game, and opportunity was once again knocking at his door. But what might be, could be, what should have been, was a mystery. Playing well against Everett would open all kinds of recruitment possibilities, give him chances of a lifetime to be recruited for top NCAA 1 football programs. However, playing in the Everett game had high-stake risks. It could become an athletic career suicide for him because his leg was less than 100 percent.

Unaware of the circumstances, newspapers hyped the game by reporting Poly's two aces—Hank Lefebvre and Jazz Lawson—had recovered from their injuries and were healthy to play. Hank knew better, but was never one to retreat from a risky situation. Sitting in his backyard with the Lefebvre crew plus Forrest and Cristina, pleasantries carried the conversations. The family reminisced about Henry's past Arizona territory war stories, with Hank's getting all the laughs. Even pa, all liquored-up with a pint, joined in. "Believe me, Hank. I've had some real thumpers."

On this afternoon, even Ma got into it by telling how she met Pa, and how they married in Bisbee and lived on Chihuahua Hill where half-breeds and penniless drifters could find shelter. She described, "We'd be hearing all the goings on every night from those red-light districts and all the ruckus coming from the center of town when miners got angry and started shooting up the place."

Cristina chimed in with memories of Morales, Mexico, how they dressed up in beautiful, swirling dresses, flaunting themselves in town squares, dancing to *mariachis con the hombres jovenes*. She smiled and said, "Yes, no football, Hank. Those young men dreamed of becoming *toreros...profesionales*. They'd go all the way to *Española* to fight *el grande los toros* to break the monotony of small-town life. But it was a good life. Just like yours, señora Lefebvre?"

Ma nodded. "Yes, it was a good life...so is this."

After a few moments of quiet, Hank broke in. "So, Mama. Now we know where you—"

Lily laughed, clapping her hands while the family joined in to tease, "Yes, Mama, now we know."

"I didn't say where!" Ma added, continuing the charade.

She'd grown so socially sensitive in these past few years that Hank joked, "Mama, you really are beginning to believe your own stories about how you came from Spain, then got into those covered wagons while hitchhiking around Arizona."

Again, the family got to laughing, even Ma, until finally she broke the news: "Looks like we'd be getting a new family member soon."

Everyone gasped, and Lily spoke first, "No, Mama."

"Yes, I am again, going to have another child."

"Mama, how did that happen?" Lily teased.

"Best take that up with your pa. He'd have a better way of telling you youngsters."

Soon, everyone cajoled and gave hugs of encouragement, until Ma tired and went on to bed. When the lights slowly dimmed and Lily finished with her giggling friends, Hank continued sitting outside with Cristina, Forrest, and Alfred as the stars came out, which always got him thinking about his adventures in remote parts of the Chiricahua Mountains out under those same stars. To his friends, Hank remembered the little campfires and talks about dreams, but he rarely let himself reveal anything below the surface of these simple memories and emotions. When reaching a precipice that might lead anyone to despair or depression, he'd slip in a joke and carry the conversation another direction.

Eventually, the topic of their futures came up, and Forrest asked, "Hank, how's your leg? I see you're still a little timid with it in practice."

Hank grinned. "The leg's problem is...well...you see the leg and I got different ideas. And if it doesn't want to follow mine, then I think I'll just not let it play with me."

Forrest paused and seemed to think about Hank's comedic response for a while, then faintly smiled at his friend's attempt to cover up the dilemma. But, Cristina's facial expression seemed to give very different thoughts away. She showed not a hint of a smile, just concern—like one of those caution signs at the side of the road. This was the first time they'd witnessed Hank engulfed in circumstances that just may corral him in. Could Hank's ego have gotten a little ahead of itself?

Hank dialed out of that uncomfortable conversation by drifting to another when he said, "Cristina, it's not Forrest's fault. He let it slip out over casual talk."

Forrest tried to help. "Sorry, Cristina but we were talking with Hank and he asked what Syriana and I had going on after high school, it just came out."

"What is it that came out, Hank?" Cristina questioned.

Stumbling for time to gathered his words, Hank said, "That...well...there is talk about you and Syriana leaving us after school's out, instead of college, then the two of you going back to Morales, Mexico?"

Cristina's her feelings snuck out of her big brown eyes and ran down her cheek. She stood abruptly. "Hank, can we talk about this some other time?" Her emotional state choked any further conversation, and with downcast eyes she simply turned and left.

"Forrest, please go with her. Make sure she gets home safely. Tell her I said that yes, there will be some other time for just me and her. Okay, friend?"

"Okay, Hank."

Those who couldn't could get sideline tickets had to be content to sit by the wireless anywhere one could be found. They would soon be read telegrams that carried the game's activities quarter-by-quarter, or were telephoned in from Burcham Field. But before that would be the pregame hype.

"It is a supreme day in Long Beach football history. The fiery, superb gridiron machine of Poly High is steady—ready to hurl its full power against Everett High, champions of the Northwest, on Poly's field this afternoon to compete for the football supremacy of the Western United States.

Twenty thousand people, stark mad and raving with football, surround the field upon which the two of the most powerful prep teams in the West, probably in the United States, are fighting a traditional game.

The stands that encircle the field are seething with movement and color. Spectators press against the steel fences eager to snatch glimpses of the battling men. Impatient crowds of people are still storming the gates in hope of gaining entrance, though it seems as if not one more man could be pried into the field.

Fans are swaying as the three white-garbed yell leaders twist and writhe through their movements. Green and gold pompoms are waving frantically as the great boom of sound grows in volume. The cheer has finished now, and the crowds are screeching into song, carrying a cry for victory and is almost jubilant, although the teams have not yet come upon the field. Long Beach could almost be glorious today, even in defeat.

All the Long Beach boys are in wonderful shape, with Lefebvre, the crack halfback, and Lawson, the wide receiver, both recovered from injuries that kept them out of earlier games during the season. But there's some consternation. Much to everyone's surprise, Hank Lefebvre is not in the opening starting lineup. Coach Kienholz's response is that he's holding him for a time when his return of yards count the most, after wearing down the Everett defense."

The next day's newspaper article said it all.

Within just five minutes of the game, two quick turnovers by the Jackrabbits gave Everett an early 14-point lead. The rest of the game was a Herculean struggle of defenses, even when Poly attacked the Everett goal with Lefebvre, who'd entered the game during the second quarter in an effort to stem the Everett tide.

In his first carry, Lefebvre went down, his thick leg twisted and tore, then he was carried off the field—after two plays.

Though the Long Beach football team fought bravely, they went down in glorious 28-0 defeat, not because she was the worse, but because Everett was better and there were no apologies needed.

Superintendent W. L. Stephen's splendid statement expressed the sentiments of the entire Long Beach community: "We are as proud of our boys in defeat as we would have been in victory. It is not a question as to whether they won or lost, but as to how they fought. Their spirit in the contest was the finest I've ever seen on the gridiron and my heartiest congratulations are herewith extended."

On January 1, 1921, Everett defeated East Technical High School of Cleveland, Ohio 16-7 for the United States High School title. Enoch Bagshaw went on to be named head coach of the University of Washington.

CHAPTER 22

CHET DOLLEY

S ome pundits of the sports world loved scrambling words on typewriters, often without truth, insight, or even a rational basis for the stories they created. As long as an article filled a column and held a reader's attention long enough to stray across the page to a neatly placed advertisement that paid the writer's way, it would make it in the paper.

Apparently, attempting to deflect responsibility for the loss, one such reporter suggested that the reason Long Beach couldn't do much against the aggressive Everett team was the "quarterback's punk judgement in his choice of plays."

These speculations didn't matter much to Hank. His pa already cautioned about such superficial endeavors, calling the pundits "nothing but 'Monday coaches'" and said, "it don't take too much brain matter to explain the obvious."

Fortunately, the Everett loss didn't take the wind out of the Long Beach Jackrabbit sea sider's sails. On the contrary, the Jackrabbits had traveled further out into the sports world than any other high school football program in the nation. And it was the heart of those previous warriors, the beacons of the Big 102, that kept them on the road to success.

Hank's bravado was heralded throughout the city. "He risked it all until a torn and mangled leg wouldn't allow him to play on," his fans said.

"If they'd let him, he would have tried crawling over the goal line to scratch out a victory."

Now that his high school career had just about run out of eligibility, the question of where he was headed was also big on everyone's mind.

During all this, desolate thoughts never entered Hank's mind. No, there was no self-pity from this maverick who had the unapologetic confidence to cut his own path out of his former frontier life. For sixteen years he'd lived in Douglas as if he were Kit Carson, an Indian scout, and a conquistador—all wrapped up in one. While others faced with what might seem to be insurmountable obstacles would give into despair and depression, it wasn't in Hank's character to stoop to such indulgence. His current predicaments—the loss of the Everett game and his leg injury—were just stitches woven into life's wonderful journey, challenges that delighted in each new sunrise.

For Hank, the antidote was always to reset his bearings and move on. Some called it motivation. Hank thought of it as recalibrating. That's what worked best for him anytime things got tough and few choices were available. In her most recent letter, Doris Mae exemplified the same frontier spirit that Hank never left behind after moving out West to California almost five years before.

> *...Knowing you Hank, I probably need not write this. But, because of you, I just don't get discouraged or let depression in when things appear to be going wrong. Life for us, as you know, has not been easy. There have been many obstacles in our way and crosses to bear. How you've carried yours has shown all of us here in this remote corner of Arizona so much about your character. I pray for you each night. Keep the dream alive for all of us Lefebvres. Your next chapter, I know, will come soon.*

A lot of colleges had been paying attention to where Hank might head as well. For one thing, it seemed, wherever Hank played, the football program began a winning tradition. At Poly, Hank had helped create a legacy, a link in a chain for other Poly grads to follow. Winning at sports was clearly in Hank's DNA, which of course in those days was a medical conspiracy theory. Many colleges jumped at a chance to recruit Hank. He received letters from Pomona, Occidental, Stanford, and of course, the USC Trojans. Even a few Midwest teams vied for his services.

Early one morning Ma said to Hank, "get your best on. We're going to get a visitor."

Pa couldn't contain his excitement. "Someone's going to be around today, hoping to convince you to play for USC. And guess who's head of recruitment? Chet Dolley!"

"Really, Pa? But, he's their star player."

Ma said, "Well, you know he been part coach when Kienholz gone off to the war and probably needs a summer job, just like you been doing with Sonny at his produce company. They say he's responsible for recruiting all of you Long Beach players for USC. Makes sense, now don't it?"

"Mama, how'd you get to know all these things."

"Hank, I never missed your games. Especially those years when Chet was the captain. Besides, Pa and me do talk some. But, 'cause Pa's not been…well…quite as sharp these last few years, I needed to know more, and that's where your sister Lily filled me in on all the other matters going on."

"Lily? What does she know about this stuff?"

"She knowed about you and Cristina."

Hank smiled a little then asked sarcastically, "And, what does she know, Mama?"

"Well, for one, Cristina be going in a different direction than you after high school. She's been talking about going back to Morales, Mexico…maybe find herself a farmer and get married or something."

"Lily told you this?"

"Yup, she did, Hank."

"Well, truth is, me and Cristina got a lot of talking to do about our future. And Mama, since you're in it now, maybe when you're down to St. Anthony's lighting candles, light one for me."

Ma gave a big smile. "Hank, you know I always do. How'd you think you made out all these years?" Hank laughed and ma reached over to say, "Now, Hank, give your mama a kiss and mind your manners 'cause Mr. Chet Dolley is coming over later…says he wants to talk to you, me, and Pa."

At a half past one o'clock in the afternoon, Pa set himself out on the front porch to research the daily horse race entries, "hoping to make a small investment in the family's future," as he put it. Sure enough, a shiny black car pulled up in front of the house. Ma had cooked up an apple pie and had vanilla ice cream prepared for the occasion.

Chet was pleasant to Pa when he said, "Good afternoon, Mr. Lefebvre. First time I get to be able to talk to you away from the Poly bleachers during practice."

"Yep. Time is moving on real fast since then, Mr. Dolley."

"Please, Mr. Lefebvre, just Chet. I feel more like family that way."

"Well then, Mrs. Lefebvre has us set up in the backyard patio. Let's go through the house and join her and I'll get Hank."

"That would be swell, Mr. Lefebvre."

Ma was dressed for the occasion and casually brought back her Parisian style of speaking, like she did on the train out to California. Pa asked, "Where's Hank?"

"I believe he's listening to a phonograph record in his room. I'll go get him."

A few minutes later, Hank stepped out the back door, appearing quite agile on crutches, but slowed as he moved toward the table. Chet stood and joked, "Well, Hank, so that's what Everett left you with. At least you had an excuse."

Hank smiled back and said, "It wasn't the ending we'd wanted. Not like the Arizona game for sure."

"There will never be another game like that—102 to nothing! You and Tierman, nine touchdowns. And all I had to do was hand off the ball."

"It was a team effort, Chet. What about the defense? They never played up the defense who shut Arizona down."

"Well that was then. Now sit down, Hank. We've got a proposition for you. Of course, I'm sure no one else has been talking to you about college yet," Chet said with a sarcastic smile. "I know better. I bet Stanford and Cal and all the rest have already called or sent letters."

Hank grinned. "I've had some offers."

"Well, they can't beat ours, Hank. Let me lay it out for you. And by the way, we've got Tierman on the USC campus. I'm sure you've heard about it."

"I've heard Jazz Lawson is going to the Stanford farm."

"Dang, we'd loved to have him at USC. Anyhow, well folks," Chet turned to include Henry and Adela, "here's the spiel: USC, much like Long Beach City Commerce Department did for Poly, wants to promote their school by greatly improving their athletic programs. The intercity LA Chamber of Commerce are on the same page. As you know, USC has recently become a member of the Pacific Coast Conference, which means it will eventually play teams from the Northwest, like Oregon, Washington, and other regional division teams besides Stanford and California already on their schedule. Gus Henderson has stressed USC's need to begin serious recruiting programs all over the country to get some of the best athletes. Coach Henderson says 'okay, let's go out and get these guys and tell them what we have to offer.'

"First, USC has fine academic programs. Knowing Hank and you have ambitious business ideas, Mr. Lefebvre, I want you to know the school has one of the finest business education departments on the West Coast. Now, on a more personal note, I told Coach Henderson that you have a big family and it would be hard on you because...well, now looking at your pa, health looks like a major concern. It would probably be a financial blow for Hank to move away, knowing how everyone in the family needs to work to keep it together. So, consider this. We have rules and guidelines that we'll need to follow, and we can only go so far in offering financial packages without violating those rules, but we can offer some perks."

Pa leaned forward and said, "And what are some of those perks?"

"Now, before I go into that, know that I don't want you to make a decision right now. I want you to give all of this some thought for a couple of days." He had their full attention now. "I'll get straight to it. How would you like to move your family to a place right off the USC campus?" Chet held up his hand to make his point and to wait for the rest. It's one block away. You can see USC's Bovard Administration Building right from your doorstep and Hank could walk to practice."

"What? Move to downtown LA?" Ma said.

"Yes, Mrs. Lefebvre. That's it. Now, think for a moment, Hank and Mr. Lefebvre have their ongoing business delivering produce, milk, and stuff daily. Most of your supply line is from the LA produce district, which would be closer. And the girls will have no trouble finding jobs in LA's booming economy. Also, Mr. Lefebvre can still spend time at his day job on Signal Hill. As you know sir, Mr. Doheny is a big sponsor of athletics, especially USC."

Ma still couldn't seem to quite get it across her mind about the move. "But, we just got here five or six years from Douglas."

"I know, Mrs. Lefebvre. But LA and USC is beckoning for Hank. Coach Gus Henderson says Hank could be one of the key pieces of the puzzle in USC's scramble to get credible enough to attract top college teams to come out West to Hollywood's Tinseltown and play in front of national media—in the Rose Bowl."

Chet leaned over to Hank. "How'd you like the chance to play in USC's new home field, the Los Angeles Coliseum! It will be ready by the 1923 football season. Bovard Field will be our exclusive practice field. Plus, the Coliseum is just a few blocks walk from your house."

"But, how can you do this knowing, as you said, there's these 'rules and guidelines' you mentioned?" Hank asked.

"Well, that's where a great fan of USC and the Lefebvre family comes in. Mr. Girard not only runs a very successful pool hall, but his wife manages three houses next to USC's campus. And they want you as a neighbor."

"You don't say," Pa said with amazement. Ma's eyes revealed her excitement.

Chet went on, "With a handshake, Sonny Cardinale can assure the family his boys will keep your trucks supplied for that home delivery produce and dairy business you have. Oh, I've left one of the best for last. Hank, we have a lot of connections at the film studios and you'll also be able to work as a grip, a stand-in, moving props around, or sometimes as a stunt guy at the studios during summers."

After a long pause, Pa asked, "Well, what do you think, Mama?"

"Well, that's something. All because of Hank's football. Who would've ever known." Even with such a grand offer, Ma asked, "What about Lily and the younger kids schooling?"

"Oh, believe me, Mrs. Lefebvre. There's wonderful grade schools, junior highs, and Manual Arts High School is just a few blocks away. Oh, and by the way, Manual Arts is a lot like Poly, with strict academic and athletic programs that USC will recruit from soon. And Lily, with her good grades, we got her covered. She'll attend USC with Hank."

"So, there you have it. Bottom line is, Coach Henderson says he's certain that Henry Lefebvre Jr. will be a future star at USC and says, don't worry about the leg. Hank will spend most of his first year at USC rehabilitating with the best orthopedics sports doctors at USC and get some time playing with the frosh/sophomore team. Now, Mr. and Mrs. Lefebvre, have I addressed all your concerns?" After a short pause, he continued, "I know this is a big decision for your family to make. But when opportunity comes knocking at your door, you got to think about the possibilities. All right, then." Chet stood and pulled business cards out of his wallet and handed them around. "Can I impose on you to give me an answer in a week or so? Sooner the better." Then Chet bent down to look directly at Hank, who seemed to have lost concentration during the details. "What do you think, Hank?"

Hank smiled and nodded, trying hard not to give away any bargaining chips. But what was resonating, as his heartbeat found its way to the back of his mind, was the tune, 'Coliseum, you'll be playing in the Los Angeles Coliseum.' He remembered the conversation Ma had with the stranger on the train about the new Coliseum that was to be built in LA. He thought it strange how much it had perked his interest back then and how he was hearing about that very same Coliseum now.

Later in his letter to Doris Mae he wrote: "*Maybe there is something to that providence thing mama is always talking about. Better not talk it down too much.*"

Before Chet left he turned again to Hank. "Remember the

first time I saw you play? It was the scrimmage game and you intercepted the pass Bullet Baker threw and ran it back to the end zone."

Hank smiled. "You remember that?"

"I sure do. A lot of coaches did too. Hey, what ever happened between you and Herb. The guy you got into a tangle with that day?"

"Well, we never talked much after that. He left school and got married. Last time I'd heard, he went off to fight in Europe."

"Oh," Chet laughed, "you know, I talked to Sonny about becoming a recruiting sponsor."

"Really?"

"Funny thing, he tells me you knocked out Tony Valachi, Sonny's nephew, a ways back. That so?"

"Yes, sort of. But Tony and I became good friends since then. So, all is good there."

"Okay, can't wait to get you over to campus. Coach has big plans for you."

"We'll talk it over."

"Good. I'll take you around if you want a visit. Oh, one more thing. What's your take on Morley Drury?"

Hank answered passionately, "Good player. You'd better get him quick. Don't let Stanford get to him first, not like they did with Jazz Lawson." On their way out to the car, Hank asked something that had been weighing on his mind, "Chet, what about Forrest?"

"Don't worry about Forrest, Hank. They know who kept you in school with satisfactory grades. This year, we have recruits coming in from all over the country with similar issues, and besides being your best friend, he'll be busy helping a lot of you through a rigorous educational program, hopefully keeping everyone eligible. We've got him covered. Not much to worry about there." With that, Chet said his good byes and left.

Later, Ma and Pa called the family together and took turns telling them what USC had offered. "What do you kids think about that?" Ma asked, now taking the lead on the discussion. Each family member brought up concerns that would need to be resolved.

It was on this Saturday that Hank's future had been laid out. He called Forrest and told him all about the USC offer. Forrest said, "Take it, Hank, 'cause, I'm planning on enrolling right away. It's four more years that you and I and could be enjoying a really fun college campus life and all."

"Sure could, Forrest."

"But what's the story with Cristina?"

I don't know, Forrest, haven't talked to her lately."

"It's been only a few days since she broke down."

"Yep. I'm going to ask her out for a walk along the strand tonight and see how it goes."

"Be careful with her, Hank. She's tender on this idea to leave for Mexico."

"Okay. Thanks buddy."

That night, Hank picked Cristina up at her house. As they drove to the beach, they didn't discuss anything about USC or going back to Mexico. Actually, there was little conversation at all. Once they parked, Hank helped Cristina put on her sweater to keep her warm as the chilly ocean air breezed off the Pacific. They strolled together until they found a bench with a view of the star-studded night. With only the pleasant roar of the breakers, the stage was set.

Hank broke the deadlock of silence first. "Cristina, I've told you this before but tonight it's important you look up there at the stars with me. They've been around for so long, it makes life seem slight alongside of them. Do they have a future or has it passed on, no matter, the light doesn't go out. I know this is awkward, but, Cristina, what do you see in those stars?"

"What do you mean, Hank?"

"Cristina, what is your future in years to come?"

After moments of silence, she finally gave an answer. "I see a girl working on a farm with kids gathered around, helping with the planting. I see a cozy little house with a white picket fence and the smell of chili simmering over a hot fire that is far away from the lights of the city, much like here tonight. Somewhere I can hear *mariachis* playing at some festival not far away. And what do you see out there in those stars, Hank?"

After a deep sigh, he answered softly, "I see myself out there traveling in space, bouncing from star to star, uncovering and challenging its mysteries. An unlimited adventure that would take more than one lifetime to finish."

"And family, Hank?"

"They're always with me. Like my father and his rambling stories, the family is always in my thoughts and concerns. Because of that, I need to go as far as I can in this life. I've got just this one chance to find out what footprints I can leave."

"And that is most important to you, Hank?"

"Cristina, If I don't take this opening—or as Mama calls it, 'providence,' and Chet calls 'opportunity,'—what happens to my family?"

And with baby brother Everett here...it's just that, they're dreaming high on what I do. Does Charley Jr., Doris's brother who she's so fond of, does he not dream too, back there in Fort Huachuca and Tombstone? And my friends in Douglas...what about them? You see, my life is in some ways not mine. Because what good would I be to them married, planting and sitting in my rocking chair, telling my kids I gave up my dreams for yours.

Hank turned and looked Cristina in the eyes. "Cristina, believe me, I loved my days in Bisbee and Douglas. They gave me roots…good and bad. But now, I need to bear fruit. Do the best I can do until there is no more. Then I'll find that rocking chair. Will I end up lonely? Yes, maybe. But when I look up into those stars on a night like this, I'll say, 'see, this is what you gave me, and others will follow what I do and remember.' Isn't that life?

"Children, home, and tradition is all that's asked from you, Cristina. Me? I don't have that leisure. Each day demands more of me. I know you must go home to Morales and I also know I'll always think of you and the times we've spent together. Now, it seems as though you must take a certain path while I take another. We've had adventures and good times. We'll reminisce on what we had these past years while we were so young and free, knowing all we'll have are memories to lighten us when we're down, and delight us when we're up. That's the price we pay and the compromise we make, living one life at a time."

Cristina took hold of Hank's hand and looked deep into his brown eyes when she said, "Just think, I will tell them I knew Hank Lefebvre, one of USC's greatest."

They sat for a while in silence under a heavenly night accompanied by the chorus of Pacific breakers and fresh ocean breezes there along the Long Beach strand in 1921. They hugged and kissed just once more to last a lifetime, promising to write. But about what? It would just get in their way. It would never be.

PART III

USC

Bovard Administration Building 1921

CHAPTER 23

THE LOS ANGELES TIMES

To suggest that Los Angeles wasn't a booming town in the 20s would be a monumental distortion. Angelinos' advancements were so numerous that to make a list would at best, be cursory.

Film and entertainment industries led the way with at least 90 percent of all movie productions done in LA's suburb of Hollywood. The oil and petroleum sectors became giants due to drilling and abundant gushing of black gold at Signal Hill and Huntington. The Los Angeles Harbor became the second largest deep-water port of entry into the United States, receiving and sending goods from all over the world and cashing in on the growing West Coast markets. Aviation took off, with various exploration and research companies establishing headquarters around the seaside community of El Segundo. Add to that LA's large naval base, which housed thousands of US navy personnel, and you've got an unrestrained and ever-expanding LA County market.

Intercity LA had grown from 577,000 to almost two million in just a few short years, causing the Wilshire District's clothing, manufacturing, and investment banking interests rush in to share the wealth. Exploding real estate values caused venture capitalists and railroad developers to supply opportunistic residents with a variety of affordable housing.

Business throughout the city was flourishing at such a rate that labor couldn't keep up with demand. It's even been said there wasn't a ghetto to be found in Los Angeles County during California's "second gold rush." Entertainment opportunities became just a matter of how fast construction would take to set out venues for their display. The Hollywood Bowl was built to suit a growing demand for holding outdoor events, while the Los Angeles Philharmonic Orchestra offered regular performances and new traditions with their Easter morning concerts, and eventually the Shrine Auditorium was refurbished to host even more concerts. Even the off-shore resort town of Catalina Island was at last ready with the completion of a spectacular casino that provided an amazing backdrop. Entertainers from all over the continent performed here for dignitaries and celebrities, like Clark Gable, Mary Pickford, and Douglas Fairbanks. And, thanks to Sid Grauman, the Chinese Theater in downtown Hollywood was open to immortalize the iconic characters of show business along city sidewalks.

How did all this effect the life of Hank and the Lefebvre family, who'd recently accepted USC's offer of a scholarship and all its 'perks'? A lot. This innovative and exciting part of town was now Hank's backyard and playground. USC's location was settled just a few years back in 1917 when the its board of trustees decided against moving the university to a more rural environment. They chose to leave USC right dab in the middle of LA, maintaining 'USC should be a city institution…a university which tries to solve the problems from the city.'

When Hank signed the commitment letter, Rose Bowl games had a new home. Instead of playing New Year's Day Bowl games at Tournament Park, they now had a state-of-the-art Rose Bowl stadium in the city of Pasadena, just up the road from the Los Angeles Civic Center. More important to

Hank, though, the new Los Angeles Coliseum—expected to hold a crowd of over 90,000 roaring fans—would be USC's home field. Also just up the road was the Olympic Auditorium, soon to host some of the greatest boxing matches of the century. Of course, the nearby sprawling LA Market District had a wide diversity of wholesale products like textiles, jewelry, meat packing, and perishables picked from local farms, of which Sonny Cardinale and his trucking interest were in full control. For the Lefebvres, coming up the coast from Long Beach to Los Angeles was an immense change in lifestyle and a formidable task of readjustment.

Due to its labor shortage, LA often embraced the indigenous Mexican people, allowing them to find a variety of menial labor opportunities on the more affluent west side. Social tensions persisted between many ethnic groups, however, and often Mexicans were looked down upon as uneducated, lazy, and of low character. Most Hispanics migrated to Southern California in spurts due to upheavals caused by periodic revolutions across the nearby border. They gathered in the enclaves of East LA to such an extent that it was often referred to as the US capital of the Mexican community. Each morning, bustling traffic made up of Mexican workers flowed across the Los Angeles River's bridge to look for jobs. At the end of the day, they'd return, crossing back to their barrios for familiar food and friendships.

Other parts of Los Angeles were dissected in much of the same way. Newly arriving Jewish, Armenian, and Chinese refugees found their own neighborhoods, but in smaller pockets. The Chinese established Chinatown and many Jewish settlers found their home in the Fairfax District. Italians generally spread throughout the town, some going on to the more brazen enterprises of boot-legging and a variety of protection rackets for speakeasies and other reprobate, underworld ventures.

Doris Mae continued writing letters to Hank during this time. Perhaps to help quiet his family's concerns about uprooting themselves again, she wrote:

> *When I was in primary school, there were only ten kids in each class. Now my high school is miles away and I must sit on a bus for over an hour each way. The school is so much bigger and it feels strange to try and fit in. I can hardly bring up the courage to think of moving from the comforts of our home in Fort Huachuca to attend Ohio State University when the time comes. Yet, I can see, it will be time to move on. Over the past few years, towns out here in the Arizona Southeast only survive if they become a showplace of a past frontier, and they are constantly hoping to avoid becoming mere ghost towns. I can understand your uncomfortable feelings about the move, but to have your family live so close to USC's campus, sounds wonderful.*

The University of Southern California was their new home. USC had been called "The Methodist," or "Wesleyans," up to just a few years before, but neither name was held in high regard by the administrators. No, they needed a new brand, something that would catch the spirt of their game. So administrators ventured out to the local news media and asked one of the *Los Angeles times* sports editors, Owen Bird, to select an appropriate nick name for the growing college. At the time, the athletic department was at a complete disadvantage because besides playing Cal and Stanford, weak scheduling otherwise handicapped their accomplishments in sports. Although when they faced bigger and better-equipped teams, they had a splendid fighting spirit. Therefore, when Owen Bird came out with an article just prior the USC-Stanford game that called attention to their fighting spirit: "…and, with my journalistic liberty, I referred to that spirit as the Trojan Spirit…" It stuck and applied to USC, because "whatever the odds or whatever the conditions or competition, they carried on to the end. And those who strive must give all they have and never be weary in doing so."

Now, that might've gotten to the bleeding hearts of USC football's die-hard fans, but to Hank it simply meant: "This is the place and type of team I want to play with," and he continually reminded himself that it was with this kind of passion the Big 102 Eleven had lived and played by.

As the family pulled up to the curb of their new house and climbed out of the packed car to the street, Hank looked around at the incredible view. Chet was certainly right. They were close to the action. From their front yard, they could see directly across the road to the refined architecture and iconic structure of the USC Bovard Administration building. Before everyone could take it all in, out from the neighboring house flew three girls followed by Mr. and Mrs. Girard, all holding their hands up in a welcoming gesture. Ma said, "My goodness, Henry. I think we're almost outnumbered." Everyone laughed heartily and introduced themselves.

Mr. Girard began, "This here is my wife, Louisa, and my girls, Virginia, Mary, and the youngster is Loraine."

Then it was Henry's turn, "Here's our girls. Lily, Mary, and Esther. This boy's Alfred, that's Gilbert, Benjamin, and our youngest, Everett. And you already know our oldest college boy, Hank."

Louisa spoke up, "So, you're the one my husband and this town is talking all about."

Hank smiled. "I guess so, ma'am."

"Well, I hope you can help our local football team get some notice."

"Yes, ma'am. I intend to do my part."

"Okay then. Let's get you into your new home." Mr. Girard motioned and led the way.

Early the next morning, Hank had to shake himself out of bed. There were no familiar neighborhood roosters crowing out the rising of the sun, only the roar of traffic and a few sirens screeching somewhere off in the distance. Hank put on his shoes, then while standing on the big front porch, he looked over to see Mr. Girard coming in from his billiard parlor.

"Well Hank, here you are. What do you think?"

"I think sir, that it's a long way from where I woke up yesterday in Long Beach, and a lot further than Douglas."

"Oh, don't you worry. Once you get on with your classes and football, you'll be too busy to look back.

"What's on your schedule today, Hank?"

"I got a meeting with Coach Gus Henderson this morning, sir. Plus, Dean Cromwell wants me to come in for a talk, he's also the track and baseball coach. So, I guess I got a long day of introductions."

"Sounds good to me. Again, welcome to USC, Hank. I got to get in and get some rest."

"Good day to you, sir," Hank said, then went back into the kitchen where Ma had already started breakfast with eggs, potatoes, and a big slice of ham.

Hank continued into the bedroom to look after the boys, but decided not to wake them, knowing this might be the last day they'd be sleeping in. Their produce business was about to keep the boys busy—especially in the early morning hours. When Hank walked back into the kitchen he said, "Mama, this is a fine place."

"Yes, it is, Son, coming from a covered wagon, living in a one-room shack on the side of the Chihuahua hills, to Douglas on dirt floors, then Long Beach with wooden floorboards and an indoor washroom and toilet. Now here, yes, this is the best so far. We're moving up, that's for sure."

Later that morning, Hank found his way to the athletic department. While passing Bovard Field, he was pulled like a magnet through an open gate onto the practice field. He stood on the fifty-yard line, much like his first day at Poly, to give his traditional acclamation.

"Here I am, USC. Let's play!"

A voice from the end zone yelled back, "Who is that out there?"

Hank brought up his hand to shade the sun from his eyes. "I'm Henry Lefebvre, but everyone calls me 'Hank.'"

"Then 'Hank' it is." As the figure moved across the field to greet him, Hank took notice of his appearance.

The man looked like a gentleman of moderate age that one might imagine getting off a street car, wearing a fedora that was struggling to stay abound. When closer, Hank recognized the man from newspaper photos. It was the acclaimed coach, Gus Henderson.

Hank thought he was a stout man in appearance, and decidedly not particularly athletic. His spectacles floated about his face, trying to find the resting spot—or was it just his eyes flirting to find their focus? He was dressed to fit with the best from the ivy league. Light sweater vest and a coordinated sport coat over khaki pants and shoes that, though worn, didn't take much notice. But, it was his pleasant smile and his genial presence that brought you to his way. Not the usual football robust, sturdy, over-powering or intimidating presence at all. He was almost a comical figure for a head football coach.

Once he came close, Henderson said, "Hank, welcome to USC. I see you found your way here. Out for an early practice?"

"No sir…aw, yes…maybe, just, but right now I'm on my way to your office."

Henderson smiled, then chuckled. "Well, this should be my office. Especially if you knew how many hours I spend here. And you, Hank, is this much different from the fields of Douglas?"

Surprised, Hank said, "Well sir, it's a long way from here in many ways."

"They tell me your parents were one of the first pioneers in that region of Arizona. Also, they were there before it was a state, fighting off Indians and Mexican bandits and watching Western legends being made." Hank stared blankly without knowing what to say. The coach smiled. "I love those western stories. Maybe on our way back to the office you could share some with me."

Hank eased into the moment. "Yes sir. I've got a lot of them." This was Hank's first impression of Gus 'Gloomy' Henderson, who would become—and still is—USC's leading percentage-winning coach. He thought of Coach Henderson as a friendly, likable—almost comical at times—caricature of a happy hooligan who made each team member feel like he was needed. You wanted to play for him 'cause you liked him, and that made all the difference in the world.

CHAPTER 24

SORORITIES, FRATERNITIES, AND RUNNING TRACK

"Welcome to the Epsilon chapter of Alpha Chi Omega, the longest standing sorority at USC, having been here continuously since 1895. Alpha Chi Omega enriches the lives of our members through lifetime opportunities for friendship, leadership, learning, and service. Every day we are inspired by our sisters to fulfill our Alpha Chi motto, to become 'Real, Strong, Women.'"

Symbol: The Lyre

Colors: Scarlet Red and Olive Green.

"What is this your reading, Lily?" Hank asked, while sipping a cup of coffee.

"If you must know, I'm looking over the possibilities for next year."

"Come on. Those are just a bunch of girls who can't get dates on their own and my God Lily, you have to swat them off with a fly swatter."

"And you, Mr. Athletic Hero, why don't you want to rush for one of those astute fraternities?"

"Are you kidding? What for? I've got a whole football team to…what do you call it…oh yeah, socialize with."

Lily jumped back, "And look at them. They're most likely rough guerillas who bully themselves into affairs."

"That's a pretty limited approach, Lily, like bulls in a

China shop?" Hank laughed. "And Lily, who gets the first peek at these girls…those sorority types."

"Okay, so there's a few cheerleaders willing to drop their knickers for a night out with a football number, but when you get out of the game, what will you have then? They'll just jump the train and get another ride."

"Since when are you so concerned about my relationships?" Hank joked.

"Since I'm at a new school and I'm making new friends. So, when I introduce you to one, just be nice."

"When have I ever not been?"

Lily grinned. "Well, I do admit, you sure got the charm when you want to."

"You think so?"

"Hank, you know, when you flash that wily, wild, cockeyed smile of yours, it attracts all sorts of girls to come on across the track."

"You got it all figured out don't you, Lily?"

"Yep. I know more about the birds and bees then you, and more about what nice, proper girls want, like Cristina."

"Come on, Lily. Let's not go there. That's been left back in Long Beach."

Perhaps sensing she'd gone too far, Lily let off the pedal. "So, are you going to get into some kind of Greek fraternity or not?"

"What do you think, Lily? Like I been telling you, I've got teammates, school, and practice, besides, there's so many rules for frats out there, I'd have trouble keeping track. And why would I need some preppy, egotistical group of condescending, pernicious, supercilious tots and social demagogues telling me what I should say and do?"

"My goodness. Listen to that," Lily joked, which didn't distract him from rambling on to finish making his point.

"Where'd you hear them big words?" Ma asked, coming in. "You got them from Forrest?"

"Yep," Hank said with a smile. "He's good at them big words. Now, Mama, you shouldn't let your ears be so sensitive when Lily and I are talking about such things."

Ma chuckled. "Well son, I've got a lot of kids around here and if I don't keep in touch that way, no telling where you'd all end up, 'cause Pa, even when he's around, he's always talking too much about them oil fields, which I don't mind. It's Clifford's billiard parlor, a-gambling, and hitting the bottle—now that's something to worry about."

"Aw, Mama, he's done that his whole life. Not to worry."

"But his health's a-failing with that emphysema acting up every day. So, I worry."

"Okay, Mama. I'm not getting much done here. Got to run over to the school and get my classes in order, then the bookstore. Also, I need to sit in on a team meeting with our offensive coordinator, Coach Cromwell. Coach Henderson's got this new scheme." Hank turned to leave. "See you later," he said, then stopped. "By the way, Lily, Forrest and some of the freshman and sophomore boys want to hang out at Sonora's tonight. You know that place over on Wilshire Boulevard?"

"Sure."

"Could be fun if you get some of your girlfriends to meet us down there. We'll have a few margaritas to keep the party going. And you girls will be drinking colas. Right, Mama?" Hank called out to the kitchen.

"Okay sounds like fun, Hank…after work. I'll try."

"Come on, Lily, don't let me down. Oh, I forgot, I'm going to see if Dean Cromwell is in—he's the baseball and track coach. I missed him yesterday. He sent me a note saying he'd really like to have a talk…thinks he's got something that might interest me. So, Mama, sorry, won't be back for dinner."

"But Lily, we're still on at Sonora's. Hear that?" Hank shouted, as he threw open the front door.

"Yes, Hank. I heard you. I'll bring some of my friends."

"A little after 7!"

"Okay, okay!" Lily shouted back.

Hank picked up his class schedule, stopped by the bookstore, and sat in on the frosh/soph meeting. Then later in the afternoon he found his way to the athletic department office from reading the list of room number locations on the directional down in the lobby. After walking up two floors, he entered another lobby where he quickly noticed the receptionist—a cute blonde—sporting a USC cardinal sweater that wrinkled only where it should on a girl. She was fingering through stacks of papers. He tried to get her attention and see if the rest of her would be at least half as pleasantly inspiring. Using his special smile, he said, "Miss?"

That's all it took. She turned and looked up at him, and a circus parade went off in his mind. She was just plain beautiful, tanned by the California sun, and Hank's presumption that it was a result of beach bathing was an unmistakable conclusion. Her blue eyes twinkled when she smiled back, causing a cheesecake interlude. He held his smile, drawing her in to focus on his eyes, and she stared unquestionably at him. To break her trance Hank asked jokingly, "Miss, do you talk?"

She finally spoke with a streak of enthusiasm, as if she was just having a break from what she'd been doing. "Yes, I do. Sorry, you remind me of someone."

"Well, I hope it was a good friend."

"Oh, as a matter of fact, yes it was. So, may I help you? My name is Miss Lillian." She blushed.

"Miss Lillian, I've come to see Coach Cromwell."

"Oh, he's been called out on a personal issue."

Hank tapped twice on the front of her desk, then asked,

"Is Chet Dolley in then?"

"Oh, now I know who you are," she said, flirting now.

"You do?" Hank smirked.

"And, we need to get together."

"We do? And why's that? Because you know me?"

"Sure do. You're Henry...sorry, Hank Lefebvre from Long Beach."

"Now, how do you know that, Miss Lillian?"

"Well, I work part time for USC, meeting new recruits. I'm the one who makes sure all is going well and class schedules are set, you know, all of that kind of stuff."

"Part time?"

"Kind of, you see, Mr. Lefebvre, I'm a part-time volunteer because I'm also a student. I've been around just one semester."

"Are you from a sorority or something?"

"Yes and no."

"How's that work?"

"Well, I'm kind of the coordinator between the Greek clubs on campus, those who want to help and volunteer for athletic events."

"Really? So, why do you know me?"

"Because you're on my list."

Never one to shy away from a conversation that strayed too personal, Hank ask casually, "How do I look? Like you expected?"

"What?" She laughed.

"Well, do I look like what you expected?"

"Okay, Mr. Hank Lefebvre, let's see," she said while pulling out a file. "It says here, male. Yep, there's no doubt there. 5'8", hum, maybe in football cleats. It also says you're 180 lbs., plus you're fast and quick. Well, that's for sure...even before I had a chance to say hi." She laughed.

Hank added, "Does it say there that I make friends fast, because, I only got four years left at USC?"

"Not sure if that's here. Maybe in the fine print." She smiled.

"Well now then, since we've been introduced and we're on our way to becoming good friends, might I ask, Miss Lillian, do you date?"

"What do you think?" she said and blushed again.

"Not married I hope."

She held up her left hand showing proudly there was no ring.

Hank pressed on. "Well, that's good, so your answer is?"

"Yes, is my answer. I do date."

Hank broadened his smile while he attempted to penetrate her eyes with his.

"However, Mr. Lefebvre…"

"'Hank' will do. Remember Miss Lillian, we're good friends now."

She quipped back, "Here's where the devil is in the details. I date, but never with USC athletes. Especially, ones who require a professional relationship. Sorry, but it causes rumors."

Hank smiled back. "Now, Miss Lillian, I know just how you feel."

"How's that, Hank?"

"Well, me too, I don't date anyone I work with. Don't want to make things too complicated."

She dropped her pencil, flipped back her hair, and rolled her eyes. "You're really something."

"Well, thank you. May I call you 'Lillian' without the 'Miss'? We're friends now."

"I think you've worn out that friend thing, Mr. Lefebvre."

"Since nothing's coming out of this, Miss Lillian, I'm pleased to have met you. Now, could you let Dean Cromwell and Chet Dolley know that all is fine on campus…no negative comments about our move here. By the way, Miss Lillian, are you from here?"

"Santa Monica."

"So that explains that beautiful tan. Well then, it's been fun talking with you, Miss Lillian, and I sure hope we meet again."

She smiled, and Hank found a future opening when she said, "I'm certain we will," then skirted back to a business-mode, "are you going to freshman orientation later today?"

"Sure am."

"I'll be checking on you, Hank."

"Don't you worry, I'll be there, just for you," he said.

Hank started to walk away, then turned to ask, "Lillian, have you ever been to Sonora's over on Wilshire?"

"Yes."

"You like it?"

"Yeah, a lot of students hang out there. I've been there myself a few times."

"Okay, 'cause I've got a few of the frosh teammates going with me tonight. I'm sure you know most of them by now. Just thinking…"

"Well, you just keep thinking, Mr. Lefebvre."

Waving goodbye, he said, "No need to be calling me 'Mr. Lefebvre.' I'm not in the military yet." While walking back down the stairs, Hank thought he'd made his usual good impression on that lovely girl 'cause he'd made her smile and laugh so much.

At 6:30 that evening, Hank, along with a load of other freshman athletes, found their way to Sonora's. Mexican food, along with towering Margaritas dashed with lime and salt, combined with an upgraded-style of dining created the per-fect atmosphere for a casual party.

USC recruited these freshmen from all over the coun-try, and each took turns telling tall tales that drew awe and laughter. The restaurant became increasingly cluttered as each minute crept later into the night. Hank dealt out some of his Douglas stunts, claiming his allegiance to the Southwest Territories, while glancing at the restaurant entrance door each time it swung open and closed on passing customers. He hoped his charm and his suggestion for the night had got its way with Miss Lillian.

At one point in the evening a lovely couple came in. Be-fore they could be seated, a rather distinctly irreverent Ivy League type immediately approached them. He was adorned in a printed Polo shirt, punctuated by a checkered sweater of contrasting colors and a pair of Oxford two-toned shoes that gave him away. Now that might sound superfluous, but here in sunny California where causal wear was vogue, he stood out. Hank felt Forrest watching him carefully as he keenly followed the encounter between this couple and the Ivy League guy. Soon Hank could tell by their body language there was some kind of confrontation going on. Forrest kept scoring Hank, who quickly got a take on what was going on.

Hank turned to his teammates and asked, "Does anybody know who that guy is by the door, in the Oxfords?"

One of his team members said, "You don't know from his fashion? That's Ray Price. He's the president of some presti-gious foreign Greek frat house around campus. I think its 'Alfa Bagobango' or something." Everyone laughed. "He's also Ray Price, the English prizefighter who's rumored around campus to be contracted to fight the undercard for a Dempsey fight when the Olympic auditorium opens later next year."

"Really? So, what's going on over there?" Hank asked.

"Looks like Price is badgering a pledge."

"For what?"

"Probably for bringing a Mexican girl with him in a place like this."

"Why?" Hank asked.

"Because this is the west side of Los Angeles, and most Mexicans have their place on the eastside, across the bridge."

"What? So, that's the way it is here? Well then, let me see about that," Hank said, as he pushed back his stool and walk over to the altercation.

"Where the hell is he going?" another player asked Forrest.

"Oh, no. Not again. I know what he's doing. You guys haven't seen his play but you're about to witness a car crash. Just watch and listen," Forrest said.

As Hank got closer, he overheard the prickly Greek frat president scold the pledge in front of his Mexican date. His behavior became even more insulting, peeking into intimidation.

"What's going on here?" Hank asked.

The entire room went silent, as if a Neanderthal had walked in to take center stage. By now, all the patrons had turned to listen to the heated conversation.

"Son, this is none of your business or your concern," said Ray Price, in a condescending manner. "I'm just having a private little chat with one of my pledge friends here."

Hank stepped forward. "Well sir, it is my concern."

"And why's that?"

"Just a healthy respect for humanity," Hank shot back.

"Humanity? What humanity?" Ray asked sarcastically.

"Yeah, humanity, and I bet that's the first time you've used the word, limey."

Price looked back to the table where Hank had been sitting and saw the others streaming in on the action. "Your friends?"

"Yes, all of them."

"Oh, I see. Football players?"

"Yep."

"Well, football is a barbaric unskilled team game where—"

"And boxing is?" Hank cut in.

"It is, of course, a highly skilled and civilized sport."

"Is that so?" Hank challenged. "And insulting this lovely girl in front of her date is civilized? Is that another one of your skills? If so, then maybe it's best we go out there in the parking lot and settle your confusion as to what the word 'humanity' means."

Ray looked startled, backing up a step. "Now, that's not the way gentlemen go about this, my friend."

"Well, seeing that you're not a gentleman, nor my friend, your rude behavior to this fine gent and this Mexican girl appears to need immediate attention. Or, will you coward under the skirt of mere pretense?"

"Listen to you. Big words for a frag tot." When Hank didn't back down he added, "Okay, okay! Let's do it outside. One three-minute round. That will do it. I assure you."

Hank had never backed off in his life. "Let's go!" he agreed.

The restaurant emptied out the door and joined Hank and Ray outside. While peeling down to their undershirts, Ray repeated, "You know there's no need for this."

"A Mexican girl goes to a Mexican restaurant and you rank through this, embarrassing her? You are in need of a lesson on good manners. Now, Limey, quit the talking and let's get to the fightin'." Hank gave Forrest his sport shirt and said, "Check your watch. Three-minute rounds. Round one!"

The two met each other in the middle of the parking lot and the crowd watched. Rice back-peddled about, smiling as if Hank was a duck swimming in the middle of a pond, ready to be engulfed by a swift crunch of an alligator. Rice bounced about while Hank stood still. Finally, Price jumped into attack mode, taking the offensive. He gave a short jab, then another, then threw a left hook followed by a powerful overhand right. His punches catching nothing but air, Price began to bounce more and smile.

"You got away with that 'eh? Now, try this," he said, as he went in on Hank again. Instead of jabbing, this time Price faked a left hook, then threw a sweeping right hand, keeping his left hand low, which now exposed him to to Hank's powerful right. Price stopped dead in his tracks and down he went—no ten-count necessary.

As Price lay there, some of his friends came over to pamper the pitiful warrior with a glass of water from the restaurant bar. The crowd was silent and Hank waited until Price slowly revived before putting his shirt back on. "Sorry to disturb you all, but sometimes these kinds of things need a bit of settling," Hank told everyone.

With that, the patrons filed back in to the restaurant where the Mexican owner announced: "One round, so only one round of margaritas is on me. And for Hank—a dinner for two!"

"*Gracias, señor.* But no, *señor,* a dinner for two for that gent and his beautiful Mexican date," Hank said, while nodding to the couple. The festivities picked up then, much like they do when a bullfighter is carried out of the ring on the backs of his fans, holding ears in both hands.

As the night wore down and people slipped out in their separate directions, the Mexican girl approached Hank. "Thank you for what you did for me," she said.

"No, *señorita.* You did that for yourself. I thank you for your courage to come here. What I did tonight was for that Englishman who needed to be taught a lesson in humility. I hope he learned it well."

"Thank you anyway," she said, then smiled as she leaned over to give Hank a kiss on the cheek. "*Via con dios, amigo.* You come to the eastside of LA and *mi familia* will welcome you to the best Mexican dinner you have ever had. *Muchas gracias.*"

The next morning, Hank rushed over to see Coach Cromwell at his office, but in the back of his mind he also hoped he'd get another chance to bait on Miss Lillian. This idea made his trip over even more pleasant. When he arrived at the second-floor lobby, he saw her, frantically fingering through more stacks of files. This time she looked up at the sound of his footsteps and immediately opened the conversation. "So, Mr. Lefebvre, I'm glad I didn't accept your invitation yesterday, which I admit at the time seemed very inviting. There's a story going around here about a certain USC rookie football player defending a Mexican girl from the eastside. That certain player caused a ruckus in Sonora's parking lot last night."

Hank smiled and stopped her from going on. "So, Miss Lillian, where did you hear that rumor?"

"Oh, it wasn't a rumor, Mr. Lefebvre. It's here for all to read about. Listen to this," she said, picking up the *Los Angeles Times.* She read: "USC freshman knocked out the talented prizefighter, Ray Price, over an unknown altercation inside Sonora's restaurant last night." Lillian put down the paper and looked at Hank, "It's all over campus, so when you talk to Coach Cromwell, just be prepared."

"And you…your thoughts?"

Her smile gave her away before she could speak. "Oh, I loved it—a noble cause. And beating the stuck-up, obnoxious Ray Price! To tell you the truth, I wish I'd been there myself to drink down a few of those margaritas with you to celebrate."

"Really?" Hank asked, crowing like a conquering hero.

"Now, Mr. Lefebvre, don't let that cause you to think you

have any priorities with me."

"But…but, okay Miss Lillian. I'll make sure to not take priorities," Hank smiled.

Just then Coach Dean Cromwell walked in. He was the "Maker of Champs" at USC who'd coached many different sports and was a luminary figure on campus. And what were his first words you ask? "Did I hear you say something about butts?"

"No, no, Coach Cromwell. I said, 'but because…'" Hank stumbled, as he scrambled for a defense.

"No need to explain, Son. It was a joke, just a joke. Did I break up the conversation between you two while you were admiring each other?"

They all laughed and Lillian blushed. Then Cromwell said, "Take a walk with me, Mr. Lefebvre, around the track."

"Sure, Coach."

As they stepped down the stairs and out the building, crossing over to an open gate, Dean Cromwell gave Hank a history of all the fine athletes who had passed his way. He'd trained them on this very same track, some had even brought home Olympic medals. After a few times around, he stopped and turned and said, "You know Hank, I went to that Big 102 game."

"You did, Coach?"

"Yes, I did, and I saw you dashing about. You sure are quick. Then it hit me just last week. You see, I've got a problem you could help me out with. I have a runner who is very fast and has proven himself at the Olympics and World Games in the 100- and 200-meter dash. But lately he's been slow to get off his mark compared to some of the other nationally known runners. Sure, he kicks in at the end and wins, but I need him to get quicker in the first forty yards. That's where you might come in. Hank, I haven't seen anyone as quick as you at forty meters, so I'd like to ask you to join the track team and train with this guy. If you agree, as an incentive, our booster club has offered to pay you two dollars a workout. What do you say about that?"

"Sure, Coach."

"And by the way, I've talked to Gus Henderson. He loves the idea."

"Sounds okay by me, Coach. Can I ask who this person is I'd be training with?"

"I'm sure you know of him, Hank. I held back on giving you his name in fear that it might prejudice the whole project." Cromwell paused then revealed, "It's Charley Paddock."

"Who? Charley Paddock!"

"You've heard of him then?" Dean Cromwell smiled.

"Heard of him? Charley Paddock? Who hasn't? They call him the fastest in the world! Fastest human to ever run a race. Gold medals in the 1920 Olympics—the 100-, 200-, and 4x100-meter races!"

"Well, that's settled then."

"It will be a pleasure, Coach."

"Hank, you're going to play a big part in getting him ready for the 1924 Olympic Games in Paris."

When they were about to leave, Dean Cromwell asked, "Hey, curious where'd you learned to fight like that."

"Like what, Coach?"

"Like I heard you did with Price last night."

Hank chuckled a little. "My pa, he always fought prizefights in Douglas and he'd taught me a lot about fighting, since I was first wearing breeches."

"Really?"

"Yes sir. And Pa was real good."

"Really," Cromwell repeated with amazement. "Well then, I hope you won't need those skills out here on the track too regularly."

"No sir, I don't see the need. I'll be running so fast around this place, trouble will have a hard time finding me."

"You know kid, I'm quickly becoming fond of your pre-sentation, your exuberance—your flair. It will be infectious for the spirt of our track team, I'm sure of it, and you haven't even put on a pair of spikes. Come to think of it Hank, do you play baseball?"

"Yes sir. Doesn't everyone?"

Dean Cromwell's smile was about to burst. "Of course they do."

Hank couldn't wait to get home to check on his budding produce home delivery service. It was finally taking shape and running on time. All of his brothers, except young Everett, were now working in the business. At dinner, Hank broke the news about Charley Paddock and the family received it with a big "Woo-hoo!" Even Lily looked impressed. This news easily upstaged the Ray Price fight of the night before, which had already run out of vigor.

Hank got to bed late but couldn't sleep because of all the exciting news. There was just too many events to move out of his mind. So he went out to their Victorian style front porch and stretched out on the swing to look up in the sky. He carried on a conversation with himself. "Don't matter where I've been, from Douglas to Long Beach to USC, it's the same stars out there. Imagine, they haven't changed up there for millions of years. That keeps me going, 'cause that's where my dreams are floating about, with all kinds of unlimited 'ventures. And to think, they will always be there, the same and something to believe on, maybe, God. Surely, for me, it's not there in Mama's candles." Then a melan-choly thought invaded Hank's mind. It was Cristina, visiting through his memories. He tried to reconstruct her image. It begged him on to query, to philosophize, as he attempted to reconcile a troubled thought. He'd abandoned her dreams for his, was it all worth it?

CHAPTER 25

A Star is Born

L ife was anything but routine for the Lefebvre family, now living just a stone's throw from the USC's Bovard Administration Building. No need for the roosters to greet them each morning, that job was given over to a progressive city on the move, scheduled and orchestrated by bustling sounds and smells that—even before sunrise—habitually came to life. Sounds of automobiles cranking out RPMs and the collective voices of an enthusiastic populace percolated the ambience of a new generation of Angelinos, ready to take charge of their bright futures. Oh, stress still came from an untamed LA social climate, but people seemed to find a way to stay clear of other's interests. For there wasn't so much of a struggle between the "haves" or "have nots" now; this period was more like an Easter egg hunt—as everyone tried their best to fill their own baskets without tripping over someone else.

Hank was not only working on his blooming relationship with Miss Lillian Ludlow while attending college his freshman semester, he was also successfully managing his upstart produce business with help, admiration, and generous financing from Clifford Girard. Who, thanks to new prohibition laws, was now the renowned and prominent owner of the "finest billiard parlor in Los Angeles." On more than one occasion, Cliff's pool hall was mentioned as "a bright spot for visitors and tourists."

Henry 'Hank' Lefebvre

Not as well-advertised, but well-known, were the locals from the Los Angeles political spectrum who attended lively betting lines and games of chance, all provided in the comfort of Girard's back room. There were even rumors a speakeasy was in the works, all under the protection of LA's finest law enforcement agency.

Of course, there were those times Hank'd spend proctored by Sonny Cardinale, who often reminded him about the difference between his business and the sins of Joey Ardizzone, the reputed underworld figure. Sonny shared his new mantra with Hank: "My interests are not in competition with Joey's underworld of vices because I have the blessings of "The Accountant" from New York, to become an upstanding member of LA's Chamber of Commerce. I'm now the proprietary of a legitimate business!" he'd state proudly, though it simply meant that his companies would be able to pass any audit the Feds could throw at him.

Hank's promising athletic career was off to a good start and worth attention by the town's sportsmen, enabling his football prowess on the gridiron to become more than just a footnote at the bottom of the *Los Angeles Times* sports section. Naturally, his altercation with Ray Price only added to the chorus of enthusiasts.

Ongoing escapes and antics of this brash young collegiate on and off the field attracted the public's affection, eventually finding their way to social gossip columns. Yet even bigger games were waiting for him, and these, along with his personality and talent, propelled his popularity to blossom in a variety of ways on the campus of USC in 1923.

One bright Saturday morning, on the spur of the moment, Miss Lillian made a special request to Hank. She'd love to visit the Pike at Long Beach. "I've spent most of my time in Santa Monica and passed through the city of Long Beach a few times, but I've never ridden the infamous roller coaster." She suggested Hank bring Forrest and his girlfriend along, "Let's make it a double date!" Hank was much obliged and further enticed by Lillian's attempts to persuade him on such an endeavor. If he agreed to the trip, she hinted she just might disclose a conversation she'd overheard in the athletic office. "And Hank, I promise, you'll find it very interesting, if not pleasing."

So off they went, all four spending the day walking along the Long Beach strand. Lillian was impressed by Hank's popularity around town, especially when locals stopped them along their walk to ask about USC's upcoming football season prospects and how the leg was coming along. It wasn't until they got to the Pleasure Pier that eager solicitors once again drew upon Hank's charm to pull in customers with their sales pitches that she realized the fun side of his talents. One female vendor, noted for pandering her physical attributes, told the girls, "You should've seen the crowds he'd bring in just by throwing those beanbags and soft balls and shooting this rifle right here, winning about all we had to give out. Remember that, Hank?"

Hank smiled back and said, "It wasn't nothing, ma'am. Hope I didn't run you out of business."

"He did and the crowd loved it!" Forrest jumped in.

"Girls, you should've seen this navy officer taking home all those cutie dolls Hank won, just for them," the vendor continued.

"Then the officer gave the whole Lefebvre clan money to ride the coaster," Forrest added.

The vendor stopped abruptly and asked, "Hank, whatever happened to the beautiful Mexican girl you used to bring here all the time? What was her name?"

This took Hank by surprise. After a few moments to restrain his emotions, he cleared his throat to mumble, "Cristina."

A nervous silence fell on the group. Perhaps feeling Hank's disposition chilling, Forrest changed the conversation quickly. "Okay, now girls, it's your turn to ride the monster!" Both girls appeared as good sports and more than willing to show that no coaster was about to break their spirit. After waiting in line, hearing the screams, and witnessing the effects on the exiting passengers, Hank suggested the girls take the front seat, explaining how safe and more comfortable the ride would be.

Sure enough, when their time came, the girls slid in front while Forrest and Hank jumped into the second row, chuckling under their breath as the coaster slowly crept up the tracks. After reaching the peak and giving a short pause, it dropped fast and gyrated around corners of the rails that overlooked the ocean. The girls never caught up with their screams as each corner felt like it would be the last before flying out of their seats into the water below. Suddenly, the ride was over. Disheveled and wide-eyed, the girls sat there until Hank laughed and said, "Alright girls, were done here, so if you don't mind, can we get on our way?" Later, as the four of them strayed to the end of the pier, grubbing over cotton candy, each picking at the sticky treat, Hank asked, "So, tell me, Miss Lillian Ludlow, what's the secret you have for me?"

Lillian looked over at Forrest as if he might not be trusted with such inside information. Hank said, "Never mind him. This is our town and we men don't hold back from each other. That's what friends do out here."

"Okay then, get a hold on, Hank."

"Oh, come on Lillian, can't be that bad or so good."

She paused, keeping up suspense, then finally blurted out, "Here it is: the 1923 football schedule is out for athletic director approvals before it goes public. In October, USC will play its first home game in the new Los Angeles Coliseum."

"What?"

"Yesss and the frosh-sophomore team will be playing its game *before* the varsity, against Pomona College."

Hank stood to yell as if intoxicated. "Woooo-Hoooo! The Los Angeles Coliseum! Just like them Romans!"

"AAAnnnd, Hank, it gets even better. The Rose Bowl Game will not be played in Tournament Park, but in the new stadium in Pasadena. They'll call it the Rose Bowl. Get it? It looks like a bowl? And it will be played on New Year's Day, after the Rose Parade. See? It fits."

"What?"

"Yes. There's even more."

"Really? More?"

"Yes there is. You see, I heard Gus and Chet say that if Hank Lefebvre plays as good as he did at Long Beach Poly, we need to bring him up from the freshman team to play in the Rose Bowl. That is, if USC can get there."

Forrest cheered. "Now Hank, the ride don't get any better, now does it?"

Hank couldn't help but second guess the information Lillian just shared. "Are you sure?"

"Oh, yes, because, I heard it from the horse's mouth," Lillian said, with laughter all around. (Because, everyone knew, Lillian was scared of horses.) Nevertheless, her news held such exciting possibilities that Hank set his practice and rehabilitation program into the speed zone.

Ever since the Los Angeles Coliseum was built in 1923, USC has played all of its home games there. The very first football game ever played in the historic stadium would be against Pomona, and USC beat them 23-7. Gene Dorsey is credited as scoring the first touchdown ever in the Coliseum, but few remember that the USC frosh-sophomore game was played first that day in an earlier game. The first two touch-downs of that game were scored by Henry 'Hank' Lefebvre, which of course put him in the conversation with Dorsey.

As the year progressed, Hank's adjustments weren't the only ones people took notice of on the football field. USC's recruitment efforts began to stretch way beyond California borders, to places like Ohio, Wisconsin, and Washington. This growing community of star high school talent, ambitiously pursued, increased competition and diminished the security of any one position on the team. It kept players on their toes, always trying to catch the eye of the coaches and hoping to keep their place in the starting lineup. But this never bothered Hank. He'd been competing all his life, starting back there on the streets of Douglas. What was any different here? Yet, Hank found the politics of collegiate sports unsettling. Sports columnists, who'd never played the game, were always fond of Monday morning quarterbacking, second-guessing and suggesting who should play where and when. Hank felt that was none of their concern and people took notice when he responded to their questions after games: "I played the best I could every time my number was called. Never mind the rest."

This caused Hank to be considered a real maverick with an attitude that allowed him to play on his own terms: "If I'm good enough, produce for the team, and hold the coaches' and players' respect, there's no need to matter about the other.

Local newspapers would repeat that, "It was [Hank's] ef-fervescent flair and confidence in his talents on and off the field," that made him even more of a celebrity.

As time passed, outside interests took notice and became a major part of sports, especially now that USC was on the rise and Coach Gus Henderson was on the move. One could meet up with regular, everyday fans gathered around corporate coffee pots, talking up their favorite college teams, and to help break through the monotonous daily business routine, they might even put a few bucks on the upcoming game. And there was always the assorted few that would be happy to encourage a wager or two, creating a thriving underworld enterprise. Therefore, tampering with a player's performance could make for a very profitable venture. Responding to such concerns about the trustworthy performance of his players, Gus Henderson stood up in a team meeting and preached honesty and integrity of the game, and the university, knowing there still could be one or two players who'd get lost in the 'get rich fast' temptation. "But those schemes have a cost—the sacrifice of the team's effort to win."

Hank was not insulated from such suggestions daily by outsiders, who'd ask if he'd thought about his future, "after your fame is left in a college yearbook" then they would answer for him, "nothing, that's what's left. Let me help you out…make a little money to put away for those years up the road…" Hank would admit there was no money to be made in pro-football contracts at that time, and as his popularity became entwined with USC's, the price went up on his stock. Patrons at Clifford's billiard parlor and other places about town offered: "We'd be making you a deal you can't turn down."

It was a letter from Doris Mae about her father wanting to bring Charley Jr. out to California to see Hollywood and meet with Hank to talk about Charley's future in sports that probably made the most difference in Hank's decision. How could Hank introduce an impressionable young man like Charley Jr. to college athletics if he was on the take? They didn't do that back in Douglas, where life was true and virtuous, and although sometimes strained and clothed in different suits, stayed the same. That was the pioneer life. Here where a man's character could be lost to the game, life was different.

As the football season progressed, so did Hank's thrilling runs. His fantastic speed and husky frame played well with his slight height, so if a tackler ever got a hand on him, the punch from his strong thighs would leave them holding air at the goal line. It wasn't until late into the season Coach Gus Henderson called Hank into his office. "Remember the time I met you on the football field?"

"You remember that?" Hank responded.

"Yes, I do. It was then that I knew you had the right stuff. We just needed you to salt away for a while…get your legs under you once again, from the beating you took in that Everett game. You know Hank, I think Long Beach Poly could at least put some points on the board if you'd been well.

When I talked to Coach Kienholz after the game, he told me that you just being suited-up, and the way you carried yourself into the game gave your team more confidence. Hank, what I'm leading into is this: For the first time in USC's history, I think we have a chance to play in the Rose Bowl this year, and I want every edge I can get. I'm sure it will be against Penn State's Nittany Lions—a good team—and I want you on the varsity roster, suited up for the game. You may not get as much play time as you'd like, but every member of the team remembers what you and the Big 102 Eleven did to Arizona. And that plays well for morale. All our starters have earned their position for this big game. But if one of them breaks down and there's time on the clock for one more play on the one-yard line, I'd call Lefebvre's number. Chet Dolley tells me when he recruited you, he promised you a chance to play in the Coliseum and the Rose Bowl. Well, here it is Hank, just like we promised. So, what's your take?" For the first time in his football career, Hank's eyes teared up and his mouth found no reason to speak. He just nodded with a broad smile. Coach Henderson finished his meeting. "Good. No go on, tell them all. But first, we need to win a few more games, then we'll all have something to smile about."

After losing its first ever Pacific Coast Conference game to their millennial rivals, California, USC went on to an impressive winning streak, ending an 8-1 season. When the University of California, winner of the PCC, declined the invitation to play in the 1923 Rose Bowl because of financial hardship (having already traveled to Southern California three times), and considering it unnecessary to play a team they'd defeated earlier in the season, USC got the conference bid to take on the 8-2 Penn State Nittany Lions. Even though there'd been eight previous Rose Bowl games played in Tournament Park, this was to be USC's first ever Rose Bowl appearance and, coincidentally, it was to be the first ever bowl game played in the new stadium.

On the day of the game, the Nittany Lions, while in transit from their Los Angeles hotel to the stadium, got lost, delaying the game by forty-five minutes. Gus Henderson and Hugo Bezdek, the Penn State coach, almost came to blows over Penn State's demands to be allowed extra time to warm up prior to the game. The game finally started and Penn State scored first on an early field goal. However, the rest of the game belonged to the Trojans, with Campbell and Bullet Baker scoring the final points to seal USC's first Rose Bowl victory.

This would be the bright beginning of one of the most prodigious football programs in collegiate history. The *Los Angeles Times* reported: "Henry 'Hank' Lefebvre and Chet Dolley, of the famed Long Beach Poly Big 102 Eleven, though played in spots, showed the future of USC football was in good hands." And rightly so, for the events of the following 1924 season would propel USC football to even new heights that proved they'd belong with the best of those powerful Midwest teams.

After the game and after the locker room excitement had faded, Forrest said, "Hank, let's take the girls over to Kappa Alpha and celebrate!"

"You go ahead, Forrest. But, can you do me a favor?"

"Sure, what's that, Hank?"

"Would you escort Lillian over there with you? Tell her I'll be over later."

"Will do, Hank."

"By the way Forrest, thanks for jumping in the other day in Long Beach."

"How's that?"

"You know, about Cristina."

"Oh, that. I knew that vendor would ask you about her."

"Yeah, I should have known too," Hank mumbled.

"I did notice you got a little tongue-tied with emotion."

"Well, I just wanted to say thanks, Forrest. Now, you get going to the party."

"Okay, Laffy. See you later."

"Yep, maybe so, but first I need to get together with the family on the front porch for a while, like the old days in Long Beach, in the backyard, after games. Remember, Forrest?"

"Yeah, I do Hank…some good times."

A few moments passed, giving them time to resurface to the present, before Forrest asked, "The party, Hank?"

"Oh, I'll be there, Forrest. I just need some time to think things out."

"Okay, sure," Forrest said, as he walked away, knowing what Hank had on his mind.

CHAPTER 26

CHARIOTS OF FIRE

With the passing of the torch by USC's graduating seniors, a new generation of gridirons surfaced. Acclaimed celebrities from Long Beach Poly—Hank Lefebvre, Chet Dolley, and Phil Tierman—were looked upon to carry the mantle for the advancing Trojan football program. But it would be in the off-season that Hank would be offered an additional, and unexpected, opportunity to display athletic valor besides that of football, and, yes, baseball—where his reputation for hitting long balls over left-field walls drew quiet a following. So, at the request of Dean Cromwell, Hank joined USC's 1923 track team to give full attention to the prestigious privilege of helping train world record holder, Charley Paddock, for the 1924 Olympics.

Following his service in World War I as a lieutenant in the field artillery of the US Marines, Charley Paddock chose USC to further his education and track and field endeavors. After winning gold and silver medals in the 1920 Olympics (held in Antwerp, Belgium), Charley Paddock left for an international tour to break as many world track records as he could find. Heralded as "The Human Meteor," "The Prince of Spirit," "The World's Fastest Human," and "The Super Athlete of Modern Times," Charley was surprisingly deceptive.

Charley outsized the distraction of his slight frame—5'8"

and mere 165 pounds—by his athletic performance on the track. Between races he was equally influential in the social realm, as he discarded silks and turf spikes and used his public persona to interview—and then become friends with—many famous figures, including Jack Dempsey, Calvin Coolidge, Babe Ruth, Red Grange, and the Prince of Whales. His fascinating articles went on to be published in a variety of popular periodicals, such as Colliers Magazine. It was his exclusive access to some of the best of Hollywood's movie moguls, like Douglas Fairbanks and Mary Pickford as they traveled about Europe together that gathered such a large fan base. Later, Paddock would become an actor, playwright, and Hollywood critic—even a radio announcer at one point. Since eulogized as an international sensation and well-known phenomena around Hollywood and LA, what better place for Charley Paddock to perfect his skills than at USC. And all under the tutelage of Dean Cromwell, who would go on to coach a total of ten Olympic gold medal winners and twelve NCAA National championship teams, nine of which were in a row.

With this formidable backdrop, Hank was brought in to participate in Charley Paddock's world. He was to be the rabbit for Charley to chase down—at least for the first forty meters—improving his burst of speed from the starting blocks, which Dean Cromwell had detected, "was in need of improvement if he hoped to compete with the likes of Eric Liddell or Harold Abraham of England in the upcoming 1924 Olympics games in Paris."

Hank Lefebvre's arrogance and confidence was unusually subdued at their first introduction. Hank would later say, "Can you imagine our first meeting on the track, this bigger-than-life celebrity, dressed in silk running shorts and gold track shoes, shielded by track fences to keep out spectators and unwanted paparazzi interruptions?" So, after Dean Cromwell took them through an extensive warm-up exercise, Hank finally got his introduction. The three of them sat in the stands while Coach Cromwell discussed the purpose and objectives of Hank's participation. "Charley, this here fella is one of the quickest football players around, bar none. We need to get you out of the blocks and quicker in the first forty meters, and I think working out with Hank will get you there. So boys, get to know each other 'cause you'll be spending a lot of time together on this field."

To Hank's surprise Paddock's first comment was, "I've seen you play, Hank, and believe me, I'm one of your biggest fans. You're going to have a good year next year with the football squad, and I'm very happy that Coach got us to work out together."

Hank didn't quite know how to respond, except to smile and say, "Thanks, Mr. Paddock."

"No, Hank. It's just 'Charley.'"

Coach Cromwell stepped in. "Now that we got introductions well in hand, let's get to work. From now on, Hank, you need to follow Charley's workout patterns. Okay?"

"Sure enough, Coach."

As the days went on, Charley and Hank became good friends, kidding each other yet always looking after and caring about the other's performance. Years later when Hank shared with others about their friendship, he'd say, "You know, Charley was a Bible teacher in Pasadena and that certainly showed up in practices. Between sprints or just setting around the grass at the infield, Charley let me in on stories about his travels and the great personalities he'd met and athlete's he had heard about or competed against." Hank also noted, "Charley always came back to talking about Harold Abraham and Eric Liddell of England. These potential competitors stood out, 'not because of their natural talents, but what was on the inside,' Charley would say, and he called it the 'Olympic spirit.'"

One story Charley told was of Eric Liddell, a Scottish minister who would not run on the Sabbath. By chance the Olympic finals for Liddell's race ended up being scheduled on a Sunday, and though he was a 200-meter man, the English team suggested that rather than him going home without a medal, he might try his talents at the 400-meter race. Now of course, 200-meter men are not trained to run 400 meters, and the inside track analysts shamed such an idea as ridiculous. However, England, unable to convince Eric to change his mind about the Sunday race, had no other choice; they went with the decision that Eric Liddell would run the 400-meter race on Monday. Somehow Eric made it through to the final gold medal race. On the day of the race, his teammate was overheard asking Eric if he thought he'd win. Eric replied, "I have honored God, His providence will take care of the day."

As the final gold medal race began, Liddell, inexperienced at the 400 meters, ran with the speed of a 200 man. Most felt sure that after 200 meters he'd become flushed of strength, and, as the saying goes, "the bear would jump on his back," slowing him down dramatically. But Liddell went on running until all was spent. Charley told Hank that it must have been something spiritual working on his side, 'cause none of the other runners caught up until he'd past the finish line. Charley would tell Hank, "If I didn't see it myself...well it was about to make a believer out of me, and it did."

"Then there was Harold Abraham," Charley would tell Hank, "who was beaten in the prelims so readily, that I looked to the others in the contest to compete with. But he had whatever drives a man to beat me by a step, even when he knew I had the talent and records. It sure was an admirable lesson for me on passion and the calling of faith in this divine providence that would rule the day."

Charley would share more than stories about winning in sports with Hank; he'd also talk about winning outside of the arena—about business, for instance, and how to maintain his image and flair. Hank was often entertained by Charley's stories about the Paris nightlife, such when he met the icon of the Moulin Rouge, Helen de Garonne, after a remarkable performance. Charley and his friend joined Helen at her Paris apartment where she was entertaining a young English lad. When the lad left, Charley asked Helen who the fella was she had been visiting with. Helen laughed and answered, "You Americans, Mr. Paddock, have you no eyes or ears?"

"I guess not," Charley said.

"Of course not. That was the young Prince of Whales, silly. You see, when you're a celebrity, socialites want you around to keep the conversation going. But take my advice, Charley, don't overstay your visits because too much will slip away and you won't be invited back again."

One day on USC's track in the spring of 1923, however, Charley was curious about one of Hank's stories. "Hank, you know there are rumors you knocked out Ray Price defending a Mexican girl. Is that so?"

Hank chuckled. "Well yes. But I think Mr. Price underestimated my boxing past with my father back in Douglas. He put his guard down and that was that."

Charley laughed and told Hank, "I met Price once in a Kappa Alpha chapter house some time back. He seemed nice, but a little too assertive. Well done, Hank. Now, let's stop the storytelling and get on with the work."

Charley would often ask Hank about other stories he had from Southeast Arizona, about Douglas, Bisbee, and Tombstone. Charley was also fascinated that "the Big 102 game must have been one of the most monumental Long Beach Poly games ever, with you coming from Arizona."

Charley seemed to love it when Hank explained, "Tierman and I scored so many points that we decided to play on the line and give our lineman a chance to score some touchdowns."

"Really? You did? So, what's coming out of Long Beach Poly these days?"

"Well, we got some all-round great players who followed me for the last two years, but remember this name: Morley Drury. He's a good one. Played a great game in the Everett loss."

"Wow! You got him here?"

"Sure enough, Chet Dolley talked him into coming to USC."

In between perfecting each other's athletic skills, the conversations between the two went on and on. Hank and Charley had quite a bit in common. Both were about the same age, and both came from unusual backgrounds—Charley had served a stint in the military, and Hank had, of course, an adventurous early life on the frontier along the Arizona borderline. Now, on USC's track field, they were friends with a common goal, which, of course, was to get Charley ready for the Olympics.

Hank and Charley's friendship lasted their lifetimes. Later, after USC, whenever their tracks would cross, they would spend time together sharing stories. Hank would tell others, "When Charley and I first became acquainted there at USC, he kind of mentored me. He'd already tasted the good and bad of heralded athletics. And from time-to-time he'd leak out some tidbits—or golden kernels—of wisdom. Like the time he told me what the first girl he ever kissed told him: 'Charley, they will praise you as a hero as long as you win. When that time is no longer, they will forget you in a minute and move on. So, Charley, prepare yourself for your life after the running.'" Hank took that to heart, knowing how true that was about fans and remembering his decision to let Cristina go back to Mexico without him on that star-filled night back in Long Beach.

Hank also never forgot another of Charley's mantras: "All good athletes do their best to save the moment. They rise to the occasion when everything is on the line. Like you, Hank. Coach Cromwell tells me where Hank Lefebvre goes, the team wins. Think about it, Hank. It's true."

Charley would also often become philosophical or theological. He put his biblical scholar hat on when he said, "Hank, I've learned so many things about people, what got them to where they are and what made them what they are. And I've found that there is something to be said about that divine providence that Eric Liddell talked about." Hank continued to think on this thought on many a night, eventually deciding it might be so. Anyway, it made more sense to him than lighting candles, as his ma always did. To believe God took notice of those burning sticks of ten-cent wax required a lot of faith. Hank thought he must have some of this providence that Charley talked about, and it must come from God. Yet he also realized to become partners with God would require some kind of human response, and that we must prepare ourselves to do our best to make that important occasion work out best for the both of them. Hank would smile when he'd add, "Hey, that's the best I can come up with."

Hank's conversations about his good friend Charley Paddock always ended with the same finale: "You know, one day, after we'd just finished training on the track with Coach

Cromwell, Coach, holding on to the stopwatch, said, 'By gum Charley, you put up good times today.' Charley smiled and said, 'Well there you go, Coach. What do they say about me in those newspapers? That Charley Paddock is the fastest man in the world?' Then Charley turned to me and said, 'Think about it, Hank. Since I'm reported to be the fastest man in the world in the 100 and 200 meters, then that must mean you are the fastest man in the world in the 40 meters, because you beat me there all the time."

Hank would say, "Now, that really got me to laughing uncontrollably. I couldn't stop, so Charley said, 'Why is that so funny, Hank?' I told him, when I first came to Long Beach Poly's PE class, Coach Capron said he thought I was fast. I told him I was the fastest boy in the world. Coach Capron probably thought I was stretching it. But I guess since it came from you Charley, it's finally true."

That gave Hank had his favorite lifetime story. He'd start out by saying, "Did I ever tell you the story about what Charley Paddock told me one day, while we worked out on the USC track?" It didn't matter if you said, "yeah, I've heard it all before," he'd just continue, as if he never heard your answer, always ending by saying, "Imagine Charley telling me that in front of Coach Cromwell," then he'd laugh and laugh every time he told it.

CHAPTER 27

AN OFFER YOU CAN'T REFUSE

Unforeseen but to a few, 1924 would become an epic year for USC's football program, and a defining one for Hank Lefebvre. Things started unraveling with the announcement of USC's schedule to play Cal Tech, Pomona, Nevada, Washington, Stanford, California, Arizona, and Idaho—in that order. The events that would transpire placed a lug nut, not only around USC's destiny, but also that of St. Mary's College—and push that year's Pacific Coast Conference into a row.

USC and Stanford's athletic departments had been building toward a confrontation over alleged PCC eligibility infractions. This time it was USC's questioning of the "amateur" status of Stanford's star player, Ernie Nevers. Stanford's coach, Glenn Scobey "Pop" Warner, had hailed Ernie Never as an outstanding football player, without fault. Warner countered the perceived criticism by questioning USC's recruiting practices, and in another apparent act of retaliation, on November 1, Stanford and Cal Tech announced they would sever athletic relations with USC at the end of the 1924 football season. USC reacted swiftly on November 3 by canceling their upcoming game with Stanford. Since this gave Stanford just five days to respond, this cancellation threw the Pacific Coast Football Conference into turmoil.

As the two schools frantically searched for opponents to play that weekend, rumors abounded—with little-known and uncelebrated St. Mary's mentioned as a possible foe for each. On November 4, Stanford announced their game against Utah, and on that same date, USC revealed Coach Slip Madigan had agreed to bring St. Mary's football team to Los Angeles. Coach Madigan likely saw this as a shot at the big time and wasn't going to let anything stop the Saints from boarding that train to LA. With his twenty-man squad, Madigan left the evening of November 6 toward a historic date with destiny.

On November 8, over 27,000 fans flocked to the Coliseum expecting an easy win for the Trojans. And after the second play of the game, when USC's Henry 'Hank' Lefebvre cut off a left tackle and set sail on an eighty-yard touchdown run to stun the Saints, this easy win looked certain. Later in the quarter the Trojans returned a punt for another score, but it was nullified by a penalty. Yet, enthusiastic USC fans continued to cheer for a rout. The momentum quickly changed, however. Perhaps due, in part, to over-confidence from the Trojan's early score, and in part to the stiff defense and strong offense by St. Mary's captain and fullback, Norman "Red" Strater, USC soon found itself fighting back furiously from a 14-10 deficit. Then, on the five-yard line with just seconds to go, USC gave the ball off to Lefebvre for a final plunge into the end zone for the win. To everyone's disbelief, however, he was stopped just inches from the goal line. The gun sounded on one of the most unbelievable college upsets of the day.

Although USC went on to post a 9-2 season—with the only other defeat from their nemesis, University of California, in a 0-7 thriller—Stanford got the pick to play in the 1924 Rose Bowl game against Notre Dame and their highly acclaimed Four Horsemen.

USC, much like Long Beach Poly a few years earlier, now had to become creative. They would not allow themselves to be upstaged by one upset and one close game against Cal Tech, and surely would not be upstaged by the caustic exchange within the Pacific Coast Conference. So what else to do but plan a Christmas Bowl game to be held in the new Los Angeles Coliseum on December 25, just six days prior to the Rose Bowl game in Pasadena.

USC would only need to entice a prominent, nationally recognized football team to take the bait. And they did. The Missouri Tigers, who came in with a 9-1 record, having played against some of the most prestigious Midwest teams available, agreed to play the post-season game. It seemed a stroke of genius for the Tigers, but once the game was set, Angelinos went into a frenzy. USC immediately took on the scathing of the local press, berating the Trojan's risky decision: "Be careful what you pray for because if you're demolished by the mighty Tigers and unable to beat either Cal or St. Mary's, well, then USC better get to practicing something new."

Bookies took and gave record-breaking odds, and fans set more bets than ever before. Hank confided with friends, "We know we're a good team, but playing Missouri seems much like when I played against those Everett Meat Eaters, where a turnover here and there could cost us the win and national recognition for future games."

Coach Henderson spoke about this to energize his team. "A lot is riding on this game. We can make no mistakes. We can't get down or overconfident like we did with St. Mary's. If we can do this, we'll win." He'd also taunt his players, "Execute, Execute, Execute! This game will be close!" he'd chant after every practice, much like Coach Kienholz did before the Big 102, "Right Hank?" he'd say after.

"Yeah, Coach. That's right!" And with that, the team

would cheer wildly as they roared out onto the Bovard practice field.

The team worked hard to prepare, and the days passed slowly until, finally, Christmas was less than a week away. That was when a precarious situation was pushed right into Hank's face. Hank had been going over and picking up his pa from Clifford's Pool Hall more often now. Henry's health was becoming increasingly worse, like dying without being sick. Ma had to depend on Hank taking the lead more than ever before. Oh, his sisters and younger brothers helped, but daily decisions that affected the family had to be made by Hank. His pa was in no condition to take on any more of the stress. One morning, Pa stopped Hank before he left for early practice. "Clifford Girard says if you got the time he'd like it if you'd come by the pool hall Monday the twenty-second, after five."

"Sure thing, Pa. What's it about?"

"I don't know, Son, but Clifford was just askin', so..."

"Don't worry, Pa. I'll be there."

When Hank arrived at Clifford's, he noticed a bunch of expensive, black cars in the parking lot—many more than usual, and especially for a Monday. He walked in gingerly and noticed the slow pace around the dimly lit room. There were few familiar faces at the unusually empty pool tables.

A voice behind him spoke up, "Listen, Hank. I got nothing to do with this." It was Clifford Girard. "You see, the boys come in and out. The mayor...all of them. So, as you know, they like to go upstairs, play out their luck and skill with a hand of poker. Now, Joey Ardizzone, you know him, Hank?"

"No sir. But Sonny Cardinale talks about him."

"Well then, you know his reputation."

"Kinda. I don't like being around that kind of trouble."

"This has to do with your pa. They want to talk to you upstairs. I don't know what for or what troubles your pa has with them. I don't ask no questions. What I hear stays inside theses walls and business is good. Prohibition has been good to me."

"Okay, got it. Upstairs?"

"Yeah, Hank. You know the way."

Hank stepped up the stairs slowly, one by one, much like he'd done before while getting his pa out of those games. At the top he noticed the door was closed and a grim, pin-stripe-suited fellow stood watch.

After looking Hank over, he said, "Hey kid. You must be Hank Lefebvre, the football player."

"Yes, that's me," Hank mumbled.

"The boss is waiting for you. Go on in," he said, while turning the doorknob.

A swish of cigar smoke choked his entrance. Once he could see well enough, Hank navigated to the round game table at the back of the room. He noticed all eyes watching him as he walked toward the man in the center, who looked to be duplicating a scene from the last supper. He had surrounded himself with a group of men who looked like pandering knuckleheads, all wearing hats that caved into their faces apparently attempting to disguise their identities. The man in the center welcomed Hank with a gesture and said, "Hey kid. Sit down. Have a seat." Hank looked around the table for an empty chair.

"Hey Paluka! Get up and let the kid sit down! Here…sit here, just across from me, huh?" the man said with a voice raised as if to scare the pigeons from the fish, and a guy across the table jumped up and offered his seat. Hank slowly set himself down and looked straight across the table at the man in charge. "You're a fine football player. I've seen you play…I don't know how many times. I'm Joey Ardizzone. You've heard of me, no?"

"Yes."

"From who? Sonny Cardinale?"

"Yes."

Joey gave a short smirk and continued, "Well then, now that we've been introduced, I'd like you to think of me as your friend. I'm going to make you a very lucrative offer that could help your family out. You see, I know, after another year playing football, what's left for you? There's no money in the pros, your pa's health is terrible, and soon you're going to have to pay the bills around the house. So, like I said, I'm a great football fan. Right fellows?"

They answered in chorus to his prompt, "Right, boss!"

"You see, Hank, what I'd like to do is help you out, and, of course, get a little for me and the boys. This Christmas Bowl game is bringing in a lot of cash bets. I plan to make a killing on this game. Now, if we play our cards right, we—meaning the both of us—can make a lot of dough here. All you have to do is fumble the ball here and there to give us the edge in the game. You do that, we'll all make out. And after this game, and when college life is over for you, you'll have a big nest egg to start up on. It's that simple. What do you say to that, champ?"

Hank, with his back to the corner, tried to find an answer to evade the situation, a way to simply leave unscathed from the smoky comradery of these mobsters, knowing all too well their dangerous appetites.

"Well, what's your answer?" Joey asked again, sounding this time like he was coming short of losing his temperament.

"I don't know, sir."

"You don't know? Kid, this is a chance of a lifetime! And you don't know! Okay. Here it is kid. Sammy, let me see the note." A man next to him passed over a folded piece of paper.

"Hank, you know what I have in my hand here?"

"No sir. I don't."

"Well, let me tell you. It's an IOU signed by your pa…

some hundreds of dollars he lost in a poker game here with one of the boys who owed me money. Now, I got it. I need to collect from your pa, you see. And you know and I know, he hasn't got a penny to spend—not a nickel!" Joey lowered his voice to make his point. "Now, this issue can all go away—plus you make money—if you play ball with us. You see. It's simple, right?"

"Yeah, simple."

"I heard about you and your play. You're a tough family, but not here. Maybe in Douglas, but not here in LA. Joey Ardizzone runs things here. Okay!"

"Okay. I got it. Now can I go?" Hank asked.

It became deadly quiet as Hank felt Joey search his eyes for confirmation that he understood the plan. With a wave of his hand, Joey said, "Of course you can go, kid." As Hank walked toward the door, Joey called out, "Now remember, we're betting on you. And if you don't come around, we'll be around, right after the game. Either way…it's your choice. We'll be giving you money or collecting on this paper here. Capiche?"

Hank nodded his understanding, then proceeded down the stairs. Clifford met him at the bottom. "Hank, again, this is not my play."

"I know, Mr. Girard. It's Pa's and mine. Anyway, this isn't our first rodeo, and it won't be our last. We've been here before. It'll all be fine. No need for you to worry about us."

"Thanks for the understanding," Clifford said.

Hank went straight home.

"Mama, where's Pa?"

"I sent him to the store. He should be back soon. Why?"

"Oh, it's nothing, Mama."

With a voice that said she knew better, his ma said, "I'll let you and Pa talk it out, when he gets back."

Hank went to his room to think and found Doris Mae's unopened letter waiting on his bed. He tore at the seal and went out to the front porch swing to read. Though she couldn't have known when she wrote it—her letter gave Hank exactly what he was looking for…answers: *"Hank, always try and do what's right. If you're not sure of the right and wrong of it, weigh the consequences. Ask yourself, is it okay to do this? If there is a bit, even a teeny-weeny doubt that it's wrong, don't do it. There are lots of hurdles and crosses to carry in life, but that's what builds character."*

Pa walked up the steps then holding onto grocery bags.
"What's up?"
"I—"
"Hold it right there, Son. Let me give these to your mama and be right back." When he returned, he asked, "So, what's on your mind?"
"Pa, I went to Mr. Girard's today and met Joey Ardizzone and his men. Joey wanted me to help him get an edge in the Missouri game, 'cause Joey's been placing a lot of bets on the game."
"Well, what did you say to that, Hank?"
"I told him I needed to leave and have some time to think about it. But I just wanted to get out of there."
"What have you decided to do since you've had some time to think about it, Hank?"
"Pa, you know what I'll do. But that Joey Ardizzone says if I don't go along with him, he'd be holding some IOU's from your gambling debts and he'll get someone…Pa, he'll come to collect on you."
Pa gave out a hearty laugh as he sat down next to Hank on the swing. "Really? Joey Ardizzone said that! Well now, let me tell you something. Remember back in Douglas, the day I thrown that fight and ended up getting the Ham Radio for the family?"

"Yeah, Pa. I remember."

"You asked me about my honor? I said, 'Look what I got for the family.' No one cared. They just be betting for greed or pleasure at the fight. Hank, it's not about the praising or honor. No son, it's only about family. The rest is nothing but pride. The bible says pride is the beginning of a man's fall. Mind you. I've been prideful many a day and believe me, Hank. I've had some mighty big falls."

Hank smiled. "Pa, this be the first time I heard you cite from the bible."

"See, Hank. I did spend some time with your mama going to church before we been married. She'd always be saying, 'Henry you be fighting too much for pride and honor. Those are just flattering words, they mean nothing and surely don't pay the bills.'" They both laughed. "But she was right, Hank. What you lose in the ring or what you throw on the table or leave at the betting window at the track or playing odds on football games...that be flattery and greed. Some men do most anything to be praised or make money. It plays on a man's mind. But, that's all you. Don't mean nothing, just words, and words are always negotiable. That's all, Son. It's how you handle the situation on the inside, that's what really counts, 'cause, that inside struggle is what defines your character. Now that's not something a man can bargain with."

"I know what you're trying to say, Pa, but what about... they be coming after you?"

"Son, I've been intimidated all of my life. That's the frontier way. From the blasting for gold in Pearce, to working those creaky mines in Bisbee, to the smelters in Douglas, and the prizefighting just to make an extra dollar to keep the family afloat. I'm here today, aren't I? Joey Ardizzone may break a few bones. Sure, it'll hurt for a few days, but he will never curse my soul. That'll carry me to my grave. You got that

Hank? For certain. You got that straight, Hank?" They both laughed again. Hell, Hank, did I ever tell you the story about my misfortune at poker that led old Johnny Ringo to come lookin' for me, just before me and Uncle Joseph was leaving Pearce?"

"I reckon not, Pa."

"Well, Johnny found me and I said, 'Johnny Ringo, I be much younger than you, but my honor is as big as yours. You can beat me to a pulp, kill me, but all you'll have is nothing. You ain't getting even a penny by wrangling out my poor pockets, except maybe prison time or a hangin'. But, you can trust on my honor that if my luck gets better, I'll pay you back every lick I owe yah.'

"Now Johnny, he hesitates then says, 'can't get water from this cactus. Henry Lefebvre, shucks I don't need that kind of a problem.' He starts to walk away, but then turns back to say, 'If your luck gets better, yeah, I'd much appreciate the repaying of my debt.'"

"Really, Pa? Johnny Ringo said that?"

"Son, I swear, that's the dying truth. Just ask your mama. What I'm saying, Hank, is go out and beat the Missouri Tigers, give them the best you can and all you got. Remember, you got a lot of Lefebvres here in California and Arizona depending on you."

With that problem put to rest for the moment, Hank had only one bit of concern. It was personal. For Miss Lillian Ludlow was less interested in the Christmas Bowl game and more interested in the vendor at the Long Beach Pike bringing up the question of Cristina. He assured her that it was just a high school sweetheart. Even asking if she didn't have one in high school? She did, and they both got a laugh out of that. So they got back on track, talking about all the publicity and outrageous interest in the Christmas Bowl.

Hank might have fooled Lillian about Cristina, but he could never fool himself. For every time her name came up, a hurt took over Hank, then a regret, then a wondering of "what might have been" seeded his thoughts. He'd always reconcile that maybe someday that providence thing would magically work its way for them. But for now, it had other things left to untie.

Henry 'Hank' Lefebvre

CHAPTER 28

THE 1924 CHRISTMAS BOWL

The stage was set. There would be no more formidable task to face during the early days of USC football. All was on the line. They'd rebutted the Pacific Coast Conference over allegations of recruiting and eligibility tampering. They even had the audacity to shun their suspension by upstaging the Rose Bowl's season climax by inventing a Christmas Festival Bowl game. The venue: the new Los Angeles Coliseum, right in USC's backyard. And—to top it off—they had persuaded one of the most talented teams out of middle America, the Missouri Tigers, as their rival.

To further raise speculation and intrigue for the upcoming season finale, it was rumored that the USC booster's enthusiasm for Coach Gus "Gloomy" Henderson had soured. The fifth consecutive loss to the University of California was enough to place his head on a platter, and if his underdog, the underperforming yet talented Trojans took another demoralizing and embarrassing defeat in front of a national crowd like they had earlier in the season against St. Mary's, Gus would find his coaching stint at USC coming to an abrupt end.

As for Hank, it would be an understatement to say that the pressure was personal. Even though it was never publicized nor reported that certain reputed Los Angeles mobsters had begun to take an unusual interest in collegiate football, attempts to tamper with players of Hank's stature, in the hopes of affecting the scoring odds, were becoming all too common. And, if matters couldn't be worse, history was about to come around again for Hank.

Just like the Everett game years earlier at Poly, the *Los Angeles Times* acknowledged Hank's predicament in its December 19, 1924 edition. The lead read: "LEFEBVRE ON INJURED LIST." Reporter Braven Dyer wrote:

> Coach Gus Henderson drove his USC gridders through a stiff workout last night in preparation for the Christmas Day game with Missouri at the Coliseum, and Lefebvre, the bounding halfback, was not among those present. 'Laffy' was on the field, but he wasn't in a uniform, and a football player in civilian clothes is of about as much use as a book on etiquette is to a Fiji Island cannibal. The hard-hitting ball carrier will not be able to don a 'unie' until the day of the game because of injuries received in the Syracuse scrap, and that means the Trojans are going to be rather severely handicapped against the Tigers from the snow-bound Middle West.

Henderson wasted no time mourning when Lefebvre reported with instructions to let his injured shoulder rest, and immediately shoved Bill Cook into Laffy's position at halfback during practices.

The night before the game, while he huddled with his family, all seemed in an upbeat mood. Not so for Hank, but he hid his deception well as he thought about the win-lose or a lose-win outcome that lay ahead. Unlike the night before the Everett game, this situation was unbelievably complicated and the response could be much more ominous. Most trying to Hank was the fact that, besides his dad and himself, every other member of the family was left out of the loop. Not even his girlfriend Lillian was clued in. He'd decided that disclosing the dilemma would create more problems and expose his father to unnecessary ridicule. As the day of the game closed in, thousands of tickets had already been sold, and a nation of football pundits had taken their stories to print.

On the morning of the game, Forrest found Hank resting on the locker room floor. He sat down beside his friend. "Laffy, this is like déjà vu."

Hank laughed and said, "You got that right."

"Except the stakes just seem to get higher and higher."

"Not really, Forrest. Just the characters have changed."

Switching subjects, Hank quickly asked, "Forrest, you ever think about Syriana?"

"What do you mean, Hank?"

"Oh, just how things might've worked out if…"

"No, not really, 'cause we were different then. We were…"

"Go on, Forrest. Say what's on your mind."

"Hank, you already went there. Can't get the toothpaste back in the container. I mean…"

"Maybe so, maybe not, Forrest. Have we really changed that much? Cristina and I had something special. Maybe we just had to work out our differences. She wanted the farm, and me…I looked forward to other challenges, and there have been so many, one after another."

"How long will you go on, Hank?"

"As long as it will take me. Until one day football will end when I don't become part of the winning. The challenge of winning game after game isn't what's bothering me, though. It's all the garbage you pick up on the way. That's when I start thinking about that farm in Mexico. Or, the Douglas life that was simple, exciting, demanding, but not because of the crowd's pleasure, but the pleasure you get inside. You don't get that here."

"What about days like today, Hank? Isn't it worth it?"

"Yes, but it's not all about me. Here it's about them out there...what they get from all this. Are we giving up too much of ourselves just for the game? We love the game, but do they... really? 'We're number one!' They yell, and never actually play the game."

"Hank, I think a better way to look at it is, this game will be even more pivotal for USC and how it allows the university to grow and the educational opportunities that USC's growth will offer others."

Hank chuckled and said, "Damn, Forrest. You should become a preacher."

"That's a good one, Hank. Me a preacher, yeah right."

Just then Coach Henderson walked in holding his clipboard up in the air. "Okay, let's gather together. Round it up."

When the team had circled the wagon, Gus stood in the middle and began. "I can't tell you how important this game is for the future of USC's football program. Hell, all our sports programs. We've kind of put ourselves out on a limb here. This Missouri team is good, real good. And we can't let them get an early lead...let this one get away from us."

He paused to look over at Hank. "Now, Laffy, I've been talking to your high school coach, Eddie Kienholz. He said the problem he had with Everett was he let them get ahead too early by turnovers. And he also said 'I should have played Lefebvre earlier in the game, not when we had to come from behind.' So Laffy, how's that shoulder?"

"Should give you at least a good half of the game or more, Coach."

"Good. I knew you would say something like that 'cause

all we need is to get a good start in the first half. So, Cook, you'll get some of the glory in the second half. Now, all the rest of you healthy guys need to play the game of your life. Remember, the pain you live through today on that field will last just a couple of days, but the pain of failing out there today will last a lifetime. USC will always talk about how you play out there today. Good or bad, it's your choice. This is quite a unique day, and gentlemen, let me say one more thing: This game is more personal than others because I believe it will be my last game as your coach."

Gus raised his hands to quiet the low groans and hushed murmurs. "You've been reading newspapers, I'm sure. So, I ask you, make my last run out of that tunnel a memorable one. I would be most appreciative of that. Just give them your best, boys, and I know we'll come out as winners. Okay then, are we ready?"

When the Trojans ran out the tunnel into a stadium of 47,000-plus fans, a roar went out that could be heard from miles away. The California sun shone bright with enough chill in the air to make it a perfect day for an epic game. Straight from the first kick-off, the USC Trojans took charge, letting Missouri know they were in a fight.

Braven Dyer would write the next morning in his column:

> It was Lefebvre who carried the brunt of the Trojan attack in that game with Missouri. It was Henry 'Hank' Lefebvre who dashed and smashed his way through the Tiger line. It was Lefebvre who ran the visiting ends goofy with his dynamic bursts of speed inside and outside of the wing positions. It was Lefebvre who dazzled the Bengals with his running back of kick-offs. In short, it was Lefebvre all the way through

until he was injured and removed, late into the third quarter when the game was well in USC hands. USC won, with touchdowns by Lefebvre, Badgro Pythian, and Pat Hawkins. By settling that issue with Missouri on Christmas day in the Coliseum, USC posted one of its biggest wins in its history."

A wild celebration overtook the locker room, but all went silent and came to a standstill when Coach Gus Henderson walked in. He spoke of his gratitude for all the players who played for him, especially this year with all its ups and downs. His voice quivered. This would be his last time in this locker room as head coach of the team. After he finished, John Hawkins, the team captain, spoke up. "Coach, we want you to know, all of us here, that the win was for you. Then he handed over the game ball. Gus held it tight, looked at all the teammate's signatures, and teared up. Unable to speak, he nodded his appreciation and turned to walk out of locker room door. Then the cheers and celebrations began again.

This was not the emotional crescendo of the night but more of a ritual for the changing of the guard. The team knew the next time someone came through that door and took charge with their clipboard in hand, it would be a new head coach—trained and ready to lead the team toward its promising future. A blend of excitement cozied up with a sense of consternation and floated about the locker room as the players showered and dressed for what promised to be a festive evening back on campus.

But not for Hank. Winning the game left him vulnerable to a sinister mob lurching outside somewhere—one that held a dire and direct relationship to his and his family's well-being. He wished the problem would just pass away, but he knew it wouldn't. There would be a reckoning. Unfortunately, though

Uncle Joseph's influence had managed to quell it some, Hank's temperament would still often draw him toward spontaneous and explosive responses, a bleak contrast to his ma's constant reminder to follow the biblical admonition to be 'slow to anger.'

The sun had gone down on the remarkable afternoon, and when Hank and Forrest were about to leave the Coliseum locker room, Phil Tierman and Chet Dolley came over to congratulate Hank on his play. They told more stories and relived the Big 102 game they'd played together five years earlier. Eventually the two of them peeled away, agreeing to meet up on campus later.

"Bringing Lillian?" Chet asked.

"What do you think?" Hank answered then added, "God willing."

That remark didn't get much attention from Phil or Chet as they said their good byes and rushed out of the locker room, leaving Forrest and Hank alone.

As Hank started to zip up his athletic bag, Forrest asked, "God Willing? What's that all about?"

"I know what you're going to say, 'what's the matter?', right? Well, Forrest, let me just say that it has nothing to do with you. Just stay out of this. Trust me. I've got a handle on it."

"It's that bad?"

"Well, it could be. Then again it might just go away or play itself out. Now, when we leave the locker room, if anything happens on our way back to campus, just go on your way."

"Why? What's going to happen?"

"Listen to me, Forrest. I'm serious. Just go on your way. I'll be going home to sit for a while with the family before I make it over to the parties."

"Okay, Hank. You'll fill me in later?"

"Right, buddy. Will do. I promise. Now, let's get out of here."

As they were leaving, a janitor said, "You'd best get going quickly now 'cause they might lock the gate at the end of the tunnel soon…not much lighting…security has already left, and its gets dark in that tunnel."

Hank and Forrest breached the locker room door and stepped out into the cold December night. The dim light at the top of the tunnel encouraged them to move quickly.

"Walk softly and slow. Don't talk until we get pass the gate," Hank said. Hank couldn't help but quicken his steps as they closed in on the gate.

"Better stop, Forrest," Hank whispered.

Hank heard the scratch, then saw the light of a match in the darkness. It gave off just enough light to reveal the silhouette of a man wearing a hat. His cigarette glowed and then suddenly a bright flashlight turned toward them. "Let's go, Forrest. Walk fast, but don't run. It'll give us away," he whispered.

They put their heads down and slipped through the crack in the gate. "Hold it there, fellas!" a man called out. Forrest and Hank froze when he added, "Is by chance one of you Hank Lefebvre?"

"Yeah. That be me," Hank yelled back.

"Who's that with you?"

"Just a friend."

The man who seemed to be in charge said, "Okay boys. Let the other one go. Kid, we don't have no dealings with you. Lefebvre, you come with me."

Forrest looked at Hank. "No, Forrest. Get on now. This is not your fight." When Forrest hesitated, Hank added, "Now go!"

The man walked up to Hank. "Come on, Lefebvre. Someone wants to have a conversation with you."

Hank could now make out three men wearing overcoats

gathered behind him, and then they walked him over to the far corner of the parking lot toward three parked cars. The interior of one car lit up, revealing more men inside puffing away on their tobacco. The men led Hank to one of the cars and opened the back door. A familiar voice spoke in a surprisingly friendly manner. "Come on in and have a seat. We've got to talk."

"Yes sir, we do," Hank replied and slid next to Joey Ardizzone in the back seat.

"Hank, I thought we were partners. You know, I put some big dough on today's game. We could have been happy lugs tonight, and your pa's debts…hell, I'd be tearing them IOU's up right now. But it seems you didn't want to play it that way. So Hank. What do I got to do to convince you to go along with me? I don't want to rough your pa up, but what choice do I have? Can you help me out here…or if not me, your pa?" he said, his friendly tone now changed into outright and deranged anger.

Hank baited him anyway, "So, how could I do that now, Mr. Ardizzone?"

"Kid, it's easy. Just, from here on, play ball with us. We can make the dough back on next year's games."

"I'm sorry, sir. Not tonight, not next year, not ever. My pa might have a gambling problem. He likes to win. But he has his good name and it's been too long in the making to give in to your kind. I won't let you destroy him that way, or me. You're messing with the wrong *hombres, señor.*"

"Wooooo. Hey, boys! You hear this kid! He thinks he's back in Douglas with some of his posse around to back him up. But I keep telling you, you're in LA now and this is Joey Ardizzone territory. So, what you going to do, write letters to those frontier friends with six shooters?" he said as he laughed.

Now, if timing has anything to do with luck or providence

has anything to do with the boldness of a man's behavior, then the events that were about to unfold proved both of those theories out. Right then, four cars screamed across the grass and shone their headlights on Joey's front windshield. Ardizzone's men were surprised, and they stiffened as car doors flew open and men jumped out brandishing long weapons. Behind the men, glaring lights continued to focus on Ardizzone's men and cars.

A voice, loud and clear, said, "Hold it boys! We've come here to talk. Back down or we're going to have a blood bath here for no reason. Okay? We just want to talk to Joey—to reason with him. Not start a war. Okay?"

Then he shouted, "Joey, you got that?"

"Yeah. I got that. Boys, let's hear him out," Joey called. When the man came closer to the car, he raised his hands to show Joey's men he was clean.

"Open the door," the man ordered.

Joey nodded approval to his men.

The voice said to Hank, "Stay calm, Son. Let the game play its way out." Then he turned and said, "Hey, Joey. It's me, Rocco. You see, Sonny got news of the problem here just a few hours ago. He's taken an interest in the kid and his pa. Sonny says no need to get crazy over this thing. You lost some money tonight. So, Sonny says to tell you, he'll cover your losses on the game. Just send a man over and it will be done. Now, if you don't see things that way and that's too much trouble, he'll wire it over to fix things and make it right. Your decision, but there's no need for nobody to get hurt here. Let the kid go, and his pa."

"So, Rocco, what's this got to do with Sonny? Why, did I mess up his hair over this?"

I'm not sure, Joey, but Sonny says to tell you this is personal, the kid's family."

"Oh, so Sonny's getting sentimental these days?"

"I wouldn't rely on that, Joey. But remember he's gone legit these days."

"So, what you're saying, Rocco, is—"

"Sonny wants this to end tonight. Capiche? No harm. You'll get your money." Dead silence took over the situation, as Joey turned and looked out the side window. The tension could be cut with a knife as everyone, especially Hank and Rocco, waited patiently for an answer.

Finally, Joey turned to Rocco and said, "You know, I don't like this much…Sonny doing this. But, okay, as long as everything is settled. And Rocco, if you ever want to make some real money—"

"I know, Joey. No dice. I'm fine where I'm at."

Then Joey looked at Hank and told him, "Next time I'll bet on you, kid." Hank didn't say anything as he stepped out of the car, but Joey continued, "Kid, it was just business… that's all. Okay, boys. Let's get out of here." Slowly, Joey's cars moved back and then screeched down the street, leaving tire treads on the payment.

After watching them disappear into the night, Hank got in the car with Rocco. "Tough night, huh Hank?"

Hank took a deep breath and said, "You bet."

Both men laughed, then Hank asked, "How did Sonny know?"

"You got Clifford Girard to thank for that. He slipped the word to Sonny after some drunk mug loosed up his tongue and told him what went down on the upstairs meeting. So, where can I drop you off?"

"A block away…don't want the family to know…might embarrass Pa. No need for that. His health is enough to worry about." Rocco did what was asked, stopping the car one block away.

When he stepped out, Hank said, "Thanks, Rocco."

"No problem, kid."

"And, please tell Sonny—"

"Tell him yourself, kid. He'd like that. Oh, and hey kid, the guys love your play, even Tony Valachi."

"Really?"

"Yeah him too. He's doing his best to keep on the right side of you, now that you're some kind of celebrity."

"Thanks again Rocco, and stay out of the reach of that overhand right."

Rocco chuckled, then rolled up the window and sped off.

CHAPTER 29

SHOWTIME

After that night's menacing drama, Hank turned his attention back to family obligations—especially now that his dad's health wasn't getting any better—as well as a few other prospects.

It was funny how this thing called "networking" had played out its hand in Hank's life. In Douglas he'd met Sonny Cardinale, then later landed a job with him; his pa had made friends with Roger the train conductor, who sent him to Clifford's Pool Hall where a friendship with Clifford Girard was formed when they learned they had both been fighters. The Big 102 Poly game had also opened several doors for Hank and led to his invitation to USC where he met Charley Paddock and Coach Cromwell, and those connections led to Hank landing a job in the movies. Douglas Fairbanks and Mary Pickford were ardent fans of USC and traveled extensively so as not to miss USC's athletic events. So, it was natural that much of the movie industry's summer hiring jobs went to aspiring USC athletes.

Hank remembered Charley Paddock's wise words: "You're only as good as when you are winning, and a good athlete only has about five years to make the most of it." Therefore, like so many other USC protégées, Hank intended to use his football celebrity to catapult himself into a future career at

Hollywood's movie studios. Some of Hank's teammates at USC were Marion Morrison (John Wayne) and linebacker Ward Bond, all introduced to the studio business by USC's upcoming head football coach, Howard Jones. These football players became grips and gofers, running around, passing out scripts and carrying props. Sometimes they were extras, or even stuntmen. Now, this may not be what you'd call "making it in the movies," but since many athletes were big fans of the silent movie stars, they had great fun working around personalities such as Charlie Chaplin, Buster Keaton, and of course—the gourmet of romance—Rudy Valentine. There was also the prurient glamor of it all, with beautiful females flaunting their wares about town, aggressively looking for a path to be discovered.

That's where Hank intended to be, right at the trailhead. It didn't take long for him to be quite well-known in and around the studios, famous for telling stories about his adventures. Once the movies changed from silent to speaking, a new cast of characters took over and Hank spoke of the fun he had being on first-name bases with the likes of Ronald Reagan, Cary Grant, Humphrey Bogart, and even Greta Gable. But it was those budding actresses who seemed to comprise most of Hank's social life. Meanwhile, Miss Lillian Ludwig's personal ambitions in Hollywood also grew keenly during her senior year at USC.

In 1925, Hank seemed to have everything in place when Doris wrote him again, summing up the Lefebvre family equation:

> *Hank, you probably know that since your father took you all to California, Grandpa Joseph has been sending your mother money when you came up short needing tuition or such. You be-*

came a football star at USC and your brothers, like you, I hear are becoming very successful. Now you've become involved in the movie and entertainment industry because of your talent and are famous. We read about you in the newspapers all the time and your brother Alfred, the acrobat, he'll be traveling around the world performing and what we hear is your other brothers may follow in your footprints. Somewhere out here, we've got the notion that our California Lefebvres are snobbish and don't want anything to do with the poor Arizona Lefebvres. I keep telling our family here in Arizona it's not really so. It would be fun someday to get both sides together. It's a shame that the family has been split up for such a long time.

That leads me into what I wanted to tell you about my brother, Charley Jr. As I wrote before, he's big for his age, and a great musician. He can play several instruments good, especially the sax. He looks like a movie star, but he's also great at baseball. And you know how our family loves baseball, just like yours. So, Grandpa said he's going to send Charley Jr. to a baseball school in Los Angeles to get some professional coaching. It's at a baseball clinic held right there at USC, under the guidance of your coach, Dean Cromwell. They promise he'll be chaperoned in the USC dorms.

As I mentioned before, Grandpa says his good friend, Congressman Carl Hayden, will sponsor Charley Jr. for an appointment to West Point once he gets out of high school. He's so smart, athletic and musical. Everyone loves him and he's a big hit with the girls from Tombstone High as well as here at home on Fort Huachuca. We go to all his baseball games and my dad is so excited for him. I told dad that if Charley Jr. goes to California, maybe you could show him around town. Hank, he would be thrilled and so would we. Hope you can make that happen.

Love, your cousin, Doris Mae

Hank was inclined to help anyone who took the effort to become somebody, but after all he'd heard from Doris Mae, he'd become exceptionally sentimental about Charley Jr. Hank was proud of Charley's efforts back home and his dedication to travel all the way from his neighborhood in Southeast Arizona to improve himself and knew he'd love to spend time with him.

In Hank's mind, there was always something more for him back in Arizona. He never wanted to leave what his past had taught him, and realized that Douglas, Tombstone, and Bisbee values would never be mainstream in California. Time stood still in his birth place and, the way he saw it, that was a good thing. When Charley arrived in Los Angeles, Hank knew a part of his frontier past and those Arizona values would arrive with him, fresh, and the idea both comforted and excited him.

As the train rolled into the station, a glassy, sprite-eyed teenager peered out the train window at a crowded collage of buildings and people, all choreographed to nonstop noise with no musical attraction. The air's scent had slowly changed flavors some miles out of Arizona, to one no longer as fresh. As the train came to a halt at the station, the teenager's attention fell upon a person waving to nobody in particular. When the passengers extracted themselves on to the platform, one of the guys Charley Jr. had befriended on the trip tapped him on the shoulder and said, "Look. That man has a sign that reads 'Lefebvre.'" Charley looked over toward a well-dressed man with his tie squarely in place—and a fine top hat to boot—holding a sign. A young, beautiful damsel hung about his arm with a smile that upstaged the spring air.

Could that really be his cousin Hank? He must have wondered. It had been such a long time, and Charley had been so young the last time they saw each other. Charley hesitantly approached his famous relative and Hank's bubbly personality overrode all awkwardness as he corralled his cousin with a big hug, then pushed him back to take another look.

"My God, you've grown," Hank told him. Then Hank turned to Lillian and said, "This is my cousin, Charley Jr. Charley, this is Miss Lillian."

She smiled and held out her hand. In doing so, Charley, who'd looked fatigued by the fright of the big city, now looked more comfortable, and soon became animated.

Hank's calling card always made people feel special. And no doubt, Hank had considered what could be going through Charley's mind as a young teenager, rolling into this strange place—the same one he and his family had rolled into some nine years earlier. Hank told Charley Jr. that he'd talked to those in charge of the five-day baseball clinic, and they'd given him the okay to pick him up and take him over to campus, and that after the orientation and practice session was done tomorrow, Hank would be his guide to the sights around Southern California.

Lillian slid into the back seat and Charley Jr. sat up front with Hank. As they got on their way, Hank said, "Yep, Lillian, my cousin Doris wrote me that Charley here loves baseball, and that he's smart in school, like me."

"Well, I won't hold that against you, Charley," Lillian said with a laugh.

Charley Jr. smiled back and added, "And music."

"So, here's what we're going to do," Hank said, taking charge, "first, we'll check Charley here into the dorm and get him acquainted with the campus. Then when he's squared away, we'll take him to meet what his family calls, 'the California clan of Lefebvres, the snobbish bunch,'" Hank teased.

Charley, hopefully you'll find out we're not that way at all. Just busy going about making ends meet. Much like they do back home in Fort Huachuca. After your practice tomorrow, we'll head off to Long Beach to see the Pike. Hey Charley, you've heard about the Pike?"

"Some," Charley Jr. answered.

"The monster roller coaster. You in for it?" Hank asked.

"You bet, cousin," Charley Jr. answered eagerly.

"Okay then, the day after that, we're going to drive just a short way out to what they call 'The Ranch.' You'll get to see a Hollywood movie being filmed."

"Really?"

"Did I say we were?"

"Yes, you did," Charley Jr. agreed.

"Then it's done. Lillian is into acting and her friend Gladys is playing a part in a Western. You'll be able to meet her, plus see what we USC athletes do for extra money when there's time.

"Next, we'll travel over to Santa Monica and visit a famous beach where it's popular to hang out. Lots of Hollywood connected people live there along the coast, all the way up to Malibu. If there's enough time we'll have you sit in on one of my football practices over on the Bovard Field.

"On your last night in town, we have tickets close up to see Rudy Vallée at the famous Palomar Ballroom on Vermont Street. And, due to my celebrity status, by which my prospects are failing each day thanks to our new coach, Howard Jones, but no matter…" Hank laughed, "just maybe, you'll be allowed to sit in on one of the band's sets. Hope you're ready for that! So, Charley, what do you think about them apples?"

Charley didn't speak. Not only were the prospects of the next few days likely more than a boy from a remote corner of Arizona could hope for, but his favorite and famous cousin would be taking time to personally show him around!

And show him around he did. First, it was on to the USC campus, where Lillian took care of Charley Jr.'s arrangements at the dorm, informing him of the schedule and rules, and making introductions with the staff. Second, the three of them strolled about the campus where Hank and Lillian gave Charley Jr. little chance to be bored. After they walked across the park to the entrance of the Coliseum tunnel, a security guard greeted Hank handsomely. "Hey Lefebvre, how you doing? So, what's going on with this Howard Jones guy? He's nuts. You playing as a guard?"

"We'll see. Hey Stan, this is my cousin, Charley Jr. Don't ask me if he's a first, third or whatever, but he's a junior like me, Charley Jr. I'd like to show him the Coliseum. He's from Fort Huachuca, Arizona…goes to school in Tombstone."

"Where Wyatt Earp hung out?"

"Yep. That's the place."

"Well, welcome, Charley Jr."

Hank patted Charley on the back and said, "I'd like to show him where all this notorious USC football takes place."

"Sure Hank, go on in. Only the grounds keepers around."

As they walked down the darkened tunnel, Hank stopped a moment to tell Charley, "That's our locker room, behind that door." They continued down the tunnel until the bright sun blinded them for a few seconds, then walked across the running track onto the lush green football field.

On the fifty-yard line, Hank yelled, and an echo sounded about the empty stadium. "This is where it all happens Charley. Right here. What do you think?"

Charley was short on words and high on the vision as he did a 360 to take it all in. "So, this is it. You, Hank, playing right here?"

"Yep, Charley. Right here."

"Well, I'll be," Charley whispered.

Lillian added, "Yeah, and you know, Charley. Hank's never brought me out here."

"Really? You've never been in here before?"

"Oh, I've seen all of his games from up there in the student body section, but not here…especially when thousands of people are screaming and flaying about after each play."

"Okay, you two novices, let's get going. Lots more to see. We need to let Lillian go to her voice and acting class. She's telling me that the future of movies will be talkies."

"Really. You don't say."

"Yep. That's inside information you can take home with yah. Now, go on Lillian. Charley and I have a bunch of Lefebvres waiting at home anxious to greet him."

After leaving the stadium and walking across the park, they said their goodbyes for the day. "See you tomorrow, Charley. Have a good clinic in the morning. Coach Dean Cromwell is a great 'maker of champions.'" She smiled, then moved on.

When Hank and Charley Jr. arrived at the steps of the Lefebvre house, the front door flung open and the family poured out. After lots of hugs and handshakes, they scrubbed out of Charley all the details about what was going on back in Arizona, then Ma called them inside. She'd fixed a fine tamale dinner with chili con carne, chips, and salsa. "I'll never be the cook as your mother, Maria Figueroa Lefebvre," she told Charley Jr., "but I want you to feel at home."

After dinner, they all sat out on the front porch and told favorite stories, all starting with, "did you know…or did you hear about…" When storytelling had run its course, it was time to take Charley Jr. back to the dorms. He'd had a long day and he had his baseball clinic early the next morning.

Hank got up at sunrise the next morning, dressed, told

Ma to forget breakfast, then ran over to the baseball venue to watch young Charley Jr. work out. When he arrived, the players were fully engaged. Each position had its specialty coach, guiding the boys through the intricacies of their position. One by one, boys were called into the cage for hitting evaluations. Once Charley's name was called, Hank found a seat in the stands, hoping not to draw attention. But just when it appeared to work, a voice called over.

"So, Hank, I see you there. What you looking at? Training to be a scout?"

"No, just had some extra time, that's all," Hank said with a smile.

When Charley got to the plate and belted a few out to left, Dean Cromwell looked at the roster and asked, "Say Hank, who's this kid, Charley Lefebvre? Some kin of yours?"

"Yep. A cousin, Charley Jr."

"Well from the look of it, he's got a family pedigree. In a couple of years, make sure we get him here."

"Sorry, Coach, I think his grandpa's got a plan to get him into West Point."

"Really?"

"Yeah, seems the Arizona Lefebvres have a military legacy."

"Well done. His grandpa must be a man of some importance in Arizona."

"Yes sir. Very important, knows all of those politicians and business types…has plenty of friends with pull."

After practice, Alfred and Lillian arrived and Hank took the group off to the Long Beach Pike. Hank narrated their journey down the coast while Charley kept his eye out for the infamous monster roller coaster. Once they entered the Pleasure Pier, the familiar hawking barkers called out to all passing by. "Throw these balls. Hit the milk cartons, and get your girl a prize, a teddy bear, something to hold dear, won by your champ."

Hank's notoriety being unforgettable, one of the barking gents called out, "Hey, Lefebvre, been awhile!"

"Couple of weeks," Hank said, smiling back.

The group walked over to the gent and he asked, "Who's this fine lad you have here with you today?"

"Charley Jr. He's my cousin."

"Well then, pay up, give him a chance to win a prize…see if he's a chip off the old block." They all laughed and Charley agreed to play.

"Okay, Charley. Do you think you can knock all those bottles off with three throws of those beanbags?" Hank asked.

"Nah cousin, just one will do."

"What? Now Charley, you sure? Maybe your confidence needs better odds."

"No, cousin. One will do."

Some in the crowd overheard the exchange and began to gather around. "Okay, mister," Hank told the man, "give my cousin just one beanbag."

"That'll be twenty-five cents."

"One beanbag for twenty-five cents? How about five cents?" Hank asked.

The man knew his sell. "You know, Hank, I once read there are plenty of good five-cent cigars in this country, the trouble is they cost a quarter. What this country really needs is a good five-cent nickel."

"That has nothing to do with beanbags now does it?" Hank said and smirked.

"That's the point," the man said as he chuckled.

"Okay, give Charley a twenty-five-cent beanbag."

When Charley got hold of the bag, Hank noticed Charley squeeze it, just like he always did to prepare for a throw. Then Charley took a good look at the bottles, practiced a few simulated throws—more like a golfer than a baseball player—and quickly geared in and threw the bag where he intended. Sure enough, all three milk bottles flew in the air and off the table.

Hank gave a proud smile. "Well done, Charley! Want to try again?"

"No way, Hank. Like you, this kid will break me. No more today," the vendor said,

"Okay, Charley, pick your prize," Hank said.

"No, not me. Lillian, you go ahead and pick one," Charley said.

Lily looked thrilled, picked a smiling stuffed bear, and held it tight as they moved on to the monster coaster—which today especially seemed to hang over the Pacific solely to increase the fright of spectators and prospective daredevils.

Hank thought he'd have a little fun. "Hey Charley, you sure you want to do this? This coaster has the tendency, from time to time, to go off those tracks and into the Pacific Ocean."

"No matter, cousin. I'm a good swimmer," Charley said sincerely.

Hank shrugged his shoulders and said, "All right then, let's go."

As the coaster came to a halt and they prepared to board, Hank, for once, thought to be cautious for his young cousin. "Hey, Charley. It's best to sit in the second seat."

"If it's okay with all of you, I'd like to sit in the front seat with Alfred," Charley said while climbing aboard. Hank grinned, but was secretly concerned that maybe this time Charley's shoes might be too big for his feet. But once that coaster came over the first drop and Charley had both hands raised over his head, Hank gave way on that idea. This was a feat of courage that he'd seen little of, even while playing in the pits of a football scrum.

"Look at that, Lillian," Hank kept saying while the coaster rumbled and rolled on. After the coaster ride, Hank's endearing perception of Charley Jr. changed considerably to one of admiration, not only his talent and family ties, but now also for his brave character.

The next day, Hank and Lillian took Charley on a trip to a nearby desert outside Los Angeles referred to as 'The Ranch.' Charley and Miss Lillian Ludwig were well-received on the set by the crew who was taking a break from filming a silent Western movie. The crew knew Hank well; not only did he work there in the summer months, but his celebrity at USC matched most of the co-stars. Miss Lillian was at her best on the set, showing young Charley around and explaining what actors and actresses do in preparation for shooting a scene. Lillian's friend Gladys saw her and called out, "Come on over here Lillian. Let's chat. I've got some dead time," then she switched to a whisper, "plus, at twenty-five dollars a picture, I'm not getting rich."

Lillian took Charley by the hand to introduce the two. Gladys looked eager to talk to such a handsome young man, asking all kinds of questions about his relationship with Hank and some of the Arizona legends. The conversation came to an end when the directors said, "The sun's right. Let's get the scene in."

Everyone said their goodbyes with lots of "Please come again" and "See you later in class, Lillian."

Hank, Charley and Lillian stood back to watch for a while, then got back in the car. During the drive back, Charley prattled on about what an exciting day it was. "Miss Lillian, what classes are you taking to be a movie star?"

"Acting, but silent movies may be a thing of the past. The future will be in talkies."

"Talkies?"

"Yes, Charley. Imagine that. Some of the actors are taking

language and speech classes to work on their voice, which will be important in the talkies."

Hank noticed Charley taking in every word, as if storing it in his memory bank for future reference. Then Charley asked Lillian, "I saw, on your friend Gladys's seat, a script titled 'Jean,' was that the character she was playing for that movie?"

"How amusing, yet perceptive. No. You see, actors like catchy names, so they give themselves screen names. Now Gladys's real name is 'Gladys Georgianna Greene.' That's hard to spell and say, right? So, since her favorite characters from history were Jeanne of Arc and King Arthur, she claimed as her screen name, 'Jean Arthur.'"

"But Miss Lillian, wasn't it Joan of Arc?"

Lillian giggled. "In English yes, in French no. Someday, you might see her name headlined on a theatre billboard. But times are changing for the movie industry. Who knows."

"What about you, Miss Lillian. Will you be changing with the times?"

"Well, yes I guess I will. I've got a lot to learn and who knows, maybe my name will be up there too, one day. What do you think, Hank?"

Refusing to fuss over it, Hank kept driving on.

As promised, Hank took a left then drove on to Pacific Coast Highway. "We're going to pass through Malibu where the rich and famous live, then onto Santa Monica. That's were Lillian grew up. It's much like Long Beach but with a very different sort of crowd. You'll understand what I mean when you see some men with big muscles and girls with less bathing suit material," Hank said with a laugh. After amusing themselves by watching a few surfers ride their big board's down the crashing waves, Hank suggested it was time to eat, so it was on to Sonora's Restaurant where Hank was again well-received.

He showed off his cousin Charley Jr. with delight, telling everyone, "If you think I have stories about the Southeast, Charley's got even more! His father's been the quartermaster at Fort Huachuca for a long time. Got a story to tell them about that, Charley?"

"Sure," Charley's eyes lit up, "did you guys know that the troops from Fort Huachuca, with the help of Indian scouts, trailed down Geronimo and brought him back to the reservation? They also brought back all kinds of Indian relics, and then my father would trade them for whatever they wanted… money or such. In one of those trades, my father acquired a musket once owned by Geronimo himself. He has it hanging over the mantle back home. And Villa relics are all over. Just ask Hank. He's famous in Douglas for trading Villa's war memorabilia." The stories went on throughout a wonderful evening. Hank became enamored by the wit, the interest, and quiet assertions of his Arizona cousin. Charley's self-assurance with regards to his place in time, as well as that of his future, was infectious—much like Hank's own self-assurance was known to be.

For the finale on Charley's last night in town, Hank took Charley, Alfred, Lily, Mary, and Lillian to the Palomar Ballroom. It was to be a festive occasion to see Rudy Vallee, actor, singer, composer, and band leader. They sat at stage right, and as the music played on, the girls tried out their dancing steps, each taking Charley out to the floor to show him the latest 1920s ballroom dance moves.

Hank went about unnoticed on a special conspiracy, meeting with Rudy Valle for a talk, then bringing him over for an introduction to Charley.

Rudy was beside himself at meeting someone who'd just walked out of a Western novel. He even asked to have a flash photo taken with him and offered to make a copy for Charley if Charley would sign one for him. Hank offered to send it along to Charley, and Charley graciously accepted the deal. The big conspiracy of the evening was revealed when Rudy Valle stepped up to the microphone. At the end of his last set he mentioned that he had a wonderful surprise for the audience. Now he said, "I've been informed that a fine new musician has come into town for a short engagement before traveling back to Arizona. They tell me he plays the sax like no other from those parts. We would be pleased to have him sit in on our last set of the night and jam where he'd like. Please give a warm Los Angeles welcome for CHARLEY LE-FEBVRE!"

Charley looked over at Hank and pointed. He knew who set this up. Then he reached into his pocket, pulled out his mouthpiece, stripped the reed out, and began the process of wetting it in preparation. While stepping up on the stage, he put the moist reed back in his mouthpiece and placed it on a waiting saxophone offered up by one of the band members. Charley said "thanks," and nodded to Rudy he was ready to get it on.

Rudy announced: "How about a little boogie-woogie. Let's dance!" The band played on with Charley, who never missed a beat. At one point, Rudy even asked Charley to stand and play a solo. After Charley took him up on the offer, the crowd hooted and yelled their approval as they danced on.

With Charley safely aboard, the train back to Arizona pulled out of the station. Hank couldn't help but continue watching till it moved off into the horizon. Even Miss Lillian's gentle grasp on his arm went unnoticed. Hank's emotions played tricks on his mind again. Watching this boy—so much like him—go home was overwhelming for him. Home was more than a place to Hank, more than history, it was the essence of his innocence and a way of life that gave substance to his memories. Home was pure, untainted, and unblemished, even with its past tragedies. Home made sense. Here in LA there were opportunities and options, but not without costs. Oh, how easy it would have been to step back on that train with Ma and the family.

At this point though, could Hank afford to entertain these types of emotions? What he'd learned from Uncle Joseph still sounded in his mind: "When life comes to a fork in the road, stay in control. As long as you keep going, you'll get somewhere." Hank thought he knew what his pa would have done.

CHAPTER 30

CHANGING OF THE GUARDS

THE FRENCH FLASH

USC football boosters were intent on taking their team to a higher level. Gus had taken the Trojans from a fledgling embryonic stage, to a highly recognized national football program, and even with the perpetual inability to beat the California Bears, Gus Henderson had plenty of success to crow about. But, that wasn't enough for the athletic steering committee who were determined to lead USC to a national title. They had decided Gus was not the man to get the job done and forced him to resign.

Finding a coach with the credibility of Stanford's 'Pop' Warner or the stature of Notre Dame's Knute Rockne was an ambitious maneuver. They even tried to seduce Knute to come to USC as head coach, with promises to give him whatever he needed. Knute said no, but he offered up a name. Howard Jones' Iowa Hawkeys had recently beat the Irish and USC was impressed enough to take Knute's advice. Howard Jones was offered—and accepted—the position, but when personalities got in the way, his transition as head coach of the Trojans didn't happen as smoothly or as swiftly as most would have liked.

Besides both being head football coaches, Henderson and Jones were cut from entirely different fabrics. Gus Henderson was warm, witty, and personal. Howard Jones was straight-talking, conditioned, and distant. Gus was middle-class bred, holding a common bond with his players, and this contrasted with Jones's Ivy League pretenses and experience. Gus's acclaim as a "happy hooligan" was a factor of life that found a home among USC football. Howard Jones, on the other hand, gave the impression of entitlement to his position. It was said of Gus that he'd give you the shirt off his back.

"Not true!" replied one of his players. "He gave the *coat* off his back. Yeah, one cold day I was walking to practice and he stopped his car and offered his coat to me. Once I got to practice, I presented it back to him. His reply? 'You like it?' 'Yes,' I said. Then he said, 'It's yours.' Now, I can't even get Howard Jones to stop his car for a player in a blizzard. He's always too consumed with the intricacies of the O and X to even give players a name."

As to his field of play, Gus was an adventurous soul when working between the lines. His variety of plays, trickery, and diverse selection offered suspense to the game and gave the Trojans their unique tag as "the creator of the emerging west coast offense." On the other hand, Howard Jones's mantra of 'The Thundering Herd' was a predictable slant on smashmouth football's reputation for running it right at them. It was said, regarding Howard Jones's national successes, that his opponents knew where and what USC's herd was going to do, they just couldn't stop them from doing it. This was a precursor to USC's offensive style of "student body right" and "student body left" attacks.

For Lefebvre, the new coach would prove to be a real adjustment. Not only because of the amicable relationship he'd had with Henderson, but because of the complications created by Howard Jones's propensity to adjust the offense to meet his new system. Hank woke to this new reality with an early morning *Los Angeles Times* headline that clearly proclaimed his predicament:

"LEFEBVRE TO PLAY GUARD: Rumor Has It That Halfback is Slated for Line Berth on Howard Jones's 1925 Eleven" The obviously disgusted critic Braven Dyer reported:

> Mr. Feg Murray, the well-known cartoonist, says—believe it or not—but the latest football rumor at USC has it that Lefebvre will play guard this season. Lefebvre, it might be stated, was just about the rip-snortingest halfback the Trojans had last year. His eighty-yard jaunt to a touchdown in the St. Mary's game is still a vivid picture in the minds of thousands of fans who saw the stocky Trojan athlete dash through Slip Madigan's men for the longest local run of the season. Lefebvre is speed personified and his smallness, it has been pointed out by those of stature, would make him an asset. Howard Jones, the new Trojan grid mentor, thinks that short stocky men are his ideal type for the guard berths and Lefebvre fits that qualification perfectly. But Jones also dotes on speedy athletes to lead his offense. With the possible exception of Morton Kaer, there is no faster man on the Trojan squad than the brilliant halfback from Long Beach."

Hank wasn't impressed by the flattery in the article. He was too consumed by his replacement for the halfback position. He and his pa talked and they both agreed it was a setback. But Ma, bless her soul, graced the day by never mentioning she'd light an extra candle at downtown's St. Vincent. Things felt promising when she told him, "No need to fret, Hank. It will work out for you. Hasn't it always?"

Hank never really understood how this providence factor

that Charley Paddock talked about worked. Hank just trusted what his pa said, "As long as you go to practice, buy into the system, positive things will happen." So, Hank took on the challenge and disguised his contempt. Fortunately, it only took three games to get back to the position he left off.

Another one of sports reporter Braven Dyer's articles prompted Forrest to arrive early to the Lefebvre house one day and call Hank to come out to hear the latest news:

Fullback, Stocky Frenchman, Replaces Lee in Practice.

Due to the manner in which he punched holes in Stanford's line last Saturday, Lefebvre has been installed in the fullback position of the USC Eleven by Coach Howard Jones. The stocky Frenchman replaces Bob Lee, who seemed to lack the driving ability to penetrate the Cardinal line. The change took place at last night's practice, the first since Saturday's battle. How long Lefebvre stays at the position depends entirely upon his own actions. If he continues to make good, there is no reason why he shouldn't hang on to the job, as long as he's able to hobble about. So, he's back. If our memory serves us correctly, it was Hank who carried the brunt of the Trojan attack in that game with Missouri last season. It was Hank who ran the visiting ends goofy with his dynamic bursts of speed inside and outside of the wing positions. They say that it takes Lefebvre just a little bit longer than his mates to adjust himself to the task at hand. Gus Elmer Henderson didn't use him much until late in the season when Hank showed he knew quite well how to roll or dazzle defenders at will. Lefebvre is by now undoubtedly familiar with Howard Jones's system.

Forrest stopped to hand Hank a flyer torn from a sports magazine. "Read this. You won't believe what they're saying."

Henry 'Hank' Lefebvre, the 'French Flash,' is one of Howard Jones's many backfield stars. The ancient Trojans played football along with the Spartans about 2,300 years ago. A team known as the "Trojans" have been playing football along the Pacific Coast for the past quarter of a century. Trojan athletes traveled East to win the intercollegiate track and field championship in Philadelphia last May, and now another Trojan band, called by Knute Rockne, 'The finest material I have ever seen,' is cutting a wide swath to gridiron fame while playing a schedule of thirteen games under the tutelage of new coach, Howard Jones. The assembly of Hank Lefebvre—a fast, chunky French lad from Long Beach—as well as Drury, Earle, Cook, Elliott, Lee, and Kaer Boren, is as good as any backfield in the country."

Hank's comeback, if you could call it that, was geared more toward adjusting to this new coach's methods—methods that felt foreign to his own way of doing things. First, unlike with Coach Henderson, Hank had a hard time connecting with Howard Jones on a personal level. Second, Jones's decisions about the future placement of the team's talent were usually made known in the local newspapers, then as a belated directive to the players at the next practice, so the team soon discovered it was best to keep ahead of their *Los Angeles Times* subscription to get information on what their roll would be in Jones's scheme of play. Hank felt this was an indignation, particularly to the athletes, and it emasculated the personal idiosyncrasies of his individual style of play. This new system worked as an anti-equation to Hank's psychology.

Was it meant to be an antidote for the Henderson way to recall the Trojan warrior spirit of the ancient world? The mantra about "The Thundering Herd" may have been an appropriate format for a mass movement or collective effort, but somehow along the way Hank thought the creativity of the athlete, actor, writer, or anyone else, had to evolve with such a master scheme so that players would lose their individuality, except in rare occasions.

One of those occasions came when Hank was leading as guard for Cook in a game against Stanford. Cook took a smashing hit by a defender and the ball came out of his hands and went airborne. It ended up in Hank's hands, and he had no choice but to improvise outside of The Herd. He dashed, stunned, and overwhelmed with punk strength when he took the ball some forty-eight yards in for a touchdown. "Was that Mr. Lefebvre?" Jones asked his assistant coach, using the proper name to add bravado.

"Yes Coach, it was Lefebvre," Coach Dolley added with sarcasm, "Coach, that's what Hank does."

"Well then, maybe we ought to give him a chance at running back," Jones quipped back. As usual, Jones made sure to let the other coaches know that it was his discovery, and his decision.

So Hank found his way back in the lineup as a running back. But his friend Paddock's advice: "The fans will only be there as long as you win," remained planted back in his mind like a proverb from the bible, continuing to prompt Hank to plan beyond the game of football, and for a future after USC's fame.

Hank had been with Lillian now for a few years and their relationship was a neat little package. She was the sorority type, attractive, and had a family with social ties. Hank was the handsome star football player and popular man about campus. It was hard to argue that this kid from Douglas wasn't a winner in whatever he'd ventured into.

Yet, there was his family predicament to think about. He had four brothers and three sisters to care for and cloud of uncertainty had begun to gather now that his pa was but a few months from dying. Hank couldn't shake the memory that not too long ago his celebrity had taken a hit when he was moved to lead guard rather than the star running back for USC. During that time, when he went with Lillian to Sonora's or other places around town, people treated him different, less congenial, as if he'd lost some relevance. It wasn't all that apparent, but the nuisances persisted. Even his conversations with Lillian began to fray during that time. She chattered on more often about her acting, and introduced him around town like a Hollywood prop. When Hank made a thing over it, she defended her actions by calling it 'networking.'

"Come on now Hank, get with it. My lovely, Hollywood's the future and your college football is the calling card that will help break you into the industry." Since Hank's interest in Hollywood only went as far as part-time grip, inevitably, Lillian's new-found wisdom didn't seem all that appealing.

But with the resurrection of Hank's glory as running back, his instincts told him that for now, there was no time to think about what came next in life; he decided to continue to do what he'd been doing best…playing sports. The future would take care of itself.

Economic conditions seemed certain to dramatically change soon, however, so Hank figured it wouldn't hurt to become engrossed in his class work as well. It was the 1920s and there was speculation that American investments in the stock market, financial leveraging, and over-extensions of paychecks were about to run their course. Hank's pa had been the gambler while his uncle Joseph put away nest eggs for just such an occasion. It was a balanced perspective inherited from both that would keep Hank one step ahead and able to make the best of situations in this volatile world.

CHAPTER 31

COOK, LEFEBVRE, AND DRURY SHINE FOR LOCALS

The latest *Los Angeles Times* sports section headline read: "COOK, LEFEBVRE AND DRURY SHINES FOR LOCALS"

Rolling up touchdowns with monotonous regularity, the USC football outfit regained the form displayed before the Stanford tussle and thoroughly chastised the Arizona Wildcats 56 to 0 before a crowd of 17,000 at the Coliseum yesterday afternoon. The Wildcats' line was very porous and stopped the smashing Trojans backs much after the manner of a stove absorbing water — with the exception of the last portion of the second quarter, when they registered four first-downs on a passing and running attack. The Arizonians were terribly busy trying to keep track of USC's ball carriers. Bill Cook, Morley Drury, and Henry (Hank) Lefebvre shared the honors with Jeff Cravath and Brice Taylor during the afternoon entertainment. Cook, running for half the contest, scored touchdowns and performed in a creditable manner as a signal snorter. Drury was responsible for the best play of the game, the bright spot coming near the close of the second quarter. Howard Elliott, who had replaced Cook with the ball on USC's forty-five, dropped back, and shot a short pass to Drury, and Morley responded with a dazzling run of more than fifty yards to the Arizona goal line. He bowled over several embryo tacklers on route and in general conducted himself in a manner that made hundreds ask why Jones doesn't use him more as a ball packer. The former high school star, Morley Drury — recruited, like his teammate, Henry 'Hank' Lefebvre, by Chet Dolley from the long list of talented Long Beach Poly Jackrabbits — had a perfect day of goal kicking, booting six over the cross bar in as many attempts. Lefebvre smashed the line in his old-style and got a big cheer from the USC fans when his day's work was done.

Life, as Charley Paddock explained, was a network of connections and an arrangement of contacts. But Hank added the importance of good timing, being at the right spot at the right season—he was an opportunist who thrived in an epic breakout period for the university, recognized as a legitimate contender in a period surrounded by some of the most notable football legends to ever put on a uniform.

For the next two years, Morley Drury would go on to become a sensation. Jones would become one of the most successful college coaches in football history, along with such names as Glen "Pop" Warner, of Stanford, Knute Rockne of Notre Dame, and of course, USC's Gus Henderson. Hank felt an especially close bond to Morley, who'd played behind him at Poly and then again at USC. Morley was three years younger. His dad had died when he was seven, and after completing grade school, Morley took a break from school and worked in the shipyards to take care of his family before enrolling in high school at Poly. Morley and Hank had a lot in common. Like so many other players of that era, they needed to work to help their families survive. Morley played linebacker, punter, and just about any other position the team needed, even center in Poly's infamous Everett game, so it wasn't much of a surprise to the coaches for him to make high school and college all-American. But it wasn't until USC, when coaches made him a ball carrier, that his notoriety took off. So much so that in the closing moments of his last game, Coach Jones sought him out to say, "Drury, you're done for the day, you can go to the locker room, but you must cross the center of the field to get there." As he walked toward the tunnel, a cheer came from the crowd, that silenced the outside world and could be heard all the way back to Long Beach. What a fitting display for this fine warrior's last march off the field. Many estimated the cheer lasted for ten minutes.

Morley was a quiet person, never one to tell or make rumors, and held a reputation for having little on conversation. But when someone brought up his days at Poly, he would talk on and on about his famous teammates, especially Coach Eddie Kienholz. The Big 102 game against Arizona was played a year before he joined varsity, so Morley often asked Hank how it felt to be part of the history making game.

Cook came in 1925 by way of Stanford after being recruited from Anaheim High. He left Stanford and enrolled at USC, playing quarterback, then running back at just about the time Morley took over as quarterback in their single-wing system, and the rest is history. Cook later went on to coaching.

Hank often enjoyed recalling when Forrest read the headlines of the day after the Big 102 game back in 1919. Reading the headlines inspired him to remember where he came from, and how far he had gone. Hank's positive personality made up for his caustic individualism that sometimes created controversy. Yet when presented with flattery, his humble nature surfaced; he needed some real prompting to talk about himself. He preferred others do that while he laughed with them about his escapades. On occasion, he'd concede, some activities weren't always commendable, but offered few regrets and seldom appeared apologetic.

The year 1925 had been a good one for Hank, Jones, and the USC Thundering Herd. Hank's billing as "The French Flash" and backfield star played out the season's entire thirteen-game schedule. One article, describing Lefebvre as a "fast, chunky lad from Long Beach, California" went on to say, "Lefebvre is one of the stalwart stars of the Trojan backfield. In my estimation Coach Jones's collection of backfield stars is as good as any in the country. Without mentioning them by name, they rival the Four Horsemen of Notre Dame."

A humorous and off-the gridiron story from the *Los Angeles Times* on October 16 noted:

Henry (Hank) Lefebvre, stocky Trojan fullback, was the first casualty of the USC football Eleven on its way to play Oregon. While the famous Trojan was practicing at the Claremont Country Club course this afternoon, Lefebvre was hit on the head by a golf ball, slipped by a female golfer who'd braved the rain to keep up her game. Lefebvre was knocked down, but quickly revived when the fair-haired beauty stood over him. Discovering that her victim was a USC star, she took the occasion in hand, asking Hank to autograph her golf glove. To wit, Hank was very pleased, then returned to signal practice. But a few minutes later, the team doctor indicated his head trauma needed nursing due to the large bump beginning to swell and protrude from his head.

Jones ended his first year at USC with eleven wins and

two losses, placing third in the Pacific Coast Conference. The losses were to Stanford, 9 to 13, and Washington State, 12 to 17. Meanwhile, the University of Washington, under the illustrious coach of the 1920 Everett High team, Enoch Bagshaw, subsequently beat Stanford 13 to 0 and won their bid for the Rose Bowl. The Huskies were beaten on New Year's Day by Alabama in their first Rose Bowl invite by a score of 19 to 20. But without question, the remarkable historic era of USC football had begun. Those early gridirons, launched a new torch—lit a flame that would be passed on by many nameless warriors for centuries.

But for the first time in Hank's life, football wasn't in the cards for the future. Prohibition was still an opportunity, the roaring twenties had just about run its course, and the American economy was symptomatic of the times and—as his early English teacher once told Hank—in need of immediate attention. Also, over in Germany, lofty proclamations made by a pied piper and comedic character resembling Charley Chaplin to a tee was about to be thrust onto the world stage.

Hank knew well his predicament, along with other recent graduates, would require him to find a job, resolve personal commitments, and navigate the minefield that current events would surely present.

CHAPTER 32

CUPID, DRAW BACK YOUR BOW

The story of Cupid goes somewhat like this: An ancient Greek writer of the second century, Plantonicus, created a myth as he scribed about the nature of love. His story of Cupid and the psyche asserted love was not brought on by virtue, but by lust pandered with sexual passion that created a terminal confrontation within the Spartan warrior. Raised to give unconditional devotion to the Spartan city-state, the men committed themselves to battle all enemies, while Spartan women knew their role was preserved for procreation. When a male offspring came of age, he would be removed from the fold to start the life of a soldier.

Now, that's where Cupid came in. If the tip of Cupid's arrow, which contained the potion of passion and desire, pierced the flesh, it would cause a man or a woman to lose their Spartan virtue by seeking a malign joy contrary to the current platonic relationships guiding and preserving Spartan society. That obsession, called "romance," was a curse that made a person vulnerable to weakness, and brought on such an irrational response they would pursue a life of blind pleasure. This romantic love was deemed a psychological "infection" that found its way into the souls of valiant defenders, making them impotent to function in a Spartan heroic life.

What's this got to do with Hank or USC football? Well, early one chilly morning just as the sun broke and the city began to orchestrate its recovery from slumber with all varieties of sounds—some detectable, others just fitting into the mesh, but each in chorus playing a different tune—Hank Lefebvre reclined on his front porch swing. Sipping from a cup of steaming java made by Ma's tender hands, he browsed the business section of the morning paper. He stayed clear of the sports section, no need to read its Monday-morning quarterbacking, unless, of course, it said something positive about his game, Hank thought, as laughed to himself for his unapologetic attitude. Pretty soon Forrest came up the driveway, appearing unusually excited and waving a newspaper in the air.

"So, what is it now, Forrest? Did your young lady last night reject your demands?" Hank quipped.

"No, no. It's about you and your mademoiselle. Have you read the sports section this morning?"

"No, I haven't, Forrest. I try to stay out of the way from those critters' story lines. They never played a game themselves, but somehow always know what went wrong in the huddles."

"Hank, It's something different this time. Listen, it's not about the game on the field. It's about your game off the field."

"Coffee?"

"No…well yes," Forrest answered.

Hank yelled into the house, "Hey Mama!"

"Yes, Hank?"

"Forrest's here."

"Forrest? What's he doing up so early?"

"Don't know, Mama, but I'm about to find out. He needs a cup of coffee."

"Coming up in just a minute," Mama called back.

"Here, sit down, Forrest. Now, what was it you were saying?"

"Listen to what it says here: 'LEFEBVRE BETROTHAL ANNOUNCED. Engagement of Trojan Star to Miss Lillian Ludwig is Announced at USC.'

Forrest paused to get Hank's reaction. After seeing his broad smile, he read on. 'Henry 'Hank' Lefebvre, demon fullback of the USC Thundering Herd, was thrown for a loss the other day, and Lefebvre is glad of it. The enemy in this case, was Dan Cupid, that all-around athlete who knocks out prizefighters, gets home runs off pitchers, noses out jockeys, and throws fullbacks for losses.

Daniel Cupid was performing at the instigation of Miss Lillian Ludwig, USC co-ed and one of the most popular young women on the campus. The effervescent Lefebvre…"

Hank interrupted with laughter, "He really wrote that? 'Effervescent'?"

"Yep, 'effervescent.'"

"Well, who knew? Go on, Forrest, what else did he say?"

'Hank and the popular Miss Ludwig announced their engagement yesterday and admitted that the date for the ceremony would be sometime in the latter part of the summer season.' Forrest looked up again at Hank before continuing. "Then it goes on about 'Miss Ludwig is the daughter of Mr. and Mrs. H.W. Ludwig of' such and such social distinction."

"So, why aren't you congratulating me, Forrest?" Hank joked.

Before he could answer, Ma pushed out the screen door with a tray of hot coffee and cream. "So, what brings you out so early today, Forrest?"

"Well, Mrs. Lefebvre," Forrest stuttered, handing over the newspaper, "here Mrs. Lefebvre, you can read for yourself."

"Well, well, well. What do we have here?" she said, then

read without expression. "Is it true, Hank?"

"I guess so. That's what it says there in the paper so it must be."

"Don't you be funnin' with me now, Son. You've decided to marry Lillian then?"

"Well, maybe, Mama. So, don't go telling this to too many people, 'cause it's only an engagement."

Ma shook her head. "Okay, I'll go inside and think about this while fixing you boys some breakfast."

After she left, Hank asked, "So, Forrest, what's your concern here? You don't have any skin in this."

"Well, Hank. I thought you and I were going into the gold business after graduation. Remember what you said about a depression coming and needing to put our efforts in gold? That it will never lose its value?"

"Yeah. So, what's that got to do with me marrying Lillian?"

"Well, you know…Miss Lillian has hopes of becoming a big Hollywood star, and lately you've been talking about that too. I'm sure that won't make for a good marriage, being away and all, leaving her to mess around with them unscrupulous producers."

"Okay, Forrest. I get your drift. But, as I told Ma, it's only an engagement. I've got a reprieve until late summer. Right, partner? Don't worry, we're still going to be interested in that gold."

Forrest seemed relieved for the moment.

Ma yelled from inside the house. "Come on in, boys, *pronto*—before the food freezes."

The two young men rushed into the kitchen to the smell of sizzling bacon, toasted bread, and simmering eggs bursting from the busy stove. Once seated and served, Forrest said, "So, Mrs. Lefebvre, what—"

"Let's pray first," Ma said firmly.

After prayer, she looked over to Forrest. "Now what is it you were saying?"

Forrest smiled and asked, "What do you think of Hank marrying Lillian?"

"To tell you the truth, I kind of like the girl. She's a bit too ambitious on the acting though. But, I leave those kinds of decisions to my children. As long as I don't have to live with them," she added with a smile. "There were a lot of people who said I shouldn't have married Hank's pa. But, with all his forgivin's, I'd never do different. So, we'll see. Knowing Hank, nothing will surprise me."

After breakfast, Hank and Forrest took off to practice. Before entering the locker room the teasing began. "Hank's going to turn in his cleats for a lunch bucket," Bagro taunted, and Cook kidded, "Who knows, maybe Miss Lillian will get him in the movies, like Morrison and Bond." They all had good laughs, even stuffy Howard Jones joined in. "So, Hank's finally going to become an honest man."

Hank couldn't let that one get by without a response and the team loved his comeback: "So, Coach, you do read the torrid *Los Angeles Times* sports section after all!"

When the day ended and Hank saw to it that his brothers completed their produce deliveries, he went back to relaxing on his porch steps. While he pondered about the future, Pa sat down alongside. "So, Hank, you going to do it?"

"Maybe so, Pa, but don't worry. I'll make sure I still can take care of Ma and the family. What do you think, Pa?"

"I know you can handle the responsibility, but times have changed so much, in just what—maybe ten years from Arizona? In that dusty border town we'd seen a lot of people, all kinds and a lot of squabbles, some shootin's and hangings and some fine noble people amongst those goings on. They all were apart of building what we are and what we think is true. Now, that's the world we'd been brought from, much like Clifford's world in the small Minnesota town he come from. But Hank, that was then. Now, we live in a different world. Cars—and some say airplanes—will be as common as flies, carrying people all over the world...talking movies too, hey Hank? Some say we'd be having a depression sometime soon. Remember, Hank, what I said about—"

"Yeah, Pa. I remember what you said about gold."

"Yes, Son—gold. Paper money won't mean nothing then. So, you go on thinkin' out here. I'd be getting some rest. Goin' down to Signal Hill tomorrow early. Clifford wants to visit the oil field and meet Mr. Dohney. I promised him such. Oh, by the way, Hank, Mama told me to have this chat with you and when I'd finished to give you this letter she got in the mail today."

Pa got up and opened the screen door.

"Hey, Pa?"

"Yes son?"

"Thanks, Pa."

"For what? I never gave you advice on the matter."

"I know that Pa, but thanks for reminding me of what you and Mama have done to get us here." As his father said good night and walked back into the house, Hank, for the first time ever, saw his father's eyes glass up and heard his voice crackle.

Hank sat there for a while, gazing at the stars as each came out from hiding. He then looked over at the letter lying beside him as if it was an intruder violating his respite. Eventually his hand wandered over and slowly picked it up. The letter had an Arizona postmark, but wasn't the same type of envelope he was accustomed to receiving from his cousin Doris Mae.

Intrigue set in and he quickly broke the seal. Thrusting the torn envelope to the side, Hank unfolded the paper.

Hank, I bet you're surprised to hear from me. We just had the second anniversary of the passing of old Villa, being killed in his car on the way back from a political meeting. I kind of miss that old bandit. Both of our families had a lot of good stories to tell about him, and we'd made a lot of money rummaging about that battlefield. I was down at the Gadsden the other day and ran into Emiliano. Remember Texas John Slaughter's right-hand man? He lives in Sonora now. He was just visiting his old stomping grounds, since Mr. Slaughter has moved in to town 'cause of the murdering going on just outside his ranch. We got to talking about how Emiliano first met you. He remembered me falling into those bushes and that he asked if I was from Ireland and I told him no, Poland. He laughed really hard, then asked about you. He said, "Now Hank, there was a real hombre. Calm as the snowflake, but when you got him going, he was like a thunderstorm." He went on with some stories about when you and him took the trip to Tombstone, then Bisbee, and back here to Douglas, then said your goodbyes after a wonderful picnic in Benson. Seems you had some trouble there. I told him all what I heard you're doing and said goodbye.

That night I told Chata about running into Emiliano and our talking about you and that got her going about remembering when Hank was racing across that field with those Villistas and Federalies firing at us. Wow. Them where the days. We had lots of fun then, didn't we Hank? Now, times have changed. You and I have moved on. Chata asked when I thought you'd settle down, maybe even come back to your real home in Douglas. I told her I didn't know but to remember that Hank's chipped from a different block. That you're always wandering off on a journey to some place and when you get there, you need another journey to keep going. I told her, 'Hank's not like you and me, with a family and all. No, I think he'll travel all over the world and at night, like we done so many times in the Chiricahua Mountains, he'll see those stars. And, as the Indians would say, that be where his spirit meets his soul and the dreamin' and wondering of another adventure takes place.'

No, I told her, 'This life we have, it's not for Hank. We've had to give up so much.' But since Chata and I have always been together, somehow that makes it all worth it. We have something more than romance, something more binding. Maybe though, after you've been around the world you'll find someone like I did. And, then you'll come back home just to say hi. No? Well, my compadre, mi amigo, yup and the Gipper, we miss you every day.

Josiah and Chata

Hank settled back in a confrontable position, looking at the galaxies, searching for something. However, it was more like looking into a blemished mirror. He couldn't make out who he was anymore. Josiah's letter took him to a place he'd hadn't been for years. Was it all worth it, these past years of USC fame? Then the image of Cristina that night on the boardwalk explaining her vision for the future came to him. He could almost hear her soft voice asking him if he could see himself in that place...raising a family like hers. No, it just wouldn't fit, not then nor now. But where was the love and romance he'd felt back in Long Beach. Why did he feel so incomplete when morning papers gave favorable reviews of last night's deeds? Had he bartered away Cristina's imprint on his heart? Could he someday resurrect what he'd had with her?

His mind began to wonder, maybe someday he'd wander into Mexico, find a small farm and there would be Cristina mending a cornfield, with her dark black hair blowing about her face from a warm summer breeze. The mystery of an un-announced visit would give her a tingling, a clue that someone had entered her space. She would turn to take a precaution-ary glance, then look beyond the stalks of corn to see him walking up the road. She would focus in disbelief, disrupt all she'd been doing, then thrust away the threshed corn she held in her hand and let it fly into the air. She'd begin a ceremonial march, walking slowly at first, so her vision wouldn't escape, run from her approach, or merely disappear from her mind. Could it be? Once convinced that it wasn't an illusion, she would break into a sprint toward him. She would throw her beautiful, tan, strong arms around him with hands longing to caress, but no kiss nor words would be offered. Words would have lost any meaning. What would they say? An embrace would do fine. Feelings that pressed out all restraints. Her firm hands would reveal a soul that had resisted hope for too long, how she'd needed him without conditions. Feelings he'd al-ways thirsted for, not the ones that merely graced him when he won a football game.

Reality hit as he resurfaced from his crevice. "No," he thought, "I can't keep replaying this again and again when her name is brought up. I can't let this sustain me all my life." Yet, like always, he'd reconcile his discontent with a compro-mise that he'd never let that dream go, nor would he go to the dream. The image was too real and haunting. Instead, he'd convince himself that chances and probabilities could make it happen. Pretending to be rational, he surmised what he'd learned from his pa: "Take a spin on the roulette's wheel. Not dependable, but what a ride." Oh, how could it get much bet-ter if he beat the odds on this. If somehow all those stars out there lined up for him, giving him that chance. Even if he was too old to toil the journey, what a finale it would be.

CHAPTER 33

GRADUATION

"Now graduation…" Hank explained to Ma. "It's a ceremony that that students go through when they've finished all the required classes for a degree."

"I know that Hank, but what degree did you finish?"

"A Bachelor of Science in Business."

"Well then, Hank, what business are you going to be in?"

"Not sure, Mama. I guess, I don't know yet."

"What? You spent four years on USC's campus thinking about business and you don't even know what business you're going to be in? Well, I'll be. Maybe you should work for Sonny Cardinale in the produce business. You and the boys been selling and delivering produce, milk, and eggs in your truck for three years. And everybody needs to eat, that's for sure now."

"I know, Mama, but the economy doesn't look promising in the near future. Maybe I'll go and work full-time in the movie studios, move up from a grip to whatever."

"Now you're starting to sound like your potential wife, Lillian."

"Yeah, she's sure been bitten by the Hollywood star bug. That's all she talks about these days…how she met this producer or that person who's going to give her a chance in the movies."

"Well Hank, I suppose that's one way to start."

"I know, Mama, but she's been using my name as her calling card for the meetings and I'm getting tired of playing up to some of those schmucks." Hank thought for a while before he added, "Well, I guess, I can always open a billiard parlor, like Mr. Clifford."

"Now, you're talking Pa's talk. And you know what it got him. No need for that, Hank."

"Well then Mama, I think I might just go gold hunting with Forrest."

"Gold hunting?"

"Yeah, Mama. When the money dries up, remember, 'you're worth your weight in gold,' and gold will always have value."

"You're not serious, are you Hank? Quit playing with me. Gold hunting...and what's the family going to live on while you're out there...yonder."

"Yuma, Mama. Out there in Yuma."

"Yuma?"

"Yep. In them mountains there's gold. Lots of it. I'll be sending you packets of gold."

"Hank, just tell me you'd be thinking this over real long and hard 'cause you know your pa is not going to last much longer. His breathing is hard to come by now."

"I promise to think and plan before I do anything, Mama. But today, I've got to get over to the athletic banquet for graduating seniors. I'm going to take Alfred with me."

"For what?"

"To help me carry all my trophies back home," Hank said with a smirk.

Ma laughed and gave Hank a hug. "Okay, take Alfred, but keep Lily and Mary here to help me with Pa."

The *Times* reported on March 20, 1926: "AWARD TRO-JAN FOOTBALL MEN SWEATERS, EMBLEMS FOR WORK.

Twenty-one members of the USC football team of last season received cardinal and gold sweaters for their efforts at a rally in Bovard Auditorium yesterday afternoon. At the same time, four of the men were awarded gold footballs and life-time passes to all Trojan athletic contests for their three years of service on varsity teams.

Those receiving the gold emblems were Capt. Hobbs Adams, Honey Earl, Newton Stark, and Henry (Hank) Lefebvre."

Hank was also noted for his past contributions to California football's prominence at Long Beach Poly and for being, technically, the first ever Trojan to score a touchdown in the Los Angeles Coliseum. Additionally, Hank had played on the USC football team's first year in the Pacific Coast Conference and in first ever Rose Bowl. There was more. Hank Lefebvre was given standing ovations as the star that led USC to national notoriety in 1924's first and only Christmas Festival Bowl against the Missouri Tigers under the leadership of Coach Gus Henderson in his last game of USC tenure. USC's Coach Howard Jones came to the podium to speak of Hank's warrior mentality and even said that because of Hank's efforts, there was no finer backfield in college football. He even went as far as to say that Hank's talent playing backfield was as good as or better than the Four Horseman of Notre Dame. Another presenter stood and reminded the audience that Hank was also noted for his defense of "damsels in distress" when he took on the torrid Ray Price, who got an undercard with Jack Dempsey at Shrine Auditorium. Everyone laughed and cheered when the presenter described how Hank knocked Price out in Sonora's parking lot one Friday night. Another presenter described Hank as having some unnoticed athletic talents in baseball in his freshman year, and how he ran track for two years under Coach Dean Cromwell, and that by Dean Cromwell's and Charley Paddock's own admissions, Hank was the fastest man in the world at the forty-meter dash. That story had been around for a while and got another great cheer then laughter when Charley Paddock stood to shout, "That's the truth!" while pointing at an exuberant Hank, who sat there smiling from ear to ear. What a night it was.

Hank's graduation ceremony, with all the festivities to follow, was held the next day on campus. His pa was too sick so Ma insisted that Hank's sister Mary watch him so she could attend. Clothed in his graduation gown, Hank escorted his ma over to campus with Lily and Alfred. At first, Hank felt a little feminine in the flowing cardinal material, but soon it didn't matter because he realized this day meant a lot more than he ever expected. Life was calming down and becoming increasingly tame for him now, he realized as he talked and joked with acquaintances, saying "goodbye" to some and "hope to see you someday" to others. Never thinking men were made to be so sensitive, Hank was surprised how often he had to fight off tears as he hugged, patted shoulders, and shook hands. All of his significant experiences these last few years had been athletic achievements. Yes, today was an accomplishment all right. He knew it was entirely unique and remembered how often he'd shied away from academic activities back in Douglas. Fortunately, he also remembered Emiliano's words on that long automobile ride: "Hank, education is the way to go. The frontier life is about to change. The future will be for those who are educated."

Ma sat through the graduation in tears, especially when Hank's name was called to receive his diploma. "Getting all those sports accolades was expected. But this was unexpected.

Hank is the first in the family to get one of them college diplomas. That's what makes it so special."

When the last name was called and the ceremony was over, the crowd began to gather about. Forrest was the first to rush over to Hank and his ma. "Well, Mrs. Lefebvre, I bet you never thought you'd see this day."

She nodded because no words could be said through her tearful joy. After Hank gave her another hug he said, "Lily, you and Alfred walk Mama back home. I'm going to socialize for a while then be home for supper. Okay?" After his family left, Hank leaned over to Forrest and said, "Let's go and do us some real socializing!"

Forrest agreed. "Why not? We've earned it!"

But just as they moved forward, Hank got a glimpse of a beautiful Mexican girl being pushed back by an usher. Forrest saw it too and said nervously, "No Hank. Don't do it."

"Don't worry, Forrest. It will be fine."

"Hank, its graduation day. Give it a break."

Hank paid no attention to his plea and walked over to the altercation, while Forrest shadowed him step-for-step. When Hank reached the roped-off area he asked, "What's going on here?"

"Oh nothing. Just telling this young lady this is no place for her." The girl pulled her arm away from the man's grasp and looked hopefully at Hank.

"Why do you say that?" Hank challenged.

"Well you can see—"

"See what? She's with me." Hank pounced with his hands held out toward the girl, working hard to hide his rising temper.

"Is that so? Then where's her pass, mister?"

Hank turned to Forrest, "You have her pass, don't you?"

"Yes of course," Forrest said, playing along with Hank's game, "sure I do. It's right here," he continued, while digging into his pocket and eventually producing a pass that he held up to the face of the unconvinced usher.

"That's just fine, but now where's his pass?" the man growled, looking at Hank.

"He gave it to another usher when he came in. Can't you see he's wearing that ridiculous cap and gown?"

The usher was angry and looked about to become un-hinged when Hank turned on his charm and offered a solution. "Look, we don't need this nor do you. What's the girl going to do, drink too much Kool-Aid or eat too many cookies? Come on, see it our way. Nobody's going to be put out over this."

Reluctantly the usher sighed and stood back to let the girl in. "Okay, but you're responsible for her."

Hank smiled and offered his arm for the girl to take and walk with him toward the festivities. Once they reached the refreshment table, Hank supplied her with a glass of Champagne. She shook her head no and in a soft voice said, "Thank you, but Kool-Aid will do."

"No, it won't," Hank replied and handed her a glass of the sparkling drink and a plate of cake.

Apparently seeing that it was time to leave the two alone to get to know each other better, Forrest lost himself in the crowd. Hank smiled when he saw a cute petit blonde, who wasn't shy about inviting Forrest over with a wave of her hand. The girl and Hank were left alone to encourage a conversation, which Hank never had much trouble doing with a person of the op-posite sex.

"Let's go over and set down on the lawn," Hank offered.

"Just for a short while," she replied.

"Why? Are you in a hurry to meet someone?"

"Oh no. It's not that, but I work in the county hospital and today is the day I work."

They both sipped their drink and tasted the cake. "Not

bad," Hank said, breaking the silence. He turned and searched the girl's dark brown eyes. She looked back into his as if in a trance, begging Hank on. A balloon hanging about from the decorations popped and Hank lost what her eyes were giving him.

"You don't remember me now, do you?" she said.

Hank stumbled to find an answer. "I'm so sorry. You tell me."

Smiling, she leaned forward, as if she had a wonderful surprise for him, then jumped in confidently, "I know who you are. You're Hank Lefebvre…football star. What do they call you?" she paused then became deliciously animated, "oh yes, 'The French Flash!'" Since half of USC's campus knew that, Hank waited for her to tell the rest of the story—if she had one—for his lack of memory. "Let's go back two, no three years ago. I came to Sonora's Restaurant and we had a little problem."

"Really? We did?"

She had Hank in suspense so he begged her on. "You somehow got away from your football buddies and intruded into an ongoing conversation. You said something about humanity and the fellow questioned your concerns. So, you took your dissertation out on the man in the nearby parking lot."

"You were there?"

"Yes, I was. Now what was that all about?"

Hank ran his hand through his hair and smiling from relief he explained, "Well, to tell you the truth, it was over a girl."

"Yes, a Mexican girl."

"How do you know about that?" Hank ask curiously.

"How do I know? Because I was that girl."

Hank threw himself back laying on the grass laughing. "You were the girl?"

"Yes, and you don't remember," she said with a smile.

"How could I? I was so heated over that guy, I couldn't think about anything else but to teach him a lesson."

"See, you do remember. And I came to you later to thank you for what you did for me and you told me, 'It was not for you, that guy needed a lesson in humanity.' Now do you remember?"

"That's right. I did say that."

"Why? What did you mean by that?" Her eyes turned sad.

Hank sobered and sat up tall to answer. "Well, let me tell you," Hank stopped and looked hard to identify who he was about to trust with his secret.

Perhaps sensing Hank's anguish at the change in mood, she offered her name, "Leticia."

"Leticia, yes, I'm called 'The French Flash.' But my hypocrisy only goes so far. You see, that's only half the story. The other half is my mother…she's part White Mountain Indian. The other part, well who knows. My pa says it's Mexican. You see, I was brought up in the frontier of the Arizona territory, even before it became a state. And, in those days, being a half-breed was the bottom of the list of desirables. We are half this and half that, not whole of anything, so we got no respect and a lot of rude behavior. My cousin, Doris Mae, whose father is French but mother is Mexican, had to wait until all the white *gabachos* drank from the faucet before she could get a drop of water.

"But we made out okay. Her mother always told the family to 'hide the tortillas,' to cover up for our heritage. We had to fight *gabachos* for every ounce of respect. That was the only way. That night at Sonora's, when I saw what was happening to you, all I could see were my sisters, Mary and Lily. That you were in the right and that guy needed a-learning. Because you are Mexican, you knew what it was all about, but that guy didn't. And so he paid for it in that parking lot. Not by me knocking his lights out, but by him being embarrassed and looked down upon. At least that's what I hope he learned."

Tears lost their way from Leticia's eyes, showing stored-up hurt. "Yes, yes. Thank you so much for that. I watched you play so many times, but your words…when you said, 'not for you.' Those words have haunted me, but now I understand."

Hank reached over and pulled her to him and hugged her until she let up the tears, then asked, "Leticia, why did you come today?"

"Every year, for the last three, I come here on graduation day. It is a dream of mine to go to college and become a doctor. This is my ritual to keep that dream alive. To come here and see all the faces of the people who dreamed as I do and get the feeling of what they did. It keeps me going. I will be there too, someday."

"What about your boyfriend from Sonora's…that night, the fraternity guy?"

"Oh, he was a good friend. But his parents came from the west side…not much chance for us. He didn't want to say it when we broke up, but we both knew it. Well, Mr. Lefebvre do you always go around saving Mexican girls from such circumstances, saving their virtue?"

Hank laughed. "You know my sister Lily says so. She wonders why they always are the beautiful ones."

"So, then that must be a compliment for me." Leticia smiled.

Hoping his words would reach her soul, he said, "Especially for you."

"Do you mind if I kiss you?" she asked, "only for respect, that is."

"Respect me all you want." Hank grinned and leaned forward to receive her lips. The kiss went beyond respect and she pulled back.

She enticed him to visit her someday in the hospital, "Not

as a patient, please." Then she stood and said, "I'm in a hurry. I'll be late." Leticia turned to walk away, then looked back and said, "Goodbye Hank, French-Mexican-Indian guy. I will never forget this moment. Just think, I knew Hank Lefebvre, one of USC's greatest. No one will ever believe it."

Hank was dazed. He'd heard that before and it took him a few moments to shake off the memory. Then Leticia dashed back into the crowd, like a magician disappearing into the traffic of the city.

Hank found Forrest fumbling around with the enchanting blonde he'd just met, but he appeared to be wasting his time so Hank didn't mind interrupting. "Come on, Forrest. Let's go back to my house. Ma's got us a fine meal, then we can catch a trolley to go down to Long Beach and visit with your folks."

Forrest agreed and on the way over asked, "What about that hot-looking girl? What's her story?"

"Not one I'm going to tell."

Forrest chuckled. "Okay, buddy. How about telling me if you're going to play pro football on your next stop?"

"No way. There's no money in it, Forrest. Suckers game… my vanity has to quit enabling my football addiction. The physical price has simply become too high. Maybe a game or so just to pay a few bills. No, I've got something else in mind. My friend, just as you said—you and I are going gold hunting!"

"What?"

"Yes, gold hunting. An old friend of mine from Douglas tells me he knows where to find it. Mining is a bit dangerous, but when you see that gold glitter, your eyes will pop out and your heart will pump faster than ever."

"And what does Miss Lillian Ludwig think about your future business escapade?"

"Lillian is now only concerned with Lillian Ludwig. We gave up on our mutual plans. She's going to Hollywood to be a star. And me, I'm going on a journey to Arizona. Yes, that's our first stop on our venture."

"What do you mean our first stop?"

"Just that, Forrest, you and me are partners in gold mining, then it's the world."

PART IV

THE FINALE

CHAPTER 34

3:10 IN YUMA, ARIZONA
THERE'S GOLD IN THEM HILLS

Henry Lefebvre Sr. died April 5, 1927 from acute, chronic emphysema, and buried in the Sunnyside Cemetery in Long Beach, California. His life was built on contradictions, yet his name resides alongside other pioneer legends. For Hank, carrying a torch that included a responsibility to care for the legacy of the Lefebvre crest would be a heavy load. He knew, with the help of his sisters and brothers, they would manage, but for now Hank needed a reality check to bank on.

On November 11, 1926, the *Los Angeles Times* announced his reluctant decision:

> HAWKINS AND LEFEBVRE SIGN CONTRACT TO PLAY PROFESSIONAL FOOTBALL: Ex-Trojan Stars on Local Gridiron Team!
>
> Johnny Hawkins, former University of Southern California captain and Henry (Hank) Lefebvre, another ex-Trojan grid performer, yesterday signed contracts to play professional football. For Hawkins, who captained the Trojans from the quarterback positon two years ago, the plunge was not a new one as he played with the General's professionals against 'Red' Grange here last fall with Lefebvre. However, it was another matter, Lefebvre, who has been strictly

an amateur since his graduation last June and at one time said he would never play professional football. Apparently 'Laffy,' like all humans, is not entirely immune to the lure of the banknotes. While on the gridiron he confines himself to the backfield.

Ultimately, Hank played just two games with the Hollywood Generals. The $123 per game didn't pay the bills, and in those hard economic times, he would have to take a different chance. What else was there to do but roll the dice, as his pa often did, and go looking for gold.

"And where would that be?" Forrest asked.

"Arizona!" Hank answered.

"Why there?" Forrest quizzed.

Hank shot back, "The Dutchman did, and look at what he found. There's gold in them hills! Now, Forrest, I know, what you're going to say. That it's dangerous with all them rustlers and *banditos* jumping claims. But that's just it. I know that country and dealt with them type of varmint's all my young life. Yup, another spellbound venture. The more trouble, the better the stories of the journey."

"Okay, so where in Arizona are we going to mine all this gold?"

"No, no, no, Forrest. You've obviously been way too long in the city. There will be no mining. We're going "placer" gold hunting. Meaning, no one's going down a mine shaft. Not like my pa and his brother done. No, we'll build a sluice and let the water run down and gold nuggets will shine at the bottom."

"Really? That's all there is to it?" Forrest asked, now getting into the idea.

"Sure thing," Hank declared.

Forrest paused, then replied, "If it's that easy, why aren't more people doing it?"

"I'm not sure. You'd got me there, partner," Hank answered and looked down to think about that some more. "Maybe, they don't have the start-up money that's needed for such a venture."

"And we do?"

"When I get through talking up the idea with Clifford and Sonny, I think they will go along."

"Yeah, I'm sure they will," Forrest mocked, then added "by the way, you're talking real peculiar, Hank. What's that all about?"

"That's the way people talk down in the Southwest. I'm just trying to remember how it was. That English teacher, what was her name anyhow?"

"Miss Mary Christine Ellis?"

Oh yeah, that's it. Anyway, she told me the first day I was in her class that my English needed immediate attention. Can you imagine that?"

Hank and Forrest spent the rest of the conversation reminiscing about the old days around Long Beach, when they weren't really that old, at least not by age, but by experience.

"Well, Hank, my life's been like a cat with nine lives around you…"

A few days later Hank approached Forrest with a big smile. "So, our new investors are a one-time ex-billiard parlor-entrepreneur-bootlegger and a converted mobster-now-legit produce businessman." The young men laughed, delighted with the idea of these unlikely investors enabling the latest exploits of one Hank "Laffy" Lefebvre, who continued to trip into the headlines with a certainty that was at least as entertaining as a Charley Chaplain matinee.

The dramatic economic downturn came like an

unsurprising flash flood from a monsoon. Many desperate individuals, rather than gamble away their stashed savings, kept it well-hidden under the mattress as a firewall from untrusted bankers, institutes, and federal monetary policies. They remembered Hoover's proclamation that "Prosperity is just around the corner," but unfortunately, that corner's block kept getting longer and a certain sense of impatience became an epidemic when the stock market crashed in October of 1929.

So, the Son of Douglas followed through with his promise to Forrest and turned his eyes to the sedentary desert mountains and the mining of precious metals that had supported the Southwest Arizona territory well.

The men would start their search around Yuma, Arizona, eventually settling down to work on Claim #56. It was a depleted mining region, but was covered in a rich residue of flash from the Puerto Blanca Mountains, which just happened to be in the proximity of Hank's former hometown of Douglas.

Besides the predators, indigenous reptiles, and members of the cat kingdom who vanquished victims for want of tasting homosapiens, there were the two-legged concerns of bandits and local vultures. They came in many flavors in this remote land, ready to ambush unassuming visitors who were untrained and unaware to the nuisances of the region. With that in mind, and under the supervision of Forrest and the leadership of USC's "Flash" Hank Lefebvre, Benjamin, Gilbert, and few previously unknown acquaintances undertook the mission to get rich and ride the Lucky Lady of chance.

After a few weeks in the great outdoors shoveling dirt and rocks into a mining sluice box that was fed water from a nearby stream, nothing seemed desirable anymore. The sun was scorching hot and the food tasteless, even with a few Mexican beans and splinters of jerky as condiments. Then there were the predators crawling about, looking for a cooling by the shade, loitering under rocks for cover from the unrelenting heat, and irritated by the interruption of these men who turned over each protective stone in their quest for any fortune or treasures the heartless earth may have been hiding.

When the others felt displaced, Hank felt at home and joked with them around the campfire. "Imagine when the Indians came out here to feel free. And how about when the troops arrived at Fort Huachuca praying for their first quick fix of bravado in battle. One Indian asked his leader how many more would venture out this way to experience the wild Southwest. 'More than the buffalo,' the wise chief would say.'" Everybody laughed at Hank's animated attempts to lighten the mood. However, temporary moments of comedic relief would soon drift away at the sight of unfamiliar creatures, like the well-represented scorpions who inched their way into camp. Also, trying to rest under the dark sky while listening to the disturbing cries of some poor critter being devoured by a starving predator was impossible, to say the least. A trickling stream provided the only toiletry needs, and by sunset, complaints and grumbles about the risk, investment, and emotional struggles they were enduring would begin again.

Yet Hank, who'd grown up in these territories, seemed to grow stronger with each challenge. As time passed and resentment billowed throughout Claim # 56, Hank, seeing discomfort had its limits for the other men, attempted to squash their dismay. "Boys, why not take the truck and a few of you go up the road aways. There's a friendly looking bar I saw last week while getting supplies. Go on ahead. Maybe there's some farmer's dau—no—miner's daughter ready to be taken for a dance or a wild walk into the desert." With that pardon, the other men took off, hopefully hearing Hank's last-minute instructions to take care of the truck. Forrest and a few of the most noble stayed behind and settled in around the campfire to enjoy hearing more of Hank's stories of the past—not only his, but his father's, Emiliano's, Jack Slaughter's, and other legends who'd passed this way.

It wasn't long till all this boredom and self-fulfilling prophecy of doom came to an abrupt end. Forrest was first to find a considerable-sized gold nugget while scooping a load of dirt into the sluice. The camp was beyond itself with cheers of joy, applause, and celebratory hugs. Finding that precious gold nugget reminded Hank of the grumblings that went on during football when the team took a loss that changed to cheers of joy when the team took a win. Sure enough, finding the nugget completely changed the atmosphere around camp. The members of the gold hunting team went slightly mad, digging and shoveling like well-greased machines, looking for that next nugget, which they eventually found within a few yards from the other. They were rich, and their heads swelled with dreams of what they now could afford. What a day it was!

But Hank and Forrest knew better. This was just enough gold to make it through some bad spots. They'd need more to keep them going. Gold had dropped to only eighteen dollars an ounce, so there would be a lot more work to do, but Hank and Forrest decided to keep those uncomfortable facts to themselves.

Later, while the boys were in town again, they apparently began to loosen up on the spirits and offered drinks to some less-than-savory folks. Upon their return, Benjamin whispered to Hank that he had some concerns. They stepped away and Hank said, "Okay Benny, let's hear it."

"Well, Hank, when the boys were at that bar, you'd think by their excitement they'd found the Lost Duchman's mine, and they let the place know what we'd found. Some were listening a little too careful and even asked where our claim was."

Forrest overheard Benny's concerns. "Well, what should we do, Hank?"

"Wait here boys. I'll be just a minute," Hank said, then went to his tent and came out with a pistol. "If any unsavory folks want trouble, this here is going to do the talking."

Hank saw that Forrest couldn't hide the fear welling up, so he smiled to reassure. "Not to worry Forrest...been through this a time and a bit. Even seen men hanging from trees." Hank spoke with a calm urgency and tried to appear undisturbed at the prospect of an altercation, "Why, didn't my Pa, Emiliano, and John Slaughter help tame this land from unwanted moral retards? And none of them pleaded for the law to protect them. They appointed themselves as proxy for the law. So, look. I have this fine Colt M1911 semi-automatic pistol. It fires .45-caliber bullets, good enough to be used by the US military. It has stopping power. Rest assured, if these bad hombres think of coming to our camp, they'll be in mighty big trouble." Hank knew Forrest had seen his bravado and skills as a fighter and ability to smash opponents in football games, but never had he shown him his frontier warrior pretense. He didn't want Forrest to be afraid, like the others seemed to be, that if the chance came, it would be a serious situation.

Once the sun set and shadows disappeared, the sounds of animals that had survived the previous night's carnage came alive. This time the boys welcomed the familiar commotion. Hank already cautioned his companions about loose talk—especially when it concerned gold—but he reminded them again: "Gold has a way of making people crazy and act in peculiar ways."

At about the last flicker of the fire, Forrest came over to Hank. He was stirring the fire and settling in. When the sparks gave out their remaining burst of heat and light, Hank said, "It's too quiet. Can't hear the critters. They've stopped."

"Yep, me neither," Forrest whispered.

Hank instructed Forrest to walk around camp. "Tell everyone to take cover behind something that will stop a bullet. But tell them to move naturally and put out their cigarettes."

"Why Hank?"

"Just get at it. And you get back too. I'll be right here to greet any intruder who comes this way. Now go Forrest, do as I say."

Forrest slipped away, leaving Hank to set alone, keeping the hot embers between him and the desert. The glow gave him just enough light to see them. There they were: men... approaching. Hank didn't move. He just let them come closer, closer, until they were a safe distance, about some thirty yards. Still sitting, Hank spoke up, "So what you folks doing out here this time of night?" There was no reply, but they stopped their advances. Hank noticed one was carrying a shotgun in his right hand, a short barrel...not much use for killing critters, and another man had a holstered pistol. He saw another two men stay back in the shadows. Hank broke the silence again when he asked, "Best tell me what is your business, coming on our claim."

The man holding the shotgun spoke up, "Well, we'd heard you found some nuggets."

"Maybe so, maybe not," Hank taunted and continued, "I don't see it's any of your business now, do you folks?"

"This makes it my business," said the other man as he unholstered his pistol.

"So, what makes you think that you can come in here and steal a few nuggets that easy? You know we've got many men around," Hank said in a composed manner.

"'Cause, señor, we'd seen that they all be but tenderfoots

and after tonight, be running back to LA where they admit they come from. That's why!"

"So then, you didn't ask about me…who I am?"

"No matter. You's all the same Californ-i-a greenhorns," The man mocked, his features still guarded by the night.

Hank slowly stood. "Well, you should've asked, see, I'm Henry Lefebvre Jr. You heard of the Lefebvres in these parts?"

"Can't say I have."

"Well, you should have. See, I ain't one of those city dwellers. I've been born and raised in and around these parts."

"Is that so?" the man sniped back.

Hank had no more patience for this man. "YOU SON OF A BITCH. I'M A REGAL SON OF DOUGLAS, THAT WHO I BE!" Without pausing, Hank did as as his cousin Charley had done at the Long Beach Pike and threw out his left hand that held the Colt, went to his knee, and let the bullets fly.

Caught by surprise, the *banditos* froze for a moment. Hank stayed on the man holding the shotgun, hitting him first with two rounds of the .45 shells, throwing him on his back. By the time Hank turned and directed his deadly shots at the man holding the pistol, he'd gotten a round off. Still, Hank never gave way, peppering him with another round until the man fell to the ground.

Everything went still until a man's voice pleaded from the shadows, "Stop the shooting!" He came into view with raised hands. "Damn, *hombre*, you shot them both," he said, as he stumbled over a body.

"I had good reason, and if any of you bastards come back here again or talk to my crew…you know what to expect. *Comprende*? Now, get those *hombres* out of my sight before I send the rest of you bandits to your maker with them. *¡MUY RAPIDO!*"

The men obeyed, hastily gathering up their fallen comrades and carrying them out into the night. It took a few moments before Forrest and Gilbert came out from hiding. No one seemed surprised at what Hank did except Forrest, who stated the obvious several times, "Hank, you shot those guys."

"Like I said, Forrest. I come from this part of the world. We play the game a little different out here. Justice is swift and direct. No need for a pampered judge or nervous jury. That be the only law I'd grown up with. Seems nothing changed much since I was here last."

"So, what about those guys you shot?"

"Forrest, do you really think they are going to go to the authorities and tell them they tried to rob us with guns in hand and get thrown in jail for who knows how long? Believe me. They will go back and lick their wounds, if they can, and tell their bandit friends to stay away from Claim #56. It's not healthy there. There's other fish for them to fry." Suddenly, Hank stopped to look around and said, "Hey Benny, get out of that chair. I need to sit down. I think I took one in my stomach. Here, take a look Forrest."

"You have a small puncture mark, Hank."

"Now, check my back."

"Yep, you got hit there too."

"No, Forrest. It's the same bullet. He only got off one. It must of went straight through."

"We got to get you to a doctor."

"Not in Yuma," Hank ordered. "Let's drive on to Tucson. I've got a friend there."

It took about an hour to get to the hospital where they waited patiently for the doctor. Hank was as much a celebrity in Arizona, and for as many reasons, as he was in LA or Long Beach. After a lot of concerned greetings, the doctor confirmed the bullet had passed right through. Hank let the staff in on what happened and asked if maybe they could write this up as just an accidental shooting, that way there would be no need for explaining.

The January 7 edition of the *Chicago Daily Tribune* quoted the January 6 edition of the *Los Angeles times*, which reported that: "Henry (Hank) Lefebvre, #33, the famous fullback of the University of Southern California football teams of 1923, 1924 and 1925 accidently shot himself in the abdomen last night while inspecting an automatic pistol in the home of a friend. The bullet cut through the abdominal muscles, but did not strike a vital organ and surgeons said his recovery was considered certain."

Ultimately, Hank pursued the gold-hunting venture long enough to make a respectable living. But sensing there was no fortune to be made there, he would eventually travel back to the Hollywood studios where his reputation could at least get him a steady income. This would be another temporary engagement, of course, for Hank firmly believed in that old adage: "America is paved with streets of gold." He just needed to find the right address.

CHAPTER 35

LAST BUGLE CALL
THREE GUN VOLLEY

The fort was established back in 1877 in the Huachuca
mountain range to protect settlers and fellow travelers
from the plunder of native Apaches, Mexican *banditos*,
and the worst American *hombres* who made their headquarters
in the string of remote and lawless towns of Southeastern Arizona. Pearce, Tombstone, Bisbee, and Douglas were yet to be
tamed and benefited the most from the young warriors who
came to fulfill their duty in a time of great danger. And, like
so many others who ventured to this remote post, it was often to be their final resting place, alongside early cavalrymen,
pioneers, Apache Indian scouts, teamsters, packers, and the

families that supported their efforts.

On this warm July day, a special formation of troops dressed in Class A's were corralled at Fort Huachuca's cemetery. Colors flew, and buglers stood at the ready to commemorate, with full military honors, one of their own. High-ranking military officers, notable state dignitaries, senators, and congressmen gathered to console the grieving family. Most were in shock. The suddenness of this death prevented adequate preparation for this moment.

As the sun set high across the crowd, the pastor stood, cleared his throat, and attempted to wipe his swollen eyes while tears escaped and trickled down his cheeks. His voice cracking with pain, the pastor tried to explain and make wisdom from scriptures.

There's one indisputable fact. Life is dynamic. It continually preys and challenges emotional and physical mobility. Only death can prevent this discomfort. What more do we have then? For, it is certain that what is today will change from what is, or what was before as rapidly as a flick of a switch or seconds on the clock. It offers untimely and indiscrete drama to the heart.

Hank's flirtation with the prospects of life would be interrupted after opening the next letter from Doris Mae. The letter had trouble reaching him. It was outdated, obviously rerouted over a period of time. The postal markings on the envelope gave a clue as to its journey hoping to find him in the remote Arizona area. Sensing somehow, as instinct does, the fright of what she might reveal in her letter, he read:

> *Dear Cousin,*
> *I don't have the emotion or words to know where to start...*
> *so I will just begin.*

On July 13th, Charley Jr. died at the Fort Huachuca hospital after only a month's illness. It started with a sore throat that developed into an ear infection. I'll never forget the shock my mother got one morning when she took his temperature and it was 106! We rushed him to the hospital and they were not sure if it was a mastoid disease or polio or what. There was a new drug called "sulfa" and every day, Uncle Ernest would drive to Tucson—80 miles away!—for a vial of the drug. The doctors thought the new miracle drug might save him, but it didn't. They decided he died of streptococcus of the bloodstream. He was sick for one month, then buried in the fort's old cemetery with all those fallen frontier soldiers, and honored with a volley and bugle call.

I've been so distressed that I can hardly write about his death. It was the worst tragedy to ever hit our family. All our family fell apart. My mother almost lost her mind. Right after the funeral, my dad sent Mom, Joe, and me to El Paso where my aunt and uncle lived. He thought the change might help my mother. We stayed one month. My younger cousin, Rueben (one year younger than me) and I became close and he tried so hard to cheer me up when I would think of Charley Jr. He would take me to the "Heap O'Cream" ice cream parlor every evening and buy me an ice cream cone. Every time we would hear the song, "What a difference a day made," Rueben would say, "That sure reminds me of Charley Jr.," and we would both cry! Little did he know that a month later he would be with Charley Jr. in heaven. We left El Paso on Aug 13th in the morning and when we arrived home that evening, there was a telegram waiting for us that Rueben had been killed by his best friend while his friend was showing him his dad's gun. His friend's father was a policeman.

My mother was in no condition to make the trip back to El Paso for his funeral, so my dad sent Uncle Albert and me, and we stopped in Douglas and picked up Uncle John and two close friends of my cousin Rueben's mother, and the five of us motored to El Paso. We were about halfway there near Deming, New Mexico, when we were in a head-on collision. A reverend with no insurance ran into us. Luckily, no one was seriously injured, but the car, a new car that my dad bought just before Charley Jr. got sick, was totaled. Some nice strangers picked up the three of us women and took us to El Paso, but my uncles caught a ride on a freight train. I can't describe what a horrible nightmare all this was. My dad immediately put in for a transfer. We had to get away from all these memories. It was on Sept. 13th that we left Fort Huachuca for Columbus, Ohio as pop got his transfer to Fort Hayes. It certainly was a different world. It was bitter cold and so dirty. We hated it but it did serve the purpose. We became so busy trying to adjust to this new life that the wounds started to heal.

Even to this day I can recall the hurt and pain that we all felt at the old cemetery at Fort Huachuca. The military so loved Charley Jr., they paid him honors at the burial site. Not only did they present arms with a three-gun volley, but the bugler played taps. It was such an emotional moment that the bugler interrupted to expel the tears running down his face, then proceeded after gathering the breath he needed to finish. I think some of the military's dreams and aspirations were buried with Charley Jr. in that grave that day. Grandpa Joseph was so bereaved. He built a rock arch around the entry of the old cemetery in Fort Huachuca, which he said will stand and endure for centuries. It's quite a tribute to pass under that arch, to see all the limestone grave markers lined in formation, and the white headstones, so disciplined, so erect, and to read about all the acts of bravery carved in granite. It's as if they're all standing at attention as a memorial to the other soldiers that lay there. Charley Jr.'s grave is the only one encased by white concrete. The marker is simply inscribed, Charley Lefebvre Jr.

I'll always remember Charley Jr. I can't, and won't, let his memories fade. However, there's no wisdom on replaying them too often. Terrible things happen, we all know that. But every time I hear our favorite songs, "What a Difference a Day Makes," "Solitude," "I Was Lucky," "Lazy River," I can't help but dwell on him. In the notes, the lyrics and the rhythm, I remember Charley Jr., my brother, and what life could have been for him.

I am sorry to have to write you of his passing. But you're so hard to find these days. Just hoping this letter will find you well and safe.

Love, Doris Mae

Late that night, back in camp, with those timeless stars twinkling above, Hank held that letter, going over it many times, trying to read between the lines, hoping to come up with an answer. For what, he didn't know. But he did remember the book that his cranky high school English teacher had loaned him, which he'd never returned and still carried with him. The *Anthology of Poetry* seemed useless to him at the time and he'd replied to her offering, "What use would I have with poetry? I can't understand any of its ramblings."

"Someday, Hank, the moment will come when you will need to take time to fondle its pages," She had assured him.

Hank felt that time had come. Emily Brontë, an eighteenth century poet, gave him the peace he so desperately needed that night. Passages from her work, "Remembrance" echoed through his mind: "But when the days of golden dreams had perished and even despair was powerless to destroy, then did I learn how existence could be cherished, strengthened and fed without the aid of joy, then did I check the tears of useless passion."

CHAPTER 36

HOLLYWOOD'S GOLDEN AGE

"All the world's a stage and all men and women merely players; they have their exits and their entrances…" Shakespeare's famous monologue best explains the sleight of hand where commoners can become revered as kings and queens merely by pretensions offered by personas displayed on the big screen. Caveat, it's nothing but a thespian ruse, nothing but an act, not necessarily chimed into the pragmatic world. For the cinema performance is scripted so that thieves and liars can become the virtuous hero, simply framed by the magic of the pen, passionately massaged and animated to where tenacity, regrettably, becomes most compelling.

By luck or charm, Hank had been going through life like a wandering gypsy. This boy from Douglas, Arizona first entered Hollywood's world of fantasy and entertainment when it was but an infant, and now publicized as "The Gold Days of the Movies." In the early 20s, while Hank worked as a camera grip, all films were silent and produced in black and white. A pianist would sit in the orchestra pit, beating away a mood as the action took place on the screen to signal moviegoers on how they should feel at any given moment. When United Artist and Warner Brothers began gobbling up distribution outlets, the competition was on. In 1927, talkies were introduced with Al Jolson in *The Jazz Singer*, and when producers began choreographing film with sound, they found that most actors desperately needed voice lessons—that is, if they wanted to remain employed for the going rate of $125 a movie.

When Hank returned from the goldfields of Arizona, he was happy to find most of his celebrity status was still in the studio's memory, however Hollywood was quite a different place. Douglas Fairchild explained to him that Technicolor spacing and other camera innovations were about to change the face of the industry. Once again, by mere product of timing, destiny, or his keen Douglas instincts, Hank was at the right place in 1939 when Hollywood sprouted wings with the making of two important movies. Gone with the Wind and The Wizard of Oz were both milestones for voice and Technicolor's intrusion into motion pictures. Something more personal to Hank was the new brand of celebrity these technologies created—celebrity that surpassed the Gables and Chaplins of the early days. This new band of performers came from far-off places, such as Winter, Iowa; Benkelman, Nebraska; Northern Bristol England; and Plattsburgh, New York. Hollywood's new stars often had marquee names that needed amending from their parent's identification, however. Unappealing monikers wouldn't fit neatly with the sale, so actors like Marion Robert Morrison would be introduced as "John Wayne," and nicknamed "The Duke." Like earlier screen talents, such as John Sidney Blyth, who became known as "John Barrymore," the likes of Archibald Alexander Leach would now be known as "Cary Grant," and perhaps the most talented survivor of the silent screen B movies, Gladys Georgianna Greene (later acclaimed as "America's Greta Garbo"), followed court by receiving her screen name of "Jean Arthur." For the first time, this new brand of actor or actress became bigger than the movies they played in. The big screen became a magical experience for audiences where personalities and chemistry between actors became larger than life. Names on billboards became familiar and enticed people off their couches to rush eagerly into theatres for each new production. Even athletes like Babe Ruth became giants among men through the magic of cinema.

Thus, the celebrity was born...a new reality, a reset for many. These new status holders would become relevant beyond the big screen, emulated for their lifestyle and fashion choices. Hank asked his friend Gladys, who was still as shy as when Lillian first introduced them, why she stayed in the business so long. Her reply became her anthem and carried by many other famous people of film. "I guess I became an actress because I didn't want to be myself."

Back in Hollywood, Hank bustled about the studios on a first-name basis with budding stars and busy production crews. His charming personality was well-received on the sets of Warner Brothers, United Artists, and even Columbia. During the transition between the Golden Age and Technicolor films, Hank stayed mostly behind the camera where producers sought him out for his athleticism, his contagious good humor, and his unique pioneer background—especially when they needed script and scenery advice for the popular western movies. Sometimes Hank even served as an extra, riding here and there as a nameless cowhand. Over time he was promoted to grip boss, stuntman, background barber, painter, or whatever was needed in those days when unions were almost void in the growing industry. But most often he was known as a behind-the-scenes comical character that loved to play pranks on actors as they waited long hours to hear the word "action."

Hank performed one of his biggest ploys on his closest friend, Ronald Reagan, the sports announcer who became known as "The Gipper," from his Knute Rockne movie. In one scene, the script required someone to grab a pail of water and pour it over Ronny's head. Hank sat patiently through a couple takes, then set his trick to work. When the actors were in place and the director called "action," an actor dumped the pail over Ronald Regan's head. But instead of water, the pail had been mysteriously filled with milk. That brought the cast and the production crew to a standstill with laughter, knowing immediately who the culprit was. Studios loved having Hank around because he was one of those unique characters who could keep a crew entertained while catering to puffed-up celebrities, who often became consumed with themselves to the point of tedium and movie-making threatened to turn into encumbered and laborious propositions. Hank always kept track of his friends from the movies and USC, never forgetting that Ward Bond, John Wayne, and he had played alongside each other at USC. All remained great alumni until the end.

He had access to, and dated, all kinds of young actresses, so his social life needed no attention. However, it wasn't long before he would need a new challenge beyond the movie industry. He understood that, as with his former football popularity, glamor and fame would eventually fade and he would need something more to push him forward. His Hollywood work and small produce delivery business managed to steer the family through the depression. But the idea of working in management with Sonny or procuring a place with Clifford in the declining billiard business was not Hank's calling. Also, as he watched the politics of the times, it became evident that sooner or later, events in Europe would find their way across the pond.

Signs of war were all around, and Hank remembered from his high school days how the first world war came home. Lately, his mother had been expressing concern about how

Hank would turn out now that his father had passed. But there was no need for worry about Hank's devotion to family. His instincts were always "family first," and he was anxious that if war came again, this time his brothers would likely be drafted. His oldest brother, Alfred, was touring Europe in a gymnastic exhibition and training for the decathlon in the upcoming Olympics, while his youngest brothers were following in Hank's footsteps as football standouts. But their futures were still as uncertain as his. The family was still living hand-to-mouth, just meeting each day's needs.

About this time, another one of Doris's letters found him.

> *Dear Hank,*
>
> *It's been a while since I've written to you. Life has been more complicated since Charley Jr.'s death. I can remember how it was back in Arizona before he died, going to high school in Tombstone 30 miles away. Even the bus trip we took every day was fun. I would look out the window and daydream en route. I liked school in Tombstone. I was popular and the only girl in the band. I think I got the best education in that one year then all the rest of my school years. I left there and finished my high school in Columbus Ohio, then attended Ohio State University. It was a waste of time because all I concentrated on was trying to have fun. I was thrown in with a class of 2,500 students. It was a rat race. What I really liked was the band. I played the baritone sax, the heaviest instrument, and I was the smallest in the band. Imagine all those marches and parades, carrying around that big sax. But thoughts during my leisure time always went back to when I was a little girl visiting my family in Douglas for weekend picnics. Christmas with them was real special, and so was the post chapel at Fort Huachuca. Since it was so small, we'd either travel there, or the priest and nuns would visit us. Then there was the post commissary. My dad ran the whole commissary and*

sometimes after school, I would stop by his office and he would take me through the store where he had access to everything. Best was the Post bakery and I can still smell it and the gallons of ice cream. Since my father procured all the food at the fort, we as a family were invited to many officer festivities, quite a treat for us since my mother was Mexican. But on those occasions, our heritage didn't seem to matter much. During the depression, my dad was the only one with a steady job and about once a month he would load up the car, a Hudson Super 6, with groceries and we would take off to Douglas. Mother would gather all her hand-me-down clothes and toys to give to our more unfortunate relatives once we arrived in Douglas. They must have thought it was Christmas. Speaking of Christmas, we'd order things from the PX catalogs, from Sears and Wards. Speaking of earning money, I learned how to give finger-waves. There were no beauty shops on post and once the word got around, I had many customers, mostly officer's wives. And then there was Mother, who was always there when we needed her. She devoted her whole life to us kids. She was born June 29th, 1898. Being of Mexican decent, she helped me cope with the national tension that persisted in the Northeast Arizona. In time…Gosh Hank I'm rambling on such. I hope you have patience with me, but it does me good to get things out, probably more than you reading this.

Well, back to the present. I'm married now and the war is on. With my husband being a pilot, not knowing when he might be deployed is our big concern. Father says he can arrange a transfer for him to be closer to home. Hopefully soon. So, I'll let you go for now in the hopes to not have such boring details in my next letter.

Always take care, your cousin, Doris Mae

CHAPTER 37

AMERICA GOES TO WAR

It was a usual Sunday morning ritual with Hank, his sisters, Lily and Mary, and his brothers kneeling quietly together. Ma had reluctantly stayed home to tend to a persistent cold while the siblings said mass under the rotunda of the St. Vincent's Cathedral. Its parishioners could feel the sun gaining strength as it threw rays like rainbows through the cathedral's stained-glass windows. Warm light flowed about, attempting to overcome the chill of California's December morning. Serenity fell on the crowd after communion, leaving members time alone to search out God in their hushed prayers.

An abrupt interruption shattered what was left of the service when a visibly upset parish priest hastily took to the podium. "Regretfully, I need to pass this important news on to you…no better place for you to hear it than here before God." He paused while someone passed a note to him, then he stood silent, appearing to take it all in. He read somberly to the anxious crowd: "This morning, in Honolulu, bombers suddenly and without warning struck our naval fleet from the sky and sea at Pearl Harbor. The Japanese bombs took a heavy toll on American lives. Cannonading offshore indicates a naval engagement in progress. Wave after wave of planes streamed over Oahu in an attack, which the army said started at 8:10

Gene Westall

a.m. Honolulu time and ended around 9:25 a.m., an hour and fifteen minutes later." He carefully set the note down on the podium and bowed his head as parishioners gasped. Then he raised his hands to silence them and continued, "Now, more than ever, we need to spend time in prayer for our brave young men and to search out God's peace."

After some time on their knees digesting what the priest had just revealed, members vacated the church in haste, except for the few who remained at the side alters to light candles. This time, Hank was one of them—for Ma's sake. Then the family hurried home to sit by the radio, to take in each momentary sketch of the battle across the Pacific as it played itself into history. It was soon an incontrovertible fact that the United States would go to war, and the world would change once again. Ever since congressional passage of the Selective Training and Service Act of 1940, war had been at the center of many Lefebvre family discussions. Requiring all men between the ages of 21 and 45 to register for the draft had surprised many, since it was the first peacetime draft ever in the United States' history. Once again, Hank's instincts would come into play.

The war took its toll on lives all over the world, and the Lefebvre family wasn't indifferent to its effects. Not only was the war costly in terms of lives lost, this war would also severely disrupt the traditional social fabric of the United States. For the first time, women were brought out of the kitchen and into the world of commerce and production. With the absence of men who were off fighting wars on foreign soils, women were left to tend the home front, work in the defense industries, and make ships, guns and ammunition.

Hank's first thoughts were about his brothers. Gilbert and Benny found themselves exempt from duty because they were married with children now and worked in defense factories down in Long Beach. However, Everett, the youngest, would soon find his way by joining the Army. Alfred joined the Navy.

The year before the war started, to most everyone's surprise, Hank had decided to marry a quiet, unassuming nursing student by the name of Agnes Schultze, and to no one's surprise, her family was well-off. Even though Hank was forty-two years of age, his patriotic passion and past ROTC training at USC compelled him to duty. So, on December 10, 1942, he applied for enlistment, vacating his busy schedule as a film technician, part-time USC physical director, and backfield coach for Page Military Academy. For his experience and celebrity, the military rated him in to the Ninth Company Coast Artillery Corp as Chief Petty Officer and ordered him to report immediately to Norfolk, Virginia for basic training. After instruction on the 20 mm cannons, Hank returned to Long Beach and was stationed in Terminal Island with the Coast Artillery Unit. Even with earpieces to muffle the blunt of training young recruits to fire big guns, his hearing became impaired for life. Combined with his lingering Poly High and USC football injuries, the loud noises took a toll on his body and eventually landed him in nearby Long Beach Naval Hospital alongside an insurmountable number of war causalities that poured in every day. Hank found himself in the position of celebrity patient and staff asked him to talk with patients about the despair and desperation they were feeling. Soon he found himself bedside, addressing their psychological needs, and desperately trying to give hope and meaning to the injured men. Hank even went a step further, organizing the talents of local athletic stars and Hollywood entertainers for visits to the busy hospital wards.

Since D-day, Everett, had been serving somewhere on the European front, causing Ma and others to spend far more time lighting candles in desperate prayers and wishes that, miraculously, their loved ones would survive. Throughout the country, personal dreams and love were displaced and put in abeyance as the war dragged on.

While in the Long Beach Naval Hospital, Hank and Agnes found a love relationship, not so much built on the passions between men and women, but upon a shared compassion for the work they did at the hospital, where she'd also become a volunteer. Through his volunteer experience during the war, Hank's frontier spirit was tamed, but for other Americans, much more was at stake. For many, the war unfolded events that were tragic and life-altering. From the beginning until the end of the war, people waited with hopes and dreams for letters that were never scheduled and always arrived at unexpected times. The anticipation to unseal, unfold, then read a message that was a matter of life and death often produced only a whimper of hope that there would be a next letter, then a next.

Doris's letters continued to weave their way into and make an impact on Hank's life. The two cousins were very different, yet also much alike. Even though they'd met briefly back in Tombstone, the words she wrote in her letters took him back and humbled him with reminders of his upbringing. Her honest voice revealed where life was really lived—in the heart—and they shared comfort with each other. Unfortunately for Doris, this war would strike a diabolical note—one she would bear throughout her life.

> *Dear Hank,*
>
> *The first time I met Gene Westall was after an Ohio State band practice. He didn't play in the band, but his good friend, Harry Kellenberger, played trumpet, as did my brother Joe. Harry introduced us. It was Harry that wanted to escort me to the bus stop and be my boyfriend, but I wasn't interested in him. It*

was love at first sight when I saw Gene. I thought he was the best-looking boy in school and he was so nice and mannerly. I had started teaching a dance class and asked Gene if he cared to join it. Soon we were going steady. He would call me every day and come over every Tues, Fri, Sat. & Sun. He would take me to the movies and then we would walk up and down High Street and stop and eat hot fudge sundaes. Our favorite ice cream places were Dorsum's and Walgreen Drug Store. Gene and I had a perfect relationship. We liked the same things and had the same beliefs. We planned our life together. It was going to be the perfect marriage. We made a budget and set a goal for when we could afford a pretty church wedding. We designed our home (in our minds) and planned how many children we would have—we even had names for them. Everything was going to be just great— but things don't always work out the way you plan.

It looked like America might become involved in a war so the Ohio National Guard, of which Gene belonged, was activated and he was sent with the 134th field artillery unit to Camp Shelby, Mississippi for one year. I thought I was going to die. A year seemed like such a long time in those days. I promised him I'd wait for him and he bought me a beautiful diamond engagement ring. What a sad day it was when I went to the Armory to see them leave. There were a lot of tears as the G.I. trucks pulled away loaded with soldiers. We wrote to each other every day. I quit my job at the theatre where I was a cashier and went to work at a defense plant, Ranco, Inc. I kept very busy working there and also playing with bands at night, all the time counting the days till he would return. His year was up and he returned December 1, 1941. What a happy day that was. We started to rebuild our plans, but when the Japanese bombed Pearl Harbor, the whole world came apart! We knew the National Guard would be the first to go, and we knew the Field Artillery was like a Suicide Squad, so Gene immediately enlisted in the Air Force. My dad got busy right away and contacted his connections at Fort Hayes to help speed up the process for Gene to get in the Air Force. There was no time to waste because boys were being shipped away in all directions every minute. He was accepted and had to report for primary training at Coleman, Texas the last of January. We still weren't ready for marriage, as we didn't have the time or the money for the way we had planned. But when we realized that this was war, no one knew what the outcome would be, so we better grab what happiness we could right now! We decided to get married on my birthday, January 17th. There was no time for plans or arrangements. His mother worked at the County Court House and she helped us cut down the red tape. There were a lot of couples getting married then (some probably thought a married man might get exempt), but with her help we didn't have to wait in long lines to get a marriage license. We were married at his house by a minister friend of his family. Don Calendine and Thelma Kuhn, our friends, stood up with us. I wore a pretty blue velvet dress. After the simple wedding, the folks brought out the drinks and food and we had a big party. Gene and I left for Cincinnati on a short honeymoon. We stayed at the Gibson Hotel. Shortly after we returned, he had to leave for training so we never really had a married life. I went to Coleman, Texas and shared a house with five other young military wives, but the cadets could only come in town on weekends, which were wonderful, but putting up with some of those snobbish wives was not very pleasant during the week.

We went to several other bases and eventually ended up in Tallahassee, and from there he would leave for overseas. We stayed in a hotel because we weren't sure how long we'd be there. Everything was very Top Secret and we'd only know they left when they didn't show up some evening. Every morning when he left for the field we'd say goodbye, not knowing if this was the final one, and in the evening when he'd show up again we were so happy. But it was slow torture, each day wondering if this would be the day. This went on for about three weeks, then one evening he didn't show up. This was my signal to leave for Columbus the next day! I had just arrived home in Columbus when he called me from New York City to tell me his final goodbye.

What a depressed girl I was at home. Every day the paper listed the casualties of local boys. Almost every house on the street had a red, white, and blue star on their window (that meant someone from that house was in the service; quite often it would be a gold star, meaning someone from that house had been killed in action). I just lived for the letters that came every day from him. But about two weeks later the letters quit coming. I was frantic, but my mother told me, "He's alright, it's just that they're busy... maybe the mail isn't getting thru," etc. One morning, very early, the doorbell rang and I heard my mother say, "Oh dear God, does it have a star on it?" When I heard that, I jumped out of bed and ran downstairs. By this time mother and dad were both crying and my dad was telephoning Gene's mother. Yes, the telegram had a star on it but we still had hope because he was "missing in action." I heard from a lot of people who tried to build up my hopes. Some said that a lot of pilots were captured and treated well, or some were with the French underground, etc. Betty Oakley gave me the most hope—she called and said she received a letter from Bob (Bob & Gene were in the same squadron) and he told her that Gene had radioed in and said his P-51 Mustang had been hit, so he was bailing out over Dunkirk, and so the chances of him being alive were very good. These false hopes went on for six weeks, at which time I would not leave the house for fear some word would come and I might miss it. I couldn't eat or sleep over the worry that he might be a prisoner or worse yet—dead. My sister-in-law, Mary, was visiting her brother in Kentucky (where Gene's family lived) and my friends talked me into spending a few days with her. It would do me good to get away, and they would get in touch with me right away if any news came.

I had only been in Kentucky a couple days and Mary and I were coming out of a theatre when I saw Mammy and Pappy Westall. I was so surprised to see them. Mammy said, "Do you want me to tell you here or wait till we get to the house?" I said, "It's bad news, isn't it?" She nodded yes and from then on I can't remember. He was only overseas two weeks and was killed on his third mission. Out of his squadron of fifteen, only three returned from that mission.

I enlisted in the WACS right away and left home for Fort Des Moines, Iowa on Oct. 10, 1944. This was the smartest thing I ever did. I was so busy that there was no time for grieving or feeling sorry for myself.

Life in the Army was very hard. The first day there they gave us shots and vaccinations. Then we had to scrub the floor of the barracks on our hands and knees. Girls passed out right and left from reactions to the shots, but not little puny me. The first few nights, I sobbed, and heard other girls sobbing as well. We were so tired and homesick and thought the Army was hell! No sooner would we cry ourselves to sleep than the darn whistle would blow and bright lights would come on. We had to get up at 4:45 a.m. Then we would all stampede into the latrine and get ready for breakfast at 5:00. It was twenty degrees below zero outside and we had to march to the mess hall. This was suffering! We were forced to eat all our meals. Some girls tried to hide food they didn't like under their hats, but guards started checking all hats, purses, pockets, etc. It didn't take long for me to gain the weight I had lost, and more!

The three months' basic training at Fort Des Moines brings back bad and good memories. Doing KP was no fun. We had to report to the mess hall about 2:30 a.m. and peel potatoes or wash garbage cans to get ready for breakfast. Then we had to

*stay until after the dinner hour and clean up—until 10:00 p.m.!
Worse than that was guard duty. At 2:30 a.m. I went on duty
and although it was only two and a half hours, we had to patrol
the area in twenty-five degrees below zero without a break. Once
in a while we would find an open boiler room and sneak in for
a few short minutes to thaw out. There were always two of us
(armed with a flashlight and a whistle). We put on every piece
of clothing we could, starting with flannel pajamas, ear-muffs,
gloves, under mittens, etc., and were still so cold we couldn't have
blown the whistle if we had to! It was a miserable experience.*

*One time I was called to report to the orderly room. My com-
manding officer had a telegram in her hand and asked if I knew
Albert Lefebvre. I said, "Yes, he's my uncle." She told me he'd
been wounded in action at Omaha Beach on D-day and was in
a hospital in England.*

*I was on KP one day and the mess Sgt. asked if any of us
were artistic. I said I was, and she handed me a bunch of red
and green crepe paper and said, "Here, decorate this mess hall for
Christmas." What can you do with so little to work with? Well,
I cut red pedals and green leaves and glued sticks or wires, whatever I could find for stems, and made poinsettias. I must have
made hundreds of them, for every table had a big bouquet. And I
hung steamers around the tables. The next day at formation our
platoon leader called out, "Private Westall, step forward." I was
scared and wondered what kind of trouble I was in. She said,
"We wish to commend you on the beautiful job you have done
decorating our mess hall!"*

*That evening I was called to the orderly room again. I was
nervous again, but my commanding officer put me at ease. She
said, "I've heard you play the piano in the day room and wonder
if you could play an accordion for Christmas music?" I told her I
sure would try. She found me an accordion and I rode in a jeep all
over the post playing Christmas carols on Christmas Eve. I got*

a commendation for this too. It wasn't easy playing with gloves on, but it was fun, and we brought a little Christmas cheer to the homesick soldiers! This was my first Christmas away from home, and like so many others, a very sad one.

CHAPTER 38

BASKETS OF GOLD AND BLUE BIRDS

Henry "Hank" Lefebvre's life proves that persistence and optimism has its place. When the direst of situations appeared to leave no safe course for recovery, he would offer this advice: "If you find a fork in the road, just take it."

After the war ended and soldiers went home to receive lots of well-deserved attention, mostly unnoticed also came boatloads of unused materials once manufactured to sustain war efforts in the Pacific. Hank settled back in Long Beach then and continued his efforts at the Naval hospital. Persuaded by his wife not to return to the studios, Hank pursued a new business venture. He remembered his talent at trading with Indians in the Chiricahua Mountains and selling Villa relics to the tourists. It had been a matter of supply and demand, and the war hadn't dented that economic proverb one bit. One day, Hank announced to Agnes: "I'm going down to the docks at Terminal Island this morning to check out the Navy surplus sale."

"What? Why would you do that?"

"They're selling all kinds of items in bulk, for pennies. That's why."

"And what in the world would you do with the lot of them?"

"I don't know. Just looking. So after lunch I'll be gone for a while from the hospital. Just cover for me."

"Okay Hank, but mind your business. Don't you dare bring me back military equipment we have no need for."

While wandering around the docks that afternoon, looking for a good buy, Hank noticed rolls and rolls of large green mesh. He figured they must have been used to protect the troops from the mosquitoes that brought the dreaded malaria. He questioned the auctioneer about the price of a roll and was told they were sold by the ton. Without hesitation, Hank bought enough of the mosquito net to protect a couple divisions or so. He found a storage location in Sunland, California, and soon this city became his new home. What followed was an unbridled surprise for his wife, who'd been disgusted by the purchase of those "useless rolls of green stuff."

While visiting his brother Benjamin and his wife, Virginia, Hank found a solution for the use of his risky investment. Benjamin and Virginia both worked for the LA Recreation and Parks Department, and Virginia managed the Olympic swimming pool next to the Coliseum that had been built for the 1932 Olympics (Previously, she had also trained such notables as Johnny Weissmuller and Ester Williams.). As Virginia described an ongoing problem at the pool that needed a solution, Hank listened. "The swimmers have trouble keeping their clothes in order when they come in. They change into their bathing suits in the dressing rooms, and then after swimming have a hard time finding their clothes again; usually when they do, they're wet from lying about. If only we had some kind of basket to put belongings in, then we could hand them a ticket like they do in restaurants for coats."

"I think you've got something there Virginia!" Hank said, "I've got some green mesh, why don't you design a basket and let's see what we can do. Maybe green mesh will work."

Virginia replied, "That will work fine! Bathing suits will dry out when they hang in the sun." So Hank, using Virginia's pattern and his popularity, set about presenting the idea to local city recreation departments. The city of Los Angeles placed their first order for 1,500 green baskets, and soon Hank was traveling throughout the country selling millions of those baskets to almost every city in the US.

Then Benjamin, a recreation leader at Rancho Playground in Los Angeles, came to Hank with another idea. "We only have a string across the middle of our Ping-Pong table, and when people play, they argue about whether the ball goes under or over the string." So Hank came up with the first patent for the Ping-Pong net. Once again, Hank sold millions—this time not just to city recreation departments, but also to happy table tennis fans throughout the world. This led to so many more uses for the green mesh that Hank published a catalog containing over 125 different products.

A favorite of the family, especially nieces and nephews, was his next business venture. Drawing from past experience at the Long Beach Pike, Hank found that his new hometown of Sunland had a perfect location to build the first extra-large swimming plunge and amusement park—no monster roller coaster, but it did have an exciting go-cart racetrack.

It wasn't but a short time later that Hank and his wife Agnes started traveling around the world, just like Emiliano told him he would do years before. And boy did he travel. He and Agnes went to almost every country, to every mountain that he could climb, and crossed all the mighty seas. He loved taking photos of all the places he'd visit and sharing them with anyone who would take the time to enjoy.

Once while sharing his photos to me, Uncle Hank explained, "I don't think it was too much of divine destiny, or a result of Mama lighting all those candles over the years, nor chance, that I've been able to do all that I have. My religion is more of a common-sense, garden-variety faith in God, and I hope that He is pleased with the efforts."

Describing his visit to Rome when the Pope had just died, Hank said, "Now, I'd come to Rome to see the Pope, so I wasn't going to leave that place until I did. I lined up outside of the Sistine Chapel for hours. Even though signs warned us that photos were prohibited, I decided, while passing by the open coffin, that this was worth remembering. So I took out my camera that I'd concealed under my coat and took a few shots of the deceased Pope. I promise you, it wasn't in defiance of God that I broke the rules, it was because of the pretentious claim of those who thought they were unquestionably speaking on God's behalf." Hank went on to admit, "I'm guilty of obtaining some of the blessed holy water, which I fed into my overheated sedan radiator several times, which then miraculously carried me through some tough European mountain climbs."

I surmised that Uncle Henry "Hank" actually did believe in God, but much like Martin Luther, wanted to meet Him on his own accord.

Late in life, without children of his own and a firm belief that what was left of his family was doing just fine, Hank began to give his money away to organizations he felt could do the most good. His first love was education, so his beloved USC was first on his list. The Boy Scouts, Joplin School for Juvenile Offenders, and Rainbow Acres School for Retarded Boys also benefited from his generosity. He also gave thousands to the YMCA, always remembering the opportunities they offered to him and his father back in Douglas.

Hank continued to be an artist as well, scripting oil

paintings around covered wagons, cowboys at round-up time, and Indians on the warpath. His paintings also depicted Mexican ranch hands sipping together over a coffee break in unclaimed, lonesome San Bernardino plains. When asked by reporters, "Why the covered wagons?" Hank would say, "My parents were pioneers in Bisbee and Douglas, where I grew up over eighty years ago. When I was a boy that was our way of life. I like the memories."

Doris Mae's life, although cast in the same vintage of the Southwest and shaped by the values and struggles of a harsh land as Hank, took a much different direction. Yet she navigated her life with similar grace, dignity, pride, and conclusive sense of optimism as Hank, which she shared in the last pages of her memoir titled: *Hide the Tortillas.*

Far left Doris Lefebvre Westall

In January, I was sent to Wright Field, Ohio, which was only about 50 miles from home. I was assigned to the Air Force. I worked in the post office and played with an off-duty band made up of GIs and a couple officers. I played saxophone. We also had a little symphony orchestra and an all-WAC dance band. I was assigned to a DS (detached service) national show as a model. It was a show that went all around the country showing military equipment, and I modeled nurses' uniforms. It was fun because when I wore that uniform, I could go into officers' clubs and pass as an officer (I was only a private!). In other words, I was impersonating and officer! But I had permission to do it!

A lot of well-known bands (Stan Kenton, Benny Goodman, etc.) used to come to the field to entertain the soldiers, but I never wanted to attend. I was still too much bereaved over Gene.

One Friday in August, 1945 we were all alerted that the war was over! It was V-J Day and all the soldiers could have leave. The end of the war was a very depressing time for me. I felt so empty when the gals' husbands returned from overseas, and was envious and bitter because mine would not be coming back. I didn't want to leave the Army. I felt I would never fit in with my old friends. I signed up for as long as they would let me, which was until November, 1946. I hated to leave Wright Field (It had become Patterson Field by then). It had been my refuge. I was certainly a lost soul when I returned home.

I'll never forget meeting Jack Valentine for the first time. I hadn't been out of the service long and neither had he. A girlfriend of mine from Dayton, Ohio (Rhea Anthony) was visiting me, and I took her downtown to the Deshler Wallick Hotel to hear the good band that was playing. As we left the hotel, we entered the revolving door and two good-looking guys entered with us. They kept the door revolving and would not let us out. We were dizzy and laughing. They finally stopped the door and when we got out, one of them said, "If you girls would like to meet us, I can arrange an introduction. My name is Pete Popovich, and this is my friend Jack Valentine." They were so cute and such gentlemen. They walked us to my car, which was parked a few blocks away. They told us they were students at Ohio State University, and also Navy pilots at Port Columbus. They didn't have a car so I offered to give them a ride to the campus since we were going by there anyway. They were such delightful company and asked if they could call us someday. Early the next morning Jack called me and told me his fraternity was having a formal dance in a couple weeks and would I go with him. I was so excited! I bought a gorgeous gown and felt like it was the first date of my life. He was a good dancer and we had a wonderful time. He'd call me every day, and soon we saw each other every night. My folks loved him and my mother would say, "When does the poor boy ever study?" I soon started feeling as though Gene was back. They were so much alike. They both treated me like I was very special. I never thought I could fall in love again, but I did. Gene's parents loved him too, and treated him like he was the son they lost. Jack took me to Painesville to meet his family. They were just great. Soon I had them come to Columbus to meet my folks and the Westalls. They hit it off like old buddies! My girlfriend, Phea, came from Dayton a few times to date Pete. They really hit it off too, and probably would have become serious over each other, but Pete was killed on a training mission one Sunday when he and Jack were flying. I'll never forget the look on Jack's face when he came to my house right after he landed and told me Pete had crashed over his hometown, Lorain, Ohio. Pete was Jack's best friend.

I was going to Capitol College of Oratory and Music and also working at Arthur Murray Studios teaching dancing at this time, a busy schedule with all the activities at Ohio State that I attended with Jack. He was majoring in Mechanical Engineering. He spent more time with me than studying, but it didn't seem to bother him and he graduated with honors. He too was a genius, I found out later! He was very witty. The first time he kissed me after several dates he said, "I bet I can kiss you without touching you, I bet you a penny. Close your eyes." So I closed my eyes and he kissed me on the mouth and then handed me a penny! The next date we had, he pulled out a roll of pennies and handed them to me!

We had been going together about a year when he asked me to marry him. First, I said, "Are you kidding?" Then I said, 'Of course I will!" A few nights later on Valentine's Day, 1948, he took me to dinner at the Deshler Wallick Hotel and proposed.

I said that I would not remarry until Gene's body was sent back and buried in his family plot. They had notified me four years before that his body was on the way, and every month a shipment of bodies would arrive at the Columbus Depot. My dad would rush down there and check out the list and tell us, "No, he's not on this one." This was another ordeal we went thru for several years. It certainly wasn't going to be easy to bring him home in a box and have a belated funeral. Jack and I had been engaged almost a year and could not set a wedding date because we did not know when that funeral would be.

One day, Gene's mother and dad gave me a talking to. They said, "You don't know how long it's going to be before Gene's body arrives. It could take years and you are not being fair to Jack to keep him waiting, you should set a wedding date!" So we did. We decided to get married during Christmas vacation on December 27th when we would have time off for a short honeymoon. It was a beautiful wedding in Holy Name Catholic Church on December 27th, 1948. We flew to New York City and spent New Year's Eve in Times Square, something I had always wanted to do. We were both so happy. We had a real cute apartment waiting for us when we returned. I enrolled at Ohio State University in the Fine Arts department. We were both students, but since we were both going under the GI Bill of Rights, and had his reserve officer's pay and my small widow's pension, we managed very well financially. We had been married about a year and a half when Gene's body arrived. I was so glad to have Jack by my side all this time, and he was a big comfort to Westalls. Jack was considered next of kin and sat with the family at the funeral service. Several of Gene's old buddies were there and they met Jack and liked him so much and were so happy for me.

Jack graduated from Ohio State in May 1950. My dad retired from his Civil Service job in 1952 and they moved to San Diego. Two months later, Jack and I (and our new son, Jackie) followed them. Jack found a job at Convair in Pomona, California. I didn't like having to live so far from my folks (130 miles), but it was certainly closer than Ohio.

We left Ohio in August 1952 in our new Pontiac Convertible. I was three months' pregnant. We were so happy that I was going to have another baby, and it was scheduled to be born on Valentine's Day of 1953. We were in Montana heading for Yellowstone when I became very ill. I was in excruciating pain till we reached Ogden, Utah, where Jack took me to the emergency hospital and they told me I miscarried that baby. I stayed in that hospital for four days, meantime Jack and Jackie stayed in a motel. This was a terrible trip and I have never liked Yellowstone National Park because it reminds me of that time. When we arrived in Pomona, we rented a nice apartment. We loved California! Right away we looked for a house to buy. We fell in love with the new houses that were being built at Kellogg Park. After looking at many homes, we bought one and watched it being built from beginning to end. About three months later it was ready for us to move in. What an exciting time that was! These were the happiest years of my life. Our next three children were born in Pomona Community Hospital. Everything was just great and then in November 1959, Jack died!

A terrible, terrible death that I have been trying to forget for twenty-eight years, and I cannot talk or write about it! He was the nicest, smartest person I ever knew, and he loved his little family more than anything in the world! I had felt so secure in this marriage because I just knew lightning couldn't strike twice. Jack and I both being Catholic, absolutely did not believe in divorce, so it could never end that way. Besides, Jack was four years younger than I, so I knew I would go before he did! Well, lightning did strike twice. Unless you have lost a loved one to death, you cannot possibly know the terrible feeling. You cannot describe it. It was as though I was torn inside into little pieces, and all at once, like someone gave me a shot and I became numb all over and remained in this stupor for the duration of all the arrangements. I could not have made it if it hadn't been for the fortification of my family and his family, who came from Ohio. They were by my side all the time, as were many of my friends. Right after the funeral service at St. Joseph's Catholic Church, I packed as many of my belongings and my children in my station wagon as I could and took off for San Diego. I just wanted to get away from Pomona as fast as I could. My nephew, Butch, drove Jack's car, and although my brothers insisted on driving my car, I would not let anyone drive but me. I was so afraid no one would be as careful driving my children as I would be. I guess that is when I became the over-protective parent that I am. I just could not live if something happened to one of my kids. I would never leave them with a babysitter unless it was my mother.

Jack's body was sent to San Diego a week later for burial at Fort Rosecrans, so I attended his funeral there. Again, I had to sit through the gun salutes and listen to taps and receive the American Flag. To this day, the sound of taps seems to pierce my heart!

I found out that the best way to overcome a grief like this is to not let yourself think about it. Always change your thoughts when you start to think of what's happened. But you cannot control your dreams, and to this day, I have nightmares and flashbacks of those horrible days.

Jack left me well-taken care of financially so there was no hardship that way. However, I did not want to touch a cent of the children's money that they were getting thru VA benefits, so I put it in trust for them till they were twenty-one, and then I opened them their own bank accounts. I knew I had to go to work, but I would never take a job that would take me away from them during the day, so I decided if I learned to play the organ, I might find work in a cocktail lounge and the hours would be while my children were asleep with my mother and dad watching them. My plan worked out perfect. I was soon playing in the best places in San Diego. Rudy's Hearthside Mission Valley Inn, Kings Inn, Town and Country, Officers Clubs, etc. Working nights and busy as a mother in the daytime was certainly good therapy for me, for no one can imagine how lonely and empty I felt. When you're a widow, you are almost like an outcast. You no longer fit in with other couples, and they exclude you a lot more than they do divorcees. I guess they think you'd put a damper on their party, whereas divorcees are more eager to pick up their heels and show their ex's they are living it up!

The hardest time was always 5 p.m. I would see the neighbors' husbands come home from work and I would be envious, even of my mom and dad. They were always doing things together, working in their garden or whatever, and my brothers did the same with their wives. I was happy for them, but felt sorry for myself because I was sure I would never, ever remarry again. Every day it seemed like something would happen to make me ask, "Why did this have to happen to me?" My heart broke the day Elaine rushed home from her little friend's house and said, "Today is Teddy's birthday and her daddy just had a bouquet of flowers delivered to her. Can my daddy send me flowers on my birthday?" How do you explain to a three-year-old child that her daddy is gone forever? At times like that I would reflect back to the day of Jack's funeral in Pomona when an older lady who lived up the street from us came to my house to offer her condolences (Mrs. Leezer). She had heard this was the second husband I lost and she said to me "Someday, somewhere there is a blue bird of happiness waiting for you!"

I was working at the Spinnaker Room in Shelter Island and one night this good looking, charming man came in with his date. They didn't stay long. It was quitting time and I was getting ready to leave when the door flung open and in rushed this charming man. He said, "Oh, I was afraid I missed you. I took my date home and hurried back. Are you married?" I said, "No." He said, "Can I take you out to dinner?" I said, "I don't go to dinner with strangers!" He said, "Can I buy you a drink?" I said, "I don't drink." My boss stood nearby and said, "Go ahead and have a cup of coffee with him," so we sat down at the end of the bar and I had a coke with him. He said, "I love your music, let me introduce myself and tell you something about myself so we won't be strangers." He gave me his card, told me his name was Richard Flemming and worked for Bank of America. He said he graduated from USD and had recently passed the bar. Then I said the magic words: "My brother went to USD and recently passed the bar too, did you know George Lefebvre?" He lit up like a Christmas tree and said, "Did I know George Lefebvre? He was one of my best friends, he sat in front of me in class!" This broke the ice.

I told him a little bit about myself. Told him I had four children. He said, "I love kids—always wanted a big family." He insisted on taking me to dinner so I told him to call me the next day at noon and ask me. I figured by that time he'd be sober (if he was inebriated) or probably wouldn't remember. I didn't give him my phone number but told him it was in the phone book under the name Lefebvre. I was sure I'd never hear from him again.

Who can spell Lefebvre? Anyway, I went home that night and called George right away and asked him if he knew a fellow in his class by the name of Richard Fleming? George said, "Oh yes, he's a heck of a nice guy, very reserved and intelligent." Anyway, sure enough, at noon the next day he called me and he sounded very sensible and repeated the invitation for dinner. We made a date. He took me to the Admiral Kidd Club and we had a wonderful time. He was a good dancer and didn't smoke. He really swept me off my feet! He started talking marriage right away and would not take no for an answer. I told him I never intended to marry again and besides I couldn't marry him because he was a divorced man and my church would not allow it. What I didn't know was that he was a good friend of Bishop Buddy and he had other connections that would cover all angles! To go through all the red tape to get permission to marry a divorced man sometimes takes two years, but Dick was so persistent and determined that he did it in two months. The final consent did not arrive until two hours before we were to be married, and then my church could not find a record of my baptism. They finally located it at Benson, Arizona listed incorrectly under the name of "Maria Adoratin"! We were married at St. Mary Magdalene Church November 25th, 1964.

After the brief ceremony, we boarded a plane for our honeymoon in Acapulco. We spent Thanksgiving Day in Mexico City and then continued on to Acapulco. We stayed at the "El Presidente Hotel." It was great. We danced and a group of violinists followed us around the dance floor and serenaded us with romantic gypsy music. Later, I couldn't believe my eyes when we walked into our room. The wallpaper was all blue birds! I immediately thought of what Mrs. Leezer had told me in Pomona five years before.

CHAPTER 39

BREAKING NEWS

OB's Mysterious Ashes Belonged to Star College Football Player and Inventor of the Ping Pong Net

Posted 11/8/2012
By: Dan Haggerty San Diego 10News has uncovered
major developments Wednesday in the bizarre case of a
box of human ashes left at a car wash in Ocean Beach.

The Amazing story of the mysterious ashes left at the OB Suds Car Wash has had a dramatic turn. We now know much more about Henry "Hank" Lefebvre, whose ashes were in a gold metal box discovered by the carwash owner more than six months ago. After Dan Haggerty of 10News broke the story, a family in Orange County claimed the remains and told 10News an account to rival that of "Forest Gump." Since Lefebvre's remains were found at the OB Car Wash on Voltaire Street in San Diego, the story has circled the world.

As you may recall, the ashes were found and then turned over to the Ocean Beach MainStreet Association for safekeeping. The OBMA then publicized the information about the mysterious ashes and the rest is history, sort of. Members of the family have stepped forward to claim the remains, surprised that Lefebvre had not been buried back in 1995, as some of them had attended his memorial service.

Born in the frontier mining town of Bisbee in 1900, Henry "Hank" Lefebvre was the oldest of eight children raised in a dirt-floor home in one of the last cities the vestige of law reached: Douglas,

Arizona. Smelters, railroad men, and construction workers helped support brothels and gambling salons that became magnets for the worst kind of outlaws. Other parts of the US didn't take much notice of Douglas until the infamous Pancho Villa attacked the bordering Mexican town of Agua Prieta, just five blocks from Henry's home. Enchanting stories in the cosmopolitan press encouraged northern tourists to visit this rugged southwest territory.

At the age of sixteen, Hank's family moved to Long Beach, California, where, as legend has it, Henry "Hank" Lefebvre became an instant sports figure because of his part in the iconic 1919 Long Beach Poly High School Jackrabbits "Big 102" football game against Phoenix High School Coyotes. He matched this skillful play in the 1920 season during the game for the national title against Everett High, alongside Morley Drury, Chet Dolley, Jazz Lawson, and coached by legendary Eddie Kienholz.

Lefebvre went on to attend and play football for USC from 1923-25 under coaches Dean Cromwell (acclaimed maker of champs), Gus "Gloomy" Henderson, and Howard Jones. At USC, Lefebvre picked up the nickname "The French Flash" and achieved football glory as a star running back. In 1923, Lefebvre infamously made the very first touchdown during the first Rose Bowl game ever played in the newly built LA Coliseum in Pasadena. And guess who else was on that remarkable USC team? John Wayne. Yes, John Wayne. "The Duke" and Lefebvre remained good friends for years after.

Henry also played baseball and ran track at USC, becoming friends with track's world-record holder Charley Paddock of Chariots of Fire fame. After USC, Henry worked in Warner Brothers studio and befriended the likes of Jean Arthur and Ronald Reagan. In addition to knocking out famous prizefighters from time-to-time, when WWII came, Henry joined the Navy at the age of forty-two as a Chief Petty Officer and served for the duration of the war.

Lefebvre went on to become a millionaire and inventor of many products sold by his Sun Aired Bag Company. He began by turning military surplus malaria netting into mesh bags with hangers for holding clothes and other belongings at public swimming pools throughout the world. His most incredible invention, however, was the Ping-Pong net, for which he held a patent.

Henry spent his later years giving away his money to charities that focus on education and youth development. He was also an artist and traveled the world.

Henry "Hank" Lefebvre's life is an amazing story, but we still haven't revealed how his ashes turned up at the OB Suds. According to ABC, here is the story:

Henry died in San Clemente, California in 1995, at the age of 94. Relatives still remember his funeral — complete with a casket — at a cemetery in the LA suburb of Sylmar, so the discovery of Hank's ashes in a San Diego car wash some 17 years later took everyone by surprise. The name "Lefebvre" sounded familiar to the local press because of Henry's famous nephew, Jim Lefebvre. Jimmy had been a LA Dodgers Rookie of the Year and had recently coached the San Diego Padres, which heightened interest in solving the mystery.

Eventually the mystery of Henry's ashes was unraveled. In 1940, Henry purchased several burial plots at Glen Haven Memorial Park, where he would later bury his mother, Adela, and first wife, Agnes. Love ones didn't know that the ceremony they attended in 1995 was a mock funeral, and that Henry had been cremated and his remains had gone to his third wife, who had other ideas about where his final resting place would be. However, the third wife suffered a brain aneurysm two months after Henry died and was incapacitated. Two years later she died of cancer, then was cremated by the same crematorium company as Henry. When her children went to pick up their mother's ashes, they were befuddled that Henry's ashes had never been claimed. They then took his ashes back to their home in Dana Point, California until their finances took a turn for the worst. At that point, they put all of their stepfather's remaining possessions, along with the metal box containing his ashes, into a local storage unit. When they were unable to pay storage fees, the contents went up for auction. Henry was sold to the highest bidder, who apparently found his way to the OB Car Wash. Deciding the metal ash container had no real value, he or she left it there and drove off. Henry's nephew, Gary Lefebvre, retrieved the ashes, and now Henry "Hank" Renaud Lefebvre has found his final resting place with dignity and honor in the Riverside Veteran's Cemetery.

We, his family, are curious as to what response Henry would give if we had the chance to ask him about the predicament of his ashes. My guess is that Uncle Henry would probably smile and give a chuckle. For, whoever had the chance to get their story out twice in one lifetime?

CHAPTER 40

REFLECTIONS IN A
REARVIEW MIRROR

With each passing year, the contrast between past and present accomplishments became less relevant in Hank's life. He realized the next generation would set standards based on their own merits, with little need for taking the time to notice what came first. This became the bedrock of Hank's choice to live life in the present and accept that his illustrious past could never be relived, even though it would sometimes be replayed in old photos, films, and award ceremonies. As for the future, it would never be without the present, and Hank held tight to it as his last defense.

Hank's reality was the dream of others. He made history, while Doris Mae survived history. When opportunity came, she responded to its presence. She made a lot of money playing the organ she'd worked so hard at, and she realized she'd accomplished a milestone when, on one summer night in San Diego, someone yelled over, "Hey, Doris! Look up on the scoreboard!" And there she was—a live shot of her at the Padres' baseball stadium keyboard. A voice announced over the loudspeaker, "We would like to introduce our beautiful organist, Doris Lefebvre!" The crowd cheered as she shyly waved back.

Both Hank and Doris Mae cast large footprints in the parts they were destined to play. Neither boasted, beat their breast, nor took pride in their achievements. They knew events in life would come and go like the tides. In the end, for the profound lives they lived, they hoped with prayer not to become relics, like pyramids stagnating in the desert, nor to become residents of unmarked graves, encased in anonymous cemeteries, with nothing more to tell.

When warm, dry winds blow across the hot desert, high into the rugged mountains and across the plains around Douglas, Bisbee, and Tombstone, or wrestle trees in an attempt to give shade to the old graveyard at Fort Huachuca, this part of the country can seem so desolate, so unreconciled. But then the cooling comes year after year in late July from monsoons and tempers the hot air of Southeastern Arizona territories, leading the territories into fall as the winds have done for thousands of years. You must listen with your heart to sounds fueled with history, and if you do, you will hear distant voices crying out, proclaiming emphatically, "We was here!"

These are not voices from ghosts of the past exploited as props in museums to entertain tourists. Nor are they voices from dust-covered books, pandering out antiquated scripts for gossipers to tell exaggerated tales. But these are voices from the spirits of those rare lives that have been bound by notches in this remote region's topography—notches from unclaimed graves that rise up around this desolate land. They're voices of frontier men, soldiers, farmers, Indians, Mexican rancheros, and yes, even immigrants sailing mighty seas to breach this land for gain. Their spirits cry out, "Look at us! We lived! We stayed the course to tame this frontier. It's not that we did, but that we tried," for who could take on God's creation? It was their challenges that made these spirits special, that made them regal enough to take on the torments and pleasures of the quest that that poets and sentimentalists write about.

"That was us," Hank would say while remembering those special moments outside Bisbee, on his way home to his beloved Douglas when he stood with Emiliano looking out into the orange sky, sharing the same view as those who'd come before; and when he, Josiah, Benjamin, and Alfred were bedded down for the night at the pond on Slaughter's ranch, looking up toward the night sky into a world beyond, where hopefully God was looking back. He wondered, when he came to the end of his life, would he have done enough to be remembered, and more importantly, would God be pleased?

So, what do poets and sentimentalists have to say about what is a regal life? Would Shakespeare not agree that to be regal is to have the presence of honorable behavior, excellence, or magnificence suitable for a king? Hank thought it was more than that. "Though we be just peasants, we'd be the Regal Sons of Douglas." And surely His goodness and mercy had followed them all the days of their lives, and they will dwell in the house of the Lord forever.

REGAL SONS OF DOUGLAS
TALLY, NOTES, RECOGNITIONS

TEXAS JOHN HORTON SLAUGHTER

American lawman, poker player, rancher, Indian fighter, confederate soldier, and financier. "Though short in stature...when in pursuit of outlaws, he was like a spider spinning his web for the unwary fly." Lawmakers have called him "The meanest good-guy who ever did live." He saw no need to contend with biased, unsavory quiverings of nervous juries, for justice rode with him. He rendered his verdict swiftly on the villains he hunted down, returning only with horses and empty saddles.

After the death of his first wife, Eliza Adeline Harris, on August 4, 1971 in Tucson, Arizona of small pox, Slaughter remarried at Tularosa, New Mexico. The marriage to his new wife, Cora Viola Howell, produced no children of their own so they took care of several homeless children, including their beloved, adopted Apache daughter, "May," who they raised on their San Bernardino Ranch. May's premature death would become another epic story in this legendary figure's life.

In his later years—uneasy from recent murders of local ranchers, and having become ill—Slaughter moved into an apartment on Twelfth Street in Douglas. There, on the morning of February 16, 1922, he was found dead of natural causes. He defiled all his prognosticators by dying with his boots off.

Texas John's beloved San Bernardino Ranch has been well-preserved as a national landmark and visited by many a tourist who wonder about Douglas, Arizona. The ranch is located just a fair ride outside Douglas—a mere fifteen miles east—at 6153 Geronimo Trail. The Ranch is a beautiful historical monument, an epitaph to the culture and lives of those early pioneers who braved life and death in this untamed corner of Southwest Arizona, and truly is a "must see."

PANCHO VILLA

Pancho Villa, the revolutionary bandito, ranchero, populist politician, and commander of the Metro Division del Notre, was assassinated on Friday, July 20, 1923 while doing business at a bank in the municipality of Hidalgo del Parral, located just outside of his 25,000-acre hacienda, "Canutillo," in Chihuahua Mexico. He had recently married Maria Luz Corral. Mariano Azuela, Mexican historian and writer whose works chronicle the Mexican Revolution, acclaimed: "Pancho Villa was this archetype of an anti-authoritarian, and Villa was an indomitable lord of the Sierra. The eternal victim of all government, the bandit who passed through the world armed with the blazed torch of an ideal: To rob the rich and give to the poor, for it was the poor who would build up and impose the legend about him, which in time would increase and embellish as a shining example, from generation to generation."

Octavio Paz, Mexican writer, diplomat, and 1990 Nobel Prize winner, wrote: "Villa still gallops through the North in songs and ballads, especially around the border town of Douglas. Tombstone may have had the Earps and the gun fights, but Douglas has the lore, the footprints [Villa] left around her streets and them steps at the Gadsden Hotel to show off. His legacy was as much part of the history, flavor, and the daily yearning and fears of those early dwellers living in this border town."

CARL HAYDEN

Carl Hayden, born October 2, 1877, died January 25, 1972. He was the first Arizonian to serve in the House of Representatives for eight terms before entering the Senate. In fact, Hayden set a record as the longest serving member of the United States Congress. President John F. Kennedy referred to Hayden as the

"Silent Senator." Every Federal program that has contributed to the development of the west—irrigation, power, reclamation—bears his mark, and the great Federal Highway program that binds this country together and that permits Arizona to be competitive east and west, north and south, is—to a large measure—his creation. (notes from Doris Mae memories, *Hide the Tortillas*: "It was the same Carl Hayden, a good friend of Uncle Joseph Lefebvre, who nominated Charley Jr. for an appointment to West Point.")

EDDIE KIENHOLZ

Eddie Kienholz came into the football spotlight in 1917 when Long Beach Poly announced him as their new head football coach. His coaching career was interrupted when the United States government drafted him into World War I. After returning from the war in late 1918, Kienholz coached the team that will forever be a topic of conversation as the greatest in the History of America's high school football teams. In 1919, Kienholz's Poly Jackrabbits out-scored their opponents 549-21. Also, they won Poly's first of three CIF titles, first state championship, and American Southwest championship by a score of 102-0 in a game that will be replayed over and over again in high school football lore. The following year, Eddie's ambitions took the Jackrabbits into national recognition by playing the Everett, Washington high school team. A year later, "Laffy" Hank Lefebvre, and the new upstart center, Morley Drury, led the Poly team. The Poly football team's early success under Kienholz's tutelage was the beginning of a grand reputation for California's Long Beach Poly High School, which was acclaimed by *Sports Illustrated* as "the 20th century's number one high school in the United States."

CHESTER CHET DOLLEY

From Gregory Crouch, Obituaries, April 03, 1988, *Los Angeles Times* staff writer,: "Chester 'Chet' Dolley, who led the Poly Jackrabbits under the coaching of Eddie Kienholz's 1919 Big

102 to 0 victory over Arizona High, and then quarterback of the first USC football team to ever play in the Rose Bowl, died Friday from an aneurysm. He was 87. Dolley helped lead the Trojans to a 14-3 victory over the Penn State Nittany Lions on Jan 1, 1923, even though he was suffering from an injured knee."

The times also reported that Dolley, "stepped into the ranks, and handled the team in a high-class manner without complaint, although every step spelled pain."

Afterward, Dolley told a biographer: "There must have been 60,000 people in the stadium, every one of them hollering." He was named team captain the next season.

Dolley became student body president of USC Law School in 1926. After graduating, he became a practicing attorney until he founded Atlantic Oil Co. in 1933.

Atlantic is a Glendale-based oil and gas production company with thirteen rigs scattered through the San Joaquin and Sacramenoto Valley. Dolley was president at his death. Family members said Dolley, who was born in Long Beach, was a rugged and tough-minded man. He journeyed to Africa on thirteen occasions for safaris, and his homes in Baldwin Hills and Palm Springs are decorated with his trophies.

MORLEY DRURY

From Mal Florence, "'Noblest Trojan of Them All,' Dead at 85," *Los Angeles Times*,.

January 24, 1989: Morley Drury, former Long Beach Poly Jackrabbit football fame, and great legendary USC tailback who was called, 'The Noblest Trojan of Them All,' died of a stroke late Sunday night at Santa Monica Hospital. Drury, 85, had been an invalid for about 12 years and was preparing for a knee operation when he was stricken. Drury is survived by his wife, Louise; a daughter, Margaret; a brother, Harold; and two grandchildren, Tom and Carol.

Many credit Drury with pioneering the Trojan tailback legacy that has produced four Heisman Trophy winners. Drury

434 | THE REGAL SONS OF DOUGLAS

received a stirring standing ovation at the Coliseum when he left the field after his last game in 1927.

An All-American, Drury finished his college career by running for 180 yards and scoring three touchdowns as USC beat Washington, 33-13. The public-address announcer told the crowd that Drury was coming off the field for the last time and should get "the hand that he deserves.

Drury later recalled that emotional moment: "I reached the track and looked up at all those people. I tried to wave, but my hand jerked, so it wasn't much of a wave. My knees got weak even if I did feel as fresh as a horse. And I bawled like a baby."

A big running back at the time—6 feet and 185 pounds—Drury was the first Trojan tailback to gain more than 1,000 yards rushing in a season, piling up 1,163 yards in nine games in 1927. A USC tailback wouldn't gain more than 1,000 yards in a season again until Mike Garrett rushed for 1,440 yards in ten games in 1965.

Drury is identified with Howard Jones' "Thundering Herd" teams of the late 1920s. Jones used his tailback extensively in a single wing formation, and no one, past or present, was as durable as Drury. He played every position in the backfield at one time and was a safety on defense. It wasn't uncommon for him to play all sixty minutes in a game. Drury also passed and punted as a triple-threat tailback, but he was best known for his power running. In one game in his senior season, he carried the ball forty-five times. Forty-one years elapsed before another Trojan tailback, O.J. Simpson, would work as hard. Simpson had 47 carries in a game in 1968."

Ahead of his time in productivity and work ethic, Drury lived most of his life in Santa Monica and was confined to a wheelchair in his later years. He received a rousing ovation when he was introduced on the floor of the Coliseum last August in a celebration of USC's centennial year of football. He had some memorable games, such as the 13-13 tie with Stanford in 1927 when he gained 163 yards.

Drury came to USC in 1925, the same year that Jones became the school's coach. During his three years on the varsity team, the Trojans had a 27-5-1 record.

Mark Kelly, a former sports editor of the Los Angeles Examiner, is credited with immortalizing Drury in Trojan lore when he wrote of the running back: "He's the noblest Trojan of them all." The nickname endured over the years and was a constant source of gratification to Drury, who was recognized as such at every function he attended.

Morely Drury was born Feb. 5, 1903, in Midland, Ontario, Canada. His father died when he was 7, and the family—his mother and brother, Harold—moved to Long Beach when he was a teenager. Drury was older than most students when he enrolled at USC because he had spent two years working in the Long Beach shipyard after finishing grammar school before attending Long Beach Poly High School. At Poly, Drury established his credentials as an outstanding running back, and the ovation he received in 1927 as he trotted off the field to the locker room for the last time is a moment he always cherished.

EDWARD I. DOHENY

August 10, 1856-September 8, 1935

Edward Doheny was a California oil tycoon who, in 1892, drilled the first successful oil field in the city of Los Angeles.

Discovery of Oil

Signal Hill changed forever when oil was discovered. The hill would soon become part of the Long Beach Oil Field, one of the most productive oil fields in the world. On June 23, 1921, Shell Oil Company's Alamitos #1 well erupted. The gas pressure was so great the gusher rose 114 feet (35 m) in the air. Soon Signal Hill was covered with over 100 oil derricks, and because of its prickly appearance at a distance became known as "Porcupine Hill". Today, many of the oil wells and pumpjacks are gone, although quite a few still remain. Signal Hill is now a mix of residential and commercial areas.

Oil magnet donates 1.1 million in 1932 to the University of Southern California to build the Edward l. Doheny Memorial Library in remembrance of his deceased son.

FORT HUACHUCA ARIZONA –Old Post Cemetery

The brochure reads: "The old cemetery is a hallowed spot on the old military reservation. Records, over a century old, show that 3,056 known and 96 unknown dead have been interred here since 1883." It is the final resting place of rugged, early-day cavalrymen, pioneers, Apache Indian scouts, teamsters, packers, wagon masters, as well as our modern-day military and their families. The tree-shaded Fort Huachuca Cemetery is a peaceful, quiet place. A winding native stone wall borders the entrance, with two rock pillars supporting the cemetery crest. The pillars embrace the inscription of that hallowed ground to welcome visitors. It was constructed in 1935 as a quaint tribute, an epitaph, by Joseph Lefebvre to his beloved fallen grandson, Charley Jr. Lefebvre, on July 13, 1935.

CHARLEY WILLIAM PADDOCK

Born in Gainesville, Texas and later serving in World War I as a U.S. Marine first lieutenant of the field artillery, Paddock studied and trained at the University of Southern California under the tutelage of Dean Cromwell. Paddock was a gold medalist in the 1920 Antwerp Olympics and medaled in the 1924 Olympics held in Paris. He participated in his third Olympics in 1928. During his athletic career, he was declared the fastest man in the world. Paddock was a notable bible school teacher in Pasadena, California, as well as a radio announcer who received world acclaim for his journalistic endeavors and interviews with international personalities. While he was traveling with the personal staff of Major General William P. Upshur during World War II, both Upshur and Paddock died in a mysterious plane crash at Sitka, Alaska on July 21, 1943.

ELMER CLINTON "GLOOMY GUS" HENDERSON
March 10, 1889—December 16, 1965

Gus Henderson was born in Oberlin, Ohio. After a successful coaching career at Broadway High School in Seattle, Washington, he served as the head coach at the University of Southern California (1919–1924), then at the University of Tulsa (1925–1935), and Occidental College (1940–1942), compiling a career college football record of 126–42–7. Henderson›s career-winning percentage of .865 at USC is the best of record of any Trojan football coach, and his seventy wins with the Tulsa Golden Hurricanes remains a team record. In between his stints at Tulsa and Occidental, Henderson moved to the professional ranks, helming the Los Angeles Bulldogs of the American Football League in 1937, and the Detroit Lions of the National Football League in 1939.

Henderson also coached basketball and baseball at USC, each for two seasons. Henderson died on December 16, 1965 at age seventy-six in Desert Hot Springs, California of complications from pneumonia. He was survived by his wife, Kathryn, and their daughter. His cremated remains were returned to Oberlin, Ohio. He was inducted into the USC Athletic Hall of Fame in 2005.

HOWARD JONES
August 23, 1885- Excello, Ohio. Died July 27, 1941 Toluca Lake, California at the young age of 55.

The American collegiate gridiron football coach who made his mark on both West and East Coast football, along with his brother Tad Jones, Howard played football in Middletown, Ohio; at Phillips Exeter Academy (1903-04) in Exeter, N.H.; and at Yale University (1905-07). His early coaching experience came at Yale, Syracuse University in New York, and Ohio State University. In 1913, he became the first paid coach at Yale. During his coaching stay at the University of Iowa (1916-23), his team's 10-7 victory over Notre Dame in 1921 drew national attention.

After coaching Duke University in 1925, on a recommendation from Knute Rockne, Jones went to the University of Southern California (USC) in Los Angeles, where he remained until retirement after the 1940 season. There he developed 13 All-American players, and his teams won seven Pacific Coast Conference championships and two national championships and were undefeated in five Rose Bowl games. The success and fame of the football team were beneficial to USC president Rufus von Kleinsmid as he expanded the university during the 1920's and '30s. The Howard Jones practice field, once Bovard Field at U.S.C., is named after him for his contribution to its football program.

DEAN CROMWELL

As track coach, Cromwell's teams at University of Southern California won 12 national collegiate titles, including nine in a row. Nicknamed 'Maker of Champions,' Dean Cromwell was the head coach at USC for 39 years, developing a track and field heritage that still exists. Cromwell participated in track and field and played baseball and football at Occidental college, from which he graduated in 1902. After working for the telephone company for seven years, he became head track and football coach at USC in 1909. Over the next 39 years, his track teams won 12 NCAA championships including 9 in a row from 1935 through 1943. They also won 9 IC4A titles. From 1939 -1948, USC lost only three dual meets. During his tenure, USC athletes won national college titles and 38 National AAU crowns.

He also set 14 individual world records plus three more in the relays. He coached 10 Olympic gold medal winners, including at least one at every Olympics from 1912 through 1948, and had 36 U.S. Olympic team members. Among his athletes were such fellow Hall of Famers as Charlie Paddock, Bud Houser, Mel Patton, Vern Wolfe and Frank Wykoff.

Cromwell retired in 1948. The USC track carried his name and one of the sponsors that gave major donations to building that track came from Henry Hank Renaud Lefebvre. Dean

Cromwell died at the age of 82 at his Los Angeles home suffering from a heart attack.

SANTIGO CARDINALE

Cardinale was a true rages to riches story. An 8th grade dropout, he went on to become a giant in the produce business, owning 25 major companies. He was honored at his memorial by the memories of all those people he employed and mentored, giving generously when they were in need. This big-hearted man did it the old fashion way. Through hard work he created an empire by dicing his way through the turbulent prohibition days. Santiago was determined in his efforts to reshape the image of the Italian underworld portrayed in movies. By true grit he showed the world in which he lived and worked that Italians were men and women of integrity. This creative industrialist lived by a code of moral standards that a hand shake and the loyalty it bound was the best antidote to creating a better integrated America. He died at the age of 94, leaving a large family and grand legacy.

JOSEPH 'JOEY 'ARDIZZONE

During his time as boss, prohibition was active and many, if not most, Mafiosi were involved in bootlegging. In 1931, when the Castellammarese War between Joseph Masseria and Salvatore Maranzano was taking place, The Los Angeles crime family may have supported Maranzano. Nick Gentile notes in his memoirs that during a conference Maranzano was backed by two men from California. Joseph Bonanno (died 2002) and his son Salvatore Bonanno (died 2008) wrote of several close associates in the Los Angeles area, such as Jimmy Costa, Nick Guastella, Frank Bompensiero and Tony Mirabile. It was also during this time that a faction developed that opposed Aridizzone. In early 1931, he was driving with his friend Jimmy Basile when gunmen drove by and shot at them. Basile was killed and Ardizzone wounded. Ardizzone managed to be taken to the house of Leon DeSimone, the physician son of former L.A. don Rosario

DeSimone. He was treated and sent to a hospital. A second attempt was made on his life in the hospital, so his family came to act as bodyguards. Underworld sources indicated that he agreed to retire after these incidents. The opposing faction apparently did not believe Ardizzone, and on October 15, 1931, while on his way to a cousin's house in Etiwanda, driving a 1930 Ford Coupe and carrying a .41 caliber Colt revolver he "disappeared". An intense search followed, but his body was never found. After seven years Arizzone's wife had him declared legally dead.

ERNEST ALONZO NEVERS (June 11, 1903- May 1976)

Sometimes known by the nickname "Big Dog", was an American football and baseball player and football coach. Widely regarded as one of the best football players in the first half of the 20th century, he played as a fullback and was a triple-threat man, known for his talents in running, passing, and kicking. He was inducted with the inaugural classes of inductees into both the College Football Hall of Fame in 1951 and the Pro Football Hall of Fame in 1963. He was also named in 1969 to the NFL 1920s all-Decade Team.

Nevers played four sports (football, basketball, baseball and track and field) for Stanford University from 1923 to 1925. He was a hot topic of concern at Stanford his first year of play under Glen Scobey 'Pop' Warner. Nevers also had a long career as a football coach, including stints with Stanford (assistant, 1928,1932-35, The Chicago Cardinals (head coach, 1930-1931,1939), Lafayette (head coach, 1936), Iowa (assistant, 1937-1938), and the Chicago Rockets (assistant, 1946).

GLADYS GEORGIANNA GREENE

Gladys acted under the screen name of Jean Arthur. Her fabulous and prodigious movie career extended from silent to talkies, then from black and white to technicolor. She was truly an icon and honored by the industry as important to the "Golden Age of Motion Pictures". She will be forever remembered by her final performance in the classic western movie Shane, playing opposite of Alan Ladd, Van Heflin, Ben Johnson and Jack Palance. Gladys retired to the reclose mountains just outside of the seaside town of Carmel, California and later died of heart failure at the age of 90 on June 18, 1991.

JOSIAH AND CHATA

Josiah worked for the United States Indian Service. He died at the age of 62 in 1962 while attempting a rescue effort in the Chiricahua Mountains, leaving a family of three boys and one girl. Chata followed him just 14 months later. The medical term was heart failure but the family knew better. Those two would have wished to stay together forever and they apparently did just that.

EMILIANO GOMEZ

Forman of Rancho Bernardino, loyal friend of Texas John Slaughter, mentor to young Hank Lefebvre and driver of the Conejo. It is said, he'd cross the border many times from Mexico to Douglas just to say hi, then after Mr. Slaughter's death, he never returned.

MANY THANKS

Dan Haggerty of San Diego Channel 10 News.
The journalist whose instinct broke the story, or should I say recovered the story of Henry 'Hank' Lefebvre's life, which was then replayed and carried by international networks around the world.

Debbi Baker
Debbi.baker@utsandiego.com
Another fine article on the discovery and conclusion of those ashes found at the San Diego car wash.

Yvonne Sharp Lefebvre
Many thanks for her laborious research and for providing a map I could use to follow the Lefebvre clan, without which this endeavor would have been impossible and primarily a work of fiction.

Cindy Hayostek
For her dedicated pictorial work in her book, Douglas, which gave me a sense of imagination and direction for the backdrop of my novel.

Doris Mae Lefebvre, Westfall, Valentine, Fleming
With her hand-written manuscript of her illustrious life and the sequence of history, Regal Sons became far more interesting and credible.

Nancy E. Turner
Author of These Are My Words. Her book provided primary source examples for those 1981- early 1900's frontier dialogues.

Jack Valentine
A talented musical artist and crafted baseball athlete who procured and gave permission to include excerpts from his mother's autobiography, titled Hide the Tortillas.

Braven Dyer
Writer of The Los Angeles Times archives, whose early-day newspaper coverage of USC football filled my story with documentation and confirmed its authenticity. He also verified many of Hank's on- and off-the-field escapades.

Colby Lefebvre
Thank you to my son for his fine research, and for providing historical photos and descriptions of the Lefebvre sports legacy from his website: colbyl.com Lefebvre Family Legacy Collection.

Mike Guardabascio
Author of History of California C.I.F.S.S. Thanks for the wonderful details of Long Beach Poly Technical High School's athletic history, particularly the years 1918-1920.

Fred Murry
Author of A Long, Hard Grind. Another fine writer for The Los Angeles Times whose efforts archive and keep the many years of the USC football dynasty alive.

Department of the Army Human Resource Center at St. Lewis Missouri
Thanks for their 100-plus pages of Hank's military history drawn from his 201 files.

Eric T. Gable
From Fort Huachuca 'Old Post' Cemetery for sharing the history of those cherished lives with me, and for his part in honoring their presence in the old Fort Huachuca. This cemetery is a must see for readers who may find their way into those parts of Arizona.

Dick Kazan of DICK KAZAN/Today

Many thanks for his contemporary writing on one of California's most astute rags-to-riches story in California's produce business. His colorful life influenced the unique Santiago Cardinal character who tamed a wild and willy industry, making it a legitimate California golden enterprise.

Clifford Girard

Entrepreneur and owner of the famous billiard parlor just off the USC campus (and my own grandfather), thank you for sharing with me an oral history of Lost Angeles's intimate "backroom politics," gambling, and crime—before and after prohibition.

Nick Pappas

Nicknamed "Mr. Trojan" for his unwavering passion as a player, coach, and recruiter. Without many telephone conversations and meetings with Nick, some of the stories of Hank's career would have been less authenticated. And, without his involvement in the lives of USC athletics and financial assistance, many of the icons of USC football would never have had the chance to display their craft on the gridiron.

Henry 'Hank' Renaud Lefebvre

Thank you to my uncle, my father Benny's brother, who now resides in his grave as an honored veteran. Little did he know his life relived would be an inspiration, not only to the Lefebvre heritage but to those wonderful historical figures born and raised in the early frontier town of Douglas, Arizona, who can truly and proudly acclaim they are its "Regal Sons"—not to be forgotten.

ProQuest Historical Newspapers: Los Angeles Times

I would be remiss not to mention the many excellent books I've read in preparation for this book.

1. Sides, Hampton, Blood and Thunder (New York: Random House, 2007).

2. Grobaty, Tim, Long Beach Chronicles (Charleston, SC: The History Press, 2012).

3. Shelton, Richard, Going Back to Bisbee (Arizona: The University of Arizona Press, 1992).

4. Trimble, Marshall, In Old Arizona (Phoenix, Arizona: Golden West Publishers, 2006).

5. Ball, Larry D., Desert Lawmen (New Mexico: The University of New Mexico Press, 1992).

6. Jeffery, Robert S., The History of Douglas, Arizona (The Graduate College, University of Arizona, 1951).

7. Price, Ethel Jackson, Images of America: Bisbee (Charleston, SC: Arcadia Publishing, 2004).

8. Hayostek, Cindy, Images of Douglas (Charleston SC: Arcadia Publishing, 2009).

9. Price, Ethel Jackson, Images of America: Fort Huachuca (Charleston, SC: Arcadia Publishing, 2004).

10. Turner, Nancy E., These Is My Words (New York, NY: Harper Collins Publishers, 1998).

ABOUT THE AUTHOR

GIL LEFEBVRE

A man for all seasons, Gil Lefebvre is a veteran, a former professional athlete and an educator who has also worked in politics and law.

Now an accomplished writer, Lefebvre launched this new phase of his life and career penning commentaries, essays and poetry. His most prominent published works are five novels. The first, **Unto Caesar Unto God**, assesses the merits of religious activism. The second, **Not Too Far To Have Never Been**, delves into the challenges that defined the Vietnam generation, examining them through the lens of romance and suspense.

Catalina Summer, his third novel, is a romp through a wondrously exotic and historic island setting, á la Huckleberry Finn.

With his fourth release, **Obsessing Rufina**, Lefebvre captures the hurt and deception of post- World War II Germany as seen through the eyes of an intrepid college student. Stumbling upon art crimes perpetuated by the Nazis and their cohorts, the novel's heroine refuses to turn a blind eye to the sins. She dares to investigate and expose, with help from two intriguing yet wholly dissimilar romantic interests, a sordid past that others would just as soon forget.

Lefebvre's newest release is another well researched historical novel. **The Regal Sons of Douglas** is a true tale of individual triumph on the gridiron of the University of Southern California (USC) campus in the early 1900s – a story with as much heart as Notre Dame's beloved Rudy's.